TRAVELS IN SIAM,
CAMBODIA AND LAOS
1858–1860

TRAVELS IN SIAM, CAMBODIA AND LAOS 1858-1860

BY
HENRI MOUHOT

WITH AN INTRODUCTION BY
MICHAEL SMITHIES

VOLUMES ONE AND TWO

SINGAPORE
OXFORD UNIVERSITY PRESS
OXFORD NEW YORK
1989

Oxford University Press

Oxford New York Toronto
Delhi Bombay Calcutta Madras Karachi
Petaling Jaya Singapore Hong Kong Tokyo
Nairobi Dar es Salaam Cape Town
Melbourne Auckland
and associated companies in
Berlin Ibadan

Oxford is a trade mark of Oxford University Press

Introduction © Oxford University Press Pte. Ltd. 1989
First published as Travels in the Central Parts of Indo-China (Siam),
Cambodia, and Laos *in 1864 by John Murray, London*
Reprinted in Oxford in Asia Hardback Reprints *in 1989*

ISBN 0 19 588951 7

Printed in Malaysia by Peter Chong Printers Sdn. Bhd.
Published by Oxford University Press Pte. Ltd.,
Unit 221, Ubi Avenue 4, Singapore 1440

INTRODUCTION

In a volume which comes already with a plethora of prefatory material, comprising a dedication and a preface by the author's brother, and a long memoir by the Dutch naturalist, Belinfante, giving details of Henri Mouhout's life, an introduction may well seem superfluous. We shall try to put the work into its perspective.

Mouhot died at the age of 35 near Luang Prabang on 10 November 1861 and his faithful servants, Phrai and Deng, buried him, and took his notes and collections to Bangkok. These were transmitted to his widow and his brother, Charles, both resident in Jersey (a favourite place for exiles from the Second Empire, though their residence seems to have had less to do with politics and more to do with both brothers having married English wives). Charles Mouhot assembled the papers appearing in this edition, which supplemented the text of Henri Mouhot's journal with appendices listing the new species he had discovered, atmospherical observations, seven tales translated from Chinese (and clearly related to him by his Chinese servants), an extensive Cambodian vocabulary list, and a number of personal letters and communications to, from, and about Henri Mouhot.

A version of the text first appeared in French with the title 'Voyage dans les royaumes de Siam, de Cambodge, de Laos et autres parties centrales de l'Indo-Chine' in the periodical *Tour du Monde* in nine consecutive instalments in 1863, illustrated by engravings based on Mouhot's own sketches. The title was not exactly succinct, as was the fashion in the mid-nineteenth century, and was something of a pleonasm. The English edition the following year assimilated the 'central parts of Indo-China' to Siam and unnecessarily gave the dates of the voyage, getting them wrong in the process by omitting 1861.

The more extensive English edition, in two volumes, translated

not by his family but by a G. K. Greville (as Christopher Pym discovered from examining the publisher's accounts), was published
in London, with the approval of the author's family, by Murray in
1864. The French edition in book form, edited by Ferdinand de
Lanoye (who had probably edited the 1863 version), came out in
1868 with Hachette, but without any illustrations, the same year
that extracts were published in Russian, and an Italian edition
appeared in 1871.

There are quite considerable differences between the English
and French editions. In his preface, de Lanoye dismisses the diver-
gencies in the texts as being more in form than substance: 'They are
naturally explained by the difference in the points of view between
those in London and Paris charged with the definitive arrangement
of the numerous writings left by Henri Mouhot.' He added that he
had tried above all to co-ordinate the text, to tighten it up, to include some of Mouhot's correspondence and the journal, and group
subjects together, as well as reduce the two volumes of the English
edition to one for the French.

Not in the English edition is the French chapter on 'Games and
Entertainments'. There is a good deal more information about the
new French consul d'Istria in the French edition, and nothing about
Mouhot suffering from the itch. All twenty-five pages devoted to the
Bannavs are excised from the French version. The French edition
contains a long comment on Siamese priests and the desired qualities of an elephant. De Lanoye incorporated into the text extracts
from two letters of Mouhot, one to his wife and one to his brother
(Vol. II, pp. 259 and 270), containing details relating to the return
from Korat in the company of the white elephant recently caught
in Laos. The image of the two 'mandarins' presenting the animal
with cakes on gold platters throughout the journey, which then
had the misfortune to die of indigestion, is charming and the text
reads the better for it. The French version avoids mention of latitudes and longitudes and cuts out the series of dates given towards
the end of the English edition; it also says nothing about Mouhot's
last words being in English.

Perhaps the most apparent differences relate to the descriptions
of Mouhot's receptions in the palaces of Bangkok and Luang Prabang. In the French edition, Mouhot compares King Mongkut to
James I of England for his scholarship, quotes Pallegoix on the

palace itself in Bangkok, and describes its new Italianate building (since pulled down but illustrated in Vol. II, p. 71). He has a startling comment on the institution of the Second King:

As if it was not enough for the unfortunate country to have to maintain and support one king, one court and one royal seraglio with all its offspring, the Siamese have the double of all these institutions. Behind the first king is a second, who also has his palace, his mandarins, and his army. He is but the first subject of the true King of Siam.

He also describes in detail the Amazons (see Vol. I, p. 257) guarding the inner palace, and says they were the best-dressed regiment in the Siamese army with their Scottish berets, tartan kilts, swords and pistols, who could deservedly form the *corps de ballet* in the Imperial Music Academy in Paris.

The French edition incorporates in the text material found in Mouhot's letter in Vol. II, pp. 272-3, relating to his reception in Luang Prabang by the first and second kings. When one compares this with the very bald and brief account in the English text at Vol. II, p. 138, it is clear that the picture conveyed in the letter is far sharper, with the throne hall 'a sort of hangar like those erected in our villages on feast days, but bigger, and hung with all the colours readily available' and 'the King of the Ruminants' (as the French text has it) puffing on a local cigarette surrounded by teapots and silver spittoons. The English edition has a somewhat imaginative illustration of the scene in Vol. II, facing p. 143 (without, however, the teapots and spittoons), but this is out of context unless one refers to the letter which comes much later.

In sum, then, the two editions are more radically different than the French editor admits. The English edition (which makes no reference to the appearance of the text in the *Tour du Monde* earlier) has more scientific apparatus and less comment. This, together with the skilful integration of extracts from Mouhot's letters with the text, makes the French text the more readable. But the lack of illustrations in the Hachette edition is a serious drawback. There is clearly scope for re-examining the author's original notes and letters and establishing a new edition of the text.

The book put together by two different editors in Mouhot's name was not his first writing to be published about the region. A paper, 'Notes on Cambodia, the Lao country', is listed by Cordier as being published in the *Journal of the Royal Geographical Society*, Vol. XXXII, in 1862, that is, after his death, and translated by Dr T. Hodgkin; Pym thinks it was he who prepared Henri Mouhot's papers for publication in London, notwithstanding Charles Mouhot's own preface to this edition in which he speaks of preserving the chronological order of the text, inserting appendices, and collecting correspondence. Mouhot's posthumous communication to the Society was furthermore not the first at the period about Angkor; D. O. King, a friend of the American missionary, S. R. House, explored Indo-China in 1857-8 and read a paper at the Royal Geographical Society in London in 1859. A second paper, drawing on information supplied by a traveller, E. F. J. Forrest, and also House, was read at the same meeting, on 27 June, by James Campbell, a surgeon, who was to help Mouhot and later to write to Madame Mouhot on 27 April 1862 informing her of her husband's death (here in Vol. II, pp. 290-1). But Mouhot left London on 27 April 1858 on a ship bound for Singapore, arriving in Siam on 12 September.

B. P. Groslier, in his *Angkor et le Cambodge au XVIe siècle* (Paris, 1958), deals extensively with the early Western accounts of Angkor, which was a good deal less lost than popular legend has it. Portuguese Dominicans were present in Cambodia from about 1550; Gaspar da Cruz was in Louvek in 1555, and one Sylvestre d'Azevedo, in Cambodia from 1584, studied Khmer. Another Portuguese, Diogo Veloso, who was not a priest, was, according to the Cambodian chronicle quoted by D. G. E. Hall, adopted by King Satha (r. 1576-94). The earliest and most detailed account of Angkor was by Diogo de Couto, an official Portuguese chronicler of the Indes, but by oversight it was never included in a text of 1599 in which it was due to appear. The material dates from 1550 or 1551 and describes an elephant hunt in the forest by the Cambodian king who saw extensive walls covered with jungle. He ordered some five or six thousand men to cut the undergrowth down, and when it was cleared, went in. The city of Angkor Thom is accurately described in the text, and so is Angkor Wat.

The Spanish interventions in Cambodia from 1593 to 1599 led to three texts appearing in the early seventeenth century with references to Angkor. Marcello de Ribadeneyra, in his *Historia de la Islas del Archipielago* (Barcelona, 1601), has a brief reference to

Angkor and to it being built by Alexander the Great or the Romans. Gabriel de San Antonio wrote his *Breve y Verdedera Relacion de los Succesos del Reyno de Camboxa* (Valladolid, 1604) containing essentially the same information as Diogo do Couto, but, as his title foretells, with greater brevity. Christoval de Jaque's published account of 1606 was lost, but it reappeared in Ternaux-Compans' *Archives des Voyages* (Paris, 1840). Two other mentions of Angkor appeared shortly after, Fr. João dos Santos's *Ethiopia Oriental* (Evora, 1609) and Bartolome de Argensola's *Conquista de las Islas Malucas* (Madrid, 1609), in which the gloss speaks of 'Angòn, an ancient city of Camboxa, recently discovered in this region'. As Groslier notes, the actual sources of these accounts are virtually impossible to trace with certainty.

There is evidence therefore that about 1550 Angkor was rediscovered (after having been abandoned at a date sometimes disputed but around 1444, after Siamese attacks), and occupied for a time by King Satha. The irrigation system was still functioning and was restored. Satha abandoned the site in 1587 or 1593, and Portuguese priests working at his court saw Angkor. Merchants from different countries, including Siam, at Satha's court spread information about Angkor. The two Spanish expeditions of 1596 and 1599 to Cambodia would have acquired some information about Angkor.

In Angkor Wat itself, Groslier points out, is an inscription dating from 1587 relating to the restoration of the temple, and in 1629 pilgrims left another inscription there. According to the chronicles, Angkor Wat was restored by the Cambodian king, Ponhea Sor, and more dated inscriptions are found up to 1747. Angkor Thom appears to have been abandoned after 1629 but there is a Buddhist inscription in Pre Rup dating from 1684.

Other references to Angkor occur after the early Portuguese and Spanish accounts. There is another mention in Spanish by Navarrete in 1676, in Dutch in a letter by the merchant Indijck of 1656-7, and in Japanese by Shimano Kenryo, who was in Cambodia about 1623-36 and visited Angkor. Accounts appear in French in Chaulmer (1654) and Chevreul (1674) but neither went to Angkor, and French texts of the eighteenth century, according to Groslier, copy earlier Spanish accounts. An exception was Langenois, who went to Cambodia, visited Angkor Wat, and described it in a letter of 1783, now lost. In 1819 a translation by Abel Rémusat appeared in French of Chou Ta Kuan's thirteenth-century account of Angkor, and Bouillevaux went to Angkor in 1850 and published his account in 1858. Pallegoix, too, in his work on Siam, has a reference to Angkor (1854).

Mouhot, then, did not discover Angkor, and he did not claim to. Its existence was known, though perhaps its importance was not realized. To Mouhot goes the credit of creating a more general awareness of Angkor, of attempting to establish its significance; he was its popularizer and its assessor.

He certainly set the vogue for accounts of Angkor. Admiral Bonard followed Mouhot in 1862, and Doudart de Lagrée in both 1863 and 1866 (his account, with François Garnier, *Voyage d'exploration en Indo-Chine effectuée pendant les années 1866, 1867 et 1868* first appeared in the *Tour du Monde* from 1870 to 1872 and then with Hachette in 1873, with 250 superb illustrations). James Thomson went to Angkor in 1866 and made the first systematic attempt to photograph the ruins, an effort mentioned in his *The Straits of Malacca, Indo-China and China: Ten Years' Travels, Adventures and Residence Abroad* (London, 1875). Angkor had become so topical by 1870 that Anna Leonowens, in her book *The English Governess at the Siamese Court* (London, 1870), included as her penultimate chapter 'The Ruins of Cambodia—An Excursion to Naghkon Watt' which describes what appears to be a journey there, though there is no evidence she ever went to the country, and all her information is from Mouhot and the illustrations from Thomson. Angkor was soon the object of visits from gentlemen of leisure and means, like Frank Vincent, who describes Angkor, with an accurate plan, in his *The Land of the White Elephant* (New York, 1874), and gives credit, unlike Anna, to Mouhot.

According to Belinfante, Mouhot came across 'an English book on Siam' which sufficiently fired his imagination for him to want to go and explore the country, which then counted within its empire what was left of the kingdoms of Cambodia and Laos. Pym speculates this book was Sir John Bowring's *The Kingdom and People of Siam*, published in 1857, and his guess is probably correct: Mouhot quotes extensively from Bowring when dealing with the history of Siam. In English, only Crawfurd (1828) and, to a much lesser degree, Finlayson (1826) had published substantively on Siam before Bowring, and both books were out of print, though Mouhot seems to

have had access to Crawfurd, for his information about the accession of Rama II is identical. The slight work of F. A. Neale (1852)
is hardly likely to have inspired anyone to leave home, and the references to Siam in works of the 1830s in Abeel, Earl, Gutzlaff, Malcom, Moor, Roberts, Ruschenberger, and Tomlin would probably
not have been readily accessible to Mouhot in Jersey. It should be
pointed out that Monseigneur Pallegoix's work *Description du
Royaume Thai ou Siam* was published in Paris in 1854, and Mouhot
certainly consulted this, because he quotes from it, very extensively
in the French edition. One would like confirmation from Mouhot's
own writings that Belifante is correct about the book which inspired
Mouhot to go to Siam being in English.

But it is rather extraordinary that one book should have caused
such a dramatic change in his personal life. However, it was perhaps in character. Mouhot was born in provincial Montbéliard,
near Belfort and the Swiss border, in 1826 and went to Russia to
teach French, staying there from 1844 to 1854, and acquiring an
interest and some expertise in the new invention of photography.
The outbreak of the Crimean War caused his return and for two
years he travelled in Western Europe with his brother, settling in
Britain in 1856, as Belinfante says, 'the more willingly as they had
both married English ladies, relatives of Mungo Park'. Henri Mouhot
then took up zoology and ornithology, read his book on Siam, got
the blessing of the Royal Geographical Society for his expedition,
and weighed anchor for Bangkok. He clearly was born with wander-
lust and scientific curiosity, something his wife could presumably
understand, and appears to have had sufficient if modest private
means to satisfy both.

What was there in Bowring (if Bowring it was) which so fired his
imagination? It was a magisterial summary of all the information
known about the country, drawing on numerous sources, including
personal communications from King Mongkut himself, and with the
authority of someone who was the first to negotiate successfully in
modern times a trade treaty with the Siamese, and who had established a close personal rapport with the reigning monarch. The book
remains a classic text on the country, as does Mouhot's own work,
but for different reasons.

Once arrived in Bangkok in October 1858, Mouhot made four
journeys in Siam and its dependencies. The first was an appetizer,

going only as far as Saraburi and Prabaht (see Map), though this in itself was an adventure, for no previous traveller had got that far and recorded the journey since the French embassies went to Lopburi in the seventeenth century. From December 1858 to April 1860 he made an extensive journey by sea to Chantaboon (Chantaburi) for a three-month stay, followed by two months in Cambodia, in Udong and Pinhalu, three months in Brelum, and three weeks in Angkor. It was this journey which was his major accomplishment and for which he became internationally famous. The third journey was a filler, spending from May to August 1860 in or near Phetchaburi, as the weather was unpropitious for going to the north-east as he intended. Yet his account of Phetchaburi is only the second to come down to us (the first, by an unnamed gentleman, is found in Bowring), and the first to describe the newly built palace of King Mongkut on the hill.

His last journey, from mid-October to his death, was to be as original as his trip to Angkor, though it is not always recognized as such. He was the first person to get beyond Korat (Nakorn Rajasima) in North-east Siam and to attempt to fill in the blanks on all the maps, for cartography had made no progress in this region since the seventeenth century. He reached Korat, visited some minor Khmer ruins nearby (but not Pimai, to judge from his text, though he knew about it) and got as far as Chaiyapoom in February 1861, where a recalcitrant official refused to assist him or allow passage. So he had to return to Bangkok, acquire more letters with more impressive seals, and set off for Chaiyapoom again, which needlessly added two months to his travails. From May 1861 he was in Laos, surveying the Mekong, the majestically located Luang Prabang (still one of the most striking sites of the region) until his death in November. The superficially romantic aspects of this journey have overshadowed its real importance; he was the first person to travel overland to Luang Prabang in modern times and leave a record of his journey, and the first person to attempt to map the region.

All these travels were traced on Mouhot's map published in the Murray volume. For all its inaccuracies, it was a map of no small importance, fleshing out hitherto *terra incognita* in the blanks between Korat and Luang Prabang.

This aspect of Mouhot is often overlooked. He was the discoverer of North-east Siam and of the Lao, who occupied the region. Many

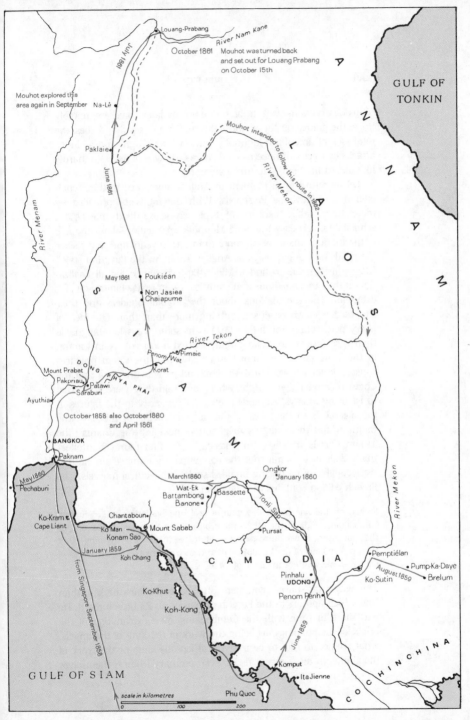

GULF OF
TONKIN

River Nam Kane

Louang-Prabang

October 1861   Mouhot was turned back
                and set out for Louang Prabang
                on October 15th

Mouhot explored this
area again in September   Na-Lè

Paklaie

Mouhot intended to follow this route in 1862

River Mekon

River Menan

May 1861   Poukiéan

Non Jasiea
Chaiapume

River Tekon

Penom Wat   Pimaie

Mount Prabat   Korat

Pakpriau   Patawi
Ayuthia   Saraburi

October 1858 also October 1860
and April 1861

BANGKOK

Paknam

May 1860

Pechaburi

Ongkor
March 1860   January 1860

Wat-Ek
Battambong   Bassette
Banone

Ko-Kram   Chantaboun
Cape Liant

Ko Man   Mount Sabab
Konam Sao

Koh Chang   Pursat

CAMBODIA

January 1859

from Singapore September 1858

Ko-Khut

Koh-Kong

Pemptiélan
Pump-Ka-Daye
August 1859   Brelum
Ko-Sutin

Pinhalu
UDONG

Penom Penh

June 1859

Komput

ItaJienne

COCHINCHINA

GULF OF SIAM

scale in kilometres
0   100   200

Phu Quoc

(From *Henri Mouhot's Diary*, abridged by Christopher Pym, Kuala Lumpur, Oxford University Press,
1966.) The spelling of place names follows Mouhot.

of his observations were to be borne out by later travellers, notably Bock: the goitres on the women, the smoking of suckling babes, the total lack of amenities. Mouhot's journey was rough, and included attacks by tigers, rhinoceros, and cobras. He was of necessity hardy, like most nineteenth-century explorers.

Let us return for a moment to Angkor, compared in the French edition to Nineva or Persepolis. With the hindsight provided by more than half a century of Ecole Française d'Extrême Orient scholarship, it is easy to deride Mouhot's speculation about the age of the monuments as being more than 2,000 years and to consider the heads on the gateways at Angkor Thom 'in the Egyptian style'. It was fashionable to find a Middle-Eastern source for all civilization at the time; one finds it in countless other texts (James Low, for example). The speculations about the original builders and their supposedly Jewish origins is nothing more than that. The idea of Jewry penetrating South-East Asia is in some ways less laughable than it seems, for there apparently existed a lost colony in Canton in the Tang period. Mouhot himself says that the Cham practices considered Jewish were also Muslim, and he was unaware that the Cham themselves were right when they said they were converted to Islam by Malays. He finds a physical similarity to the figures in the bas-reliefs to the faces of the 'savages' living in the east, the Bannavs and their various neighbours, including the Chams ('the Thiâmes or Isiampois'). But, basically, Mouhot found it intellectually difficult to admit that the contemporary Cambodians he met were capable of producing unaided such architectural marvels. The French edition contains the comment:

Seeing, on the one hand, the state of profound barbarism of present-day Cambodians, and, on the other, the proofs of the advanced civilization of their ancestors, it was impossible for me to see in the first anything other than descendants of the Vandals, whose rage was wrecked on the works of earlier people, and not the issue of these.

This was a far sharper comment on the Cambodians he saw than that which appears in the English edition on p. 23 of Volume II. He was more in tune with the Cambodians' own explanation of the origin of the buildings, as being the work of the king of the angels, what seemed to him to be a mythical leprous king, or the work of the giants. In more recent times, even ordinary Khmers themselves apparently find it hard to appreciate the feats of their forebears. As a consultant of the Asia Society in New York lecturing on Angkor to an audience of Khmer refugees in the United States in 1988 noted in a personal communication, many members of her audience had little idea that their ancestors were great architects and engineers.

Mouhot was also a man of his times in other respects. He deplores native idleness and speculates on the virtues colonial rule could bring to the countries through which he passes. Like many travellers of his time, he found the despotism of local societies, propped up by slavery, obnoxious. The young Marquis de Beauvoir, for example, in his account of a visit to Bangkok in 1868, was to write that after 'commercial, peaceful, and lawful conquest' of metropolitan powers, in Siam 'help could be found here for suffering humanity. This door must be opened to try and rouse those who are isolated behind it.' There was little evidence at the time that colonial rule was markedly superior to native rule as far as social stability was concerned, and most people were 'happy in their peaceful ease' even if they only extracted 'a tenth part of what the soil could produce'. But the doubtful virtues of colonialism were, howsoever questionably it may seem today, the justification on which nineteenth-century imperialism was built.

Mouhot was also a hunter, a profession or a sport which modern ecologists despise, though to this day hunting is regarded as a natural right of many provincial Frenchmen. He was, though, a hunter with a scientific purpose, of assembling his collections and sending them for study to Europe. At this period there was no other method available to make a collection of fauna, as Wallace and Forbes make amply clear, except by shooting his specimens dead. But he suffered a similar misfortune to that great collector (but no hunter) Raffles, whose entire collection went down at sea off Bencoolen in the *Fame* in 1824 on its way to England. Mouhot lost his collection, too; *Sir James Brooke*, the ship carrying it, foundered at Singapore, the port which Raffles himself had established. The French text twice refers back to this loss and the anguish it caused Mouhot; the more sturdy English editor mentions the event only once.

Mouhot's stays with so many French Catholic missionaries and his appreciation of their work is a little surprising when one realizes that he was a Protestant. The unifying forces of race and nationality overcame religious division. Here one wonders at his capacity for assimilation; for all his apparent sympathy with many people he met, which appears real, for all his genuine attachment to his servants, he remains a European, a White, a *farang*, separate from the people around him. However, this distancing is hardly the hallmark of the mid-nineteenth-century European; even now a Westerner going into a rural temple is likely to be greeted with the exclamation '*Farang!* Come and see the *farang!*' as he was in 1859.

Mouhot was not above the dramatic rather than the scientific. He unduly emphasizes the wildness of the 'savage Stiens', he finds the cave of Phetchaburi of undoubted volcanic origin (something every visitor for another forty years continued to repeat until Warrington Smyth put them right), and he even found an unlikely submarine volcano off Rayong. Everyone can make mistakes.

There can be no doubt that one of the chief attractions of Mouhot's volume are the splendid illustrations, most of them deriving from his own pen, since he sketched as he went along, and also took a number of photographs. Both sketches and photos were turned into the engravings by Sabatier, Boucourt, Rousseau, Thérond, Beaumont, Janet Lange, Catenacci, and others, some unidentified. Many of the views and portraits shown do not appear to relate to the text itself. This is because the plates were commissioned for the *Tour du Monde* edition, which, as we have seen, is markedly different from the English edition. Furthermore, we have always to bear in mind that we are dealing with a text, and a volume, put together not by people who knew the subject, nor by the author himself, but by dedicated amateurs (in the best sense of the word). Mouhot, had he lived, might have assembled something very different, more on the lines of Wallace, who had ample time to go to print, returning to London in 1862 and publishing in 1869. Even the inconsistencies in spelling in the English edition, where clearly the editors could not distinguish between Mouhot's 'n' and 'u', are proof of this.

But, apart from his sketches and observations of Angkor, other episodes in the book remain long remembered. His description of monkeys teasing crocodiles in the jungle, his impressions of the Cambodian kings and their palaces, the way of life in the province of Korat, the flooded rice plains near Ayutthaya, and the poignancy of the end of his account, when close to death, 'Have pity on me, oh my God!' are strongly evocative passages from the pen of a talented writer.

The book remains a pleasure to read more than a century after its appearance, and its illustrations are among the finest to depict scenes from the region of any book in the nineteenth century. Mouhot's work directly inspired the Garnier expedition in the 1860s, and also indirectly the drawings of Angkor which appeared in it. That the potential of the Mekong remains unrealized, that Mouhot died in vain or was sometimes wrong, are neither here nor there. He had the spirit of adventure and enquiry, and the book that was posthumously put together relating his travels in mainland South-East Asia remains a classic of its kind.

Bangkok   MICHAEL SMITHIES
June 1989

References

Abeel, D., *Journal of a Residenc* in China and the Neighbouring Countries, New York, 1836.

Argensola, Bartolome de, *Conquista de las Islas Malucas*, Madrid, 1609.

Beauvoir, Ludovic, Marquis de, *Java-Siam-Canton*, Paris, 1869 (reproduced in his *Voyage autour du Monde*, Paris, 1872).

Bock, Carl, *Temples and Elephants*, London, 1884; reprinted Singapore, Oxford University Press, 1986.

Bonard, Amiral, 'Exploration du Grand Fleuve du Cambodge (septembre 1862)', *Revue maritime et coloniale*, February 1863.

Bouillevaux, C. E., *Ma visite aux ruines cambodgiennes en 1850*, St. Quentin, 1863.

Bowring, Sir John, *The Kingdom and People of Siam*, London, 1857; reprinted Singapore, Oxford University Press, 1987.

Chaulmer, C., *Le Tableau d'Asie*, Paris, 1654.

Chevreul, Louis, *Relation des Missions des Evesques françois aux royaumes de Siam, de la Cochinchine, de Cambodge et du Tonkin*, Paris, 1674.

Chou Ta Kuan, 'Description du royaume du Cambodge par un voyageur chinois', trans. Abel Rémusat, *Nouvelles Annalles des Voyages*, Paris, 1819.

Cordier, Henri, *Bibliotheca Indosinica*, Paris, 1912.

Couto, Diogo do, 'Cinco livros da Duadecima decada da Asia', Cod. 537, ms. *da Livraria*, National Archives, Lisbon.

Crawfurd, John, *Journal of an Embassy from the Governor-General of India to the Courts of Siam and Cochin-China*, London, 1828; reprinted Singapore, Oxford University Press, 1987.

Earl, G. W., *The Eastern Seas, or Voyages and Adventures in the Indian Archipelago in 1832, 1833, and 1834, Comprising a Tour of the Island of Java—Visits to Borneo, the Malay Peninsula, Siam, etc.*, London, 1837; reprinted Singapore and Kuala Lumpur, Oxford University Press, 1971.

Finlayson, George, *The Mission to Siam and Hué, the Capital of Cochin-China, in the years 1821-2*, London, 1826; reprinted Singapore, Oxford University Press, 1987.

Forbes, Henry O., *A Naturalist's Wanderings in the Eastern Archipelago*, London, 1885; reprinted Singapore, Oxford University Press, 1989.

Groslier, B. P., *Angkor et le Cambodge au XVIe siècle*, Paris, 1958.

Gutzlaff, C., *Journal of Three Voyages along the Coast of China in 1831, 1832, and 1833, with notices of Siam, Corea, and the Loo-Choo Islands*, London, 1834.

Hall, D. G. E., *A History of South-East Asia*, 3rd ed., London, 1968.

Indijck, Hendrick, in H. P. N. Muller, *De Oost-Indische compagnie in Cambodja en Laos ... van 1636 tot 1670*, The Hague, 1917.

Jaque, Christoval de, in Ternaux-Compans, *Archives des Voyages*, Paris, 1840.

Kenryo, Shimano, in N. Peri, 'Essai sur les relations du Japon et de l'Indochine aux XVIe et XVIIe siècles', *BEFEO*, Vol. 23, 1923.

Lagrée, Doudart de, and François Garnier, *Voyage d'exploration en Indo-Chine effectuée pendant les années 1866, 1867 et 1868*, Paris, 1873.

Langenois, Pr, letter quoted in Bouillevaux, q.v.

Leonowens, Anna, *The English Governess at the Siamese Court*, London, 1870; reprinted Singapore, Oxford University Press, 1988.

Low, James, 'Dissertation on White Elephants', *Transactions of the Royal Asiatic Society of Great Britain and Ireland*, Vol. III, 1831.

Malcom, H., *Travels in South-Eastern Asia, embracing Hindustan, Malaya, Siam, and China; with notices of Numerous Missionary Stations, and a full account of the Burman Empire*, Boston, 1839.

Moor, J. H., *Notices of the Indian Archipelago and Adjacent Countries; Being a Collection of Papers Relating to Borneo, Celebes, Bali, Java, Sumatra, Nias, the Philippines Islands, Sulus, Siam, Cochin-China, Malaya Peninsula, etc.*, Singapore, 1837.

Mouhot, Henri, 'Notes on Cambodia, the Lao Country', trans. Dr T. Hodgkin, *Journal of the Royal Geographical Society*, Vol. XXXII, 1862.

———— *Voyage dans les royaumes de Siam, de Cambodge, de Laos et autres parties centrales de l'Indo-Chine*, edited by Ferdinand de Lanoye, Paris, Hachette, 1868 (first published in *Tour du Monde*, 1863).

Navarette, D. F., *Tratachos Historicos, Politicos, Ethicos y Religiosos de la Monarchia de China ...*, Madrid, 1676.

Neale, F. A., *Narrative of a Residence at the Capital of the Kingdom of Siam*, London, 1852.

Pallegoix, Mgr. J-B., *Description du Royaume Thai ou Siam*, Paris, 1854.

Pym, Christopher, ed., *Henri Mouhot's Diary*, Kuala Lumpur, 1966.

Ribadeneyra, Marcello de, *Historia de la Islas del Archipielago*, Barcelona, 1601.

Roberts, E., *Embassy to the Eastern Courts of Cochin-China, Siam, and Muscat; in the U.S. Sloop-of-War Peacock, during the years 1832, 1833 and 1834*, New York, 1837.

Ruschenberger, S. W., *Narrative of a Voyage round the World during the Years 1835, 1836, and 1837; including a narrative of an Embassy to the Sultan of Muscat and the King of Siam*, Philadelphia, 1838.

San Antonio, Gabriel de, *Breve y Verdedera Relacion de los Succesos del Reyno de Camboxa*, Valladolid, 1604.

Santos, Fr. João dos, *Ethiopia Oriental*, Evora, 1609.

Smithies, Michael, ed., *Early Accounts of Phetchaburi*, Bangkok, 1987.

Smyth, H. Warrington, *Five Years in Siam, from 1891-1896*, London, 1898.

Thomson, James, *The Straits of Malacca, Indo-China and China: Ten Years' Travels, Adventures and Residence Abroad*, London, 1875.

Tomlin, Jacob, *Journal Kept during a Voyage from Singapore to Siam and while Residing Nine Months in that Country*, Singapore [1832], Malacca, 1832.

Vincent, Frank, *The Land of the White Elephant*, New York, 1874; reprinted Singapore, Oxford University Press, 1987.

Wallace, Alfred Russel, *The Malay Archipelago*, London, 1869; reprinted Singapore, Oxford University Press, 1986.

Wurtzburg, C. E., *Raffles of the Eastern Isles*, London, 1954; reprinted Singapore, Oxford University Press, 1984.

Drawn by M. Bocourt, from a Photograph.

THE KING AND QUEEN OF SIAM.

TRAVELS

IN THE

CENTRAL PARTS OF INDO-CHINA

(SIAM),

CAMBODIA, AND LAOS,

DURING THE YEARS 1858, 1859, AND 1860.

BY THE LATE

M. HENRI MOUHOT,

FRENCH NATURALIST.

IN TWO VOLUMES.—VOL. I.

WITH ILLUSTRATIONS.

LONDON:

JOHN MURRAY, ALBEMARLE STREET,

1864.

DEDICATION.

TO THE LEARNED SOCIETIES OF ENGLAND, WHO HAVE
FAVOURED WITH THEIR ENCOURAGEMENT THE
JOURNEY OF M. HENRI MOUHOT TO THE REMOTE
LANDS OF SIAM, LAOS, AND CAMBODIA.

I TRUST that the members of those scientific societies who kindly
supported and encouraged my brother in his travels and labours,
will receive favourably the documents collected by the family of
the intrepid traveller, whom death carried off in the flower of his
age, in the midst of his discoveries.

Had he been able to accomplish fully the end at which he
aimed, it would certainly have been to you that he would have
offered the fruits of his travels: he would have felt it his first
duty to testify his gratitude and esteem to the worthy repre-
sentatives of science in that great, free, and generous English
nation who adopted him. Half English by his marriage, M.
Mouhot still preserved his love for his own country: there,
however, for various reasons he did not receive the encouragement he anticipated, and it was on the hospitable soil of England
that he met with that aid and support, which not only her
scientific men, but the whole nation, delight in affording to
explorations in unknown countries, ever attended by perils and
hardships. The journal of the unfortunate traveller shows his
feelings of affection for the two countries which he loved
equally, and his devotion to science, art, and the progress of
civilization.

I therefore feel it an imperative duty to express to you and to the whole English nation the sentiments of gratitude to which this good and loyal Frenchman so often gave utterance, while engaged in the work to which he spontaneously devoted himself, and in which he was sustained by your counsels and assistance.

Receive therefore from Madame Mouhot and myself, as a legacy left by her dear husband and my affectionate brother, the expression of our gratitude; and accept the work, left imperfect, it is true, but which we hope will prove how much has been lost by the death of a brave man, who, allied to the family of Mungo Park, met the same fate in the East that that illustrious explorer did in Africa. M. Mouhot's premature end did not permit him to correct and arrange his journal, which is an additional reason for claiming indulgence from you, whose enlightened minds and generous benevolence will know how to appreciate the circumstances under which this posthumous work sees the light.

CHARLES MOUHOT.

Jersey, 1*st December*, 1862.

ONE OF THE SONS OF THE KING OF SIAM.

PREFACE.

As will be seen, this work is compiled from the
private letters of M. Mouhot to his family and
friends, and from his journal. I had also the
benefit of the paper destined by my brother for
the Archæological Society of London, on the interesting ruins of Ongcor. Among the documents
which, thanks to the active kindness of Sir R.
Schomburgh, British Consul at Bangkok, of Dr.
Campbell, R.N., and of M. D'Istria, French Consul,
reached me as early as possible after my brother's
death, I found valuable sketches and drawings,
together with various unfinished papers relative to
his different scientific researches in the countries
he had visited and in districts which had only
recently been brought into notice by the advance

of commerce, and by the military expeditions which had been sent to the extreme East.

The family of M. Mouhot were divided in opinion as to the course to be adopted with regard to these varied materials. Should they be kept in a portfolio as a sacred but barren deposit, or should they be arranged in the best manner possible and laid before the public?

After grave consideration they yielded to the representations of friends of the deceased, and to myself was confided the painful but interesting task of superintending the arrangement of the notes, sketches, and documents for publication. I accordingly set about it at once, under the first impressions of grief at the loss I had sustained, and guided only by fraternal love, for I lay no claim to the title of author. I have simply classified the masses of papers, the fruit of four years' travel, and added a few explanatory notes.

I have already stated the motives which induced me to dedicate this work to the Savans of England, more especially to those with whom my brother was connected through science or literature.

Let me give a short sketch of the work for

which we claim the indulgence of the public. I have first, preserving the chronological order, divided the journal into chapters, inserting in their appropriate places such portions of the private letters as served to throw light on the subject. This forms the body of the work.

In an Appendix I have inserted the Chinese tales translated by the author during his residence in Siam—some unfinished papers which are only specimens of a zoological work which my brother intended to publish—the descriptions of the principal entomological and conchological specimens discovered by him, and which are now deposited in the Museums of London and Paris—the Cambodian vocabulary, a proof of his industry, of the variety of his knowledge, and of the care with which he collected everything which might be useful to his successors in the difficult path which he opened to them.

Lastly, I have collected the letters of my brother to his family and other correspondents, together with some letters addressed to him, a few of which were never even received, while others only reached their destination after his death, or remained in the hands of friends who were charged to deliver them. This correspondence tends, I think, to display my brother's character, the delicacy of his mind, and the goodness of his heart, qualities which have been recognised by so many, both during his life and after his death.

The engravings from his drawings will impart interest to the descriptions of the ruins and vast buildings which he discovered in the interior of Siam and Cambodia, testifying to an advanced state of civilization in former times, and which, I venture to think, deserve to be brought into notice. They will also familiarize the reader with the manners, customs, and appearance of the country. My aim has been to be useful to those who deign to read these pages ; and, if fidelity be merit in a book, I trust the reader will be satisfied.

Even should there be any errors in the numbers of the population, and similar details concerning the little-known countries which my brother tra-versed, I beg the reader to view them with indulgence, bearing in mind that most of this journal was written in pencil, sent home from a long distance, and some of it half effaced ;—illegible, indeed, to any one to whom his writing was not as well known as it was to Madame Mouhot and myself, and who were not as intimate with the heart and thoughts of the writer.

All these reasons induce me to reckon on the indulgence of the public.

The Memoir which follows was written by a friend in Holland. The historical notice which I have thus introduced, appeared to me useful, in order to give a clearer idea of the country which my brother has contributed to make better known, and where he sealed with his death his devotion to travel and scientific pursuits.

Let me add, in conclusion, that the family of M. Mouhot gladly embrace the opportunity of thanking publicly all those who have given aid to the traveller, and have testified their friendship for him ; several are mentioned in the course of the book by my brother himself, but others, from whom he received equal kindness and support before embarking on his perilous journey into unknown regions, have not perhaps been noticed as they deserved. It was neither forgetfulness nor ingratitude on his part; his death is his excuse.

CHARLES MOUHOT.

Adelaide Lodge, Jersey,
January, 1863.

Drawn by M. H. Rousseau, from a Photograph.

HENRI MOUHOT

MEMOIR OF M. HENRI MOUHOT.

ALEXANDER HENRI MOUHOT was born at Montbéliard on 15th May, 1826, of parents not rich, but respectable. His father occupied a subordinate post in the administration under Louis Philippe and the Republic, and expended nearly the whole of his salary in the education of his two sons, even undergoing many privations for that purpose. His mother, a teacher of considerable merit, whose memory is held in respect by all who knew her, died young, greatly through overwork and fatigue, incurred in providing for the wants of her family and the education of her children. Two months after the departure of her son Henri for Russia—a separation which was heartbreaking to her—she took to her bed, from which she never rose again. This was in 1844. M. Mouhot first studied philology in his own country, intending to become a teacher; but before long a strong leaning for the natural sciences, easy to be understood in the country of Cuvier and of Laurillard, gave a new direction to his mind; and this, with his ardent desire to see other countries, determined his vocation. His first profession enabled him to extend his researches, and while he perfected himself in

c 2

science he continued to follow the arduous and thorny path of the professor. Having a thorough knowledge of his own language, and being a good Greek scholar, it was not difficult for him to acquire with facility both Russian and Polish during his stay in that vast northern empire, which he traversed from St. Petersburgh to Sebastopol, and from Warsaw to Moscow.

He began as a teacher, but soon became an artist, after the discovery of Daguerre, which impressed him strongly; he mastered its mechanical parts, and determined to carry the new invention into foreign lands. This afforded to him the means of an existence conformable to his wishes. He soon made affectionate friends in the highest classes of society in Russia; took out his professor's diploma there, and in that capacity was admitted into several establishments, both public and private; among others, to that of the cadets of Voronége, &c. Devoting himself in his hours of leisure, and at night, to the cultivation of the arts and sciences, and profiting by his visits to various towns and departments of the empire, he constantly augmented his collection of drawings and photographs, comprising landscapes illustrating different parts of the country, portraits of distinguished men, specimens from museums, and buildings in the semi-Byzantine style, equally interesting to artists and to archæologists.

He scrupulously refrained from politics, and fully appreciated the difficulty of governing a country so immense, and in which the manners, religion, and language differ so much in its various parts; still he felt deeply the condition of the serfs, a condition which Alexander II., moved by generous sentiments, wishes now to reform. This state of things made a painful impression on the heart of the young Frenchman, and on his return to his own country he gave vent to his feelings in a book called 'Slavery in Russia;' and in order to engage better the attention of the reader he wove it into the form of a novel, in which he was enabled to employ the resources of illustration, and to depict the manners of the country. This work, however, which touched on many of the leading questions of the day, was never published, and is only mentioned here as an illustration of his generous feelings.

The war which broke out in the East induced him to leave Russia, although, doubtless, owing to his numerous friends, he might safely have awaited there the return of a time more propitious to the cultivation of art and science; but his feelings as a Frenchman revolted from this, and he also felt that the gravity of the events about to take place would turn every mind from all but warlike subjects.

M. Mouhot, therefore, returned to France to his father and to a loved brother, who became the companion of his new travels in Germany, Belgium, and the north of Italy; and everywhere they laboured by means of photography to make known the works of the great masters and the beauties of the country, exercising their profession like real artists. They afterwards resolved to visit Holland, where photography was less widely known than in other

countries. After staying there some time they removed
their establishment to England in 1856, the more willingly
as they had both married English ladies, relatives of
Mungo Park, and having friends willing to push on the
two young men, who, full of energy, possessed the qualities
necessary for success in an artistic or scientific career.
During some ensuing years the two brothers pursued their
calling together, and shared each other's pleasures and
cares; but Henri afterwards found in a peaceful life at
Jersey an opportunity of resuming his studies in Natural
History, devoting himself particularly to Ornithology and
Conchology. These studies revived in him the desire for
foreign travel; and beautiful as was the island where he
lived—and where his time was divided between his home,
his books, and out-door pursuits—his thirst for knowledge
made him long for a wider field of research, and one less
explored by modern travellers. An English book on Siam
came into his possession about this time, as though sent
by the hand of destiny, and to visit that country became
the object of his aspirations. The great Geographical and
Zoological Societies of London, capable of appreciating the
man of merit, approved of his project, and aided him
efficaciously in its prosecution; and M. H. Mouhot quitted
his wife, brother, and all his friends and every advantage
of civilization, in order to visit, in the cause of science,
regions little known, but where, through much fatigue and
danger, the prospect of a glorious future opened itself
before him.

He was already well prepared for the life; active, strong,

and blessed with an excellent constitution: his physical
strength was beyond the average—a result of the gym-
nastic sports in which he had taken pleasure in his youth,
and of his habitual sobriety. He had never had an attack
of fever, nor any other illness; and he resisted for four
years the effects of a tropical climate, incredible fatigue,
bad food, and nights passed in forests, without any apparent
loss of health or strength, which is doubtless to be attributed to his never taking spirits, and wine only very
sparingly.

His intellectual and moral qualities did not seem less
to promise success; both a *savant* and an artist, he was
also an indefatigable hunter, and had a degree of kindness
mingled with his courage which was sure to gain the good-
will of the uncivilized people among whom he had to live.
In all these respects M. Mouhot fulfilled the expectations
of the *savans* of England and of his numerous friends, as
is evident by the rich collections made by him in so short
a time, by the cordial welcome which he met with throughout his travels, by the respect paid to him by all learned
men, and by the unanimous feelings of regret at his death,
both in England and on the Continent. Although a Protestant, he inspired sincere friendships among the Catholic
missionaries in Siam and the other countries he visited
from 1858 to 1861, friendships which are clearly shown
in his journal and letters.

We shall not say much about his travels; they form the
subject of this work, which, even in its unfinished state,
we trust will present much important information to the

geographer and archæologist, to the naturalist and linguist.
Many capable of judging have already hastened to pay
their tribute of praise to the traveller who has enriched
such various branches of science, and displayed to the
world the riches of the extreme East.

M. Mouhot dedicated the last four years of his life to
exploring the interior of Siam; he first travelled through
that country, then through Cambodia, and afterwards re-
ascended the Mekong as far as the frontiers of Laos;
visited one of the savage and independent tribes inhabiting the district between those two countries and Cochin
China; then, after having crossed the great lake Touli-
Sap, he explored the provinces of Ongcor and Battambong,
where he discovered splendid ruins, especially the Temple
of Ongcor the Great, which is nearly perfect, and perhaps
unparalleled in the world.

Passing from the basin of the Mekong into that of the
Menam, he saw mountains of which the principal peak
was more than 6000 feet high. He returned occasionally
to Bangkok, the capital of Siam, in order to make preparations for fresh expeditions. The loss, by the wreck
of the *Sir James Brooke*, of a very valuable collection, did
not discourage him; but he set about at once to replace it.
At the time of his death, which happened on 10th November, 1861, he was *en route* for the provinces south-west
of China, when, having already penetrated far into the
interior, he was attacked by the jungle fever, and died
after twenty-two days' illness. His energetic mind, full of
the task he had to perform, remained clear to the end,

and a few last words were written by him, his strength of will overcoming his weakness.

He set out for Louang-Prabang on 15th October, and on the 18th halted at H—— (the name is unfinished in the manuscript); the next day he felt the first symptoms of the fever to which he fell a victim. From the 29th October he wrote nothing. The last words in the journal, "Have pity on me, O my God," show the religious principles which had guided his life.

All that we know of his last days and his lamentable end, was learned from his two native servants, who were strongly attached to him; and through Sir R. Schomburgh, the English Consul at Bangkok, and Dr. Campbell, Surgeon R.N., who was attached to the British consulate, and who returned shortly afterwards to England, when he placed all the papers, notes, and drawings left by M. Mouhot in the hands of his widow and of M. Charles Mouhot, whose task it has been to arrange this legacy as methodically as possible, considering the great difficulty of finding the connecting links of his various descriptions.

The 'Athenæum' and the 'Illustrated London News'* both inserted an account of the death of M. H. Mouhot; and the latter journal justly designated his death as another addition to the long list of martyrs to science. It likewise gave a short sketch of the discoveries and scientific services of this intrepid traveller.

Ornithology, entomology, and other branches of natural

* Number for August 9, 1862, which also contained a tolerably good portrait of M. Mouhot.

history, were represented in the collection sent by M. Mouhot to his agent, Mr. S. Stevens, of Bloomsbury Street,
London, and were the subject of several papers by Dr.
Gray, Dr. Gunter, Dr. Louis Pfeiffer, and other naturalists,
members of the Zoological Society of London, and published in the 'Annals and Magazine of Natural History.'
At a meeting of the Royal Geographical Society on the
10th of March, 1862, Sir R. Murchison seized the occasion
of reading some letters from the traveller relating to the
topography of Cambodia, to pay a tribute of gratitude to
his merit as a zoological collector and explorer. "His
loss," he observed, "will be much felt by men of science,
and a long time may elapse before another man will be
found bold enough to follow his steps in that country of
virgin forests and fever, and to the exploring of which he
sacrificed his home, his health, and his life."

Mr. Stevens, in acquainting the brother of the traveller
with the fact of his having received a new zoological collection which had been consigned to him, says, "I can
truly say that the insects and shells equal, if they do not
surpass, any in the most beautiful collections I have ever
received, and show clearly what a marvellously rich country
for the naturalist lies between Siam and Cochin-China."
A splendid *scarabœus* was also sent to Mr. Stevens, who
remarks, that " this insect was described in the 'Zoological
Review' of Paris under the name of *Mouhotia gloriosa*, as
a mark of respect to the late M. Mouhot, and stated to be
one of the most magnificent known."

The Society of Montbéliard hastened, on the first news

of his death, to write to his brother, and the letter contains
these words:—" His work was left unfinished, but it was
gloriously commenced, and his name will not perish!"

Amidst all these eulogiums of a life, short but well
spent, one of the most touching is a letter from M. Marie
Ch. Fontaine, missionary at Saigon in Cochin-China, who
was in Paris in August, 1862, and saw in a newspaper
the death of the man whom he had met in Siam and Cambodia, which was soon confirmed by a letter from his
brother. This worthy missionary addressed to M. Charles
Mouhot a letter, of which the whole should be read; we
only extract the following passage:—" I learned, when on
my mission, the death of my father, and then that of my
mother. I assure you that these two cruel blows scarcely
made more impression on me than the news of the death
of a man whose equal I had not met with during the
twenty years that I have inhabited that country; and to
hear of his dying without any help, and having no one
near him but his servants throughout his illness, in a
country so barbarous, was more than sufficient to make
tears flow at the memory of this good and benevolent
friend. Be assured, my dear Sir, that my sentiments are
shared by all here who knew M. Mouhot. The natives
themselves must have felt regret at his loss, for all whom
he came near praised him for his behaviour towards them,
and his gentleness and generosity; qualities invaluable in
the eyes of that people."

In a letter recently addressed by Sir R. Schomburgh to
M. C. Mouhot, enclosing the portraits of the King and

Queen of Siam, that gentleman thus expresses himself :—
" I admired the zeal and knowledge of your late brother;
and his manners were so amiable and modest that one
would have thought that every one with whom he came
in contact would have exercised all their influence to assist
him in his plans. I often regretted that he was not an
English subject, that I might have been able to do more
for him. I shall look impatiently for the publication of
his book, and have given orders that the French edition
may be forwarded to me at once."

I can add nothing to these touching testimonies, which
paint faithfully the man as I knew him in Holland. The
affectionate heart of Henri Mouhot awakened in others
an affection which the tomb does not destroy, but which
grows stronger with time.

J. J. BELINFANTE.

The Hague, December 15, 1862.

CONTENTS OF VOL. I.

CHAPTER X.

CHAPTER XI.

CHAPTER XII.

ILLUSTRATIONS TO VOL. I.

THE RIVER MENAM.

Drawn by M. Sabatier, from a Sketch by M. Mouhot.

TRAVELS IN INDO-CHINA,

ETC.

CHAPTER I.

THE VOYAGE — FIRST IMPRESSIONS OF SIAM; AND OF BANGKOK, ITS CAPITAL—RECEPTION IN THE PALACE—THE TWO KINGS OF SIAM.

ON the 27th April, 1858, I embarked at London, in a sailing ship of very modest pretensions, in order to put in execution my long-cherished project of exploring the kingdoms of Siam, Cambodia, and Laos, and visiting the tribes who occupy the banks of the great river Mekon.

I spare the reader the details of the voyage and of my life on board ship, and shall merely state that there were annoyances in plenty, both as regards the accommodation for the passengers and the conduct of the captain, whose sobriety was more than doubtful.

We arrived at Singapore on the 3rd September. The census, taken in May, 1859, of the population of this beautiful and flourishing settlement, gave the following results.—Total, 81,792, of whom only 450 were Euro-

peans, and 1995 Eurasians, or of a mixed race, such as
Indo-English, Indo-Portuguese, and Indo-Dutch. The
Chinese numbered 50,043, the Klings 11,735, and Malays
10,880; the women belonging to these races being com-
puted at no more than 3248, 963, and 3700 respectively.
The remainder of the population was composed of Ben-
galese 1236, Burmese and Siamese 14, Bugese 916,
Javanese 3408, and Arabs 117.

There are in the island 13 schools, 70 temples or
pagodas, 13 hotels and taverns, 26 pawnbrokers, 87 spirit-
merchants, 144 houses licensed for opium-smoking, and
11 houses for the sale of a peculiar spirit unknown in
France, but which is extracted from rice, and known under
the name of arrack. The fishing-boats number 750.
Facilities for locomotion and traffic are provided by 589
public carriages, 1180 passenger-boats, and 600 carts for
the transport of merchandise.

In addition to the population of Singapore itself, the
islands in the immediate vicinity, and forming a part
of the settlement, contain 1500 inhabitants, making the
entire population of Singapore and its dependencies
nearly 83,000. I made only a short stay there, my chief
object being to gain information respecting the country
I was about to visit. On the 12th of the same month,
after a very monotonous voyage, we arrived at the mouth
of the river Menam, on whose banks Bangkok is built. A
vast sandbank here bars the entrance of large ships, and
compels them to go eight or nine miles farther up the
gulf, and discharge their cargoes at great additional

VIEW IN THE GULF OF SIAM.

Drawn by M. Sabatier, from a Sketch by M. Mouhot.

expense. Our vessel, however, only drawing eight feet
of water, passed without much difficulty, and anchored
at Paknam in front of the Governor's house, whither the
captain and myself proceeded without loss of time, in order
to obtain the necessary permission to continue our route.

This formality over, I hastened to visit the forts, which
are of brick and battlemented, the markets, and some of
the streets. Paknam is the Sebastopol or Cronstadt of the
Kings of Siam; nevertheless, I fancied that a European
squadron could easily master it, and that the commander,
after breakfasting there, might dine the same day at
Bangkok.

On a little island in the middle of the river rises a
famous and rather remarkable pagoda, containing, I was
told, the bodies of their last kings. The effect of this
pyramidal structure reflected in the deep and limpid
water, with its background of tropical verdure, was most
striking. As for the town, all that I saw of it was dis-
gustingly dirty.

The Menam deserves its beautiful name—Mother of
Waters—for its depth permits the largest vessels to coast
along its banks without danger: so closely, indeed, that
the birds may be heard singing gaily in the overhanging
branches, and the hum of numberless insects enlivens the
deck by night and day. The whole effect is picturesque
and beautiful. Here and there houses are dotted about
on either bank, and numerous villages give variety to the
distant landscape.

We met a great number of canoes managed with

incredible dexterity by men and women, and often even
by children, who are here early familiarised with the water·
I saw the Governor's children, almost infants, throw
themselves into the river, and swim and dive like water-
fowl. It was a curious and interesting sight, particularly
from the strong contrast between the little ones and the
adults. Here, as in the whole plain of Siam, which I
afterwards visited, I met most attractive children, tempting
one to stop and caress them; but as they grow older they
rapidly lose all beauty, the habit of chewing the betel-
nut producing an unsightly blackening of the teeth and
swelling of the lips.

It is impossible to state the exact population of Bangkok,
the census of all Eastern countries being extremely imperfect. It is estimated, however, at from three to four
hundred thousand inhabitants. Owing to its semi-aquatic
site, we had reached the centre of the city while I
believed myself still in the country; I was only unde-
ceived by the sight of various European buildings, and the
steamers which plough this majestic river, whose margins
are studded with floating houses and shops.

Bangkok is the Venice of the East, and whether bent
on business or pleasure you must go by water. In place
of the noise of carriages and horses, nothing is heard but
the dip of oars, the songs of sailors, or the cries of the
Cipayes (Siamese rowers). The river is the high street
and the boulevard, while the canals are the cross streets,
along which you glide, lying luxuriously at the bottom of
your canoe.

GENERAL VIEW OF BANGKOK.

Drawn by M. Bocourt, from a Sketch by M. Mouhot.

We cast anchor in front of the cathedral of the
French Mission and of the modest palace of Monseigneur
Pallegoix, the worthy archbishop, who, for nearly thirty
years, without any assistance but that of missionaries as
devoted as himself, has made the revered emblem of
Christianity and the name of France respected in these
distant regions.

The sight of the Cross in foreign lands speaks to the
heart like meeting with an old friend; one feels comforted
and no longer alone. It is beautiful to see the devotion,
self-denial, and courage of these poor and pious missionaries; a blessing as they are, also, to travellers, it
would be ungrateful not to render them the gratitude
which is their just due.

For some time past, particularly since the wars in
China and Cochin-China, Siam has been much talked of
in Europe; and, relying on the faith of treaties of peace
and commerce, several French and English houses of
business have been established there. Unfortunately,
there was much deception on the part of the native authorities, which has given rise to general and well-founded
complaints from the merchants. The fact is, that they
have dangerous competitors in the mandarins and even
in the princes, who monopolise the greater part of the
trade in rice and sugar, their chief articles of commerce,
which they despatch in their junks and other vessels.
Moreover, the people were not prepared for the change
which had taken place in the laws, and had scarcely cultivated more than enough for home consumption; add

to this that the population is far from numerous, and, the Siamese being an indolent race, most of the agriculture falls into the hands of the Chinese, who flock to Singapore, Australia, and California.

The country certainly merits the reputation which it enjoys for beauty, but it is especially in its mountain scenery that nature displays its grandeur.

During a ten years' residence in Russia I witnessed the frightful effects of despotism and slavery. At Siam, results not less sad and deplorable obtruded themselves on my notice ; every inferior crouches before a higher in rank; he receives his orders kneeling, or with some other sign of abject submission and respect. The whole of society is in a state of prostration.

I was making my preparations for departure on the 16th October, my purpose being to penetrate into the north of the country and visit Cambodia and the savage tribes belonging to it, when I received an invitation from the King of Siam to be present at the great dinner which this monarch gives every year, on his birthday, to the European residents in Bangkok. I was presented by Monseigneur Pallegoix, and his Majesty's reception was kind and courteous. His costume consisted of a pair of large trousers, a short brown jacket of some thin material, and slippers; on his head he wore a little copper helmet like those worn by the naval officers, and at his side a rich sabre.

Most of the Europeans in Bangkok were present at the dinner, and enthusiastic toasts were drunk to the health

THE SECOND KING OF SIAM.

of his Majesty, who, instead of being seated, stood or walked round the table, chewing betel and addressing some pleasant observation to each of his guests in turn. The repast was served in a vast hall, from whence we could see a platoon of the royal guard, with flags and drums, drawn up in the courtyard. When I went to take leave of the King, he graciously presented me with a little bag of green silk, containing some of the gold and silver coin of the country,—a courtesy which was most unexpected, and for which I expressed my gratitude.

This King, whose official title is Somdel Phra, Paramanda, Maha-Mangkut—that is, His Majesty the King, encircled with the Great Crown—was born on the 18th October, 1804, and mounted the throne of Siam in the year 1851. The first part of his life was passed in complete retirement in a monastery, in this following the example of many of his predecessors: for all sects emanating from Buddhism think it necessary that the rulers of nations should prepare themselves for supreme power by a previous life of repose and sanctity.

It was only after the accession of Somdel Phra that the mastery he had gained over the most difficult sciences became known. After having applied himself to the history and geography of his country, he turned to the study of astronomy, natural philosophy, politics, and philology. He was familiar not only with all the dialects of Siam and Indo-China, but also with ancient Sanscrit and English, in which latter language he had written several treatises. The English journals at Hong-Kong have been honoured by articles from his pen, and no one who reads them can be surprised that the august contributor should have been elected a member of the Asiatic Society in London, a body which reckons on its list so many savans of the first rank.

His Majesty had also acquired a fair knowledge of Latin from the French missionaries, especially from Archbishop Pallegoix, who has been his friend for thirty years. He studied astronomy almost without a master, and had gained such proficiency in that science as to be able to calculate an eclipse and determine the latitude and longitude of a place. He introduced a printing-press into his dominions, in which both Siamese and Roman characters are used. His language testifies to his education and intelligence, though it more resembles the phraseology of books than that of ordinary conversation.

His predecessor had several hundred wives, and I believe the present King does not possess fewer than some dozen ; but he only bestowed the title of queen on one, whose portrait hangs by the side of his own, and whose death, soon after my visit, left him inconsolable.

A singular institution, peculiar to Siam, Cambodia, and Laos, exists in a second king, slightly inferior to the other, and having a sort of reflected authority, the limits of which are not easily defined. His official title is Wangna, a word which literally signifies " the youngest King." He has his court, his mandarins, and his little army, and they pay him royal honours ; but in reality he

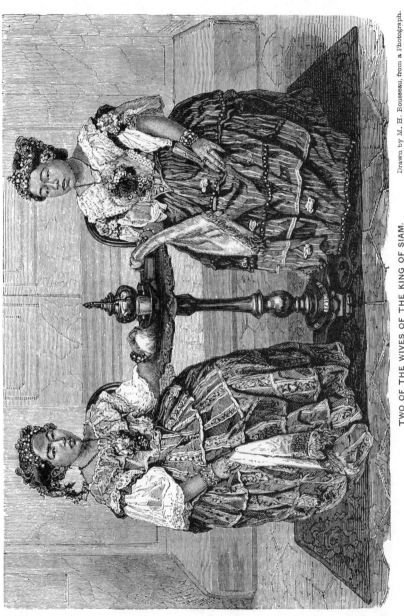

TWO OF THE WIVES OF THE KING OF SIAM.

Drawn by M. H. Rousseau, from a Photograph.

E 2

is merely the first subject of his colleague. His sole pre-rogative is exemption from the customary prostration before the King, instead of which he salutes him by raising both hands in the air. It is true, he is allowed to draw largely from the royal treasury, but never without an order from the King, which, however, is rarely refused.

The present Wangna, Pin-Klau Chan You Hona, is the legitimate brother of the First King and his intended successor. He is a perfect gentleman, of a cultivated mind, writing and speaking English, and leading in his palace—which is arranged and furnished in our Western fashion—the life of a rich, noble, and learned European. He is fond of books and scientific researches, and familiar with all the improvements of modern civilization; he possesses in a higher degree than his brother the capa-city for government and statesmanship, and deplores more than any one the sad condition in which his country lan-guishes.

Before asking the reader to accompany me into the interior of Siam, it will not be amiss, in the next chapter, to give a short sketch of the kingdom itself and of its past history.

CHAPTER II.

THE name of Siam was first heard in Europe in the year 1502. Nine years after Alphonso d'Albuquerque had conquered the peninsula of Malacca, some intercourse took place between Portugal and Siam, which, however, was interrupted by the long wars between this country and the Burmese.

In 1632 an English vessel touched at the ancient capital Ayuthia. Shortly afterwards the Portuguese at Goa sent a party of Dominican and Franciscan missionaries to Siam, and the communication between the two nations became more frequent. The King engaged in his service three hundred Portuguese soldiers, who were distributed over the country, having lands allotted to them for cultivation, and who contracted marriage with native women. The missionaries built two churches, and established a school.

After a while the Dutch power began to supplant that of Portugal in the East, and, in the course of the seventeenth century, the empire of Siam was brought into contact with the new conquerors of the Indies. The Portuguese colonies gradually became extinct; and the influence of the Batavian settlers increased so much, that they esta-

blished at Ayuthia a Dutch factory, which, under its
director Schonten, attained its greatest prosperity about
the year 1690. Various articles of merchandise were introduced into Siam, from whence, in return, were exported
skins, sapan-wood, &c. ; and the country, from its position
and the richness of its natural productions, became at
that time an important station for the commerce of the
Dutch between China and Japan, and the valuable islands
of Ceylon and Java.

France herself, at the height of her maritime power
under Louis XIV., could not equal the power of the
Dutch Company, though, at one period, chances eminently
favourable presented themselves to her. A Greek adven-
turer named Constantine Phaulcon, of whom we shall have
subsequently to speak, opened for himself a remarkable
career in Siam, where he was converted to Romanism
by the missionaries. He suggested to the King to send
envoys to Louis XIV., and their arrival in France produced a sensation, the echo of which we have heard in
our own day in the embassy from the same country to
Napoleon III. His Most Christian Majesty replied by
accrediting ambassadors to the Siamese Court—De Chau-
mont in 1685, and La Loubéze in 1687. Each was
accompanied by several Jesuit priests; and a force of 500
men, under the command of General de Fargues, was
stationed at Bangkok. The General, however, was not
able to maintain his position ; Constantine met with a
tragic end, and the Jesuit fathers were kept as hostages.
These failures destroyed the French influence for more

than a century and a half, and for a time strengthened the power of Holland.

This brief glance at the intercourse between Europe and Siam in the sixteenth and seventeenth centuries will suffice.

The celebrated German traveller Mandelslohe visited the capital Ayuthia in 1537, and called it the Venice of the East—a title which, as we have seen, is equally applicable to the modern capital Bangkok. The Portuguese explorer Mendez Pinto, who also paid a visit to Siam in the sixteenth century, gives a favourable picture of the country, and all that has since come to our knowledge respecting it shows that he merited a greater faith in his statements than was accorded to him by his contemporaries.

The empire of Siam is of great extent. Its limits have varied much at different epochs of its history; and even now, with the exception of the western frontier, the lines of demarcation cannot be exactly traced, most of the border-lands being occupied by tribes more or less independent, and there are perpetual wars between the Malay and Burmese races on the one side, and the Cambodian or Chinese on the other. As nearly as can be calculated, the country extends, at present, from the 4th to the 20th or 22nd degree of north latitude, and from the 96th to the 102nd degree of east longitude; and according to this computation, its length would be about 1200 miles and its breadth 400 miles.

The Siamese dominions are divided into forty-one pro-

PAGODA AT AYUTHIA.

Drawn by M. Thérond, from a Photograph.

vinces, each presided over by a phaja or governor, and these, again, are subdivided into numerous districts under the authority of functionaries of inferior rank, of whose administration little can be said in praise.

The northern provinces are five in number—Sangkalôk, Phitsalôk or Phitsanulôk, Kumphang-Phet, Phixai, and Tahëng. In the centre are nine provinces—Nantaburi or Jalat-Khuan, Pak-Pret, Patummatoni or Samkuk, Ayuthia or Krung-Kao, Ang-Thong, Monang-Phrom, Monang-In, Xainat, and Nakhon-Savan.

There are seven in the west—Monang-Pin, Suphan or Suphanaburi, Kan-Chanaburi or Pak-Phrëk, Rapri or Raxaburi, Nakhon-Xaisi, Sakhonburi or Tha-Chin, Samut-Songkhram or Mei-Khlong.

The eastern provinces number ten—Phetsjaboun, Bua-Xum, Sara-Buri, Nopha-Buri, Nakhon-Najok, Patsjin, Kabin, Sasong-Sao or Petriu, Battabâng, and Phanatsani-Khom.

In the south are—Pakhlat or Nakhon-Khuen-Khan, Paknam or Sananthaprakan, Bangplasor or Xalaburi, Rajong, Chantaboun or Chantabouri, Thung-Jai, Phiphri or Phetxaburi, Xumphon, Xaya, and Xalang or Salang.

Siam has been distinguished by the historians of the country under two great divisions—Monang-Nona, the region of the north, at first the more populous portion, and Monang-Tai, the southern region. The Chronicles of the south are sometimes called 'The Chronicles of the Royal City' (Ayuthia), and commence at the period when this place became the capital. De Barrios relates that,

in his time (the fifteenth century), nine states were in subjection to the monarchs of Siam, two only of which were
peopled by the Siamese race—viz., the southern kingdom,
and that of the north, whose chief city was Chaumua.
The Siamese language, likewise, was spoken only in these
two countries.

Siam is called by the natives Thaï, or Monang-Thaï,
which means "free" or "the kingdom of the free."
Archbishop Pallegoix, who is a great authority in these
matters, maintains that the modern name Siam is derived
from Sajam, or "the brown race."*

While several districts in the north and east are tributary to this country, it appears to have been itself
originally a great fief of China. Thus the King of Siam
receives from this neighbouring empire a special confirmation of his authority, much resembling the patronage
accorded by the Sultan to the Barbary states. However,
if the external forms of this vassalage are observed, it is
rather from a profound respect for tradition and ancient
custom than from any virtual recognition of the power
of the Emperor of China to acknowledge or interfere with
the rights of sovereignty. One of the dependencies of this
country, Cambodia, is also claimed by Cochin-China, and
its ruler, unable to resist either of his more powerful
neighbours, is forced to pay tribute to both.

------

* The word Siam is Malay, from which language this name, as well
as many others of Indian places, has been borrowed by Europeans. The
Siamese know it not.

SIAMESE WOMEN.

Drawn by M. Bocourt, from a Photograph.

The population of Siam cannot yet be determined with any great exactness, but it is certain that it bears no proportion to the extent of territory. Archbishop Pallegoix estimates it at only 6,000,000—a computation, however, very different from that of Sir John Bowring. The difficulty of arriving at any correct result is augmented by the Siamese custom of numbering only the men. Thus, the native registers showed, a few years ago, for the male sex, 2,000,000 Siamese, 1,000,000 Laotians, 1,000,000 Malays, 1,500,000 Chinese, 350,000 Cambodians, 50,000 Peguans, and a like number composed of various tribes inhabiting the mountain ranges.

In the north, a chain of mountains, covered with snow, extends from the province of Yunan to China, and its ramifications form two great divisions, between which is situated the fertile valley of Siam. Another chain stretches towards the west, as far as the Malay peninsula. The great river Menam, already mentioned, traverses the level country from north to south, taking its rise in the southern slopes of the mountains of Yunan, and empties itself into the Gulf of Siam. It is the Nile of this region, the great fertility of which is owing to the annual overflowing of its waters, an event eagerly looked for by the inhabitants, and welcomed as a blessing from Heaven. The Menam begins to rise in the month of June, and in August the inundation reaches its height, and then the waves of the ocean, opposing themselves to the current, force the waters of the river back upon its banks. The lands situated towards the middle of the great plain receive most benefit from this operation of nature, the higher districts being too much surrounded by mountains, while the lower are impregnated with so much salt water as to render the cultivation of rice difficult. If the regular inundations are, as a general rule, productive of immense benefit, they now and then, as in Egypt, lay waste the country: thus, for example, that of 1851 destroyed all the sugar-plantations; and the water, to a depth of three or four feet, resting on the earth for some time, a large number of cattle perished, the rice-crops suffered seriously, and many valuable fruit-trees were carried away. Some years afterwards, however, in accordance with nature's beneficent law of compensation, the produce was only the more abundant.

The ancient annals of Siam relate that, about the seventh century, Chinese junks used to ascend the stream as far as Sang-Khalak, a distance of 120 leagues from the sea; at present it is only navigable for 30 leagues at most. This alteration has arisen from a gradually-increasing collection of sand and alluvial deposit—a process which goes on in some of our western rivers, as, for instance, the Rhine and the Meuse.

The low grounds, as is usually the case in hot climates, are less healthy than the mountainous districts, and the forests especially are the seat of malignant fevers. Several other rivers, and numberless canals, fringed with bamboos and fruit-trees, round which fly a multitude of birds, give a pleasing aspect to the country, which is bounded on the horizon by richly-wooded hills.

Drawn by M. Sabatier, from a Sketch by M. Mouhot.

PERFORATED ROCK IN THE ISLE OF EBOULON, GULF OF SIAM.

The rivers are rich in fish, which, in addition to rice, forms the principal food of the people.

The shores of the sea are very picturesque, and the coast is studded with islands covered with the most luxuriant vegetation. "The Gulf of Siam," says Mgr. Pallegoix,

" is not subject to storms, nor to the destructive typhoons experienced on the Chinese seaboard ; thus shipwrecks are of rare occurrence."

Sir John Bowring recommends to his countrymen a project which he believes feasible, and which would scarcely be secondary in importance to the intersection of the Isthmus of Darien or that of Suez. It is the union of the Bay of Bengal with the Gulf of Siam. He hopes that the establishment of amicable relations between Great Britain and the Siamese Empire will lead to the ventilation and eventual solution of a question so interesting both in a geographical and commercial point of view. It would be, in reality, as he says, a noble enterprise, which would considerably shorten the voyage between India and Eastern Asia, by making no longer necessary the tedious détour through the Straits of Malacca, a passage which occupies not days, but weeks.

The soil of this country, composed in great part of alluvial earth, in Siam watered by its great river, and in Cambodia by the Nekong and many other streams, refreshed by the periodical rains, and glowing beneath a tropical sky, possesses almost unlimited capabilities. The mountains in the north contain precious metals, but the working of them is as yet very imperfectly attempted. The tin of Siam has been long in repute ; copper, lead, and iron have also been discovered. Diamonds and other precious stones exist, although the exact localities where they are met with are not known, for the natives are very mysterious on the subject; but it is supposed that diamonds are found on the eastern boundary of the Gulf.

The history of the empire, arranged in the form of chronicles, is preserved in the archives, and not permitted to be inspected by strangers. The late king made investigations into these documents, which, previously to the foundation of Ayuthia, towards the middle of the fourteenth century, only presented a mass of confused materials, in which truth and fable are curiously intermingled, as in the annals of all nations, and pre-eminently those of the Orientals, who love to substitute highly-coloured narratives, in the style of the Arabian Nights, for plain history.

The Siamese trace their genealogy up to the first disciples of Buddha (Gandama), and commence their records five centuries before the Christian era. A succession of dynasties, varying their seat of government, figure in the earlier volumes; and the miracles of Buddha, and the intervention of supernatural beings, are frequently introduced. Later on there are accounts of matrimonial alliances between Siamese princes and the Imperial families of China, and of embassies to, and wars with, neighbouring countries, the whole interwoven with relations of prodigies and marvellous legends respecting Sudra and other divinities. After the establishment of Ayuthia as the capital, history assumes its rightful place, and the succession of the sovereigns and the course of events are registered with tolerable correctness. The city of Ayuthia was founded by Phaja-Utong, who took the title of Phra-Rama-Thibaldi.*

The following dates, drawn from the annals, and marking important epochs in the sacred history of Siam, are believed to be nearly correct :—

	Christian Era.		Buddhist Era.
The reigning Buddha died on the 3rd day of the 6th month of the year of the serpent, corresponding with the year B.C.	543		
The first great Buddhist Council was convoked under Ajatra-Sutra (in India) the year of the death of Buddha ..			
The second grand Council was convoked under Hala-Sokkaraja .. .. .. B.C.	443	. . ..	100
The third, under the rule of Sri Dhamma Soka .. .. B.C.	325	. . ..	218
The fourth grand Council .. .. B.C.	143	. . ..	400
The Buddhist doctor, Phra Buddha Ghosa, introduced Buddhism into Cambodia .. .. A.D.	422	. . ..	965

It was in the year 1000 of the Buddhist era, A.D. 457,

---

* " The word Phra, which so frequently occurs in this work, here appears for the first time; I have to remark that it is probably derived from, or of common origin with, the Pharaoh of antiquity. It is given in the Siamese dictionaries as synonymous with God, ruler, priest, and teacher. It is in fact the word by which sovereignty and sanctity are associated in the popular mind. As the title Divus was appropriated by the Roman Emperor, as in most monarchies a sort of sacredness is attached to the royal person, the orientals have made gods of their kings, their heroes, and their sages, without any scruple. Image-worship is in fact only the materialising or incarnating of the idea of Deity."—*The Kingdom and People of Siam*, Sir John Bowring.

Drawn by M. Catenacci, from a Photograph.

RUINS OF A TEMPLE AND STATUE OF BUDDHA AT AYUTHIA.

F 2

that King Tuang, whose accession and glorious reign
had been announced by a communication from Gandama
himself, and who possessed, in addition to his other
claims to distinction, " a white elephant with black
tusks," introduced the alphabet Tai, which was communicated to a numerous conclave of Buddhist priests. The
ancient chronicles terminate with the establishment of
Chao-Utonng in the new city of Si-Ayo-Thaya (Ayuthia),
but leave the date of this event rather doubtful.

The following is the list of Siamese monarchs since
the foundation of this capital :—

Siamese Era.		Christian Era.	
712	.. ..	1350	Phra Rama Phiobodi.
731	.. ..	1369	—— Rama Suen (his son).
732	.. ..	1370	—— Borom Raxa (his brother).
744	.. ..	1382	—— Rama Suen II.
747	.. ..	1385	—— Phaja Ram (his son).
763	.. ..	1401	Inthaxara.
792	.. ..	1430	Borom Raxa Phirat.
805	.. ..	1442	Boronua Irai Lokharat.
834	.. ..	1472	Phra Rama Phibodi.
875	.. ..	1513	Raxa Kuman.
876	.. ..	1514	Xaja Raxa Phirat.
889	.. ..	1527	Phra Jot Fa.
891	.. ..	1529	Maha Cha Kraphat Raxa Ihirat.
909	.. ..	1547	Phra Chao Xang Phuok.
914	.. ..	1552	Mahinthara Thirat.
926	.. ..	1564	Phra Naret.
957	.. ..	1595	Eka Thotsarot.
963	.. ..	1601	Chao Fa.
964	.. ..	1602	Phra Chao Song Iham.
989	.. ..	1627	Phra Chao Prasal Ihong.
1017	.. ..	1655	Chao Fa Xai.
1018	.. ..	1656	Phra Chao Xam Phuok.
1050	.. ..	1688	Phra Phet Raxa.

Siamese Era.		Christian Era.	
1059	.. ..	1697	Chao Dua.
1068	.. ..	1706	Name unknown.
1120	.. ..	1758	Chao Dok Ma Dua.
1128	.. ..	1766	Interregnum.
1129	.. ..	1767	Phyja Tak.
1173	.. ..	1811	Phra Phuti Chao Luang (the founder of the present dynasty).
1187	.. ..	1825	Phen Din Prasat Ihong.
1213	.. ..	1851	Phra Chao Prasat Ihong.

Instead of dwelling on the ancient history of Siam, we prefer to give an extract from the appendix to the celebrated work of Sir John Bowring, 'The Kingdom and People of Siam:' the passage originally appeared in 'The Chinese Repository,' and is from the pen of the late king:—

" Our ancient capital Ayuthia, before the year A.D. 1350, was but the ruin of an ancient place belonging to Kambuja (now known as Cambodia), formerly called Lawék, whose inhabitants then possessed Southern Siam, or Western Kambuja. Ayuthia is situated in lat. 14° 19′ N., and long. 100° 37′ E. from Greenwich. There were other cities, not far remote, also possessed by the Kambujans; but their precise locality or much of their history cannot now be satisfactorily ascertained. Some time near the year A.D. 1300, the former inhabitants were much diminished by frequent wars with the northern Siamese and the Peguans, or *Mous*, so that these cities were vacated, or left in a ruinous state, and nothing remained but their names.

" Former inhabitants declared that the people of

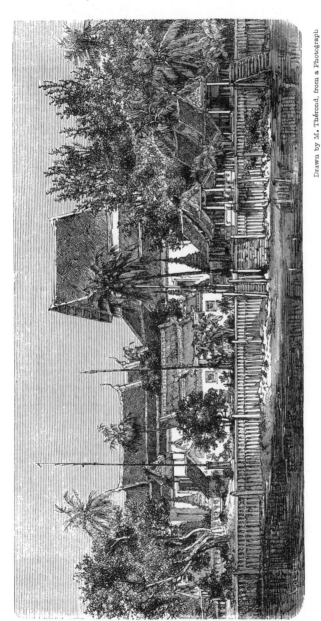

THE PAGODA OF AYUTHIA, FROM THE RIVER.

Drawn by M. Thérond, from a Photograph

Chiang-rái, a province of what is now called Chiang-mái
(North Laos), and Kampengpet, being frequently subjected
to great annoyance from their enemies, deserted their
native country, and formed a new establishment at Ch'á-
liang, in the western part of Siam proper, and built a
city, which they called Thepha-mahá-na-khon, whence has
been preserved in the national records the name of our
capital down to the present day, Krung-Thepha-mahá-na-
khon.   Their city was about lat. 16° N., and long. 99° E.,
and there five kings of the first dynasty reigned, until
the sixth, named U-T'ong Rámá-thi-bodi, ascended the
throne in 1344.   This king, it is said, was son-in-law of
his predecessor, who was named Sirichai Chiang Seu, who
was without male issue, and therefore the throne descended to the son-in-law by right of the royal daughter.

" U-T'ong Rámá-thi-bodi was a mightier prince than
any of his predecessors, and subsequently conquered and
subjected to his sway all Southern Siam, and some provinces in the Malayan peninsula.   He made Ch'á-liang
the seat of his government for six years, and then, in
consequence of the prevalence of disease of a pestilential character, he caused various researches to be made
for some more healthy location, and finally fixed upon the
site of Ayuthia, and there founded his new capital in
April, 1350.   This date is an ascertained fact.   From
this period our Siamese annals are more exact and the
accounts generally reliable, being accompanied by dates
of days, months, and years, from 1350 to 1767.

" Ayuthia, when founded, was gradually improved

and became more and more populous by natural increase, and the settlement there of families of Laos, Kambujans, Peguans, people from Yunnán in China, who had been brought there as captives, and by Chinese and Mussulmans from India, who came for the purposes of trade. Here reigned fifteen kings of one dynasty, successors of and belonging to the family of U-T'ong Rámá-thi-bodi, who, after his death, was honourably designated as Phra Chetha Bida—*i. e.* 'Royal Elder Brother Father.' This line was interrupted by one interloping usurper between the thirteenth and fourteenth. The last king was Mahíntrá-thi-rát. During his reign the renowned King of Pegu, named Chamna-dischop, gathered an immense army, consisting of Peguans, Burmese, and inhabitants of Northern Siam, and made an attack upon Ayuthia. The ruler of Northern Siam was Mahá-thamma rájá, related to the fourteenth king as son-in-law, and to the last as brother-in-law.

"After a siege of three months the Peguans took Ayuthia, but did not destroy it or its inhabitants, the Peguan monarch contenting himself with capturing the king and royal family, to take with him as trophies to Pegu, and delivered the country over to be governed by Mahá-thamma rájá, as a dependency. The King of Pegu also took back with him the oldest son of Mahá-thamma rájá as a hostage: his name was Phra Náret. This conquest of Ayuthia by the King of Pegu took place A.D. 1556.

"This state of dependence and tribute continued but

VIEW TAKEN FROM THE CANAL OF AYUTHIA.

Drawn by M. Thérond, from a Photograph.

a few years. The King of Pegu died, and in the confusion incident to the elevation of his son as his successor,
Prince Náret escaped with his family, and, attended by
many Peguans of influence, commenced his return to his
native land. The new king, on hearing of his escape,
despatched an army to seize and bring him back. They
followed him till he had crossed the Si-thong (Burman,
Sit-thaung) River, where he turned against the Peguan
army, shot the commander, who fell from his elephant
dead, and then proceeded in safety to Ayuthia.

" War with Pegu followed, and Siam again became
independent. On the demise of Mahá-thamma rájá, Prince
Náret succeeded to the throne, and became one of the
mightiest and most renowned rulers Siam ever had. In
his wars with Pegu he was accompanied by his younger
brother, Eká-tassa-rot, who succeeded Náret on the throne,
but, on account of mental derangement, was soon removed,
and Phra Siri Sin Wi-mon-tham was called by the nobles
from the priesthood to the throne. He had been very
popular as a learned and religious teacher, and commanded the respect of all the public counsellors; but he
was not of the royal family. His coronation took place
A.D. 1602. There had preceded him a race of nineteen
kings, excepting one usurper. The new king submitted
all authority in government to a descendant of the former
line of kings, and to him also he intrusted his sons for
education, reposing confidence in him as capable of
maintaining the royal authority over all the tributary
provinces. This officer thus became possessed of the

highest dignity and power. His master had been raised to the throne at an advanced age. During the twenty-six years he was on the throne he had three sons, born under the royal canopy —*i. e.* the great white umbrella, one of the insignia of royalty.

"After the demise of the king, at an extreme old age, the personage whom he had appointed as regent, in full council of the nobles, raised his eldest son, then sixteen years old, to the throne. A short time after the regent caused the second son to be slain, under the pretext of a rebellion against his elder brother. Those who were envious of the regent, excited the king to revenge his brother's death as causeless, and plan the regent's assassination; but he, being seasonably apprised of it, called a council of the nobles and dethroned him after one year's reign, and then raised his youngest brother, the third son, to the throne.

"He was only eleven years old. His extreme youth and fondness for play, rather than politics or government, soon created discontent. Men of office saw that it was exposing their country to contempt, and sought for some one who might fill the place with dignity. The regent was long accustomed to all the duties of the government, and had enjoyed the confidence of their late venerable king; so, with one voice, the child was dethroned and the regent exalted under the title of Phra Chau Pra Sath-thong. This event occurred A.D. 1630.

"The king was said to have been connected with the former dynasty, both paternally and maternally; but the

RUINS OF A PAGODA AT AYUTHIA.

Drawn by M. Thérond, from a Photograph.

connection must have been quite remote and obscure. Under the reign of the priest-king he bore the title Raja Suriwong, as indicating a remote connection with the royal family. From him descended a line of ten kings, who reigned at Ayuthia and Lopha-buri—Louvo of French writers. This line was once interrupted by an usurper between the fourth and fifth reigns. This usurper was the foster-father of an unacknowledged though real son of the fourth king Chau Nárái. During his reign many European merchants established themselves and their trade in the country, among whom was Constantine Phaulkon (Faulkon). He became a great favourite through his skill in business, his suggestions and superintendence of public works after European models, and by his presents of many articles regarded by the people of those days as great curiosities, such as telescopes, &c.

"King Nárái, the most distinguished of all Siamese rulers, before or since, being highly pleased with the services of Constantine, conferred on him the title of Chau Phyá Wicha-yentrá-thé-bodi, under which title there devolved on him the management of the government in all the northern provinces of the country. He suggested to the king the plan of erecting a fort on European principles as a protection to the capital. This was so acceptable a proposal, that at the king's direction he was authorised to select the location and construct the fort.

" He selected a territory which was then employed as garden-ground, but is now the territory of Bangkok. On the west bank, near the mouth of a canal, now called

Báng-luang, he constructed a fort, which bears the name
of Wichayeiw Fort to this day. It is close to the residence of his Royal Highness Chaufá-noi Kromma Khun
Isaret rangsan. This fort and circumjacent territory was
called Thana-buri. A wall was erected, enclosing a space
of about 100 yards square. Another fort was built on the
east side of the river, where the walled city of Bangkok
now stands. The ancient name Bángkôk was in use when
the whole region was a garden.* The above-mentioned
fort was erected about the year A.D. 1675.

" This extraordinary European also induced his grateful
sovereign King Nárái to repair the old city of Lopha-
buri (Louvo), and construct there an extensive royal
palace on the principles of European architecture. On
the north of this palace Constantine erected an extensive
and beautiful collection of buildings for his own residence. Here also he built a Romish church, on which
are still to be seen some inscriptions in European letters,
supposed to be Dutch or German; they assuredly are
neither French nor English (perhaps they are Greek, as
he was of Greek extraction, and born at Cephalonia).
The ruins of all these edifices and their walls are still
to be seen, and are said to be a great curiosity. It is
moreover stated that he planned the construction of
canals, with reservoirs at intervals for bringing water
from the mountains on the north-east to the city Lopha-

---

* Such names abound now, as Bang-cha, Bang-phra, Bang-plá-
soi, &c. ; *Báng* signifying a small stream or canal, such as is seen in
gardens.

Drawn by M. Therond, from a Photograph.

Vol. I. p. 82.

THE GREAT TOWER OF THE PAGODA WAT-CHING AT BANGKOK.

buri, and conveying it through earthen and copper pipes
and syphons, so as to supply the city in the dry season on
the same principle as that adopted in Europe. He commenced also a canal, with embankments, to the holy
place called Phra-Bat, about twenty-five miles south-west
from the city. He made an artificial pond on the summit
of Phra-Bat mountain, and thence, by means of copper
tubes and stop-cocks, conveyed abundance of water to
the kitchen and bath-rooms of the royal residence at the
foot of the mountain. His works were not completed
when misfortune overtook him.

" Many Siamese officers and royal ministers were jealous
of his influence, and murmured their suspicions of his
being a secret rebel. At length he was accused of design-
ing to put the king to death by inviting him to visit the
church he had built, between the walls of which, it is said,
he had inserted a quantity of gunpowder, which was to be
ignited by a match at a given signal, and thus involve
the death of the king. On this serious charge he was
assassinated by private order of the king. (This is the
traditional story: the written annals state that he was
slain in his sedan while faithful to his king, by order of
a rebel prince, who perceived he could not succeed in his
nefarious plans against the throne while Constantine
lived.) The works which he left half done are now generally in ruins, viz. the canal to Phra-Bat and the aqueduct
at the mountains.

" After the demise of Nárái, his unacknowledged son,
born of a princess of Yunnan or Chiang-Mai, and intrusted

for training to the care of Phya Petcha raja, slew Nárái's
son and heir, and constituted his foster-father king, himself
acting as prime minister till the death of his foster-father,
fifteen years after; he then assumed the royal state himself.
He is ordinarily spoken of as Nai Dua. Two of his sons
and two of his grandsons subsequently reigned at Ayuthia. The youngest of these grandsons reigned only a
short time, and then surrendered the royal authority to
his brother and entered the priesthood. While this
brother reigned, in the year 1759, the Burman king,
Meng-luang Alaung Barah-gyi, came with an immense
army, marching in three divisions on as many distinct
routes, and combined at last in the siege of Ayuthia.

" The Siamese king, Chaufa Ekadwat Anurak Moutri,
made no resolute effort of resistance. His great officers
disagreed in their measures. The inhabitants of all the
smaller towns were indeed called behind the walls of
the city, and ordered to defend it to their utmost ability ;
but jealousy and dissension rendered all their bravery
useless. Sallies and skirmishes were frequent, in which
the Burmese were generally the victorious party. The
siege was continued for two years. The Burmese com-
mander-in-chief, Mahá Nōratha, died, but his principal
officers elected another in his place. At the end of the
two years the Burmese, favoured by the dry season, when
the waters were shallow, crossed in safety, battered the
walls, broke down the gates, and entered without resistance. The provisions of the Siamese were exhausted,
confusion reigned, and the Burmese fired the city and

public buildings. The king, badly wounded, escaped with his flying subjects, but soon died alone of his wounds and his sorrows. He was subsequently discovered and buried.

" His brother, who was in the priesthood and now the most important personage in the country, was captured by the Burmans, to be conveyed in triumph to Burmah. They perceived that the country was too remote from their own to be governed by them; they therefore freely plundered the inhabitants, beating, wounding, and even killing many families, to induce them to disclose treasures which they supposed were hidden by them. By these measures the Burmese officers enriched themselves with most of the wealth of the country. After two or three months spent in plunder they appointed a person of Mon or Peguan origin as ruler over Siam, and withdrew with numerous captives, leaving this Peguan officer to gather fugitives and property to convey to Burmah at some subsequent opportunity. This officer was named Phrá Nái Kông, and made his head-quarters about three miles north of the city, at a place called Phō Sam-ton, i. e. 'the three Sacred Fig-trees.' One account relates that the last king mentioned above, when he fled from the city wounded, was apprehended by a party of travellers and brought into the presence of Phyá Nái Kông in a state of great exhaustion and illness; that he was kindly received and respectfully treated, as though he was still the sovereign; and that Phyá Nái Kông promised to confirm him again as ruler of Siam, but his strength failed and he died a few days after his apprehension.

"The conquest by Burmah, the destruction of Ayuthia, and appointment of Phyá Nái Kông, took place in March, A.D. 1767. This date is unquestionable. The period between the foundation of Ayuthia and its overthrow by the Burmans embraces 417 years, during which there were thirty-three kings of three distinct dynasties, of which the first dynasty had nineteen kings with one usurper, the second had three kings, and the third had nine kings and one usurper.

"When Ayuthia was conquered by the Burmese, in March, 1767, there remained in the country many bands of robbers associated under brave men as their leaders. These parties had continued their depredations since the first appearance of the Burman army, and during about two years had lived by plundering the quiet inhabitants, having no government to fear. On the return of the Burman troops to their own country, these parties of robbers had various skirmishes with each other during the year 1767.

"The first king established at Bangkok was an extraordinary man, of Chinese origin, named Pin Tat. He was called by the Chinese Tia Sin Tat, or Tuat. He was born at a village called Bánták, in Northern Siam, in lat. 16° N. The date of his birth was in March, 1734. At the capture of Ayuthia he was thirty-three years old. Previous to that time he had obtained the office of second governor of his own township, Ták, and he next obtained the office of governor of his own town, under the dignified title of Phyá Ták, which name he bears to

PRIEST'S HOUSE NEAR AYUTHIA.

Drawn by M. Thérond, from a Photograph.

the present day. During the reign of the last King of
Ayuthia, he was promoted to the office and dignity
of governor of the city of Kam-Cheng-philet, which
from times of antiquity was called the capital of the
western province of Northern Siam. He obtained this
office by bribing the high minister of the king, Chaufá
Ekadwat Anurak Moutri ; and being a brave warrior, he
was called to Ayuthia on the arrival of the Burman
troops, as a member of the council. But when sent to
resist the Burman troops, who were harassing the eastern
side of the city, perceiving that the Ayuthian government was unable to resist the enemy, he, with his
followers, fled to Chautaburi (Chautabun), a town on the
eastern shore of the Gulf of Siam, in lat. $12\frac{1}{2}°$ N. and
long. 101° 21' E. There he united with many brave
men, who were robbers and pirates, and subsisted by
robbing the villages and merchant-vessels. In this way
he became the great military leader of the district, and
had a force of more than ten thousand men. He soon
formed a treaty of peace with the headman of Báng-
plásoi, a district on the north, and with Kambuja and
Annam (or Cochin China) on the south-east."

Such is the short historical sketch, given by the late
King of Siam, up to this date, and which we must complete from other sources.

As much by stratagem as by force of arms, he gained
possession of the northern districts ; but, not deeming
himself secure enough from hostile attacks in that part of
the country, he decided on falling back towards the south,

and established himself at Bangkok, having previously surprised and put to death Phrá-Nai-Kông, the Burman governor of that place, and seized on a quantity of money, provisions, and ammunition. Its proximity to the sea afforded many advantages, one being that escape would be tolerably easy should fortune prove adverse to him. He there built a palace on the western bank of the river, near the fort, which is now standing.

After various encounters with the Burmans, he reduced them into subjection, mainly through the assistance of his flotilla; and on one occasion he overpowered their whole camp, recovering great part of the booty they had amassed, and finally freeing the country from those bitter foes, who had brought into it so much desolation and terror. The people, in gratitude to their deliverer, gladly aided him in his assumption of royal authority. He issued his mandates from Bangkok, appointed viceroys, and distributed colonists far and wide for the repeopling of the country. Thus, by the end of 1768, he found himself sovereign of all the southern part of Siam and the eastern provinces on the shores of the Gulf.

Profiting by a sanguinary war between China and Burmah, he reconquered the northern district of Horahh. He had still to contend with a revolt organised by a prince of the old dynasty, who, pending the struggle with the Burmans, had taken refuge in Ceylon. This, however, was soon quelled; and two more provinces were recovered, which had taken advantage of the foreign invasion to assert their independence. At the end of three years

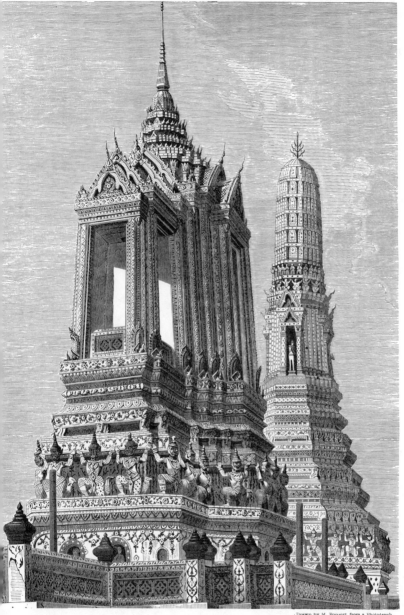

Drawn by M. Bocourt, from a Photograph.

DETAILS OF THE PAGODA WAT-CHANG AT BANGKOK.

Phya-Jak was master of the whole of the north, and had everywhere re-established peace and order. His dominion being now set on a firm foundation, it was a comparatively easy matter successfully to resist a new attack of the Burmans in 1771; and the year following he sent an expedition into the Malay peninsula to take possession of Lagor, whose governor, formerly a vassal of the king, had assumed the sovereignty, and proclaimed Phya-Jak a usurper. The governor, being worsted in several engagements, took refuge with the chief of Patawi, a town in the peninsula, by whom he was surrendered to the followers of Phya-Jak. The king himself, meanwhile, had entered Lagor, made captives of all the governor's family, and carried off his treasures. Among his relatives was a daughter possessed of great beauty: the King gave her a place in his harem; and, through her intercession, her father and all the family were spared. Three or four years afterwards she procured his reinstatement as prince of that district, which at the present day is governed by his descendants.

Phya-Jak's reign did not end happily: in the latter part of his life he fell into a state of morbid melancholy, treated his subjects with cruelty, and lost his popularity. One of his generals, Chakri, commanding in Cambodia, took advantage of these circumstances to concert a plot against the King, who was taken prisoner at Bangkok, and assassinated in the year 1782. Chakri ascended the throne, and, dying soon afterwards, was succeeded by his son. The old quarrels with the Burmans were renewed

about some disputed districts on the northern frontier;
and the Siamese monarch came victoriously out of two
encounters, but, in a third, was overcome, and lost the
western part of the country lying towards Burmah.

This king died in 1809, and his son and successor,
fearing, or feigning to dread, conspiracies against him, put
to death one hundred and seventeen Siamese nobles,
among whom were several generals who had fought by
his father's side against the Burmans. This atrocious
massacre, and the murder of a cousin much beloved by
the people, alienated their affections from him. In other
respects he ruled with wisdom and moderation: keeping
in check the turbulent Malays, he also successfully
repulsed the incursions of the Burmans, bringing his
prisoners to Bangkok, where he gave them lands to cultivate, and thus extended his capital.

The English Government, wishing to form a commercial treaty with this prince, sent Mr. Crawfurd on a
mission to Siam; but although that gentleman obtained
much interesting information respecting the country, he
failed in attaining his purpose. Allowed to remain with
his suite for some time at Bangkok, they were treated
rather as prisoners than guests. Their propositions were
rejected; and the only concession obtained from his
Majesty was a promise not to increase the export and
import duties, the' entire abolition of which had been the
object of the negotiation. The King died in 1824, and
was succeeded by his illegitimate son, Crom-Chiat.

This prince, although he feared the English, saw the

Drawn by M. Catenacci, from a Photograph.

RUINS AT AYUTHIA.

advantages of an extended commerce, and, in 1826, concluded a treaty with Great Britain, then represented by
Captain Burney; but it did not effect all that had been
desired. Direct mercantile intercourse between the two
countries was certainly guaranteed, and assistance in all
cases of shipwreck on the coast; but English subjects,
during their stay, were to be subject to the laws of the
empire; and in each province the commerce could be
extended or limited at the will of the governor. As
these functionaries constantly infringed the terms of the
treaty, and imposed heavy charges on the native articles
exported, as well as on British goods introduced, disappointment naturally resulted; and the Siamese, fearing
a resort to arms on the part of England, made preparations for defence, and fortified the mouth of the Menam.

Meanwhile France was attempting to resume her old
intercourse with Siam; but at first great distrust was
manifested of the Catholic missionaries. In 1780 they
had been ordered, on pain of death, to quit the kingdom;
they retired for a time, but again gradually insinuated
themselves, and met with considerable success. We owe
to Mgr. Pallegoix, in addition to an interesting relation
of the progress of the mission, very important information concerning this empire in the far East—its literature,
and the character and the manners of the inhabitants.
He established there seven churches and four chapels;
a seminary in which are thirty native pupils, several
other schools, and four monasteries; and has baptized
eight thousand Siamese. The King, annoyed at the

advance of the new religion, issued, in 1848, an edict against the missionaries, commanding the destruction of all their places of worship; but it was very partially carried into execution.

The Protestant mission has had a more restricted sphere of action. The celebrated Dr. Gutzlaff made a long stay at Bangkok in 1828, and finished there his translation of the New Testament into Siamese. This work was published at Singapore, and has since been widely circulated. In 1830 he revisited Siam, and translated the greater part of the Scriptures into the languages of Cambodia and Laos. At his request the American Baptists founded the first Protestant mission at Siam; the Presbyterians established a second in 1840; and a third was founded, in 1850, by the Society of the American Board of Commissioners for Foreign Missions. Their labours, however, have not yet been crowned with any great success; nevertheless, by uniting to their ministerial office the practice of medicine, they have done much good, and been favourably received by the people.

The French priests have recently made efforts to gain an influence over the government of Siam. At the death of the King Orom-Chiat, his son Chao-Fa, then twenty years of age, should have been his rightful successor, but an elder illegitimate son seized on the throne, promising his brother to resign it in a few years. This promise not having been fulfilled, the prince, as we have before mentioned, went into complete retirement, and gave himself

up to scientific pursuits. He then came into contact with
the Catholic missionaries, and, at their persuasion, made
himself acquainted with their religion.

In 1851 the King fell ill, and, in spite of the promise
to his brother, wished to appoint one of his own sons as
his successor; but he was answered that the country
had already a sovereign; and, on his decease, Prince
Chao-Fa mounted the throne, under the name of Somdet
Phra. Mgr. Pallegoix addressed to him a letter of con-
gratulation, and presented him with a portrait of Louis
Napoleon, then President of the French Republic. The
King, in return, made him a gift of money, and revoked
the decree of banishment against the five Catholic priests;
and at an audience granted to the bishop before his
departure for Europe, in 1852, he charged him with
messages to Prince Louis Napoleon and the Pope,—
intrusting to him an autograph letter for the latter,
written in English, and expressing a great regard for
his Holiness, as well as his resolution to grant full toleration in his kingdom to the Catholic religion.

He also declared to the archbishop* his intention of
assuring to his subjects entire religious liberty, with
which view he made inquiries from time to time respecting the work of the Catholic missionaries, so as to protect
the converted natives against the heathen governors.
From that time the friendship with France has never

---

* Mgr. Pallegoix died April, 1862, at Bangkok, where the king had
him buried with great pomp.

been interrupted, but has become more and more intimate.

Negotiations were commenced at Bangkok in 1856, in
the name of the French Government, which terminated
in a highly satisfactory manner, a treaty of friendship
and commerce being signed on the 15th August between
the two countries, which was ratified in the following
year. The reception accorded to M. de Montigny, the
French envoy, on this occasion by the two kings, was as
brilliant as it was cordial; nor was he entertained less
kindly by any of the authorities with whom he came
in contact, which proved that Siam has preserved a
pleasing remembrance of the embassies exchanged with
Louis XIV.

All this augured favourably for the future friendly
relations between the two Crowns; and these were confirmed in the year 1861, when his Siamese Majesty sent
an embassy to Paris, where it arrived in June, and was
received with great magnificence.

A French publication* gave the following account of
the commerce with Siam:—"According to the information obtained from M. de Montigny, the commercial and
maritime relations between the kingdom of Siam and
Europe are capable of great development. Already more
than sixty European ships have since 1854 entered yearly
the port of Bangkok, to which must be added a considerable number of junks and *prahus*, which navigate

---

* 'L'Annuaire des Deux Mondes.'   1856-1857.

SIAMESE LADIES AT DINNER.

Drawn by M. Bocourt, from a Photograph

the China Sea and the Malayan Archipelago. The markets of Siam and Laos abound in natural products, such as tobacco, cotton, sugar, spice, and dyes. The forests abound with magnificent trees, particularly teak. By the terms of the treaty with France, the duties, whether import or export, are but three per cent. on the value of the merchandise. There is therefore room for hope that commerce, favoured by the moderation of this tariff, will rapidly increase, and that the French navy will profit by it."

In 'Les Annales du Commerce Extérieur' we find the following account:—" The greater part of the commerce of Siam, Laos, and Cambodia is in the hands of the Chinese, who are much more active and intelligent than the natives. Their mercantile transactions are generally characterised by dishonesty, and we cannot too strongly warn our traders against the frauds of every kind common in this country, such as mixing diverse qualities, adulteration, and saturating various articles with moisture to increase the weight. Raw silk, cotton, and hemp, tobacco, and other merchandise sold by weight, should be carefully examined when delivered, and always compared with the samples, which it is prudent to demand beforehand. The treaty concluded between the Siamese Government and France abolishes all monopolies, and obliges the authorities to watch over the strict and faithful execution of all bargains; therefore, in case of fraud, traders should show a bold face and demand indemnity. They should be careful themselves to set an example of strict probity,

this being the surest way to improve the morality of the
Siamese merchants, who, in dealing with people of proved
honesty, will have less temptation to employ fraud.

" The best commerce will be, doubtless, that of barter;
but it will be difficult to carry this to any great extent,
as these people have few wants. Their ordinary dress,
for example, consists simply of drawers in the hot
season, to which in winter they add one or more scarves,
to cover the upper part of the body. The dignitaries
and wealthy individuals on state occasions wear a rich
suit, consisting of drawers, vest, belt, and a large tunic.
They go barefoot, rarely having even sandals. They are
not of a migratory nature, but have their fixed habitations, and are fond of elegance and luxury. Very imi-
tative in their ways, they feel a pride in putting on a
European dress; and some of those made after the
fashion of Louis XIV.'s reign are still preserved, especially among the descendants of the Portuguese, who
are numerous. The uniforms of the soldiers are copied
from those of Europe; and the whole nation has a great
taste for our Parisian furniture, cotton, silk, and woollen
fabrics, porcelain, china, glass, bronzes, cutlery, iron-
mongery, and toys. Other articles in much esteem with
them, and exported by us, are fire-arms, side-arms,
saddlery, quilts, carpets, clocks, and windows. Our
champagne, brandy, gin, and kirsch, would find in Siam
a certain and ready sale in exchange for the produce of
the country."

The efforts of the Americans to obtain from the

Drawn by M. Bocourt, from a Photograph.

SIAMESE ROPE-DANCER.

Siamese Government favourable terms of commerce were for a time fruitless, but in 1833 a treaty was concluded with the United States, which proved of but little material benefit. A second embassy from the Western Republic failed completely. Balestier, the envoy, could not even obtain an audience from the king, and consequently was unable to deliver his letters of credit. The Americans had been unfortunate in their choice of Balestier as their representative, he having formerly been in a mercantile house at Singapore, and in no favour either with the king or his ministers. A treaty was, however, eventually concluded between the two nations.

Sir James Brooke, the English ambassador at Bangkok, found his advances coldly received. Possibly the Court felt aggrieved by the attitude assumed by that gentleman; but, whatever may have been the reason, matters nearly approached to an open rupture. In September, 1850, he abandoned the negotiation, and Great Britain and Siam remained estranged, until the English Government, desirous to establish friendly relations with the Eastern monarch, despatched Sir John Bowring to Bangkok, with instructions to arrange a commercial treaty, which he effected in 1855. His travels have been published in two volumes, and contain, perhaps, the most accurate and full information we possess of Siam. It was particularly from his acquaintance with the language and manners of the nation that Sir John Bowring acquitted himself so well of his task. He was received at Court with great favour, and had several interviews with the king, whose thirst for knowledge pleased him, and whose good will he managed to secure. In all his negotiations with the Siamese ministers he displayed skill and adroitness. Knowing by experience what would be the most profitable conditions, he succeeded in effecting the ratification of an advantageous agreement on the 18th April, 1855, by which the Crown of Siam consented to the appointment of a British consul at the capital, and granted entire liberty of commerce to English merchants in all the maritime districts of the empire. All duties were lowered; those upon opium almost entirely abolished, provision being made that this article should only be sold to parties specially licensed by the Government. On the other hand, the English traders might purchase all the productions of the country directly from the producer. It is only in times of scarcity that the king reserves to himself the right of forbidding the exportation of rice, salt, and fish. English subjects are permitted to settle at Bangkok, to hold landed property there, build or purchase houses, and to lease land to others; but this last privilege is only accorded after a ten years' possession.

Full toleration in religious matters was guaranteed; and if the presence of a British ship of war was at any time thought requisite for protection of their interests, it was permitted to lie in the Gulf, but not to pass beyond Paknam without express leave from the Government.

Holland has also renewed her ancient dealings with the country, and ratified a treaty during the present year

(1862).   Even before the arrival of the Siamese ambassadors in Europe, a French publication * said very justly,
" The Government of Siam is showing itself more and
more favourable towards Europeans, who find at Bangkok
not only protection, but sympathy and toleration for
their religion.   Bangkok has become one of the most considerable markets of Asia; and the kingdom of Siam is
reaping the reward of the liberal politics which it has
introduced into the extreme East, and which is warmly
seconded by France, England, and the United States."

----

* 'L'Annuaire des Deux Mondes.'   1858-1859.

CHAPTER III.

AFTER my visits of ceremony to the two kings, I hastened to finish the preparations for my voyage. I bought a light boat capable of holding all my chests, reserving a narrow space for myself, and another for the bipeds and quadrupeds forming my adopted family—viz., two rowers, one of whom also officiated as cook, a parroquet, an ape, and a dog. One of the boatmen was a Cambodian, and the other an Annamite, both Christians, and knowing a few words of Latin* and English, so that, as I had already picked up a little Siamese, I could make myself pretty well understood.

On the 19th October I quitted Bangkok, and commenced my voyage up the Menam. The current runs very strongly at this season, and it took us five days to go about seventy miles. At night we suffered terribly from the mosquitoes, and even during the day had to keep up an incessant fanning to drive off these pestilent little vampires. They were so numerous that you could catch

---

* Latin is much esteemed among the native Christians, thanks to the ritual of the Catholic mission.

THE INUNDATION OF THE MENAM.

Drawn by M. Sabatier, from a Sketch by M. Mouhot.

them by handfuls, and their humming resembled that of
a hive of bees. These insects are the curse of all tropical
countries, but here they peculiarly abound in the marshes
and lands covered with slime and mud left by the retiring
waters, where the heat of the sun and the moisture combined, favour their rapid increase. My legs suffered
especially from their attacks.

As the country was entirely inundated, we could not
land anywhere, and even after killing a bird I frequently
could not get at it. All this was very tantalising, for the
banks of the stream are very gay and attractive, nature
wearing here her richest dress.

At this time of the year the rains have entirely
ceased, and do not return for several months. For some
days the north-eastern monsoon had been blowing, the
weather was constantly fine, and the heat tempered by
the wind. The waters, also, were beginning to subside.
It was the period of the religious *fêtes* of the Siamese,
and the river was almost incessantly crowded with long
and handsome boats bearing flags, many of them manned
by more than fifty rowers, all in new and bright-coloured
dresses, trying to pass each other, and exciting themselves
by piercing cries and all sorts of noises. In some cases,
however, sweet and agreeable music formed an accompaniment more grateful to the ear. One boat, belonging
to a mandarin, was escorted by a number of others; it
was remarkable for its elaborate carving and the magnificence of its gilding, and was carrying yellow stuffs
and other presents to the neighbouring pagodas.

The king rarely shows himself in public more than twice a year, once during the month of October, and a second time on board his barge, when a procession is formed consisting of three or four hundred boats, often containing more than 1200 persons. The effect produced by this aquatic pageant, with the rowers in their brilliant dresses, and the multitude of rich flags, is extremely gorgeous, and such as is only to be witnessed in the East.

I was surprised to see the gaiety and light-heartedness of the people, in spite of the yoke which weighs on them and the exorbitant taxes they have to pay; but the softness of the climate, the native gentleness of the race, and the long duration of their servitude from generation to generation, have made them oblivious of the bitterness and hardships inseparable from despotism.

Everywhere they were making preparations for their fishing season, for when the waters subside from the fields, the fish are most plentiful. Dried in the sun, they furnish food for the whole year, and are also exported in large quantities. My boat was so encumbered with chests, boxes, and instruments, that the space left for me was very confined, and I suffered from heat and want of air; but these were trifles compared with the mosquitoes.

On arriving at Ayuthia, my rowers conducted me direct to the excellent Father Larmandy, a French missionary, by whom I was expected. The good priest received me with great kindness, and placed at my disposal all he had to offer in his little house. He employs his leisure time in the study of natural history and in hunting, and

RUINS OF A PAGODA AT AYUTHIA.

Drawn by M. Beaumont, from a Photograph.

frequently accompanied me in my rambles. As we explored the woods we talked of our own charming country
—France.

After a long hunting or rowing expedition, we always,
on our return home, found our repast prepared by my
servant Niou, who excelled in Siamese cookery, and
which our fatigue made us doubly appreciate. Rice
and omelette, or curried fish, bamboo-stalks, haricots,
and other wild vegetables, formed our diet, with the
addition of roast fowls and game when the chase had
been fortunate. Three chickens cost a "fuand" (37
centimes).

The heat was sometimes overwhelming; for a week we
had 90 degrees of Fahrenheit in the shade throughout
the twenty-four hours, but the mosquitoes were fewer in
number, which was a great relief. In our excursions we
visited some ruins amid the woods, and I made a collection of beautiful butterflies, and found several insects
new to me. When I reach Pakpriau, which is a few
days' journey to the north, on the frontier of the lake, I
shall find a mountain country, where I am sure of a
plentiful harvest of insects and land shells.

The comet, which I had already observed on my
journey, shone here with increased brilliancy, and it was
difficult not to believe that the extreme heat was owing
to the influence of this meteor.

I drank nothing but tea, hoping by abstinence from
cold water and from all wine and spirits, to escape fever.
So far, my health had certainly never been better, not

even in the north of Russia. Since the ports have been opened. to English and other European vessels everything has been doubled in price, but still remained cheap as compared with Europe, and I did not spend more than a franc a day for my own living and that of my men. The people flocked to see my collections, and could not imagine what I should do with so many animals and insects. I have before mentioned the skilful management of boats, and the fearlessness in swimming and diving, displayed by very young children. I used to amuse myself by offering some of them my cigar-ends to smoke, in return for which they would run after butterflies, and bring them to me uninjured.

I discovered here a sort of spider, which is also, I believe, found at the Cape, from which a silken thread may be drawn out by taking hold of the end hanging from its body. One has but to go on winding; the thread is very strong, and never breaks.

It requires some time to become accustomed to the shrill chirpings during the night of myriads of grasshoppers and other insects, which seem never to sleep. There appears to be no such thing as silence or repose; everywhere is a continual stir, the gushing overflow of life in this exuberant region.

What a contrast between the subdued tints and cold skies of Europe, and this burning clime and glittering firmament! How pleasant it was to rise in the early morning before the glowing sun had begun his course; and sweeter still in the evening to listen to the thousand

Drawn by M. J. Lange, from a Sketch by M. Mouhot.

ELEPHANTS IN AN ENCLOSURE OR "PARK" AT AYUTHIA.

sounds, the sharp and metallic cries, which seemed as though an army of goldsmiths were at work!

The people here might be extremely happy, were they not kept in such abject slavery; bountiful nature, that second mother, treats them as her spoilt children, and does all for them. The forests abound with vegetables and exquisite fruits; the rivers, the lakes, and the ponds teem with fish; a few bamboos suffice to construct a house; while the periodical inundations render the lands wonderfully fertile. Man has but to sow and to plant; the sun saves him all further trouble; and he neither knows nor feels the want of all those articles of luxury which form part of the very existence of a European.

On the 13th November we arrived at a village called Arajik, where the land was more elevated. Here I killed several white squirrels, animals which I had not met with in the neighbourhood of Bangkok. It is only in the solitude and depth of the woods that one can fully admire and enter into the sort of harmony and concord which reigns in the songs of the various birds, forming such a pleasing kind of symphony that the voice of one is rarely overpowered by that of another; one can enjoy at once the general effect and the melodious note of the particular winged musician we prefer. Scarcely does the sun begin to gild the tops of the trees, when, alert and gay, they commence their morning hymn. The martins, the warblers, the drongos, and the dominicans, respond to the turtle-doves' cooing in the highest branches. Music of a less dulcet nature is discoursed by the aquatic and rapacious tribes, such as cranes, herons, and kingfishers, who from time to time utter their piercing cries.

I procured a guide in the mandarin of the village, who received me courteously, and offered me, in return for some trifling presents, a breakfast of rice, fish, and bananas. I requested his aid in arranging my purposed visit to Mount Phrabat, a favourite object of pilgrimage among the Siamese, who resort thither yearly in great numbers to adore the sacred footprint of Buddha. He volunteered to accompany me, an offer which I gratefully accepted.

The next morning, at seven o'clock, my host was waiting for me at the door, with elephants mounted by their drivers, and other attendants necessary for our expedition. At the same hour in the evening we reached our destination, and, before many minutes had elapsed, all the inhabitants were informed of our arrival; priests and mountaineers were all full of curiosity to look at the stranger. Among the principal people of the place I distributed some little presents, with which they were delighted; but my fire-arms and other weapons were especially the subject of admiration. I paid a visit to the prince of the mountain, who was detained at home by illness. He ordered breakfast for me; and, expressing his regret at not being able to accompany me, sent four men to serve as guides and assistants. As a return for his kindness and urbanity I presented him with a small pistol, which he received with extreme gratification.

Drawn by M. Catenacci, from a Sketch by M. Mouhot.
ROCK AT THE SUMMIT OF MOUNT PHRABAT.

We proceeded afterwards to the western side of the mountain, where is the famous temple containing the footprint of Samona-Kodom, the Buddha of Indo-China. I was filled with astonishment and admiration on arriving at this point, and feel utterly incapable of describing the spectacle which met my view.   What convulsion of

Nature—what force could have upheaved those immense
rocks, piled one upon another in such fantastic forms?
Beholding such a chaos, I could well understand how the
imagination of this simple people, who are ignorant of
the true God, should have here discovered signs of the
marvellous, and traces of their false divinities. It was
as if a second and recent Deluge had just abated; this
sight alone was enough to recompense me for all my
fatigues.

On the mountain summit, in the crevices of the rocks,
in the valleys, in the caverns, all around, could be seen
the footprints of animals, those of elephants and tigers
being most strongly marked; but I am convinced that
many of them were formed by antediluvian and unknown
animals. All these creatures, according to the Siamese,
formed the *cortège* of Buddha in his passage over the
mountain.

As for the temple itself, there is nothing remarkable
about it; it is like most of the pagodas in Siam—on the
one hand unfinished, and on the other in a state of dilapidation; and it is built of brick, although both stone and
marble abound at Phrabat. The approach to it is by a
flight of large steps, and the walls are covered with little
pieces of coloured glass, forming arabesques in great
variety, which glitter in the sun with striking effect.
The panels and cornices are gilt; but what chiefly
attracts attention by the exquisite workmanship are the
massive ebony doors, inlaid with mother-of-pearl of
different colours, and arranged in beautiful designs.

The interior of the temple does not correspond with the
outside; the floor is covered with silver matting, and

H. CATENACCI. del.

Drawn by M. Catenacci, from a Sketch by M. Mouhot.

RELICS FOUND ON MOUNT PHRABAT.

the walls bear traces of gilding, but they are blackene
by time and smoke. A catafalque rises in the centre,

surrounded with strips of gilded serge, and there is to be seen the famous footprint of Buddha. To this sacred spot the pilgrims bring their offerings, cut paper, cups, dolls, and an immense number of toys, many of them being wrought in gold and silver.

After staying a week on the mountain, and adding many pretty and interesting objects to my collection, our party returned to Arajik, the Prince of Phrabat insisting on sending another guide with me, although my friend the mandarin, with his attendants and elephants, had kindly remained to escort me back to his village. There I again partook of his hospitality, and, taking leave of him the day following, I resumed my voyage up the river. Before night I arrived at Saraburi, the chief town of the province of Pakpriau, and the residence of the governor.

Saraburi is a place of some extent, the population consisting chiefly of Siamese, Chinese, and Laotian agriculturists; and consists, like all towns and villages in Siam, of houses constructed of bamboo. They peep out, half hidden among the foliage along the banks of the river; beyond are rice-plantations, and, farther in the background, extensive forests, inhabited solely by wild animals.

On the morning of the 26th we passed Pakpriau, near which the cataracts begin. The waters were still high, and we had much trouble to fight against the current. A little to the north of this town I met with a poor family of Laotian Christians, of whom the good

Vol I. p. 120.

PAGODA AT MOUNT PHRABAT, WHERE IS PRESERVED THE FOOTPRINT OF BUDDHA.

Drawn by M. Catenacci, from a Sketch by M. Mouhot.

Father Larmandy had spoken to me.* We moored our boat near their house, hoping that it would remain in safety while I explored the mountains in the neighbourhood, and visited Patawi, which is the resort of the Laotian pilgrims, as Phrabat is of the Siamese.

All the country from the banks of the river to the hills, a distance of about eight or nine miles, and the whole surface of this mountain range, is covered with brown iron-ore and aërolites; where they occur in the greatest abundance, vegetation is scanty and consists principally of bamboo, but it is rich and varied in those places where the detritus has formed a thicker surface of soil. The dense forests furnish gum and oil, which would be valuable for commerce if the indolent natives could be prevailed on to collect them. They are, however, infested with leopards, tigers, and tiger-cats. Two dogs and a pig were carried off from the immediate vicinity of the hut of the Christian guardians of our boat during our stay at Pakpriau; but the following day I had the pleasure of making the offending leopard pay for the robbery with his life, and his skin served me for a mat.

Where the soil is damp and sandy I found numerous traces of these animals, but those of the royal tiger are more uncommon. During the night the inhabitants dare not venture out of doors; but in the day-time the creatures, satisfied with the fruits of their predatory

---

* Father Larmandy was the interpreter of the Siamese embassy to France in 1860-1861.

rambles, skulk into their dens in the recesses of the
woods.   One day I went to explore the eastern part of
the chain of Pakpriau, and, becoming excited in the
chase of a wild boar, we soon lost ourselves in the forest.
The animal made his way through the brushwood much
more easily than we could—encumbered as we were with
guns, hatchets, and boxes—and we ere long missed the
scent.   By the terrified cries of the monkeys we knew we
could not be far from some tiger or leopard, doubtless,
like ourselves, in search of prey; and, as night was
drawing in, it became necessary to retrace our steps
homeward for fear of some disagreeeble adventure.   With
all our efforts, however, we could not find the path.   We
were far from the border of the forest, and were forced to
take up our abode in a tree, among the branches of which
we made a sort of hammock.   On the following morning
we regained the river.

I endeavoured fruitlessly to obtain oxen or elephants
to carry our baggage with a view of exploring the
country, but all beasts of burden were in use for the
rice-harvest.   I therefore left my boat and its contents
in charge of the Laotian family, and we set off, like
pilgrims, on foot for Patawi on a fine morning with a
somewhat cloudy sky, which recalled to me the pleasant
autumn days of my own country.   My only companions
were Küe and my young Laotian guide.   We followed
for three hours, through forests infested with wild beasts,
the road to Korat, and at last reached Patawi.   As at
Phrabat, there is a bell, both at the foot of the mount

VIEW OF THE MOUNTAINS OF KORAT, TAKEN FROM PATAWI.　　Drawn by M Catenacci, from a Sketch by M. Mouhot

and at the entrance of a long and wide avenue leading
to the pagoda, which the pilgrims ring on arriving, to
inform the good genii of their presence and bespeak a
favourable hearing to their prayers.   The mount is
isolated, and about 450 feet in height; its formation
is similar to that of Phrabat, but, although its appearance
is equally grand, it presents distinct points of variation.
Here are not to be seen those masses of rock, piled
one upon another, as if hurled by the giants in a
combat like that fabled of old.   Patawi seems to be
composed of one enormous rock, which rises almost
perpendicularly like a wall, excepting the centre portion,
which towards the south hangs over like a roof, projecting eighteen or twenty feet.   At the first glance
might be recognised the action of water upon a soil
originally clay.

There are many footprints similar to those of Phrabat,
and in several places are to be seen entire trunks of
trees in a state of petrifaction lying close to growing
individuals of the same species. They have all the
appearance of having been just felled, and it is only on
testing their hardness with a hammer that one feels sure
of not being mistaken.   An ascent of several large stone
steps leads, on the left hand, to the pagoda, and, on the
right, to the residence of the Talapoins, or priests, who
are three in number,—a superior and two assistants,
appointed to watch and pay reverence to the precious
"rays" of Somanakodom. Were the authors who have
written about Buddhism ignorant of the signification of

the word " ray " employed by the Buddhists? Now, in
the Siamese language, the same word which means " ray "
signifies also shadow, and it is through respect for their
deity that the first meaning is applied.

The priests were much surprised to see a " farang "
(foreigner) in their pagoda, but some trifling gifts soon
established me in their good graces. The superior was
particularly charmed with a magnet which I gave him,
and amused himself with it for a long time, uttering
cries of delighted admiration as he saw it attract and
pick up all the little pieces of metal which he placed
near it.

I went to the extreme north of the mount, where
some generous being has kindly had constructed, for the
shelter of travellers, a hall, such as is found in many
places near pagodas. The view here is indescribably
splendid, and I cannot pretend to do justice either with
pen or pencil to the grand scenes which here and
elsewhere were displayed before my eyes. I can but
seize the general effect and some of the details; all I can
promise to do is to introduce nothing which I have not
seen. Hitherto all the views I had seen in Siam had
been limited in extent, but here the beauty of the country
is exhibited in all its splendour. Beneath my feet was a
rich and velvety carpet of brilliant and varied colours;
an immense tract of forest, amidst which the fields of rice
and the unwooded spots appeared like little streaks of
green; beyond, the ground, rising gradually, swells into
hills of different elevations; farther still to the north and

east, in the form of a semicircle, is the mountain-chain of
Phrabat and that of the kingdom of Muang-Lôm; and in
the extreme distance those of Korat, fully sixty miles
distant. All these join one another, and are, in fact, but
a single range. But how describe the varieties of form
among all these peaks! In one place they seem to melt
into the vapoury rose-tints of the horizon, while nearer at
hand the peculiar structure and colour of the rocks bring
out more strongly the richness of the vegetation; there,
again, are deep shadows vying with the deep blue of the
heaven above; everywhere those brilliant sunny lights,
those delicate hues, those warm tones, which make the
tout ensemble perfectly enchanting. The spectacle is one
which the eye of a painter can seize and revel in, but
which his brush, however skilful, can transfer most imperfectly to his canvas.

At the sight of this unexpected panorama a cry of
admiration burst simultaneously from all mouths. Even
my poor companions, generally insensible to the beauties
of nature, experienced a moment of ecstacy at the
sublimity of the scene. "Oh! *di, di*" (beautiful), cried
my young Laotian guide; and when I asked Küe what
he thought of it, "Oh! master," he replied, in his mixed
jargon of Latin, English, and Siamese, "the Siamese see
Buddha on a stone, and do not see God in these grand
things. I am pleased to have been to Patawi."

On the opposite side, viz. the south, the picture is
different. Here is a vast plain, which extends from the
base of Patawi and the other mountains beyond Ayuthia,

whose high towers are visible in the distance, 120 miles off. At the first glance one distinguishes what was formerly the bed of the sea, this great plain having taken the place of an ancient gulf: proof of which is afforded by numerous marine shells, many of which I collected in a perfect state of preservation; while the rocks, with their footprints and fossil shells, are indicative of some great change at a still earlier period.

Every evening some of the good Laotian mountaineers came to see the "farang." These Laotians differ slightly from the Siamese: they are more slender, have the cheek-bones more prominent, and have also darker complexions. They wear their hair long, while the Siamese shave half of the head, leaving the hair to grow only on the top. They deserve praise for their intrepidity as hunters, if they have not that of warriors. Armed with a cutlass or bow—with which latter weapon they adroitly launch, to a distance of one hundred feet, balls of clay hardened in the sun, they wander about their vast forests, undis-mayed by the jaguars and tigers infesting them. The chase is their principal amusement, and, when they can procure a gun and a little Chinese powder, they track the wild boar, or, lying in wait for the tiger or the deer, perch themselves on a tree or in a little hut raised on bamboo stakes.

Their poverty borders on misery, but it mainly results from excessive indolence, for they will only cultivate just sufficient rice for their support; this done, they pass the rest of their time in sleep, lounging about the woods, or

LAOTIAN.

making excursions from one village to another, paying visits to their friends on the way.

At Patawi I heard much of Korat, which is the capital of the province of the same name, situated five days' journey north-east of Pakpriau, that is about 120 miles; and I determined, if possible, to visit it by and by. It appears to be a rich country, producing, especially, silk of good quality. Caoutchouc-trees abound, but are neglected by the inhabitants, who are probably ignorant of their value. I brought back a magnificent specimen of the gum, which was much admired by the English merchants at Bangkok. Living, according to report, is fabulously cheap: six fowls may be purchased for a *fuang* (37 centimes), 100 eggs for the same sum, and all other things in proportion. But to get there one has to cross the famous forest of "the King of the Fire," which is visible from the top of Patawi, and it is only in the dry season that it is safe to attempt this; during the rains both the water and the atmosphere are fatally pestilential. The superstitious Siamese do not dare to use fire-arms there, from fear of attracting evil spirits who would kill them.

During all the time I spent on the top of the mountain the chief priest was unremitting in his attentions to me. He had my luggage carried into his own room, gave me up his mats to add to mine, and in other ways practised self-denial to make me as comfortable as was in his power. The priests complain much of the cold in the rainy season, and of the torrents which then rush

from the summit of the mountain; they are also greatly
disturbed by the tigers, which, driven from the plains by
the inundations, take refuge on the high ground, and
carry away their dogs and fowls out of the very houses.
But their visits are not confined to that period of the
year. About ten o'clock on the second night of my stay
the dogs suddenly began to utter plaintive howls. "A
tiger! a tiger!" cried my Laotian, who was lying near
me. I started up, seized my gun, and half-opened the
door; but the profound darkness made it impossible to
see anything, or to go out without uselessly exposing
myself. I therefore contented myself with firing off my
gun to frighten the creature. The next morning we
found one of our dogs gone.

We scoured the neighbourhood for about a week,
and then set off once more by water for Bangkok,
as I wished to put my collections in order and send
them off.

The places which two months previously had been
deep in water were now dry; and everywhere, around
their dwellings, the people were digging their gardens
and beginning to plant vegetables. The horrible mosquitoes had reappeared in greater swarms than ever,
and I pitied my poor servants, who, after rowing all
day, could obtain no rest at night.

During the day, especially in the neighbourhood of
Pakpriau, the heat was intense, the thermometer being
ordinarily at 90° Fahrenheit (28° Reaumur) in the shade,
and 140° Fahrenheit (49° Reaumur) in the sun. Luckily,

Drawn by M. Bocourt, from a Photograph.

SIAMESE NURSE AND BABY.

we had no longer to contend with the current, and our boat, though heavily laden, proceeded rapidly. We were about three hours' sail from Bangkok, when I perceived a couple of European boats, and in a room built for travellers near a pagoda I recognised three English captains of my acquaintance, one of whom had brought me to Singapore. They were, with their wives, enjoying a picnic, and, on seeing me, insisted on my joining them and partaking of the repast.

I reached Bangkok the same day, and was still uncertain as to a lodging, when M. Wilson, the courteous Danish Consul, came to me, and kindly offered the hospitality of his magnificent house.

I consider the part of the country which I had just passed through, extremely healthy, except, perhaps, during the rains. It appears that in this season the water, flowing down from the mountains and passing over a quantity of poisonous detritus, becomes impregnated with mineral substances, gives out pestilential miasmata, and causes the terrible jungle-fever, which, if it does not at once carry off the victim, leaves behind it years of suffering. My journey, as has been seen, took place at the end of the rainy season and when the floods were subsiding; some deleterious exhalations, doubtless, still escaped, and I saw several natives attacked with intermittent fever, but I had not had an hour's illness. Ought I to attribute this immunity to the regimen I observed and which had been strongly recommended to me— abstinence, all but total, from wine and spirits, and drinking only tea, never cold water? I think so; and I believe by such a course one is in no great danger.*

My intention now was to visit Cambodia, but for this purpose my little river-boat was of no use. The only way of going to Chantaboun was by embarking in one of the small Chinese junks or fishing-vessels, which I accordingly did on the 28th December, taking with me a new servant called Nion, a native of Annam, and who, having been brought up at the college of the Catholic priests at Bangkok, knew French well enough to be very useful to me as an interpreter. The boat was inconveniently small, and we were far from comfortable; for, besides myself and servant, there were on board two men, and two children about thirteen. I was much pleased with the picturesque aspect of all the little islands in the gulf; but our voyage was far longer than we expected, three days being its usual duration, while owing to a strong head-wind it occupied us for eight. We met with an accident which was fatal to one of our party, and might have been so to all of us. On the night of the 31st December our boat was making rapid way under the influence of a violent wind. I was seated on the little roof of leaves and interlaced bamboos which formed a sort of protection to me against the rain and cold night-air, bidding adieu to the departing year and welcoming in the new one; praying that it might be a fortunate one for me, and, above all, that it might be

---

* See the obituary notice.

PORT OF CHANTABOUN.

Drawn by M. Sabatier, from a Sketch by M. Mouhot.

Vol. I. p. 136.

full of blessings for all those dear to me. The night was dark; we were but two miles from land, and the mountains loomed black in the distance. The sea alone was brilliant with that phosphoric light so familiar to all voyagers on the deep. For a couple of hours we had been followed by two sharks, who left behind them a luminous and waving track. All was silent in our boat; nothing was to be heard but the wind whistling among the rigging and the rushing of the waves; and I felt at that midnight hour—alone, and far from all I loved—a sadness which I vainly tried to shake off, and a disquietude which I could not account for. Suddenly we felt a violent shock, immediately followed by a second, and then the vessel remained stationary. Every one cried out in alarm; the sailors rushed forward; in a moment the sail was furled and torches lighted, but, sad to say, one of our number did not answer to his name. One of the young boys, who had been asleep on deck, had been thrown into the sea by the shock. Uselessly we looked for the poor lad, whose body doubtless became the prey of the sharks. Fortunately for us, only one side of the boat had touched the rock, and it had then run aground on the sand; so that after getting it off we were able to anchor not far from the shore.

On the 3rd January, 1859, after having crossed the little gulf of Chantaboun, the sea being at the time very rough, we came in sight of the famous Lion rock, which stands out like the extremity of a cape at the entrance of this port. From a distance it resembles a lion couchant, and it is difficult to believe that Nature unassisted has formed this singular Colossus. The Siamese—a superstitious race—hold this stone in great veneration, as they do everything that appears to them extraordinary or marvellous. It is said that the captain of an English ship, once anchored in the port, seeing the lion, proposed to buy it, and that, on the governor of the place refusing the offer, he pitilessly fired all his guns at *the poor animal*. This has been recorded in Siamese verse, with a touching complaint against the cruelty of the Western barbarians.

THE LION ROCK AT THE ENTRANCE OF THE PORT OF CHANTABOUN.

Drawn by M. Sabatier, from a Sketch by M. Mouhot.

CHAPTER IV.

ON the 4th January, at eight o'clock in the morning,
we arrived at the town of Chantaboun, which stands on
the bank of the river, six or seven miles from the
mountain range. The Christian Annamites form nearly
a third of the population, the remainder being composed
of Chinese merchants, and some heathen Annamites and
Siamese. The Annamites are all fishers, who originally
came from Cochin China to fish in the northern part of
the Gulf of Siam, and settled at Chantaboun. Every day,
while the cold weather lasts and the sea is not too rough,
they cast their nets in the little bays on the coast, or in
the sheltered water among the islands.

The commerce of this province is inconsiderable, compared with what it might be from its situation; but the
numerous taxes, the grinding exactions of the chiefs, and
the usury of the mandarins, added to the hateful system
of slavery, keep the bulk of the people in a ruinous state
of prostration. However, in spite of a scanty population,
they manage to export to Bangkok a great quantity of

pepper, chiefly cultivated by the Chinese at the foot
of the mountains; a little sugar and coffee of superior
quality; mats made of rushes, which meet with a ready
sale in China; tobacco, great quantities of salted and dried
fish, dried leeches, and tortoiseshell. Every Siamese
subject, on attaining a certain height, has to pay to
Government an impost or annual tribute equivalent to
six ticals (eighteen francs). The Annamites of Chantaboun pay this in eagle-wood, and the Siamese in
gamboge; the Chinese in gum-lac, every four years, and
their tribute amounts to four ticals. At the close of the
rainy season the Annamite Christians unite in parties of
fifteen or twenty, and set out under the conduct of an
experienced man, who heads the expedition, and indicates
to the others the trees which contain the eagle-wood; for
all are not equally skilled in distinguishing those which
produce it; a degree of experience is requisite for this,
which can only be acquired by time, and thus much
useless and painful labour is avoided. Some remain in
the mountains, others visit the large islands of Ko-Xang
or Ko-Khut, situated south-east of Chantaboun. The
eagle-wood is hard and speckled, and diffuses a powerful
aromatic odour when burnt. It is used at the incremation of the bodies of princes and high dignitaries, which
are previously kept in the coffins for a twelvemonth.
The Siamese also employ it as a medicine. The wood
of the tree which yields it—the *Aquilaria Agallocha* of
Roxburgh—is white, and very soft; and the trunk must
be cut down, or split in two, to find the eagle-wood,

which is in the interior.   The Annamites make a kind
of secret of the indications by which they fix upon the
right trees, but the few instructions given me put me on
the right track.   I had several cut down, and the result
of my observations was, that this substance is formed in
the cavities of the trees, and that as they grow older it
increases in quantity.   Its presence may be pretty surely
ascertained by the peculiar odour emitted, and the hollow
sound given out on striking the trunk.

Most of the Chinese merchants are addicted to gambling,
and to the use of opium; but the Annamite Christians are
better conducted.   The nature of these Annamites is very
different from that of the Siamese, who are an effeminate
and indolent race, but liberal and hospitable, simple-
minded, and without pride.   The Annamites are short in
stature, and thin, lively, and active; they are choleric
and vindictive, and extremely proud; even among relations there is continual strife and jealousy.   The poor
and the wretched meet with no commiseration, but great
respect is accorded to wealth.   However, the attachment
of the Christians to their priests and missionaries is very
great, and they do not hesitate to expose themselves to
any dangers in their behalf.   I must likewise own that,
in all my dealings with the pagan Annamites, whose
reverence for their ancestors induces them to hold fast
their idolatry, I experienced generosity and kindness
from them, both at Chantaboun and in the islands.

The missionaries at Bangkok having given me a letter
of introduction to their fellow-labourer at Chantaboun, I

had the pleasure of making acquaintance with the worthy man, who received me with great cordiality, and placed at my disposal a room in his modest habitation. The good Father has resided for more than twenty years at Chantaboun, with the Annamites whom he has baptized, content and happy amidst indigence and solitude. I found him, on my arrival, at the height of felicity: a new brick chapel, which had been for some time in course of construction, and the funds required for which had been saved out of his modest income, was rapidly progressing, and promised soon to replace the wooden building in which he then officiated. I passed sixteen days, very agreeably, with him, sometimes hunting on Mount Sabab, at other times making excursions on the rivers and canals. The country greatly resembles the province of Pakpriau, the plain being, perhaps, still more desert and uncultivated; but at the foot of the mountains, and in some of the delightful valleys, pepper is grown in some quantity by the Chinese.

I bought, for twenty-five ticals, a small boat to enable me to visit the isles of the gulf. The first I landed at was named Konam-sao; it is in the form of a cone, and nearly 250 metres* in height, but only two miles in circumference. Like all the other islands in this part of the gulf, it is of volcanic origin. The rocks which surround it make the access difficult; but the effect produced by the richness and bright green of the vege-

---

* A metre is equivalent to 3 feet 3¼ inches.

Drawn by M. Sabatier, from a Sketch by M. Mouhot.

CHAPEL OF THE MISSION, CHANTABOUN.

tation is charming. The dry season, so agreeable for European travelling, from the freshness of the nights and mornings, is in Siam a time of stagnation and death for all nature; the birds fly to the neighbourhood of houses, or to the banks of the rivers, which furnish them with nourishment; rarely does their song come to enchant the listener; and the fishing-eagle alone utters his hoarse and piercing cry every time the wind changes. Ants swarm everywhere, and appear to be, with the mosquitoes and crickets, the only insects that have escaped destruction.

Nowhere did I find in these islands the slightest trace of path or stream; and it was extremely difficult to advance at all through the masses of wild vine and interwoven branches. I was forced to make my way, hatchet in hand, and returned at night exhausted with the heat and fatigue.

The greater portion of the rocks in the elevated parts of these islands is elementary, and preserves traces of their ancient deposit beneath the waters. They have, however, undergone considerable volcanic changes, and contain a number of veins and irregular deposits of the class known as contact deposits that are formed near the junction of stratified rocks with intruded igneous masses.

On the 26th we set sail for the first of the Ko-Man islands, for there are three, situated close together, bearing this name. The largest is only twelve miles from the coast. Some fishing-eagles, a few black doves, and a kind of white pigeon were the only winged creatures I saw. Iguanas are numerous, and when in the evening they come out of their retreats, they make such a noise in walking heavily over the dead leaves and branches, that one might suppose it caused by animals of a much larger size.

Toward evening, the tide having fallen, I allowed my boat to ground on the mud, which I had remarked during the day to be like a peat-bog impregnated with volcanic matter; and during the whole night so strong a sulphureous odour escaped from it, that I imagined myself to be over a submarine volcano.

On the 28th we passed on to the second island, which is higher and more picturesque than the other. The rocks which surround it give it a magnificent effect, especially in a bright sunlight, when the tide is low. The isles of the Patates owe their name to the numerous wild tubers found there.

I passed several days at Cape Liaut, part of the time being occupied in exploring the many adjacent islands. It is the most exquisite part of the gulf, and will bear comparison, for its beauty, with the strait of Sunda, near the coast of Java. Two years ago, when the king visited Chantaboun, they built for him on the shore, at the extremity of the cape, a house and kiosk, and, in memory of the event, they also erected on the top of the mountain a small tower, from which a very extensive view may be enjoyed.

I also made acquaintance with Ko-Kram, the most beautiful and the largest of all the islands north of the

VIEW OF PAKNAM ON THE MENAM.   Drawn by M. Sabatier, from a Sketch by M. Mouhot.

gulf between Bangkok and Chantaboun. The whole
island consists of a wooded mountain-range, easy of
access, and containing much oligist iron. On the morning
of the 29th, at sunrise, the breeze lessened, and when we
were about three miles from the strait which separates the
isle of Arec from that of the " Cerfs," it ceased altogether.
For the last half-hour we were indebted solely to our oars
for the little progress made, being exposed to all the
glare of a burning sun; and the atmosphere was heavy
and suffocating. All of a sudden, to my great astonishment, the water began to be agitated, and our light boat
was tossed about by the waves. I knew not what to
think, and was seriously alarmed, when our pilot called
out, " Look how the sea boils!" Turning in the direction
indicated, I beheld the sea really in a state of ebullition,
and very shortly afterwards an immense jet of water and
steam, which lasted for several minutes, was thrown into
the air. I had never before witnessed such a phenomenon,
and was now no longer astonished at the powerful smell
of sulphur which had nearly overpowered me in Ko-Man.
It was really a submarine volcano, which burst out more
than a mile from the place where we had anchored three
days before.

On March 1st we reached Ven-Ven, at Paknam-Ven,
the name of the place where the branches of the river
unite. This river, whose width at the mouth is above
three miles, is formed by the union of several streams
flowing from the mountains, as well as by an auxiliary of

the Chantaboun river, which, serving as a canal, unites these two places. Ascending the stream for fourteen or fifteen miles, a large village is reached, called Bandiana, but Paknam-Ven is only inhabited by five families of Chinese fishermen.

Crocodiles are more numerous in the river at Paknam-Ven than in that of Chantaboun. I continually saw them throw themselves from the banks into the water; and it has frequently happened that careless fishers, or persons who have imprudently fallen asleep on the shore, have become their prey, or have afterwards died of the wounds inflicted by them. This latter has happened twice during my stay here. It is amusing, however—for one is interested in observing the habits of animals all over the world—to see the manner in which these creatures catch the apes, which sometimes take a fancy to play with them. Close to the bank lies the crocodile, his body in the water, and only his capacious mouth above the surface, ready to seize anything that may come within reach. A troop of apes catch sight of him, seem to consult together, approach little by little, and commence their frolics, by turns actors and spectators. One of the most active or most impudent jumps from branch to branch till within a respectful distance of the crocodile, when, hanging by one claw, and with the dexterity peculiar to these animals, he advances and retires, now giving his enemy a blow with his paw, at another time only pretending to do so. The other apes, enjoying the

Drawn by M. Becourt, from a Sketch by M. Mouhot.

MONKEYS PLAYING WITH A CROCODILE.

fun, evidently wish to take a part in it; but the other
branches being too high, they form a sort of chain by
laying hold of each other's paws, and thus swing backwards and forwards, while any one of them who comes
within reach of the crocodile torments him to the best of
his ability. Sometimes the terrible jaws suddenly close,
but not upon the audacious ape, who just escapes; then
there are cries of exultation from the tormentors, who
gambol about joyfully. Occasionally, however, the claw
is entrapped, and the victim dragged with the rapidity
of lightning beneath the water, when the whole troop
disperse, groaning and shrieking. The misadventure does
not, however, prevent their recommencing the game a few
days afterwards.

On the 4th I returned to Chantaboun from my excursions in the gulf, and resumed charge of my collections,
which, during my absence, I had left at the Custom-
house, and which, to my great satisfaction, had been
taken good care of. The tide was low, and we could not
go up to the town. The sea here is steadily receding
from the coast, and, if some remedy be not found, in a
few years the river will not be navigable even for boats.
Already the junks have some trouble in reaching Chantaboun even at high water. The inhabitants were fishing
for crabs and mussels on the sand-banks close to the
Custom-house, the *employés* in which were occupied in the
same pursuit. The chief official, who, probably hoping for
some small present, had come out to meet me, heard me

promise a supply of pins and needles to those who would bring me shells, and encouraged his men to look for them. In consequence, a large number were brought me, which, to obtain otherwise, would have cost much time and trouble.

CHAPTER V.

HERE I am, once more installed in the house of a good old Chinese, a pepper-planter, whose hospitality I enjoyed on my first visit to the place, two months ago. His name is Ihié-How, but in Siamese he is called Apait, which means *uncle*. He is a widower with two sons, the eldest eighteen, a good young man, lively, hardworking, brave, and persevering. He is already much attached to me, and is desirous of accompanying me to Cambodia. Born amidst the mountains, and naturally intelligent, there are none of the quadrupeds and few of the feathered tribes found in the district with whose habits he is not familiar. He fears neither tiger nor elephant. All this, added to his amiable disposition, made Phrai (that is his name) a real treasure to me.

Apait has also two brothers who have become Catholics, and have settled at Chantaboun in order to be near a Christian place of worship. He himself has never had any desire to change his religion, because he says if he did he must forget his deceased parents, for whom he frequently offers sacrifices. He is badly off, having incurred a debt of fifty ticals, for which he has to pay

ten as yearly interest, the rate in Siam being always
twenty or thirty per cent. Besides this he has various
taxes to pay—twelve ticals for his two sons, four for his
house, one for his furnace, one for his pig. The tax on
the pepper-field is eight ticals, one on his areca-trees,
one on the betel cultivated by him, and two *sellungs*
for a cocoa-tree; altogether thirty-nine ticals. His land
brings him in forty after all expenses are paid; what can
he do with the one remaining tical? The unlucky agriculturists of this kind, and they are many, live on vegetables, and on the rice which they obtain from the
Siamese in exchange for areca.

On my return from the islands, I had been detained
nearly ten days at Chantaboun, unable to walk; I had
cut my heel in climbing the rocks on the shore at Ko-
Man, and, as I was constantly barefooted in the salt water,
the wound soon closed. But afterwards I began to suffer
from it; my foot swelled, and I was obliged to re-open
the wound to extract a piece of shell which had remained
in it. As soon as I could leave Chantaboun I hired a
carriage and two buffaloes to take me to the mountain.
I experienced much gratification in finding myself again
amongst these quiet scenes, at once so lovely and so full
of grandeur. Here are valleys intersected by streams of
pure and limpid water; there, small plains, over which
are scattered the modest dwellings of the laborious
Chinese; while, a little in the distance, rises the mountain, with its imposing rocks, its grand trees, its torrents
and waterfalls.

We have already had some storms, for the rainy season is approaching, vegetation is fresh, and nature animated; the song of birds and the hum of insects are heard all around. Apait has resigned to me his bed, if that can be so styled, which consists merely of a few laths of areca placed upon four stakes. I have extended my mat upon this framework, and should enjoy uninterrupted sleep all night were it not for the swarms of ants which frequently disturb me by passing over my body, getting under my clothes and into my beard, and, I almost fancy, would end by dragging me out, if I did not from time to time shake them off. Occasionally great spiders and other disgusting creatures, crawling about under the roof, would startle me by dropping suddenly on my face.

The heat now is quite endurable, the thermometer generally marking 80° Fahr. in the morning, and 90° in the middle of the day. The water of the streams is so cool and refreshing, that a good morning and evening ablution makes me comfortable for several hours, as well as contributing to keep me in health.

Last evening Phrai, having gone along with my man Niou to Chantaboun to buy provisions, brought back to his father some Chinese bonbons, for which he had paid half a fuang. The poor old man was delighted with them, and this morning at daybreak he dressed himself in his best clothes, on which I asked him what was going to happen. He immediately began to clean a plank which was fitted into the wall to serve as a sort of table or altar. Above this was a drawing of a man dancing and putting out his tongue, with claws on his feet and hands, and with the tail of an ape, intended to represent his father. He then filled three small cups with tea, put the bonbons in a fourth, and placed the whole upon the simple altar; finally, lighting two pieces of odoriferous wood, he began his devotions. It was a sacrifice to the manes of his parents, performed with the hope that their souls would come and taste the good things set before them.

At the entrance of Apait's garden, in front of his house, I had made a kind of shed with stakes and branches of trees, covered with a roof of leaves, where I dried and prepared my large specimens, such as the long-armed apes, kids, and horn-bills, as also my collections of insects. All this has attracted a crowd of inquisitive Siamese and Chinamen, who come to see the "farang" and admire his curiosities. We have just passed the Chinese New Year's-day, and, as there has been a fête for three days, all those living at any distance have profited by the opportunity to visit us. At times Apait's house and garden have been crowded with people in their holiday dresses, many of whom, seeing my instruments, my naturalist's case, and different preparations, took me for a great doctor, and begged for medicines.

Alas! my pretensions are not so high; however, I treat them on the "Raspail" system; and a little box of pomade or phial of sedative water will perhaps be represented in some European museum by an insect or shell brought to me by these worthy people in return for the good I would gladly do them.

It is very agreeable, after a fatiguing day's chase over hills and amongst dense forests, through which one must cut one's way axe in hand, to repose in the evening on the good Chinaman's bench in front of his house, shaded by bananas, cocoanut, and other trees. For the last four days a violent north wind, fresh in spite of the season, has been blowing without intermission, breaking asunder and tearing up by the roots some of the trees on the higher grounds. This is its farewell visit, for the south-east wind will now blow for many months.

This evening everything appeared to me more beautiful and agreeable than usual; the stars shone brightly in the sky, the moon was clear. Sitting by Apait while his son played to me some Chinese airs on the bamboo flute, I thought to what a height of prosperity this province, even now one of the most interesting and flourishing in the country, might attain, were it wisely and intelligently governed, or if European colonists were to settle and develop its resources. Proximity to the sea, facility of communication, a rich soil, a healthy and propitious climate; nothing is wanting to ensure success to an industrious and enterprising agriculturist.

The worthy old Apait has at last consented to allow his son to enter my service, provided I pay him thirty ticals, half a year's wages, in advance. This will enable him, if he can sell his house and pepper-field, to clear off his debt and retire to another part of the mountain. Phrai is delighted to attend me, and to run about the woods all day, and I am not less pleased with our bargain, for his knowledge of the country, his activity, his intelligence, and attachment to me, are invaluable.

The heat becomes greater and greater, the thermometer having risen to 102° Fahr. in the shade; thus hunting is now a painful, and sometimes impossible, exertion, anywhere except in the woods. A few days ago I took advantage of a short spell of cloudy, and consequently cooler weather, to visit a waterfall I had heard of in the almost desert district of Prion, twelve miles from Kombau. After reaching the last-named place, our course lay for about an hour and a half along a charming valley, nearly as smooth as a lawn, and as ornamental as a park. By and by entering a forest, we kept by the banks of a stream, which, shut in between two mountains and studded with blocks of granite, increases in size as you approach its source. Before long we arrived at the fall, which must be a fine spectacle in the rainy season. It then pours down from immense perpendicular rocks, forming as it were a circular peaked wall, nearly thirty metres in diameter, and twenty metres in height. The force of the torrent having been broken by the rocky bed into which it descends, there is another fall of ten feet; and, lower down, after a third fall of fifteen feet, it passes into an ample basin, which, like a mirror, reflects the trees and cliffs around. Even during the dry season the spring, then running from beneath enormous blocks of granite, flows in such abundance as to feed several streams.

I was astonished to see my two servants, heated by

their long walk, bathe in the cold water, and on my
advising them to wait for a little, they replied that the
natives were always accustomed to bathe when hot.

We all turned stone-cutters, that is to say, we set to
work to detach the impression of an unknown animal
from the surface of an immense mass of granite rising
up out of one of the mountain torrents. A Chinese had
in January demanded so exorbitant a sum for this, that
I had abandoned the idea, intending to content myself
with an impression in wax, but Phrai proposed to me
to undertake the work, and by our joint labour it was
soon accomplished. The Siamese do not much like my
meddling with their rocks, and their superstition is also
somewhat startled when I happen to kill a white ape,
although when the animal is dead and skinned they are
glad to obtain a cutlet or steak from it, for they attribute to the flesh of this creature great medicinal virtues.

The rainy season is drawing near, storms become more
and more frequent, and the growling of the thunder is
frightful. Insects are in greater numbers, and the ants,
which are now looking out for a shelter, invade the
dwellings, and are a perfect pest to my collections, not
to speak of myself and my clothes. Several of my
books and maps have been almost devoured in one night.
Fortunately there are no mosquitoes, but to make up for
this there is a small species of leech, which when it
rains quits the streams and infests the woods, rendering
an excursion there, if not impracticable, at all events
very disagreeable. You have constantly to be pulling

them off you by dozens, but, as some always escape observation, you are sure to return home covered with blood; often my white trousers are dyed as red as those of a French soldier.

The animals have now become scarcer, which in different ways is a great disappointment to all, for Phrai and Niou feasted sumptuously on the flesh of the apes, and made a profit by selling their gall to the Chinese doctors in Chantaboun. Hornbills also have turned wild, so we can find nothing to replenish our larder but an occasional kid. Large stags feed on the mountain, but one requires to watch all night to get within range of them. There are not many birds to be seen, neither quails, partridges, nor pheasants; and the few wild fowl which occasionally make their appearance are so difficult to shoot that it is waste both of time and ammunition to make the attempt.

In this part of the country the Siamese declare they cannot cultivate bananas on account of the elephants, which at certain times come down from the mountains and devour the leaves, of which they are very fond. The royal and other tigers abound here; every night they prowl about in the vicinity of the houses, and in the mornings we can see the print of their large claws in the sand and in the clay near streams. By day they retire to the mountain, where they lurk in close and inaccessible thickets. Now and then you may get near enough to one to have a shot at him, but generally, unless suffering from hunger, they fly at the approach of man. A few days ago I saw a young Chinese who had nineteen wounds on his body made by one of these animals; he was looking out from a tree about nine feet high, when the cries of a young kid, tied to another tree at a short distance, attracted a large tiger. The young man fired at it, but, though mortally wounded, the creature, collecting all his strength for a final spring, leaped on his enemy, seized him and pulled him down, tearing his flesh frightfully with teeth and claws as they rolled on the ground. Luckily for the unfortunate Chinese, it was a dying effort, and in a few moments more the tiger relaxed its hold and breathed its last.

In the mountains of Chantaboun, and not far from my present abode, precious stones of fine water occur. There is even at the east of the town an eminence, which they call "the mountain of precious stones;" and it would appear from the account of Mgr. Pallegoix that at one time they were abundant in that locality, since in about half an hour he picked up a handful, which is as much as now can be found in a twelvemonth, nor can they be purchased at any price.

It seems that I have seriously offended the poor Thaï * of Kombau by carrying away the footprints. I have met several natives who tell me they have broken arms, that they can no longer work, and will always henceforth be in poverty; and I find that I am considered to be answerable for this because I irritated the genius of the moun-

---

* The Siamese were formerly called Thaï.

tain. Henceforth they will have a good excuse for idleness.

The Chinese have equally amused me. They imagine that some treasure ought to be found beneath the footprints, and that the block which I have carried away must possess great medicinal virtues; so Apait and his friends have been rubbing the under part of the stone every morning against another piece of granite, and, collecting carefully the dust that fell from it, have mixed it with water and drunk it fasting, fully persuaded that it is a remedy against all ills. Here they say that it is faith which cures; and it is certain that pills are often enough administered in the civilized West which have no more virtue than the granite powder swallowed by old Apait.

His uncle Thié-ou has disposed of his property for him for sixty ticals, so that, after paying off his debts, he will have left, including the sum I gave him for his son's services, forty ticals. Here that is enough to make a man think himself rich to the end of his days: he can at times regale the souls of his parents with tea and bonbons, and live himself like a true country mandarin. Before leaving Kombau the old man secured me another lodging, for which I had to pay two ticals (six francs) a month, and I lost nothing in point of comfort by the change. For " furnished apartments " I think the charge not unreasonable. The list of furniture is as follows:— in the dining-room *nothing*, in the bed-room an old mat on a camp-bed. However, this house is cleaner and

larger than the other, and better protected from the
weather: in the first the water came in in all directions.
Then the camp-bed, which is a large one, affords a
pleasant lounge after my hunting expeditions. Besides
which advantages, my new landlord furnishes me with
bananas and vegetables, for which I pay in game when
the chase has been successful.

The fruit here is exquisite, particularly the mango,
the mangusteen, the pine-apple, so fragrant and melt-
ing in the mouth, and, what is superior to anything
I ever imagined or tasted, the famous "durian" or
"dourion," which justly merits the title of king of fruits.
But to enjoy it thoroughly one must have time to
overcome the disgust at first inspired by its smell, which
is so strong that I could not stay in the same place with
it. On first tasting it I thought it like the flesh of some
animal in a state of putrefaction, but after four or five
trials I found the aroma exquisite. The *durian* is about
two-thirds the size of a jacca, and like it is encased in
a thick and prickly rind, which protects it from the teeth
of squirrels and other nibblers; on opening it there are
to be found ten cells, each containing a kernel larger
than a date, and surrounded by a sort of white, or
sometimes yellowish cream, which is most delicious. By
an odd freak of nature, not only is there the first repugnance to it to overcome, but if you eat it often, though
with ever so great moderation, you find yourself next day
covered with blotches, as if attacked with measles, so
heating is its nature. A *durian* picked is never good,

for when fully ripe it falls of itself; when cut open it must be eaten at once, as it quickly spoils, but otherwise it will keep for three days. At Bangkok one of them costs one *sellung*; at Chantaboun nine may be obtained for the same sum.

I had come to the conclusion that there was little danger in traversing the woods here, and in our search for butterflies and other insects we often took no other arms than a hatchet and hunting-knife, while Niou had become so confident as to go by night with Phrai to lie in wait for stags. Our sense of security was, however, rudely shaken when one evening a panther rushed upon one of the dogs close to my door. The poor animal uttered a heartrending cry, which brought us all out, as well as our neighbours, each torch in hand. Finding themselves face to face with a panther, they in their turn raised their voices in loud screams; but it was too late for me to get my gun, for in a moment the beast was out of reach.

In a few weeks I must say farewell to these beautiful mountains, never, in all probability, to see them again, and I think of this with regret; I have been so happy here, and have so much enjoyed my hunting and my solitary walks in this comparatively temperate climate, after my sufferings from the heat and mosquitoes in my journey northwards.

Thanks to my nearness to the sea on the one side, and to the mountain region on the other, the period of the greatest heat passed away without my perceiving it; and

I was much surprised at receiving a few days ago a letter
from Bangkok which stated that it had been hotter
weather there than had been known for more than
thirty years. Many of the European residents had been
ill; yet I do not think the climate of Bangkok more
unhealthy than that of other towns of Eastern Asia
within the tropics. But no doubt the want of exercise,
which is there almost impossible, induces illness in many
cases.

A few days ago I made up my mind to penetrate into
a grotto on Mount Sabab, half-way between Chantaboun
and Kombau, so deep, I am told, that it extends to the
top of the mountain. I set out, accompanied by Phrai
and Niou, furnished with all that was necessary for our
excursion. On reaching the entrance of the grotto we
lighted our torches, and, after scaling a number of blocks
of granite, began our march. Thousands of bats, roused
by the lights, commenced flying round and round us,
flapping our faces with their wings, and extinguishing
our torches every minute. Phrai walked first, trying the
ground with a lance which he held; but we had scarcely
proceeded a hundred paces when he threw himself back
upon me with every mark of terror, crying out, "A
serpent! go back!" As he spoke I perceived an enormous
boa about fifteen feet off, with erect head and open mouth,
ready to dart upon him. My gun being loaded, one
barrel with two bullets, the other with shot, I took aim
and fired off both at once. We were immediately en-
veloped in a thick cloud of smoke, and could see nothing,

but prudently beat an instant retreat. We waited
anxiously for some time at the entrance of the grotto,
prepared to do battle with our enemy should he present
himself; but he did not appear. My guide now boldly
lighted a torch, and, furnished with my gun reloaded and
a long rope, went in again alone. We held one end of
the rope, that at the least signal we might fly to his
assistance. For some minutes, which appeared terribly
long, our anxiety was extreme, but equally great were
our relief and gratification when we saw him approach,
drawing after him the rope, to which was attached an
immense boa. The head of the reptile had been shattered
by my fire, and his death had been instantaneous, but
we sought to penetrate no farther into the grotto.

I had been told that the Siamese were about to celebrate
a grand fête at a pagoda about three miles off, in honour
of a superior priest who died last year, and whose remains
were now to be burned according to the custom of the
country. I went to see this singular ceremony, hoping
to gain some information respecting the amusements of
this people, and arrived at the place about eight in the
morning, the time for breakfast, or "Kinkao" (rice-
eating). Nearly two thousand Siamese of both sexes
from Chantaboun and the surrounding villages, some in
carriages and some on foot, were scattered over the
ground in the neighbourhood of the pagoda. All wore
new sashes and dresses of brilliant colours, and the effect
of the various motley groups was most striking.

Under a vast roof of planks supported by columns,

forming a kind of shed, bordered by pieces of stuff covered with grotesque paintings representing men and animals in the most extraordinary attitudes, was constructed an imitation rock of coloured pasteboard, on which was placed a catafalque lavishly decorated with gilding and carved work, and containing an urn in which were the precious remains of the priest. Here and there were arranged pieces of paper and stuff in the form of flags. Outside the building was prepared the funeral pile, and at some distance off a platform was erected for the accommodation of a band of musicians, who played upon different instruments of the country. Farther away some women had established a market for the sale of fruit, bonbons, and arrack, while in another quarter some Chinamen and Siamese were performing, in a little theatre run up for the occasion, scenes something in the style of those exhibited by our strolling actors at fairs. This fête, which lasted for three days, had nothing at all in it of a funereal character. I had gone there hoping to witness something new and remarkable, for these peculiar rites are only celebrated in honour of sovereigns, nobles, and other persons of high standing; but I had omitted to take into consideration the likelihood of my being myself an object of curiosity to the crowd. Scarcely, however, had I appeared in the pagoda, followed by Phrai and Niou, when on all sides I heard the exclamation, "Farang! come and see the farang!" and immediately both Siamese and Chinamen left their bowls of rice and pressed about me. I hoped that, once their curiosity was gratified, they would leave me in peace, but instead of that the crowd grew thicker and thicker, and followed me wherever I went, so that at last it became almost unbearable, and all the more so as most of them were already drunk either with opium or arrack, many, indeed, with both. I quitted the pagoda and was glad to get into the fresh air again, but the respite was of short duration. Passing the entrance of a large hut temporarily built of planks, I saw some chiefs of provinces sitting at breakfast. The senior of the party advanced straight towards me, shook me by the hand, and begged me in a cordial and polite manner to enter; and I was glad to avail myself of his kind offer, and take refuge from the troublesome people. My hosts overwhelmed me with attentions, and forced upon me pastry, fruit, and bonbons; but the crowd who had followed me forced their way into the building, and hemmed us in on all sides; even the roof was covered with gazers. All of a sudden we heard the walls crack, and the whole of the back of the hut, yielding under the pressure, fell in, and people, priests, and chiefs tumbling one upon another, the scene of confusion was irresistibly comic. I profited by the opportunity to escape, swearing—though rather late in the day—that they should not catch me again.

I know not to what it is to be attributed, unless it be the pure air of the mountains and a more active life, but the mountaineers of Chantaboun appear a much finer race than the Siamese of the plain, more robust, and of a darker complexion. Their features, also, are more regular, and I should imagine that they sprang rather from the Arian than from the Mongolian race. They remind me of the Siamese and Laotians whom I met with in the mountains of Pakpriau.

Will the present movement of the nations of Europe towards the East result in good by introducing into these lands the blessings of our civilization? or shall we, as blind instruments of boundless ambition, come hither as a scourge, to add to their present miseries? Here are millions of unhappy creatures in great poverty in the midst of the richest and most fertile region imaginable; bowing shamefully under a servile yoke made viler by despotism and the most barbarous customs; living and dying in utter ignorance of the only true God!

I quitted with regret these beautiful mountains, where I had passed so many happy hours with the poor but hospitable inhabitants. On the evening before and the morning of my departure, all the people of the neighbourhood, Chinese and Siamese, came to say adieu, and offer me presents of fruits, dried fish, fowls, tobacco, and rice cooked in various ways with brown sugar, all in greater quantities than I could possibly carry away. The farewells of these good mountaineers were touching; they kissed my hands and feet, and I confess that my eyes were not dry. They accompanied me to a great distance, begging me not to forget them, and to pay them another visit.

CHAPTER VI.

IMMEDIATELY on my return to Chantaboun, where I
was again received with open arms by the good Abbé
Raufaing, a French missionary associated as colleague
with Father Larmandy, I began to collect information as
to the best route to Battambong, the chief town of a
province of the same name, which, above a century ago,
was wrested from Cambodia by the Siamese. I made
an agreement with some pagan Annamite fishermen to
give them thirty ticals for taking me from Chantaboun
to Komput, a province of Cambodia. The Annamite
Christians demanded forty ticals, and provisions both
going and returning. After taking leave of the abbé,
who had shown me every possible kindness and attention on each of my visits, I embarked at noon, in spite of
a heavy rain, as I wished to take advantage of a high
tide. We arrived in the harbour at seven in the evening,
and were detained there for two days by a contrary wind,
too violent to allow us to leave without danger.

VIEW OF BATTAMBONG.

Drawn by M. Sabatier, from a Sketch by M. Mouhot.

Vol. I. p. 174.

Two days later we reached Ko-Khut, where, again, pouring rain and a head wind compelled us to anchor about 100 metres from the shore in a small bay which was far from promising much security to our little craft. Our position was not agreeable; our frail bark, rudely tossed by the furious waves, seemed every moment in danger of being dashed upon the rocks. Our baggage, to which we had assigned the best place for preservation from wet, occupied three-fourths of the boat, and we were crowded five of us together in the bows, with no better shelter than some palm-leaves sewn together, through which the water dripped, and kept us continually soaked. The rain falling without intermission, we could not keep the fire alight to cook our rice, and for four days remained half-lying in the boat, scarcely able to move in the narrow space left for us, and our clothes clinging to us with wet. At last, on the fifth day, we had the pleasure of seeing the sky clear up and the wind change. About two o'clock in the afternoon, foreseeing a fine night, and having revived the drooping courage of my men by a stiff dose of arrack, we weighed anchor and left Ko-Khut with a fair breeze. It was quite a comfort to be able to move and breathe freely, and I spent a part of the night under my little awning of palm-leaves, enjoying the beauty of the heavens and the rapid movement of the vessel. At daybreak we perceived, about ten miles distant, the first of the islands of Koh-Kong. It is smaller than Koh-Chang, and neither so imposing in general appearance nor having such a

splendid range of peaked hills. The island is nearly a
desert, but it produces the beautiful cardamom, as also
gamboge, collected from the bamboos, which the natives
split open when hard.

I soon forgot the miseries of the first part of our
voyage, and was amply recompensed by the shifting
scenes of beauty presented to us by the group of islands
we were passing. At length we reached the advanced
posts of the pirates of Komput, from the heights of which
they keep a look-out, and, as soon as a sail comes in
sight, make preparations for an attack. We had no
cause for fear, having no merchandise to tempt them;
and, moreover, we were all well armed. About five in
the evening we cast anchor in a little bay, where we
cooked our rice, and my men lay down to take some
repose, having had none the night previous. We were
a day and a half's sail from Komput, and at midnight
we resumed our voyage, gently rocked by the waves and
favoured by a light breeze.

After passing the island of Phu-Quoc, which belongs
to Cochin China, the view became more and more beautiful; land surrounded us on all sides, and we seemed to
be sailing on a lake. The scenery in this gulf is truly
enchanting. Eastward extend the coast and islands of
Cochin China as far as Ita Jienne, and to the north and
west are those of Cambodia, crowned by a mountain
900 metres in height, which is so like Sabab that Phrai
called out to the pilot, "You are taking us back to
Chantaboun; there is Mount Sabab." We were not,

Drawn by M. Bocourt, from a Sketch by M. Mouhot.

LEECH-FISHERS ON THE ISLE OF SAMET.

however, long permitted to enjoy the splendid picture
here displayed before us, for very shortly after our
entrance into the gulf large black clouds, gathering at
the summit of the mountain, by degrees hid it entirely
from view, the thunder growled, and a terrific wind arose,
which hurried our boat along at an extraordinary rate.
The pilot at the helm shook all over, and begged for
arrack to sustain his strength and courage. When the
storm had lasted half an hour a heavy rain began to
descend, and with it the wind moderated. We had now
arrived at the mouth of the river on which Komput is
situated.

It happened to be the day fixed for the King of Cambodia, then in Komput, to pass in review all the ships
lying in the roads; but for some time he had been
detained by the rough weather in a sort of apartment
erected for him on piles, in a place where the water was
shallow. As we passed the Custom-house, we perceived
the royal *cortége* advancing towards a large junk, which
his Majesty was having built as a trading-vessel for
Singapore.

The river leading to Komput is about 300 metres in
width, but, rising in the neighbouring mountains, its
course is but very limited. The magnificent tree called
by the Siamese Mai-Jakienne, and much prized by the
Chinese for furnishing masts for their junks, is found in
great abundance in the forests bordering its banks.
There are frequently six or seven ships loading at one
time in the roads, so that both Chinese and European

vessels may be constantly seen going up and down the stream.

Though Komput is now the only port of Cambodia, it is far from being as full of life and bustle as Bangkok, for the town boasts only 300 houses at most, and a population scarcely equal to that of Chantaboun. All its little commerce is supplied by Lower Cochin China, the ports of which are almost always closed against Europeans, so that rice, which is imported in a sort of contraband manner, some tons of gamboge, a little ivory, fish taken in the lake by the Annamites, a small quantity of cotton, and the valuable wood above mentioned, constitute the whole of the commerce of the town; and I venture to predict that, when the ports of Annam are thrown open to Europeans, the Chinese merchants will abandon Komput altogether. And yet, under a better system of government, this country might supply a great number of articles, of which I will speak hereafter. It will not probably be long before what remains of this unfortunate land will fall under the dominion of some other power. Possibly, France has her eyes fixed upon it, with the view of annexing it to her possessions in Lower Cochin China.

The comparative exemption from heavy taxes and duties which the Cambodians enjoy, when compared with the Siamese, made me imagine I should be able to live here in comfort and abundance; but I was disappointed. Almost every vice seemed prevalent at Komput—pride, insolence, cheating, cowardice, servility, excessive idleness, are the attributes of this miserable people. It is often remarked that no one should judge a country through which he is merely a traveller, and that only those are capable of doing so who have resided in it for some time. I admit that, in the first case, one is liable to make mistakes; but I state here what I see, and give my impressions as I receive them, leaving it to more experienced travellers to correct me where I am in error. Nevertheless, the first impression often proves ineffaceable, and I may mention that frequently I have trusted less to my own judgment than to the experience of others.

There are few travellers in Europe, America, or probably anywhere else, who have not had cause to complain of the offensive manner in which custom-house officers perform their duties, and often exceed them. In Europe they earn their daily bread by annoying in every possible way the unfortunates who are compelled, for the sake of peace, to submit to their insolence and tyranny: here they gain it by begging; they are licensed beggars. "A little salt-fish, a little arrack, a little betel, if you please,"— such are the petitions; and the more you give, the less strict will the search be.

After having sailed up the pretty river for about a mile, we came in sight of a house covered with creepers, and surmounted by a cross, which indicated the residence of the Abbé Hestrest, the head of the foreign mission here. Reader, have you journeyed in foreign lands? Have you ever for a time, more or less long, been separated from your friends and relatives—shut out from civilized society? Have you been tossed about by tempests or buffeted by your fellow-men? Have you narrowly escaped some great danger? Have you been unhappy? Have you lost some one very dear to you? In one word, have you *suffered*? If you have, you will appreciate the feelings with which the solitary wanderer welcomes the divine cross, the heart-stirring emblem of his religion. It is to him a friend, a consoler, a father, a brother; at sight of it the soul expands, and the more you have suffered the better you will love it. You kneel down, you pray, you forget your griefs, and you feel that God is with you. This is what I did.

I had letters to the Abbé Hestrest from several of the missionaries in Siam. We therefore anchored, and I landed; but the nine days' inactivity to which I had been forced to submit had so cramped my limbs, that for a time I had almost lost the use of them, and could scarcely walk. The abbé received me like a brother, and offered me accommodation in his humble abode until I could find lodgings elsewhere. The first piece of news which he imparted to me was, that France was at war with Austria. I did not even know that there had been a difference between the two Governments.

Scarcely had I landed when the return of the king from his aquatic excursion was announced. The Abbé Hestrest conducted me to the banks of the river; and as soon as his Majesty perceived a stranger by the side of the priest, he gave orders to his rowers to approach the shore, and, when within hail, addressed the abbé:

" Who is the stranger with you?"

" Sire, a Frenchman," replied my companion.

" A Frenchman?" repeated the king, quickly. Then turning to me, " You are French?"

" Yes, sire," I answered, in Siamese.

" Monsieur comes from Paris," said the abbé; "but he has recently visited Siam."

" And what does he come to my kingdom for?"

" He has a particular mission, which has nothing to do with politics; it is merely to see the country. M. Mouhot will soon wait upon your majesty."

After a few minutes' silence, the king, waving his hand, and saying " *Au revoir*," passed on.

I was at first afraid that the abbé had made me pass for a less humble and modest individual than I really was, and I should be forbidden the kingdom. The very name of France is full of dread to these poor monarchs; and this present one lived in daily fear of seeing the French flag waving in the roads. He is about sixty years of age, short and stout. He wears his hair cut rather close, and his countenance is good-natured, mild, and intelligent.*

The king was reclining on a thick cushion in the stern of his boat, which was of European build. Four rowers and a dozen young girls were with him; and among the

---

* Since M. Mouhot's journey, this king has died, and has been succeeded by his second son, a revolution in favour of the elder brother proving unsuccessful.

latter I remarked one, whose features were delicate and
pretty, dressed in the European style, and wearing long
hair. She would have been reckoned a pretty girl anywhere, and was, I fancy, the favourite, for she was in a
richer costume than the others, and covered with jewels.
She also occupied the place nearest the king, and seemed
to pay great attention to her old adorer. The rest were
fat, with bloated faces and vulgar features, and had their
teeth blackened by betel and arrack. Besides a kind
of petticoat, the corners of which are looped up and
fastened to the sash behind, some wore a tight jacket,
white or blue, buttoning over the chest; and had a red
scarf, which, according to the custom of the Siamese and
Cambodian women, was passed round the body under the
arms, and tied at the bosom.

Behind the king's boat, in no apparent order, and at
long intervals, followed those of several mandarins, who
were not distinguished in any particular manner. One
boat alone, manned by Chinese, and commanded by a
fat man of the same nation, holding in his hand a halberd
surmounted by a crescent, attracted my attention, as it
headed the escort. This man was the famous Mun Suy,
chief of the pirates, and a friend of the king. I was
told that, two years before, he had been compelled,
owing to some iniquities not very well known, to fly
from Amoy, and had arrived at Komput with a hundred
followers, adventurers and rovers of the sea like himself.
After having remained there for some time, keeping the
whole place in terror, and extorting by menaces all he

Drawn by M. Pelcoq, from a Sketch by M. Mouhot.

FAVOURITE WIFE OF THE KING OF CAMBODIA.

could from the market people, he conceived the project
of seizing upon and burning the town, and putting all the
inhabitants to the sword, intending then to retreat with
his spoils, if not strong enough to hold his ground.
Fortunately the plot was discovered, and the Cambodians from the neighbourhood were armed and assembled in readiness to defend the place. Mun Suy, not
liking the aspect of affairs, embarked with his band in
his junk, and fell suddenly on Itatais. The market was
sacked in a minute; but the inhabitants, recovering
from their surprise, repulsed the pirates and drove them
back to their vessel with the loss of several men. Mun
Suy then returned to Komput, gained over by presents
first the governor and afterwards the king himself, and
ever since has carried on his piratical acts with impunity,
making his name dreaded by all around. Loud complaints arose from the neighbouring countries, and the
king, either overawed by the pirate, or for protection
against the Annamites, appointed him commander of the
coast-guard. Henceforth, therefore, he became a licensed
robber, and murder and rapine increased to such a
degree, that the King of Siam sent a naval expedition to
Komput to capture the malefactor and his gang. Two
only were taken and executed. As for their leader, he
was hidden, they say, in the palace.

Some days after my arrival I was installed in a house
built by the king's orders, and at his own expense, for
the accommodation of European merchants, who, however,
do not often visit Komput. Abbé Hestrest conducted me

through the city. The market-place, occupied chiefly by the Chinese, is covered by a number of thatched huts built of bamboo, in which are exhibited for sale, glass, china, hatchets, knives, Chinese parasols, and other articles of merchandise, native and foreign. The dealers in fish and vegetables, and the Chinese *restaurateurs*, dispute the street with pigs, hungry dogs, and children of all ages and both sexes, in a state of nature, and dabbling in the mud. Mingled with these are native women, repulsively ugly, and effeminate and emaciated Chinamen, with haggard cheeks, dragging themselves painfully along to the opium-merchant's, the barber's, or some gambling-house, three requisites to the very existence of a Chinese. All the commerce is in their hands; and you meet ten of them to one native.

I was introduced by the abbé at several Chinese houses, where we were most politely received. The king was expecting a visit from me, and had sent several persons to find out who I was; his idea being, that I was an officer of the French army in Cochin China, despatched from thence to gain information about the country. I begged M. Hestrest to accompany me to see the king; for which purpose we proceeded a mile and a half up the river to Kompong-Bay, which is the Cambodian part of the town, and the residence of the governor, and where his Majesty and suite were encamped.

When we arrived he was holding a kind of levée, in a building constructed of bamboo with some elegance, and covered with red cloth, but the interior of which

looked more like a theatre than a royal abode. Finding
at the door neither sentinel nor porter, we entered
without being announced. The king was seated on an
old European chair, with two officers on each side of him,
who from time to time offered him, kneeling, a lighted
cigarette, or some betel, which they kept always ready.
At a little distance stood his guards, some holding pikes
ornamented at the top with white tufts; others with
sheathed sabres in their hands. The ministers and
mandarins knelt a few steps below his Majesty. On our
entrance, chairs similar to the king's were placed for us
close to him. Like his subjects, he generally wears
nothing but the langouti, the native dress. His was
composed of yellow silk, confined at the waist by a
magnificent belt of gold studded with precious stones.
At Cambodia, as at Siam, it is necessary to offer presents,
if one desires to gain the royal favour. I had accordingly
brought with me an English walking-stick gun, as a gift
for the king. It at once attracted his notice.

" Pray show me that cane," he said, in Cambodian.

I gave it to him.

" Is it loaded?" asked he, seeing it was a fire-arm.

" No, sire."

He then begged for a cap and snapped it; unscrewed
the barrel and examined it with great attention.

" If it would be agreeable to his Majesty," I said to
M. Hestrest, " I shall be happy to offer it to the king."

The abbé interpreted my words.

" What did it cost ? " asked the king.

" Sire, I dare not ask M. Mouhot. In Europe no one tells the price of what he gives."

The king then begged to look at my watch, and, after inspecting it attentively, again asked the price. The abbé then alluded to my design of visiting Udong, the capital of Cambodia, and of journeying through the country.

" Go to Udong; go about," said the king, laughing. " Very well." He then asked my name, and tried to write it; on which I drew out my pocket-book and gave him one of my cards. He seemed to wish for the pocket-book, and I presented him with it.

" Sire," said M. Hestrest, " as M. Mouhot is going to Udong, perhaps your Majesty will deign to facilitate his journey."

" Willingly.   How many carriages do you want ? "

" Three will be sufficient, sire."

" And for what day ? "

" The day after to-morrow, sire."

" Take a note of that, and give orders about it," said the king to his secretary. He then rose, and, shaking hands with us, retired. We returned to our hotel. I say hotel, for it is the only lodging for strangers; and M. de Montigny, when ambassador at Komput, lived there, indications of which were afforded by the inscriptions scratched on the walls by the sailors belonging to the expedition, such as " Hotel of the king and ambassa-

dors;" "Here is lodging for man, horse, and elephant
gratis pro Deo;" "Good beds, sofas, and dining-tables on
the floor;" "Sea-water bathing—in the river;" "Good
table—in the market;" "Good wine—at Singapore;"
"Nothing—for the servants."

CHAPTER VII.

ALL my preparations for departure having been completed, the Abbé Hestrest came on the morning of the day fixed, to invite me to breakfast with him; after which he offered to take me in his own boat to Kompong-Bay, where the promised vehicles were to meet us.

When we arrived there, none were to be seen. We applied to the first mandarin, who, chewing his betel, displayed his black teeth with a stupid grin, and I then perceived that I had been duped by these people, who are always and everywhere false; never yielding but to force, and holding the very name of a European in detestation. After various complaints, and remonstrances with the mandarins, we with great difficulty obtained three carriages, by courtesy so called; but the dog-cars in use in Holland would have been more serviceable to me; so I sent back the three wheelbarrows to the king, with my compliments, and hired other vehicles for myself.

Udong, the present capital of Cambodia, is situated north-east of Komput, and is four miles and a half from that arm of the Mekon which forms the great lake, lying about 135 miles from Komput as the crow flies. It is reckoned an eight-days' journey, travelling with oxen or buffaloes, and there are eight stations on the way. With elephants you can accomplish it in half the time; but only the king, the mandarins, and very wealthy persons can afford to keep these animals. The conveyances which I had engaged could scarcely hold my baggage, so that my men were obliged to make the journey on foot.

Perceiving in the shops several necklaces, bracelets, and rings formed of a material like jet, I inquired from whence it was procured, and was told that it came from the neighbouring island of Phû Quoc, where it was to be found in abundance. I afterwards handled a piece of this substance, and discovered it to be a sort of coal. It would burn well in a lamp, and greatly resembles the cannel coal of Scotland.

After traversing a marshy plain, where we knocked down several aquatic birds, we entered a beautiful forest, which stretches unbroken to the very gates of Udong. To cross this marsh I had to put on my hunting-boots, which I had not worn for some time, and consequently the leather had hardened so much, that, after two hours' walking in the heat of the day, the skin was rubbed off my feet in several places; and I was forced to take off the boots and continue my journey barefoot. Luckily, owing to the dry weather and the constant communication between Komput and the capital, the road was almost everywhere in good condition. The heat was intense, and our progress excessively slow; but at length we reached the first station, where I was lodged in a large hall, thatched and built of bamboo, which had been erected for the accommodation of the king and his suite. At night, guards were stationed at my door to protect me from robbery; and, thanks to the royal letter which I carried, I was respectfully treated. On the following morning I managed, at the cost of a franc of our money, to hire an elephant to take me as far as the next station.

From thence I continued my route barefoot, and our sufferings from the heat exceeded all I had ever imagined of the effect of the sun in the torrid zone. Its burning rays, falling on the sandy soil, became intolerable at ten o'clock in the morning, so that even the natives, the soles of whose feet were much harder than mine, could not bear contact with the bare ground, but sought for tufts of grass to step upon. The oxen could scarcely move, and showed every sign of pain and exhaustion; and, in spite of spurring and blows, often refused to stir. The water in the ponds was not warm, but literally hot; the whole atmosphere seemed on fire, and all nature languishing and prostrate. At ten o'clock we halted until three. We sadly felt the want of drinkable water, as also did our cattle, which suffered from thirst even more than ourselves. To make our tea and cook our rice, we had no resource but the stagnant pools, impregnated with unwholesome matter by the vomica-nuts which fall from the surrounding trees.

The day following I was fortunate enough to obtain another elephant; but after this there was no more help to be met with, and the greater part of the ensuing four days' journey I performed on foot, my attendants contriving to perch themselves on the corners of one of the waggons. At this dry season a broad track in the middle of the road, which altogether is from twenty-five to thirty metres in width, is beaten hard by the frequent passage of vehicles and elephants, and the fine thick dust arising from it is very annoying. The remainder of the road is covered with grass and shrubs, and on either hand is the forest, with its trees tall, straight, and majestic, surmounted by immense tufts of leaves. The effect is that of a magnificent avenue; and from the regularity of the intervals between the trees, one might almost believe that it had been laid out by the hand of art.

The stations are equidistant from each other, about twelve miles apart; and at all of them, besides the old caravanserais for the shelter of ordinary travellers, new ones, much more spacious and ornamental, have been erected for the accommodation of the king. There are also intermediate resting-places between every two stations, where travellers can obtain a welcome shelter from the midday heat.

On leaving Komput a low chain of hills came in sight on our left hand, but everywhere on our route we met with the same sandy soil, except in a single spot, which was stony, and contained veins of iron-ore. We passed

o 2

through but one village, and there, only, were a few
attempts at cultivation. In no other part of the forest
could I distinguish any traces of its being inhabited.
On approaching the capital, the prospect became more
diversified: we passed fields of rice, cottages encircled
by fruit-gardens, and country houses belonging to the
Cambodian aristocracy, who come here in the evening
for the sake of breathing a purer air than they can find
in the city. As we drew closer to the gates I found the
place to be protected by a large moat, surmounted by
a parapet, and enclosed by a palisade three metres
high. I expected to enter a fortified town, and, as my
countrymen were now engaged in giving a lesson to the
Cochin-Chinese, to be received by a sentinel with fixed
bayonet, and with the startling words, "You cannot
pass." But seeing no one, I pushed open the gate
and entered. It seemed that I was in the enclosure
surrounding the palace of the second king. The first
object that attracted my attention was a sort of cage,
something between a sentry-box and a pigeon-house, with
a small window at each of the four sides, intended for a
look-out house and signal-station in case of invasion. I
then found myself in the centre of a large square
surrounded by ramparts, and the access to which is by
two gates, one opening on the market-place, and the
other on the country. Within this walled space is, on
one side, the palace of the inferior king, and opposite
are the residence of a younger prince, his brother, and
a pagoda. All these buildings were thatched.

I hoped to find here, as at Komput, an "Hotel for the king and ambassadors," but, not seeing any sign hung out, I bent my steps to a house where many persons were passing in and out. It was the hall of justice, and the judges were then sitting. I sent my man Niou to ask if they would give shelter to a traveller, and had not long to wait for an answer, for both judges and accused came out to see me, and I was brought into the hall, where I was an object of great curiosity, all crowding round me and asking me what I sold.

The news of my arrival soon reached the ears of the king, and two pages were sent to request me to wait at once on his Majesty; but my luggage was not yet forthcoming, and I objected that I could not visit him in my travelling-dress. "Oh, that is nothing; the king has no dress at all, and he will be delighted to see you," was the reply. Scarcely had my waggons arrived when a chamberlain, followed by a page, came to say that the king was waiting for me. I went, therefore, to the palace, before the entrance of which were a dozen dismounted cannon, in whose mouths the sparrows had built their nests. Further off a crowd of vultures were devouring the remains from the table of the king and his courtiers. I was ushered into the audience-chamber, which communicates with his Majesty's private apartments, and is paved with large Chinese tiles, the walls being whitened with chalk. A number of Siamese pages, fine young men from twenty-five to thirty years of age, uniformly dressed in a langouti of red silk, were

standing in groups, or seated in Oriental fashion, waiting
the king's appearance. A few minutes after my arrival

Drawn by M. Janet Lange, from a Photograph.

PORTRAIT OF THE SECOND KING OF CAMBODIA
(NOW THE FIRST KING).

he entered, and every forehead was bowed to the
ground. I rose, and he advanced towards me, with an
air at once easy and distinguished.

" Sire," said I, " I had the honour of an interview with

the first King at Komput, and of being favoured by him
with permission to visit Udong."

" Are you French or English ? " he asked, examining
me attentively.

" I am a Frenchman, Sire."

" You are not a merchant; why do you come to
Cambodia ? "

" Sire, I came through Siam to see your country, and
to hunt here, if allowed."

" Very good.   You have been in Siam? I also have
visited Bangkok.   Come and see me again."

" As often as my presence will be agreeable to your
Majesty."

After a few more minutes' conversation, the king held
out to me his hand, which I kissed, and I then retired;
but had not proceeded far when several officials ran after
me, exclaiming, " The king is enchanted with you; he
wants to see you often."

The following day I devoted to making an investigation
of the city. The houses are built of bamboos or planks,
and the market-place, occupied by the Chinese, is as dirty
as all the others of which I have made mention. The
longest street, or rather the only one, is a mile in length;
and in the environs reside the agriculturists, as well as the
mandarins and other Government officers. The entire
population numbers about 12,000 souls.

The many Cambodians living in the immediate vicinity,
and, still more, the number of chiefs who resort to Udong
for business or pleasure, or are passing through it on their

way from one province to another, contribute to give
animation to this capital. Every moment I met mandarins, either borne in litters or on foot, followed by a

Drawn by M Sabatier, from a Sketch by M. Mouhot
CAMBODIAN CART.

crowd of slaves carrying various articles; some, yellow
or scarlet parasols, more or less large according to the

rank of the person; others, boxes with betel. I also encountered horsemen, mounted on pretty, spirited little animals, richly caparisoned and covered with bells, ambling along, while a troop of attendants, covered with dust and sweltering with heat, ran after them. Light carts, drawn by a couple of small oxen, trotting along rapidly and noisily, were here and there to be seen. Occasionally a large elephant passed majestically by. On this side were numerous processions to the pagoda, marching to the sound of music; there, again, was a band of ecclesiastics in single file, seeking alms, draped in their yellow cloaks, and with the holy vessels on their backs.

The third day after my arrival at Udong the court of justice was noisily opened at eight o'clock in the morning; and the loud voices of the judges and advocates were still resounding through the hall at five in the afternoon, having never for an instant been hushed, when suddenly two pages came out of the court of the palace, crying out, "The King!" A thunderbolt falling in the hall could not have caused a greater sensation than this announcement; there was a general hurryscurry; judges, advocates, accused, and spectators fled pell-mell, taking refuge in the corners with their faces to the ground. I laughed to see the legal functionaries, and the Chinamen with their long queues, rushing against each other in their eagerness to escape at the king's approach. His Majesty, who was on foot, now appeared at the entrance, followed by his pages. He waved his hand and called me to him. Immediately two attendants brought chairs and placed them on the grass opposite to each other. The king offered me one, and then entered into conversation with me, while the whole escort and every one near us remained prostrate on the ground; as far as the eye could reach, not a soul was standing.

"How do you like my city?" * asked the king.

"Sire, it is splendid, and presents an appearance such as I have never seen elsewhere."

"All the palaces and pagodas which you see from here have been built in one year since my return from Siam: in another year all will be finished. Formerly Cambodia was very extensive; but the Annamites have deprived us of many provinces."

"Sire, the time has arrived for you to retake them. The French are assailing them on one side; do you attack them on the other." His Majesty did not reply, but offered me a cigar, and inquired my age.

"I am twenty-three," he said to me. "I recognise you; you were at Siam with M. de Montigny."

"No, sire; your Majesty is mistaken. I have only been in Siam a twelvemonth."

I then sent for an elegant small Minié rifle, which the king's officers had examined in the morning, and presented it to him, asking him if he would deign to accept it. He desired me to load it, which I did. "It is done, sire," said I.

---

* The word *city* is here used to signify the royal palace, its appurtenances and fortifications.

" Is it possible ?   Fire, then."

He chose for a target a post some way off, and pointed
out the place he wished me to hit.   I fired, and immediately his Majesty and the pages went to satisfy themselves that the aim was true.

" When do you wish to leave Udong ? "

" Sire, I should like to depart, the day after to-morrow,
for Pinhalu and the other provinces."

" If you could remain one day longer, it would give
me pleasure.   To-morrow you will dine with me ; on the
day after I will take you to see the town of the first king,
and in the evening we will have a play."

The play, I thought, will be curious, and therefore I
decided to remain ; and, after I had thanked the king for
his kindness to me, he shook hands with me, and we
separated.   Evidently I was in high favour.   On the
following morning messengers came from the king to
place horses at my disposal, should I be inclined to ride ;
but the heat was too great.   About four in the afternoon
he again did me the honour of sending a horse to bring
me to the palace.   I wore a white coat, vest, and trousers ;
a helmet made of cork,* after the fashion of the ancient
Romans, and covered with white muslin, completed my
singular toilet.

I was introduced by the chamberlain into one of the

---

* A head-dress excessively light and cool, convenient, and shading
the face and neck from the sun.   I strongly recommend it to travellers
in hot countries.

king's private apartments, a pretty room furnished in the European style. His Majesty sat waiting for me, smoking, near a table covered with refreshments; and as soon as I entered he rose, and holding out his hand, and smiling, he begged me to sit down and begin my repast. I perceived that he intended, after the manner of the country, to do me honour by being present at the meal without partaking of it himself.

After introducing me, with much courtesy and friendliness, to his brother, a young man of fifteen, who was kneeling by his side, the king said, "I have had this fowl and duck cooked in the European fashion; tell me if they are to your taste."

All had been really exceedingly well prepared; the fish, particularly, was capital.

"Good brandy," said the king, in English (the only words he knew in that language), as he pointed to a bottle of cognac. "Drink," continued he.

The attendants then placed before me jellies and exquisitely preserved fruits, bananas, and excellent mangoes. Afterwards tea was served, of which the king also partook, having first offered me a Manilla cigar. He then wound up a musical-box, and put it on the table. The first air gave me great pleasure, all the more because I was unprepared to hear it in a royal palace. It was the *Marseillaise*. The king took my start and look of astonishment for admiration. "Do you know that air?" he asked.

"Yes, sire."

Then followed another scarcely less familiar, the air of the Girondins, *Mourir pour la patrie.*

" Do you also know that ? "

As an answer, I accompanied the air with the words. "Does your Majesty like this air ? " I inquired.

" Not so well as the first."

" Your Majesty is right; most European sovereigns have the same taste."

" Napoleon, for instance ? "

" Napoleon, particularly."

My Annamite was with me, and filled the office of interpreter, with a perfect tact which pleased the king. The young prince now asked permission to retire, and saluted his brother by bowing to the earth and raising his clasped hands above his head. The king desired him to return the next morning, and accompany us to the palace of the first king; and the prince, passing out into the courtyard, was lifted astride on the shoulders of an attendant, and carried to his palace.

His Majesty then displayed to me his European furniture, mahogany tables covered with china vases and other ornaments of a commonplace description; above all, he pointed out, as worthy of notice, two old looking-glasses in gilt frames, a sofa, and various similar articles. "I am but beginning," said he; " in a few years my palace will be beautiful."

He afterwards took me into his garden, where were some rare and curious plants, and a miniature artificial rock. Then, on returning to the sitting-room, he conducted me past the inmates of his seraglio, at least a hundred in number, whom curiosity had brought out to gaze at the stranger.

"You are the first foreigner who has ever been admitted here," he said to me. "In Cambodia, as in Siam, no one but the people on duty can penetrate into the king's private apartments."

I thanked him for the honour he had done me, and took leave. He told me to ask for all I wanted, and he would refuse no request. The only thing I desired was to have my journey facilitated; and to this end I begged him to furnish me with letters to the chiefs of the different provinces of his dominions, and one or two elephants. This he promised to do. This young sovereign is the presumptive heir to the crown. His father, who owes his throne to the King of Siam, is not permitted by that monarch to leave his own country; and as a guarantee of his fidelity, one or two of his sons have always been retained as hostages at the Siamese Court. It was thus that the young king passed many years at Bangkok, where, doubtless, he learnt the art of government, and whence he was not allowed to return to his own kingdom till it was apparent that he would prove a submissive and obedient tributary. Another brother, a prince of twenty-one, paid me a visit at night, unknown to his relatives, hoping to receive a present. He was very childish for his age, and wanted everything he saw; he was, however, gentle and amiable, and of superior manners.

The next morning the king sent for me at ten o'clock. I found him seated on a sofa in the reception-hall, giving

Drawn by M. Janet Lange, from a Photograph.

A PAGE OF THE KING OF CAMBODIA.

orders to his pages about the order of march to be observed in going and returning. When all was ready, he entered a sedan-chair or palanquin magnificently carved and painted. His head and feet were bare, his hair cut in the Siamese fashion, and he wore a superb langouti of yellow silk, with a girdle of the same material, but of a lighter shade. The palanquin was borne on the shoulders of four attendants, and another held up an enormous red parasol with a gilt handle upwards of twelve feet long. The youngest prince, carrying the king's sabre, walked beside him; I was on the other side, and his Majesty often turned towards me to point out any striking object, and trying to read in my face what I thought of the effect produced on the people by his appearance. He sat in a careless attitude, one leg hanging out of the palanquin, and with his elbow resting on the morocco cushions.

At the approach of the procession all the collected population bowed themselves to the ground. In front marched three lictors, bearing in their hands bundles of rattans (the emblems of power); behind the palanquin came, two and two, the chamberlains and pages, numbering more than thirty, all dressed in red, and bearing on their shoulders pikes, sabres, or guns in cases. In this order we arrived at the outer entrance of the palace of the first king.

His Majesty here descended from his palanquin, and, still in the same order of march, we proceeded along an avenue about half a mile in length, planted with young trees, and bounded on either side by a wooden fence. The ground slopes gradually from hence, and is laid out

in gardens and lawns, encircling which are a hundred
little cottages with walls of clay and thatched roofs.
"All these houses are inhabited by my father's wives;
there is not a man in them," said the young king.

Farther on was a lake surrounded with rich and
luxuriant verdure. On its banks, buried in foliage, which
is reflected in the clear water, stands the royal residence,
part of which is of bamboo, the rest being whitewashed.
We went through several apartments, in which poor
Annamite women were weaving silk, and, after passing
in front of the treasury and the king's magazines, finally
reached a vast hall which, here, is peculiarly called the
palace. The interior does not come up to what might
be expected from an outside view. It is stocked like a
bazaar with glass bottles, vases filled with artificial flowers
and covered by glass shades, cushions of all colours and
sizes, boxes, slippers, old sofas, looking-glasses, washing-
stands, and a variety of European articles, piled upon
tables and shelves, and on the floor. As the young king
was to spend the day at the palace, he now dismissed
me, appointing one of his chamberlains to escort me
home.

A little after sunset the people collected in crowds to
witness the play which was to be performed on the king's
return, expected at seven o'clock. The multitude was so
dense that not a single inch of ground in the courtyard
was unoccupied, and the walls, even, were all covered.
At these festivities the people are apparently permitted

to depart from the customary posture of humility, for
every one was seated in Oriental fashion. The play was
simply a phantasmagoria tolerably well managed, and
accompanied by music more noisy than harmonious; but
which appeared perfectly to satisfy the public.

Drawn by M. Bocourt, from a Photograph.

A NATIVE ACTRESS.

P 2

CHAPTER VIII.

ON the 2nd July, having taken our usual morning repast
of rice, we were ready to set off, and were only waiting
for the waggons and elephants promised me by the king.
They were not long in arriving, and we passed through
the city amidst an immense crowd of people who had
come from all quarters to witness our departure. We
were mounted on our elephants, and escorted by several
of the royal pages as far as the road to Pinhalú; all the
population prostrating themselves as before the king,
doubtless because he had paid me such marked attention.

We proceeded, at the rate of about three miles an hour,
on a good road, which was in some places raised more
than ten feet above the level of the wooded but marshy
plain which extends to the great arm of the Mekon.

Now and then we crossed handsome bridges built of
stone or wood, which certainly give a more favourable
idea of the state of engineering in Cambodia than in
Siam; for, even at Bangkok, the streams and canals are

spanned by thin, narrow planks, or by trunks of trees
thrown across by the inhabitants, and not by the
authorities.

About two kilometres from Udong is a sort of rampart
formed of earth, in the form of a horseshoe. It environs
a portion of the town, and was intended to defend the
place in case of an invasion by the Annamites, an event
which is yearly looked for at the time of the floods.

We met many pedestrians laden, probably, with
provisions for the market. The road is bordered with
miserable bamboo huts, like poultry-houses, raised on
piles, which serve for dwellings for the unlucky Thiâmes,
who were transported here by the king, a twelvemonth
since, from the plains to the east of the Mekon, as a
punishment for an attempted revolt which they were
accused of.

We arrived early the same day at Pinhalú, a village
of some size, situated on the right bank of the stream,
many of the inhabitants of which are the descendants of
Portuguese and Annamite refugees. It is the residence
of a French bishop, Monsignor Miche, Vicar-apostolic of
the mission to Cambodia and Laos. He was absent, but
I found three good and benevolent missionaries, who
begged me to wait for his return, and received me in
that cordial and affectionate manner which is so pleasant
to meet with in a strange land, and especially from
fellow-countrymen. M. Fontaine, the eldest of the three,
though still in the prime of life, had been a missionary for
nearly twenty years. He was formerly attached to the

mission at Cochin China, and I had seen him on my visit to Bangkok, where he remained some time before going to Cambodia. He was then feeble and suffering, but I was glad now to find him stronger and full of animation. I felt a true respect for this worthy man; may there be many labourers in the same vocation resembling him!

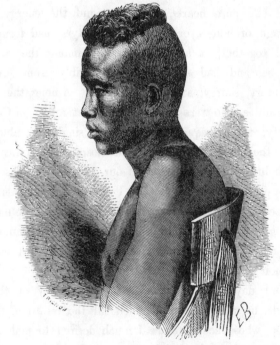

Drawn by M. Bocourt, from a Photograph.

SIAMESE OF THE LOWER CLASS.

The second priest, M. Arnoux, was not only a fellow-countryman, but our birthplaces were only distant from each other a few leagues. He was born in the department of Russey, and I in that of Montbéliard (Doubs), so that I had two reasons for being drawn towards him. He belongs to the Cochin China mission, and had come from among the savage Stiêns to renew his stock of provisions; but, having been attacked by dysentery, owing to the fatigue of the journey, he had been unable to return.   These two valiant soldiers of the Church, with good and pure hearts, iron wills, and the energy and courage of heroes, or, rather, of martyrs, had formerly lived together, at a distant station, among the savage Benous, and had suffered there terribly from fevers, dysentery, scurvy, and other diseases.   Among the fifty Annamites who were with them in that refuge of Christianity, there frequently was not a single one able to cook their rice, all being in the hospital.   On hearing these brave and worthy sons of our dear country describe their past and present misery, I was sometimes as much amused as affected, with so much liveliness was the narration given; but it is the characteristic of our dauntless nation that her sons suffer and die gaily, and with smiles on their lips.

Four days flew by rapidly in the society of these friends, by whom I was detained till the return of their bishop, whose acquaintance I much desired to make.   I knew that I should find in him a man of very superior character; but I did not expect to find in this eminent missionary a simplicity and humility equal to his talents and strength of mind.   Monsignor Miche is short and slight; but under his frail exterior exist extraordinary energy and endurance. The annals of the Cochin China mission, as well as of that to Cambodia, must contain many a page filled with the noble actions of this distinguished pioneer of Christianity, and with the persecution and captivity he has suffered. When a simple missionary, he and one of his companions were imprisoned and beaten with rods—a fearful punishment, which, at each blow, cut open the flesh and made the blood flow. They were then conducted to their cells, in order that the torture might be repeated on the following day, when their wounds were beginning to heal, for the Annamites are skilled in the refinements of cruelty.

"The suffering is dreadful," said his companion to M. Miche; "I do not believe I can bear it a second time."

"Be easy," he replied; "I will ask to receive your blows for you." He did request this, and actually did receive them.

Here the missionary is everything to the poor Christians, physician to the body as well as the soul; and every day he passes hours in listening to their disputes, and acting as peacemaker.

The rule here is, that if a man cannot pay a debt, he and his family become the slaves of the creditor. "You are my slave," said a person to a young girl whom he met.

"How so? I do not know you."

"Your father owed me money, and never paid me."

"I never knew my father; he died before I was born."

"Will you go to law?"

" Yes."

The man then consulted some mandarin, gave him a present, promised him others, won his cause, and the unfortunate girl, having no means to do the same, became a slave. It is the story of Appius and Virginia reproduced in the East. Corruption and barbarity are general in Cambodia.

I now determined to visit the savage tribes living to the east of the great river, 104° east long. from Paris, and of whom I had heard M. Arnoux speak; he had promised me a welcome from M. Guilloux, the missionary there. I sent Niou back to Udong to ask the king for the letter he had promised. He soon returned with it in due form, and on the 22nd July I quitted Pinhalú in a small boat with two rowers, which I hired as far as Pemptiélan, situated on the Mekon river, about forty miles to the north of Pénom-Peuh.

Ever since I had been in Cambodia my servants had been in a state of alarm, and it reached its height when I informed them that we were about to set out on an expedition to the savage tribes. Cambodia is much dreaded by the Siamese: and the mountains, and, still more, the forests, inhabited by the Stiêns, have a reputation for unhealthiness, among both Cambodians and Annamites, equal to that which, in France, is enjoyed by Cayenne, whither condemned political offenders and malefactors from the galleys are sent to die. I doubt very much if I could have met with any other men who would have remained with me.

Drawn by M. Thérond, from a Photograph

CHINESE MONUMENT AT BANGKOK.

On descending the great arm of the Mekon, which is here 1200 metres wide, I was astonished at seeing the current running from south to north instead of following the course of the river into which it falls. The banks of this river are peopled by the same race of Thiâmes whom I saw on my route from Udong to Pinhalú.

During more than five months of the year, the great lake of Cambodia, Touli-Sap, covers an immense space of ground : after that period there is a diminution in depth owing to the great evaporation, but its width remains nearly unaltered. Although its waters increase in volume during the rainy season, these are not swelled by the streams from the mountains on its western boundary, but by the strength of the current from the Mekon which pours into it its overflow.

As for the Malays, or Thiâmes, as the Cambodians call them, I made endeavours to investigate their origin, and also the traces which I supposed to exist in Cambodia of Israelite migrations. Monsignor Miche told me that he had never met with any Jews in the country, but that he had found, in one of the sacred books of the Cambodians, the judgment of Solomon exactly recorded, and attributed to one of their kings who had become a god, after having been, according to their ideas of metempsychosis, an ape, an elephant, &c.

The Thiâmes are the same as the ancient Tsiampois ; but these Tsiampois, whence came they ? What is the origin of this strange people, whom the conquests of the Annamites drove back, doubtless from the south of Cochin

China to Cambodia, but who form alliances with neither of the races whose country they share, and who preserve their own language, manners, and religion? On looking over the Life of the Abbé Gagelin, one of the martyrs in Cochin China, written with talent and eloquence by the learned Abbé Jacquenet, I found what I had long been in search of, and I extract the following passage :—

"In the midst of Cochin China properly so called, between the seas which surround it on all sides except on the west, where it touches Cambodia, is the ancient kingdom of Tsiampa. The inhabitants are a singular race ; they never ally themselves with the Cochin Chinese, their character, religion, and language raising insuperable barriers between them. On submitting to the yoke of the conqueror, the sovereign simply changed his title from king to mandarin, but the constitution and ancient laws remained in full vigour in his states, and he continued to exercise absolute authority over his subjects.* It is difficult for strangers to observe the domestic life of these people; but it is said that they practise circumcision, observe the Sabbath, abstain from the flesh of pork, and offer the sacrifice of the red calf.† It is even said that they possess the Pentateuch, but this I dare not affirm. Strangely, however, all these observances, imitated no one

---

* This appears very doubtful, even to the missionaries in Cochin China.

† M. Mouhot probably here refers to Numb. xix. 2.—*Tr.*

knows whence, are only vain ceremonies to these men,
enigmas to which they have lost the clue. They have
not even retained a distinct idea of the true God; and
their worship, although mixed up with some of the rites
of the Mosaic law, is a real idolatry. One wonders whence
come this people. Are they an ancient colony of Ish-
maelites or Idumeans? Are they an offshoot of Judaism
thrown on to these shores? These questions are worthy
of consideration. However it may be, their care to preserve their traditions pure from all alloy, and their
obstinate persistence in error, render them worthy of a
Jewish origin. The Jews, in the days of their prosperity,
did not guard their faith more religiously than do these
people theirs in their new Palestine; and, in order to
avoid intercourse with strangers, and escape the prose-
lyting efforts of the missionaries, they have relinquished
to the Cochin Chinese all the advantages of the sea-
shore, and retired to the mountains and the interior of
the country.

" On the eve of the Assumption I bent my steps towards
the interior, to visit the Tsiampois, and find out whether
they would still reject the good news of salvation. After
a few days' walking I arrived, I dare not say at one of
their towns, but at one of their principal dwelling-places.
These singular people have retained none of the power
ascribed to them by ancient tradition, according to which
they have held sway over Cambodia, Cochin China, Tong
King, and even Pegu, as far as the province of Canton.
Their governor has to pay a small tribute, but remains

as much ruler over his own people as before the conquest.

"I was anxious to find out the truth about their religion, but could only obtain scraps of tradition which a Christian could manage to put into form. One of these traditions teaches that the founder of their religion was a great man, a famous warrior, who worked marvels with a rod which is carefully preserved among them. I had the signal honour of being allowed to see it: it is about ten feet long, and is covered with a kind of red stuff, studded with yellow stars, having at one end an iron blade about an inch in length. With this rod in his hand, the founder of their faith controlled the elements, divided the waters, and calmed tempests; and it is pretended that this instrument still preserves its virtue of working miracles. They have, they say, a precious volume left them by this great chief. Their religious practices consist in the scrupulous observance of a seventh day of rest, in abstaining from certain food, especially pork, which they hold in abhorrence, and in the rite of circumcision which the male children undergo at the age of fifteen. When the girls arrive at the same age, the hair over the forehead is cut. They preserve a remembrance of certain days on which it was not lawful to work, nor even to leave their houses before sunset. Their prayers end with the word 'Amin,' much the same as the Amen of the Hebrews. They seem to have lost the idea of a Creator of heaven and earth, but worship the sky and the stars; there are, however, no idols in their temples. The priests who officiate there light candles on a table, burn incense, and, at certain times of the year, as in April and May, pass a month without going out of doors. Clear away from this account," says the Abbé Jacquenet, "the mists of ages, and it is easy to recognise the traces of an Israelitish origin. Comparing this with other missionary accounts, and the traces of these people found elsewhere, who will doubt that the torch of truth, which shone formerly between the great sea and Jordan, also shed its light over the extreme East? Whether, to explain these facts, we consider the commercial relations of the Jews with these countries, particularly when, in the height of their power, the combined fleets of Solomon and Hiram went to seek the treasures of Ophir (a generic name used perhaps to designate the two Indies), or whether we come lower down, to the dispersion of the Ten Tribes, who, instead or returning from captivity, set out from the banks of the Euphrates and reached the shores of the ocean—whatever ground of explanation we resolve upon, the shining of the light of revelation in the far East is not the less incontestable. Join to this light, those traditional truths carried with them as a sacred heritage by the families who were dispersed at Babel; and say what becomes of the extravagant praises lavished on Eastern wisdom by the sect of philosophers? Passion and presumptuous ignorance joining hands tried to oppose wisdom from on high, and have left behind only a faint reflection of it."

CHAPTER IX.

We left Pinhalú at eleven, and by evening had reached
the great bazaar of Cambodia, the distance being about
eighteen miles. I had little to buy, for M. Miche and
M. Arnoux had insisted on filling my boat with rice and
dried fish, sufficient to last not only for my voyage but
during the whole period I proposed to remain among the
Stiêns.

I stopped a whole day to see the city, and make a
few purchases of glass, brass wire, and cotton yarn, articles
which would be useful as barter among the savages. The
town is situated at the confluence of two great streams,
and contains about 10,000 inhabitants, almost all Chinese;
but it has a floating population of more than double that
number, composed of Cambodians and Cochin-Chinese,
living in their boats. It was the time when most of the
fishermen, returning from the great lake, stop at Penom-
Peuh to sell part of their fish, and when a crowd of small
merchants flock there to buy cotton, which is gathered in

before the rains. Having traversed the city, which was long and dirty, I arrived at an eminence on which was built a pagoda, possessing neither beauty nor interest, but from whence there is an extensive view over a large tract of country.

On one side extend, like two long and wide ribands, across an immense wooded plain, the Mekon and its tributary; on the other, another plain and thick forest, bounded on the north-west and south by small chains of mountains.

Although the missionaries often pass through Penom-Peuh, my presence excited much curiosity among the people. The war in Cochin-China was the subject of all conversations, and in every one's thoughts. The reports of the Chinese and Annamites who had seen the taking of the town of Saigou were not flattering to the pride of a Frenchman. I had not seen the glorious bulletins of our Admiral, but had the pain of hearing our enemies stigmatise us as barbarians, and, describing the burning of the market, and the conduct of the soldiery towards defenceless women, speak of it as "the behaviour of savages." Thus the evil deeds of a less civilized ally were visited upon us, and our whole nation judged of by isolated acts, all but inevitable in time of war, especially in a country where the soldier suffers from the climate and privations of all kinds.

The people, perhaps the most corrupted in all the East, expected to find in us men superior, morally, as well as intellectually and physically; and I dare to flatter myself that before long they will learn to distinguish between the characters of the true French soldiers and their allies, and that in every respect we shall recover our ancient prestige.

The next day, descending the river toward the southern extremity of the city, we passed a floating town, composed of more than 500 boats, most of them of large size. They serve as an entrepôt for some merchants, and residences for others. All their money and the greater part of their merchandize is here kept, that, in case of alarm, they may be ready to take flight at a moment's warning.

Shortly afterwards we entered the Mekon, which was only now beginning to rise, as, throughout the country the drought had been excessive, lasting much longer than usual. This great river, the name of which signifies " Mother of Rivers," recalled to my mind the Menam, north of Bangkok, but its aspect is less gay; yet there is something very imposing in this expanse of water running with all the rapidity of a torrent. A few boats, scarcely distinguishable, toiled along: the banks, generally about 18 or 20 feet high, seemed almost deserted; and the forests were indistinctly discernible more than a mile beyond. In Siam the elegant foliage of the bamboos and palm-trees shows out strikingly against the blue sky, while the songs of the birds charm the ear: here, shoals of porpoises sail along with their noses to the wind, frequently bounding out of the water; pelicans sport on the margins of the stream, and herons and storks fly silently

THE RIVER MEKON AT PENOM-PEUH.

Drawn by M. Sabatier, from a Sketch by M. Mouhot.

from among the reeds at our approach. These are the sole objects of interest.

We passed the great island of Ko-Sutin, which is distant about 40 miles from Penom-Peuh, after five days' difficult and laborious travelling. The current was so strong that at every turn in the stream we were obliged, in addition to redoubling our efforts at the oars, to hold on by the reeds to prevent our being carried away.

The farther north we went the more rapidly the stream ran; so that when the waters are high two miles a day are the usual rate of progress; and it is a common occurrence for the boatmen to seek fuel for their evening fire in the same spot where they had cooked their rice in the morning.

About 25 or 30 leagues north of Ko-Sutin, on the confines of Laos, commence the rapids and cataracts: it is then necessary to leave the boats and take to pirogues, which, as well as the luggage, have often to be carried on men's backs. I made a halt of only a few hours, in order to see another voluntary exile, M. Cordier, a priest of great worth, from the Cambodian mission, who resides here.

I felt great compassion for this good man, on entering the chapel which he had built, and seeing the poverty and nakedness around. He came to meet me, and invited me to share his repast. For the last three years the poor missionary has been suffering from a dysentery, which has become chronic. However, he complains neither of his bad health nor of his poverty : the only thing that grieved

him was the small number of converts he was called on to
baptize, so deeply are the Cambodians attached to their
idols.

"But you," said he to me; "do you know whither you
are going? I am astonished that they allowed you to
leave Pinhalú. Ask the Cambodians what they think of
the forests of the Stiêns, and propose to some of them to
accompany you: you would not find one. The rains have
begun, and you are going to almost certain death, or will
at least catch a fever, which will be followed by years of
languor and suffering. I have had the jungle fever, and it
is something terrible: even to the tips of my nails I felt
a heat which I can only call infernal: sometimes an icy
coldness would take its place: generally people sink under
it: witness M. Lafitte, a young missionary, who a short
time ago took the same journey; M. Comte, who died of
exhaustion; and many others."

This account was not reassuring, nevertheless I had
determined on my route: I knew that I should find
there land and fresh-water shells whch I could find nowhere else,* and that this tribe of almost unknown
savages would afford me a curious and interesting study;
and these considerations were sufficient to determine me
to proceed. I trusted in God, and went on my way,
M. Cordier's last words being, "May God be with the
poor traveller!"

---

* Thence come the beautiful Bulimus Cambogiensis, Ptelin Cambogiensis, and Ptelin Mouhoti.

A. ROUARGUE, SC.

Drawn by M. Sabatier, from a Sketch by M. Mouhot.

CAMBODIAN HUT AT PEMPTIELAN, ON THE MEKON.

Twelve miles higher up I left the river, and set off on my land journey at two o'clock in the afternoon, hoping to arrive the same day at Pemptiélan, a large village, where lived the mandarin to whom the king's letter was addressed. We did not, however, get there till eleven the next morning, having to pass the night at the foot of a tree, where we lighted a fire. I waited at once upon the mandarin, who is governor of the district, and he received me very well, in spite of the small value of the presents I made him, and immediately gave orders for waggons to be made ready for me. He then presented me with a quantity of tobacco and betel. His manners were, for a Cambodian, gentle and polished; and he questioned me much as to the war in Cochin-China, as well as about Europe, how long it took to get there, &c.

From the time we left Pemptiélan we had, except at rare intervals, to pass through dense forests, and at first the ground was so marshy that our miserable waggons occasionally sank deeply; and it required the united strength of the oxen and all our men to extricate them. We got over the latter part of our route more agreeably; for, as we reached a higher elevation, the ground became dry, and the aspect of the country more varied.

We had only been able to accomplish 60 miles in five days, and were still 30 miles from Brelum. I grew tired of the incivility of the inhabitants from whom I hired the oxen, and of the slowness of these animals: when we had no shelter for the night, we suffered much from rain and damp; our clothes were almost always soaked through;

and, to crown our misfortunes, my two servants were
attacked with intermittent fever; the Annamite particularly, who had a tertian fever, lasting for ten days.

The mode of life of the Cambodians is similar to that
of the Siamese : rice, as with the latter, is the chief part
of their food : they eat it with vegetables, such as pump-
kins or gourds, and wild potatoes. Those in better circumstances add to it fish, but rarely meat; and yet the
country is as fertile as Lower Cochin-China, the soil of
which yields so abundant a return for all that is put in
the ground.

The poverty of the inhabitants of these miserable
villages engenders a repulsive dirtiness : a strip of matting or an old filthy cushion thrown on the ground, and
full of vermin, some basins of coarse Chinese porcelain,
a sort of hatchet, and a piece of cotton, intended either
for counterpane, scarf, or cloak, according to the season
and time of day, are the usual contents of a Cambodian
hut.*

We arrived at Pump-Ka-Daye, on the confines of Cambodia, and inhabited by about twenty Stiêns, who have
approached the boundary in order to escape slavery in
their own tribe. Our waggons halted before a small caravanserai, open to every wind; and after having carried in
our luggage, our guides disappeared much faster than
they had come. The chief soon presented himself, followed by some men: he had all the characteristics of a

---

* Cambodian is pronounced " Khmer," in the language of the country.

savage in his face, and of a Cambodian in his nature. I
handed him my letter, but he returned it, saying that he
could not read. " These, then," said I, " are the contents.
It is the king's order to all chiefs of villages where I
shall stop to furnish me with waggons to continue my
journey to Brelum." " We have no waggons," was the
answer.

We made ourselves as comfortable as we could till the
next day, when a second interview with the chief proved
to me that I should get no aid from him. I therefore
sent Niou with two Cambodians to carry a letter to
M. Guilloux, and bring me an answer. This arrived on
the evening of the fourth day; and in it M. Guilloux
assured me of a cordial welcome, adding that he was
interested in my undertaking, and had already a great
regard for me, without seeing me, for my courage in
coming so far.* The good father sent me three waggons
from the mission settlement, and some of his Annamites,
as well as two Stiêns, to help me on my way. This letter
completely removed all fear of being a troublesome and
unwelcome guest to the poor hermit, and I set out
with pleasure and confidence. It took us two long days'
journey to reach Brelum : we encamped one night near
a torrent, lying on our mats beside a good fire, which we
lighted to keep off the ferocious denizens of these forests.
The second night we passed in a deserted cabin some
miles from Brelum ; and on the 16th August, at nine in

---

* See M. Guilloux's letter in the Appendix.

the morning, we came to a clearing of from 250 to 300 mètres square. We were betwixt two hills, at the foot of which was marshy ground. On the slope of one I saw

Drawn by M. Sabatier, from a Sketch by M. Mouhot.

CAMBODIAN HOUSE.

two long bamboo houses, covered with thatch, and with the mission-garden attached: higher up was the cross planted two years before amidst these frightful solitudes by the noble and courageous French missionaries.

Scarcely had we appeared when we were saluted by a discharge of musketry. We replied as well as we could; and while these sounds were reverberating among the echoes of the forests, poor Father Guilloux, his legs covered with bad wounds, which had confined him for above six months to his mattrass, and which he had received on the journeys undertaken through the promptings of his pious zeal, advanced with frail steps to meet me along the tree-trunks thrown as a bridge across the swamp. All honour to thee, noble son of our dear and beautiful country!—thou who bravest poverty, privations, fatigue, suffering, and even death, to bring to these savages the blessings of religion and civilization! May God recompense thee for thy painful and self-denying labours, for men would be powerless to do so; thy reward is not of this world. Besides, in these troublous and warlike times, the virtues of the soldier are more appreciated than thine. But continue thy divine work; intelligent eyes and hearts watch from afar; and if, in our day, the military career is more honoured and better recompensed than any other, there are still, be sure, Christian hearts which feel it a duty to make known to the world thy virtue and thy sufferings, thy privations, and the benefits thou conferrest on these unfortunates.

CHAPTER X.

I RESIDED nearly three months among the savage Stiêns. Is this too short a period to enable me to form an opinion of them? One would think so, on hearing Father Guilloux repeat often that, although he has lived here two years, he is yet far from knowing all their superstitions and *devilries*.

We are surrounded by forests, which are infested with elephants, buffaloes, rhinoceros, tigers, and wild boars, and the ground all about the pools is covered with their footprints. We live almost as in a besieged place, every moment dreading some attack of the enemy, and keeping our guns constantly loaded. Sometimes they come close to our quarters, and we cannot go even a few steps into the woods without hearing them. As a general rule, however, they fly from the approach of man, and in order to get a shot it is necessary to lie in wait either amongst the branches of a tree or hidden amid the brushwood near the spots where they come to drink.

Scorpions, centipedes, and, above all, serpents, were the enemies we most dreaded, and against which precautions were chiefly requisite; but the mosquitoes and the leeches, though less dangerous, were the most troublesome and most inveterate plagues. During the rainy season you cannot be too much on your guard; going to bed or getting up, you are ever in peril of putting hand or foot on some venomous snake. I have killed more than one in my house with a gun or a hatchet. As I write, I am obliged to be continually on the watch, fearing to see one reappear on which I trod this evening, but which made his exit without hurting me. From time to time, also, I stop to listen to the roaring of a tiger, who is wandering round our dwelling and looking longingly at the pigs through their fence of planks and bamboos. Again, I hear a rhinoceros breaking down the bamboos which oppose his progress towards the brambles encircling our garden, on which he intends to banquet.

The savage Stiêns who inhabit this region have probably the same origin as those who people the mountains and the table-land which separate the kingdoms of Siam and Cambodia from that of Annam, and which extend along the great river from 11° north lat. and between 106° and 108° east long. They form as many separate communities as there are villages, and seem to be a race distinct from all the people who surround them. I am myself inclined to believe them to be the aborigines of the country, and to suppose that they have been driven back from the sea and the rivers to the districts now occupied by them by the successive invasions of the Thibetans, who have spread themselves over Laos, Siam, and

Drawn by M. Bocourt, from a Sketch by M. Mouhot.

SAVAGE STIEN.

Cambodia, and nothing that I can discover leads to any other supposition.*

---

* The drawings of M. Mouhot at first sight recall those of the Polynesians of the North, and more especially of the Carolinas, as they are depicted in the works of Gutke, of Duperoy, and of Dumont d'Urville.

These savages are so strongly attached to their forests
and mountains that to quit them seems almost like death,
and those who are dragged as slaves to the neighbouring
countries languish under captivity and try every method
of escape, frequently with success. Like other savages,
they have appeared formidable to their neighbours, and
the fear inspired by them has occasioned exaggerated
reports of their wonderful skill in shooting with the bow,
as well as of the pestilential climate. However, it is a
fact that fever prevails here terribly; numbers of Annamites and Cambodians have fallen victims to it, and
I am assured that I am the only stranger who has come
without suffering from it more or less. These people love
the deep shade of the pathless woods, which they do
not trouble themselves to cut down; but if they cling to
their country, they do not to any particular locality, for
if they meet with any inconvenience in their neighbourhood, or if any of their family die of fever, they raise
their camp, take their children in baskets on their backs,
and set off to make a settlement elsewhere; land is not
wanting, and the forest everywhere alike.

These tribes are nearly independent, although the Cambodians on one side, and the Laotians and Annamites on
the other, levy on the villages near them a triennial tribute
of rice and wax. The King of Cambodia does not want
the will to treat the Stiêns as he did the Thiâmes, in order
to people some of his desert provinces.

The inscription placed—alas! so vainly—on our public
edifices is here, notwithstanding slavery, the motto of the

Drawn by M. Bocourt, from a Sketch by M. Mouhot.
SAVAGE STIEN.

people, and its sincerity is evidenced in their practice.
We use words; they act. If there is abundance at one
house, the whole village shares in it, and when scarcity
prevails, which is often the case, all alike suffer.

They work admirably in iron and ivory, and some tribes
are noted, as in Annam, for their hatchets and the
beautiful workmanship of their sabres. Their drinking-
vessels are rude, but of their own manufacture, and the
women weave and dye the long fine scarfs which they
wear, the best of which are often valued at the price of an
ox. They cultivate rice, maize, tobacco, various kinds of
vegetables, and fruit-trees, such as bananas, mangoes, and
oranges. Every person of any substance possesses several

slaves, and a field, always at some distance from the village, and very carefully attended to. In these fields, in little huts raised on piles, the Stiêns pass the whole of the rainy season, during which they can neither hunt nor fish, both on account of the inclement weather and the leeches, the immense numbers of which, as in the forests of Siam, make them a perfect pest.

Their manner of preparing a rice-field is very different from the way in which our agriculturists set about matters. As soon as the first rains begin to fall, the Stiên chooses his ground, and busies himself in clearing it. This would be a laborious task for a European; but he, with his hatchet with cane handle, has in a few days cut down a thicket of bamboos 100 or 150 mètres square. If he meets with any tree too large for him to manage, he leaves it standing. After a few days, when the canes are a little dry, he sets fire to them, and the field is soon cleared. As for the roots, he cares little about them, as no digging is required; on this virgin soil everything grows with little labour. There only remains to sow the seed, and for this purpose he takes two long bamboos, which he lays in a line on the ground; then, with a stick in each hand, he makes on each side of this line holes about an inch or an inch and a half deep at short distances. The man's work is now finished, and that of the woman begins: stooping down, she follows the line traced by her husband, and from a basket carried at her left side takes a handful of rice, of which she throws a few grains into each hole with great rapidity, and at the same time so dexterously that it is rare for any to fall outside. In a few hours the task is finished, for here there is no need of harrow or plough; kind Nature will soon send some violent showers, which, washing the soil over the holes, will cover the seeds. Then the proprietor establishes himself in his hut, where, as he smokes his cigarette (made of tobacco rolled in some leaf), he lets fly his arrows at the wild boars, apes, or goats, or amuses himself by frightening away the doves and parroquets. To this end, a couple of bamboos are so placed in the middle of the field that, by pulling a rope made of rattán, they are made to strike against each other, and the noise scares away the birds, which without some such contrivance would eat up all the seed. The harvest is reaped at the end of October. Generally, two months previously poverty and famine begin to make themselves felt. As long as provisions last they feast without ever thinking of the morrow; when they are exhausted they are reduced to eat serpents, toads, and bats, which last are found in great numbers in the hollows of the old bamboos. Often they have even to content themselves with the seeds of the maize, young bamboo-shoots, wild roots, and other spontaneous productions of the ground.

All the domestic animals of the neighbouring countries, such as oxen, pigs, fowls, and ducks, are found here, but in small numbers. Elephants are scarce; but farther north, among the tribe of the Benams, it is said that no village is without them.

When the harvest has been gathered in the Stiêns

L. SARGEANT. SC.

E. BOCOURT.

SAVAGE STIENS SOWING THEIR RICE.

Drawn by M. Bocourt, from a Sketch by M. Mouhot.

commence a series of festivities. The rice having been
piled up in oblong stacks, they take from these every
morning as much as suffices for the day's consumption.
One community sends invitations to another, and the
inhabitants of a wealthy village will often kill as many as
ten oxen for the entertainment; all must be consumed
before they separate, and day and night they eat and
drink to the accompaniment of the Chinese tam-tam and
tambourine. This excess, after a long period of privation,
brings on illness, commonly the itch and other cutaneous
disorders. Much of this, however, also proceeds from the
want of salt, which they cannot always procure. For
all internal complaints, the general remedy here, as in
Cambodia, is an iron heated in the fire and applied to the
pit of the stomach, and there are few men without scars
on this part of the body.

They are acquainted with many of the remedies drawn
from simples; they never cover up a wound or sore, but
leave it exposed to the air and sun, and it generally heals.
They appear to be exempt from leprosy, so common
among the Chinese; but then they are very cleanly, and
bathe in all weathers, often three times a day.

The Stiêns have no resemblance to either the Cambodian or Annamite races; like the last, however, they
wear the hair long, twisted up, and fastened by a bamboo
comb, in which is often inserted, for ornament, a piece of
brass wire surmounted by the crest of a pheasant. They
are usually above the middle height, are well proportioned
and robust; their features are regular, and the thick

eyebrows and beard of the men, when they do not pull out the hair from the face, give them a grave appearance. The forehead is well developed, and announces an intelligence much beyond that of the Annamites. Their manners are hospitable, and a stranger is always certain of being well received and feasted. They either kill a pig or fowl, and offer you wine, which is not drunk out of any sort of vessel, but sucked, through a bamboo cane, from a large jar; it is made from rice, fermented, but rarely distilled. To refuse a pipe when offered is considered a great rudeness, which more than one savage has paid for by a knife-thrust. It is also etiquette to eat the whole of the food set before you.

Their only dress is the long scarf I have already mentioned, and which, when worn, appears only about two inches wide. I often surprised them quite naked in their cabins; but on perceiving me they always covered themselves.

The greatest liberty is allowed to slaves, and corporal punishment is never inflicted on any one. For theft, a forfeit is exacted of a pig or ox, and several jars of wine, of which the whole village partake. If the fine be not paid, it rapidly increases in amount; the offender is soon in debt to the community for fifteen or twenty buffaloes, and finally he is sold as a slave.

The Stiêns have neither priests nor temples, yet they recognise the existence of a supreme being, to whom they refer everything good or evil; they call him "Brâ," and invoke him in all cases. They believe also in an evil

genius, and attribute all diseases to him.   If any one be
suffering from illness, they say it is the demon tormenting
him; and, with this idea, make, night and day, an insup-
portable noise around the patient, which they keep up until
one of the party falls in a kind of fit, crying out, "He has
passed into my body; he is stifling me." They then
question the new patient, asking him, first, what remedies
to give the sick man, and how the demon can be made to
abandon his prey. Sometimes the sacrifice of a pig or an
ox is required, often a human victim; in this latter case
they pitilessly seize upon a slave and offer him up to the
evil genius.

Funerals are solemnly performed, the whole village
assisting, with the exception of the nearest relatives, who
generally remain at home. All those present fill the air
with lamentable cries. They bury their dead near their
dwellings, covering the tomb with a little roof of branches,
beneath which they place gourds full of water, and sometimes small bows and arrows; and every day some
member of the family comes and sows a few grains of rice,
that the dead may have something to eat. These customs
resemble those of the Chinese.

Before every meal they take care to spill a little rice
to feed the souls of their ancestors, and in their fields and
other places formerly frequented by them they make
similar little offerings to them. At the end of a long
bamboo planted in the ground they suspend plumes of
reeds; lower down are fastened smaller bamboos containing a few drops of wine or water; and, lastly, on a

slight trellis-work raised above the ground, is laid some earth, in which they stick an arrow, and on which they throw a few grains of cooked rice, a bone, a little tobacco, and a leaf.

According to their belief, animals also have souls which wander about after their death; thus, when they have killed one, fearing lest its soul should come and torment them, they ask pardon for the evil they have done to it, and offer sacrifices proportioned to the strength and size of the animal. For an elephant, the ceremony is conducted with pomp; the head is ornamented with crowns, and musical performances on the tam-tam and tambourine, with singing, are continued for seven consecutive days. The whole village, summoned by sound of trumpet, assembles to take part in the fête, and every one is entitled to a portion of the flesh.

The Stiêns smoke the flesh of the animals when they desire to preserve it for any length of time; but ordinarily, all those taken in the chase are eaten on the spot, and within a few days; they then merely singe them whole, without skinning, and afterwards cut them in pieces and cook them.

It is rare to meet a Stiên without his cross-bow in his hand, his knife over his shoulder, and a basket on his back, which serves both for quiver and game-bag. Hunting and fishing occupy all the time not given to the cultivation of the ground. They are indefatigable in the chase, and glide amidst the thickest woods with the speed of a deer, seeming not to feel fatigue. The women appear as robust and strong as the men. Their cross-bows are very effective weapons, and they are skilful in the use of them; but rarely shoot from a distance of more than fifty paces. They use poisoned arrows for the larger animals, the venom being extremely rapid in its effects; if the beast, whether it be elephant, tiger, or rhinoceros, have the skin ever so slightly pierced, so that the poison touches the blood, it is almost certain to be found dead a few hundred yards from the place where it was struck.

They are very fond of ornaments, particularly beads of brilliant colours, which they make into bracelets. Glass ornaments and brass wire pass among them as money; a buffalo or an ox is valued at six armfulls of thick brass wire; a pig is nearly as dear; but for a small piece of fine wire or a bead necklace you can purchase a pheasant or a hundred ears of maize. Men generally wear a bracelet above the elbow and one at the wrist; but the women cover both arms and legs with these ornaments. Both sexes have their ears pierced, and widen the hole every year by inserting pieces of bone or ivory three inches long.

Polygamy is held in honour among the Stiêns, although only the chiefs are rich enough to allow themselves the luxury of several wives.

While I was among them there was a total eclipse of the sun, which, if I remember right, was also visible in England. Like the Cambodians, on the occurrence of such phenomena, they believe that some being has swallowed up the sun and moon; and in order to deliver them, they made a frightful noise, beat the tam-tam, uttered savage cries, and shot arrows into the air, until the sun re-appeared.

One of their favourite amusements is to send up kites, to which they attach a musical instrument somewhat resembling a bow, and this, when agitated by the wind, produces sweet and melodious sounds to which they are fond of listening.

Their memories are bad, and they have great difficulty in learning to calculate. If a hundred ears of maize are to be offered for sale, they are arranged in tens, to make sure that the number is correct. Their notions of geo-graphy are very limited; they imagine that white men inhabit only a few obscure corners of the globe, and, judging of them by the Catholic missionaries, doubt much if they have any women among them.

Hostilities between one village and another are not infrequent, but they are never very serious: they seek to surprise and take one another prisoners in the fields or pathways, and the captives are sold as slaves to the Laotians or Cambodians. Their disposition is gentle and timid, and at the least alarm of an enemy they retire into the forest, previously placing in the paths sharp-pointed stakes of bamboo, which often pierce quite through the feet of their pursuers.

The manners of the savages of Brelum and those of the surrounding villages differ considerably; this is owing to the influence of the good and courageous missionaries, who, although they do not make many converts—which is their chief trouble—have at least the consolation of being able by their presence, good counsel, and example, to soften and enlighten these poor creatures—in one word, to civilize them.

The Fauna of this country does not differ much from that of the kingdom of Siam; thus, with the exception of some beautiful new species of insects and land shells, and a number of interesting birds, I shall gain by my excursion nothing but the pleasure of having been able to study the habits of a curious people, and the not inferior gratification of making them known to the public, should these rough notes, written hastily, and with no claim to any merit but truth, be destined to see the light. Whether God reserves for me the happiness of again seeing my native country, in which event it will be my endeavour to put them into some sort of readable shape; or whether I fall a victim to pestilence or ferocious beasts, and some kind person takes charge of these sheets, scribbled generally by the light of a torch, and on my knees at the foot of a tree, amidst interruptions of all sorts, of which the mosquitoes are not the least annoying; in either case, living or dead, I shall need, I am aware, an indulgence seldom granted. Most readers prefer being amused to being instructed; while my sole aim has been to paint faithfully, and to the best of my poor abilities, what came under my observation.

My arrival here was—I may say it without vanity, for I was a stranger to him—quite an event in the poor missionary's lonely life; and the landing—for it did not deserve the name of room—left vacant by the departure of Father Arnoux, was placed at my disposal. I ask pardon of the good, brave, and generous priests who have aided, welcomed, and sheltered me through all my wanderings, if I have spoken too plainly of their poverty and privations of all kinds; if I have raised the curtain which, perhaps, they would wish to keep drawn, for, I repeat, they look not for recompense in this world; but I have done it that the world may know that their life is one of the hardest and most painful, and requires self-sacrifice more than any other. Exposed to the influence of pernicious climates, badly lodged, badly fed, far from their families and from their country, often ill and dying without help—such is the lot of these men.

The house of uncle Apait was at least as elegant and well furnished as that of the humble priest at Brelum: both had the bare ground for a floor, walls of bamboo canes, and dried grass for thatch. The hut was divided into four compartments, two being used by the missionaries, another by their servant, and the fourth served as a chapel. This, like the others, was far from splendid, and the whole house had been so undermined by the white ants, that it seemed menaced with approaching ruin.

Speaking of the Annamite servants, I shall quote what the Abbé Gagelin says about them, for I can testify to its truth. "All sensibility," says he, "appears deadened among them; they are very proud, however, and great cheats. There is so little affection among them, that the nearest relations never think of embracing; even a child,

Drawn by M. H. Rousseau, from a Photograph.

AMAZON OF THE KING'S FEMALE GUARDS.

returning to his parents after a ten years' absence, would
not think of such a thing.   Among brothers and sisters
it would be considered almost a scandal.   They will not
permit us missionaries to caress a child, not even a baby.
This coldness is not confined to their domestic relations;
under an ardent sky, which should warm the imagination,
they, in their stupid *sang froid*, will not tolerate in a
preacher the slightest movement or gesture."   However,
to compensate for these defects, the abbé, who, even in
the opinion of several of the other missionaries, has been
guilty of great errors in his letters, might have added that,
at times, they are capable of acts of devotion and self-
sacrifice truly great and courageous.

The French missionaries in Cochin China must have
had many proofs of this, for, hunted as they are like wild
beasts, they could not long escape the vigilant eyes of the
mandarins, nor continue, in spite of the most terrible
persecutions, to reside in the country.   It is death for
any one to be caught sheltering or assisting a priest;
but, notwithstanding, they and their goods are conveyed
in boats from Singapore, eluding all the spies set to watch
for them, and remain hidden for months and even years.
If an alarm is raised, in spite of the danger of discovery,
they are conveyed to another locality, where they find
new friends equally ready to peril their lives for them.
Missions are founded amongst the most savage tribes;
and in spite of the terrible reputation of this climate, in
spite of fevers, wild beasts, and love of home, the missionary has but to speak, and he is sure to find poor

Christians ready to follow him, often without fee or
reward. In what country in the world, among what
civilized people of the West, can you find more than
this?

Intelligent, and with a desire for civilization, the only
difficulty is to know how to guide them. From my own
experience and that of others, I believe the Annamite to
be lively, adroit, intelligent, and courageous; but obstinate, vindictive, a dissembler, a liar, and a thief; slow
to get into a passion, but terrible when he does so. His
dirtiness surpasses anything I have ever seen, and his
food is abominably nasty. Rotten fish and dog's flesh are
his favourite diet.

The tiger of Annam is terribly savage, and his strength
is equal to his ferocity. Often, however, a couple of men
will go alone to attack one, armed merely with pikes. As
soon as they see the animal, the more powerful or more
courageous of the two lowers his pike; the tiger hesitates
a moment, and sometimes, if not pressed by hunger, turns
and disappears with the rapidity of lightning; but at
other times he will make a spring at the hunter, when,
if the force of the leap do not carry him right over the
man's head, he falls upon the pike, which the hunter then
elevates by pressing the handle on the ground. The
second hunter now comes forward, and in his turn pierces
him, and uniting their strength, they both hold him down
till he dies. Occasionally the first man misses his aim,
and his pike breaks; then all is over for one, if not both.
The most common method of hunting the tiger has more

SCENE IN THE JUNGLE BETWEEN BATTAMBONG AND BANGKOK.

Drawn by M. Catenacci, from a Sketch by M. Mouhot.

actors engaged. There is in every village some experienced man who leads the attack; and if any one has
been carried off by one of these animals, the tam-tam is
sounded to summon people from the neighbouring villages
to follow this leader after the creature. As he always
sleeps near the spot where he has left the remains of
his repast, they are pretty sure of discovering his retreat.

When they have tracked the tiger to his lair, all the
hunters form a circle as large as their number will allow,
and sufficiently apart not to impede each other's movements. These preparations completed, the leader makes
sure that the animal has no outlet for escape. Some of
the most daring then venture into the centre and cut
away the brushwood, during which operation they are
protected by others armed with pikes. The tiger, pressed
on all sides, rolls his eyes, licks his paws in a convulsive
manner, as though preparing for combat, then, with a
frightful howl, he makes his spring. Immediately every
pike is raised, and the animal falls pierced through and
through. Accidents not infrequently happen, and many
are often severely hurt; but they have no choice but to
wage war against the tigers, which leave them no rest,
force the enclosures, and carry off domestic animals and
even men, not only from the roads and close vicinity of
the houses, but from the interiors of the buildings. In
Annam, the fear inspired by the tigers, elephants, and
other wild animals, makes the people address them with
the greatest respect; they give them the title of "Grand-

father" or "Lord," fearing that they may be offended, and show resentment by attacking them.

During the three months I passed in Brelum and its environs, my two poor servants were almost constantly ill with fever. I think myself very fortunate to have preserved my health, for even in these forests I have not had a touch of this complaint. In the rainy season the atmosphere is dreadfully damp and oppressive; in the thickest wood, where the sun scarcely penetrates, you might fancy yourself in a stove, and with the slightest exercise you are in a bath of perspiration.

In July and August we experienced violent storms, which burst out every second or third day; but in September and October it rained without intermission. At the beginning of November, after a change of wind, we had some refreshing nights, which made the thermometer fall to 12° centigrade. From noon to three o'clock there was little variation in the temperature.

Having paid visits to all the villages in the neighbourhood, and been visited in return by many of the inhabitants, I announced to my two excellent friends the missionaries that I must shortly leave them, and fixed my departure for the 29th November, meaning to return to Pinhalú and Udong, and from thence to ascend the Mekon as far as the great lake Touli-Sap.

CHAPTER XI.

ON the 29th I took leave of my amiable fellow-countryman and friend, M. Arnoux, to, I may venture to affirm, our mutual regret, and set off, accompanied by Father Guilloux, who had some business at Pinhalú. They both wished me to remain with them until Cochin China was open, and I could travel through the country in safety: I should have liked to do so, could I have foreseen an approaching termination of the war; but in the then state of affairs that was impossible.

As far as Pump-Ka-Daye, the first village we came to after leaving Brelum, I had the society and aid of the missionaries, and of the old chief of the Stiêns, who furnished me with three waggons for my baggage, while Phrai and M. Guilloux's Annamite attendants took charge of my boxes of insects, which, if placed among my other goods, would have been injured by the jolting.

The rains had ceased for the last three weeks, and I was agreeably surprised at the improvement in the state

of the country since August. The paths were dry, and
we had no longer to flounder through dirty marshes, nor
suffer from the wet nights which we formerly found so
unpleasant.   When we reached the station where we
were to pass the first night, our servants lighted a fire to
cook their rice, as well as scare away the wild beasts;
but, notwithstanding this, we remarked that our oxen,
dogs, and monkey showed signs of great fear, and, almost
immediately afterwards, we heard a roaring like that of a
lion.   We seized our guns, which were loaded, and waited
in readiness.

Fresh roarings, proceeding from a very short distance
off, completed the terror of our animals; and we ourselves
could not help feeling uneasy.   I proposed to go and
meet the enemy, which was agreed to, and we accordingly
plunged into that part of the forest whence the sound
came.   Although familiar with these terrible creatures, we
felt far from comfortable; but before long we came upon
recent tracks which were quite unmistakeable, and soon,
in a small clearing in the forest, perceived nine elephants,
the leader being a male of enormous size, standing right
in front of us.

On our approach he set up a roar more frightful than
ever, and the whole herd advanced slowly towards us.
We remained in a stooping position, half hidden behind
the trees, which were too tall for us to climb.   I was in
the act of taking aim at the forehead of the leader, the
only vulnerable part, but an Annamite who stood beside
me, and who was an old hunter, knocked up my rifle,

Drawn by M. Catenacci, from a Sketch by M. Mouhot.

HALT OF THE CARAVAN IN THE JUNGLE BETWEEN BATTAMBONG AND BANGKOK.

and begged me not to fire; "for," said he, "if you kill
or wound one of the elephants we are lost; and even if we
should succeed in escaping, the oxen, the waggons, and all
their contents would be overwhelmed by the fury of these
animals. If there were but two or three, we might hope
to kill them; but nine, of whom five are very large, are
too many; and it will be more prudent to retreat." At
this moment, Father Guilloux, who had not much confidence in his powers of locomotion, fired his gun in the air
to frighten the elephants; and this plan fortunately succeeded: the herd stopped in astonishment for an instant,
then turned round, and marched into the forest.

When we reached Pemptiélan we stopped at the house
of the mandarin, whose authority extends over the neighbouring district, and, contrary to the usual custom, he
offered us hospitality under his own roof. Scarcely, however, were we installed when he came to me and asked
for the best of my guns, and, on my declining to part
with it, he begged for something else, intimating that
we should have begun by offering a present. Thereupon
I gave him a suit of European clothes, a powder-flask and
some powder, a hunting-knife, and some other small articles.
In return he presented me with an ivory trumpet, and
placed at my service two elephants to enable me to continue my route more comfortably: he likewise sent off
our people with a letter to the chiefs of the Srokkhner.

We resumed our journey on the following day, the
Abbé on one elephant, reading his breviary, and I upon
another, both of us greatly enjoying the beauty of the

landscape.   Thus we traversed the beautiful plains, which, when I formerly travelled this road, were inhabited by the poor Thiâmes; but now, in place of rich harvest, I was astonished to find nothing but large trees: the villages were abandoned, and the houses and enclosures in ruins. It appeared that the mandarin of Pemptiélan, executing or exceeding the orders of his master the king of Cambodia, had kept these unfortunate people in such a state of slavery and oppression that they had even been deprived of their fishing and agricultural implements, and, being left without money or resources, experienced such frightful poverty that many of them died of hunger.

The poor wretches, to the number of several thousands, and under the conduct of a chief on whose head a price had been set, and who had secretly returned from Annam, rose in revolt.   Those from Penom-Peuh went to Udong to protect their brethren in that place in their flight; and when all were united in one body, they descended the river, and passed into Cochin China.   Orders were issued by the king to arrest their departure, but no one remained to execute them; for the whole Cambodian population, with the mandarins at their head, had fled into the forests at the first news of the rising.

Besides the interest inspired by the misfortunes of these poor people, their conduct, when all fled before them, and left Udong, Pinhalú, and Penom-Peuh defenceless, was so noble as greatly to increase this feeling. " We have no enmity against the people," said they, " if they will but let us pass and respect our property ; but we

will put to death whoever opposes our flight." And, in
fact, they never touched one of the large boats which
were moored near the market, and unguarded, but took
to the river in their narrow and miserable pirogues.

In passing opposite the island of Ko-Sutin we stopped
to see Father Cordier. The good missionary was in a sad
state: his malady had got worse; and his debility was
such that he could scarcely drag himself from his bed to
a chair. He had no food but rice and dried fish; and the
only persons to care for him, and wait upon him, were
two children of ten years old. We begged him to accompany us to Pinhalú, but he declined, on account of
his weakness. "All I regret," said he, "is, that I shall
see my poor parents no more; but for that, I should await
death calmly, and almost with joy." All our solicitations
that he would go with us were unavailing; and we were
forced to pursue our journey, very sad at leaving him in
so painful a position, and at our inability to give him any
relief.

On the 21st December we at last reached Pinhalú.

Penom-Peuh is about 103° 3′ 50″ long. of Paris, and
11° 37′ 30″ north lat. It is the great market of Cambodia, and only two or three leagues from the southern
frontier of Cochin China: it is situated at the confluence
of the Mekon with its tributary: from this point the river
flows first north-east, and then north-west, as far as China
and the mountains of Thibet. The arm, which has no
name, but which, to distinguish it, it might be well to call
Mé-Sap, from the name of the lake Touli-Sap, flows from

its source south-east to the point of junction. About
12° 25′ north lat. commences the great lake, which
stretches as far as 13° 53′. In shape it might be compared to a violin. The whole space between it and the
Mekon is a vast plain; while on the opposite side are the
great chains of Poursat and its ramifications.

The entrance to the great lake of Cambodia is grand
and beautiful. The river becomes wider and wider, until
at last it is four or five miles in breadth; and then you
enter the immense sheet of water called Touli-Sap, as
large and full of motion as a sea. It is more than 120
miles long, and must be at least 400 in circumference.

The shore is low, and thickly covered with trees, which
are half submerged; and in the distance is visible an
extensive range of mountains whose highest peaks seem
lost in the clouds. The waves glitter in the broad sun-
shine with a brilliancy which the eye can scarcely support,
and, in many parts of the lake, nothing is visible all
around but water. In the centre is planted a tall mast,
indicating the boundary between the kingdoms of Siam
and Cambodia. Before crossing the lake it may, perhaps,
be as well to say what remains to be told respecting the
latter country.

The present state of Cambodia is deplorable, and its
future menacing.* Formerly, however, it was a powerful

* This prediction is already in part fulfilled by an insurrection in
favour of the young prince, the king's brother, shortly after the departure of M. Mouhot. See the letter of M. Silvestre, 4th Jan.
1862.

Drawn by M. Thérond, from a Sketch by M. Mouhot.

TOWER AT BANOME, NEAR BATTAMBONG.

and populous country, as is testified by the splendid ruins which are to be met with in the provinces of Battambong and Ongcor, and which I intend visiting; but at present the population is excessively reduced by the incessant wars carried on against neighbouring states. I do not think that the country now contains above a million of inhabitants, and, according to the last census, the number of free men fit to carry arms is returned at 30,000, the slaves, as in Siam, not being liable to serve in the army any more than to pay taxes. Besides a number of Chinese, relatively great, there are many Malays, who have been settled in the country for centuries, and a floating population of Annamites, amounting to two or three thousand. As the calculations taken include only the males fit for active service, no exact figures can be furnished by the authorities.

European conquest, abolition of slavery, wise and protecting laws, and experience, fidelity, and scrupulous rectitude in those who administer them, would alone effect the regeneration of this state. It lies near to Cochin China, the subjection of which France is now aiming at, and in which she will doubtless succeed: under her sway it will become a land of plenty. I wish her to possess this land, which would add a magnificent jewel to her crown; but it is also my earnest desire that she may make a judicious choice of governors, and that the name of France, my dear and beautiful country, may be loved, respected, and honoured in the extreme East, as it should be everywhere.

The chief productions of Cambodia are tobacco, pepper, ginger, sugar, gamboge, coffee, silk, and cotton. The latter important article of commerce thrives here admirably; and as, according to report, America is menaced with civil war, it is a question whether we can henceforth calculate on that country for the supply it has hitherto furnished. If that supply were even partially to fail, and thousands of workmen to be in consequence thrown out of employment, what a vast field might be opened on the banks of the Mekon and of Touli-Sap for European activity, industry, and capital!

England, that great nation for colonies, could soon make of Lower Cochin China and Cambodia a vast cotton plantation; and there is no doubt that, if she set about it in earnest, with her Australian, East and West Indian, and New Zealand possessions, she might soon secure to herself the monopoly, which America now has, of this precious article: we should in that case be compelled to buy from her. Why should we not be our own purveyors? The island of Ko-Sutin alone, in which the lands belonging to the crown are let to the cotton-planters in lots for one pound per lot, may be adduced in order to give an idea of the profits realized by the cultivation of this plant. Each lot affords an income of more than 1200 francs.

The forests situated on the higher grounds abound with justly-celebrated timber, as also trees yielding resins and gums much esteemed in commerce, likewise the eagle-wood and several species of dye-woods.

The mountains contain gold, argentiferous lead, zinc,

copper, and iron, the last two in some abundance. One
is astonished to find these fertile lands furnish so little for
exportation; but the sovereigns and mandarins enrich
themselves by spoliation and extortion, and every abuse
which can ruin a country and retard its progress. If
these dominions were ruled wisely and carefully, with
probity, and with a regard to the interests of the working
classes, the whole aspect of affairs would be changed.

The taxes now weigh solely on the cultivator and producer: the more he raises, the more he has to pay: disposed, therefore, to indolence by the influence of the
climate, he has little inducement to combat this vice.
The beautiful cardamom of Poursat, much sought after by
the Chinese, who pay very highly for it, is entirely mono-
polized by the king and his ministers; and it is nearly
the same with every valuable product.

CHAPTER XII.

PRELIMINARY REMARKS.

NOKHOR, or Ongcor, was the capital of the ancient kingdom of Cambodia, or Khmer, formerly so famous among the great states of Indo-China, that almost the only tradition preserved in the country mentions that empire as having had twenty kings who paid tribute to it, as having kept up an army of five or six million soldiers, and that the buildings of the royal treasury occupied a space of more than 300 miles.*

In the province still bearing the name of Ongcor, which is situated eastward of the great lake Touli-Sap, towards the 14th degree of north lat., and 104° long. east of Greenwich, there are, on the banks of the Mekon, and in the ancient kingdom of Tsiampois (Cochin-China), ruins of such grandeur, remains of structures which must have been raised at such an immense cost of labour, that, at the first view, one is filled with profound admiration, and cannot but ask what has become of this powerful race,

---

* Sic in orig.—*Tr.*

Drawn by M. Guiaud, from a Sketch by M. Mouhot

so civilised, so enlightened, the authors of these gigantic works?

One of these temples—a rival to that of Solomon, and erected by some ancient Michael Angelo—might take an honourable place beside our most beautiful buildings. It is grander than anything left to us by Greece or Rome, and presents a sad contrast to the state of barbarism in which the nation is now plunged.

Unluckily the scourge of war, aided by time, the great destroyer, who respects nothing, and perhaps also by earthquakes, has fallen heavily on the greater part of the other monuments; and the work of destruction and decay continues among those which still remain standing, imposing and majestic, amidst the masses of ruins all around.

One seeks in vain for any historical souvenirs of the many kings who must have succeeded one another on the throne of the powerful empire of Maha-Nocor-Khmer. There exists a tradition of a leprous king, to whom is attributed the commencement of the great temple, but all else is totally forgotten. The inscriptions, with which some of the columns are covered, are illegible; and, if you interrogate the Cambodians as to the founders of Ongcor-Wat, you invariably receive one of these four replies: " It is the work of Pra-Eun, the king of the angels;" " It is the work of the giants;" "It was built by the leprous king;" or else, " It made itself."

The work of giants! The expression would be very just, if used figuratively, in speaking of these prodigious works, of which no one who has not seen them can form any adequate idea; and in the construction of which patience, strength, and genius appear to have done their utmost in order to leave to future generations proofs of their power and civilisation.

It is remarkable that none of these monuments were intended for habitations; all were temples of Buddhism. The statues and bas-reliefs, however, curiously enough, represent entirely secular subjects—monarchs surrounded by their wives, their heads and arms loaded with ornaments such as bracelets and necklaces, the body being covered with a narrow *langouti*. On a sort of esplanade is a statue, said to be that of the leprous king. It is a little above the middle height, and the prince is seated in a noble and dignified attitude. The head, particularly, is a *chef-d'œuvre*, the features perfectly regular, and possessing a manly beauty of a description seen now in very rare instances, and only amongst Cambodians of unmixed race, living in seclusion at the foot of the mountains, where the unhealthiness of the climate condemns them to a solitary existence; or among the savage mountaineers who occupy the border country separating Siam and Cambodia from the kingdom of Annam.

This place was probably chosen for the capital on account of its central position. It is situated fifteen miles from the great lake, in an arid and sandy plain, although the banks of the river would appear to have been a preferable site, more fertile, and offering greater facilities for communication.

Although making no pretension whatever either to

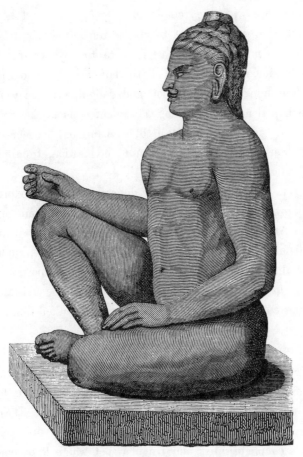

Drawn by M. Thérond, from a Sketch by M Mouhot.

STATUE OF THE LEPROUS KING.

architectural or archæological acquirements, I will endeavour to describe what I saw, for the benefit of others
interested in these sciences, and, as well as I can, to draw
the attention of Eastern *savans* to a new scene.   I shall

commence with the temple of Ongcor, the most beautiful and best preserved of all the remains, and which is
also the first which presents itself to the eye of the traveller, making him forget all the fatigues of the journey,
filling him with admiration and delight, such as would
be experienced on finding a verdant oasis in the sandy
desert. Suddenly, and as if by enchantment, he seems to
be transported from barbarism to civilisation, from profound darkness to light.

But, ere I proceed with my description, I must express
my gratitude to the excellent missionary of Battambong,
the Abbé E. Silvestre, who, with exceeding courtesy and
indefatigable energy, accompanied me everywhere, guided
me through the thick forest which covers a portion of
the site of the original building, and by whose assistance
I was enabled to accomplish so much in a limited time.

The Temple of Ongcor.

Before arriving at Ongcor from Battambong, having
previously crossed the great lake from the mouth of either
of the currents which traverse both those localities, you
come upon a stream, which, in the dry season, you ascend
for a couple of miles, and reach a spot where it becomes
somewhat larger, forming a small natural basin, which
serves the purpose of a kind of harbour. From this place
a raised causeway, still passable at the present day, and
extending as far as the limit which the waters attain at
the period of the inundations, that is to say, over a space
of three miles, leads to New Ongcor, an insignificant little

PRINCIPAL ENTRANCE OF THE GREAT TEMPLE OF ONGCOR WAT.

Drawn by M. Guiaud, from a Sketch by M. Mouhot.

town, the capital of the province, and situated fifteen
miles to the N.N.W. of the shores of the lake.

If, starting from this point, you follow for about a
couple of hours in the same direction a dusty sandy
path passing through a dense forest of stunted trees; and
having also frequently crossed the river, which is exceedingly sinuous in its course, you will arrive at an esplanade
about 9 metres wide by 27 long, parallel to the building.
At each angle, at the extremity of the two longer sides,
are two enormous lions, sculptured out of the rock, and
forming, with the pedestals, only a single block. Four
large flights of steps lead to the platform.

From the north staircase, which faces the principal
entrance, you skirt, in order to reach the latter, a causeway 230 metres in length by 9 in width, covered or paved
with large slabs of stone, and supported by walls of great
thickness. This causeway crosses a ditch 220 metres
wide, which surrounds the building; the revetment,
3 metres high by 1 metre thick, is formed of ferruginous stone, with the exception of the top row, which is
of freestone, each block being of the same thickness as the
wall.

Principal Entrance.—The edifice forms a long gallery
with a central tower, and two others, of rather less alti
tude, about 30 metres distant from the former. The
portico of each tower is formed of four projecting columns,
with a staircase. At each extremity are similar porticoes,
beyond which, but immediately contiguous thereto, is a
high door or gateway, on the same level, which serves for

the passage of vehicles. From constant use the wheels have worn two deep ruts in the massive flagstones with which the ground is paved.

Upon the west side the gallery is supported by two rows of square columns; on the east, blank windows have been let into the wall, with stone railings or balconies of twisted columns 14 centimetres in diameter. The whole of this side, within one metre of the ground, and half a metre of the cornice, is covered with sculptures executed with marvellously artistic skill.

The roof—and in this respect it resembles all the other buildings—is a double one, constructed externally of sculptured stone, the blocks in the interior being plain; they were formerly hidden by a ceiling, also sculptured, of which some remains may still be remarked. The edifice divides the wall into two equal parts; upon the other sides, and facing the monument, are three pavilions, 33 metres in length.

This imposing colonnade, which, from its great length and beautiful proportions, attracts the attention from a distance, forms a fitting entrance to the great monument.

The Temple.—Commencing from the building which forms the principal entrance, is a second causeway, 9 metres wide by 342 metres in length; it is raised 1 metre from the level of the ground. It is covered with huge blocks of stone, carefully joined together throughout its entire length, and is surrounded by a balustrade, partially in ruins, about 10 centimetres high, composed of long stones, with bevelled edges, very massive, and covered

Drawn by M. Guiaud, from a sketch by M. Mouhot.

with sculptures. On each side are six platforms of earth, ascended by several steps, upon each of which is a serpent with seven heads, some erect, others thrown back.

In the centre of the causeway are two elegant pavilions, one on each side, having at each extremity a portico 33 metres 66 centimetres in length. At the end of the causeway, and at the foot of the terrace, are, on each side of the latter, two ponds or sheets of water. A balustrade, like that of the causeway, and resting like it upon a sculptured basement, springs from the foot of the terrace, and runs all round the monument. At certain intervals there are large staircases of several steps each.

The Terrace.—The terrace is 2 metres 30 centimetres in height, and is surrounded by 112 fluted columns, surmounted by capitals, formed in each case of one single block of stone. The basement, like that of the whole building, is ornamented with very beautiful sculptured cornices, varied in style, and entirely covered with delicate carvings representing roses and arabesques, worked with the chisel, with a taste and skill equally wonderful.

This terrace forms a cross, each arm of which is 122 metres in length, and 12 metres 16 centimetres wide. There are three flights of steps, upon each of which are four lions reclining upon their pedestals.

The Portico.—This is 6 metres in length, and is supported by six columns, four of which are detached from the monument.

The temple is formed of three distinct parts raised in the form of terraces one above the other.

The Galleries.—The galleries form a rectangle, the facade of which is 180 metres in length; the sides 216 metres 16 centimetres by 4 metres 16 centimetres.

The vaulted ceilings of the galleries are raised 6 metres from the ground; those of the second roof are 4 metres 30 centimetres high. The two roofs are supported by a double row of columns, the first being 3 metres 18 centimetres and the second 2 metres 25 centimetres high by 48 centimetres broad. The columns are square, and, like all other buildings in the province, are formed of single blocks.

There are five staircases on the west side, the same number on the east, and three on each of the remaining sides.

The basement is 3 metres 90 centimetres in height, the length externally forming a terrace of 1 metre 57 centimetres.

Each portico is composed of three roofs raised one above the other, which contribute materially to give to the architecture of these long galleries a monumental appearance, producing a singularly beautiful effect.

The opposite side of the wall to the double colonnade is, from the lowest row of cornices to one metre above its base, covered inside with bas-reliefs, having externally blank windows with balustrades.

There are two rows of cornices, the first part immediately above the columns; and the space, to the extent of nearly one metre, which lies between them, is filled up by roses and other sculptured designs.

The bas-reliefs represent the combat of the king of the apes with the king of the angels : * in the centre is the king of the angels, drawn by two griffins ; he has seven heads and twenty arms, with a sabre in each hand. Some of the chiefs are seated in cars drawn by fabulous animals, while others are mounted on elephants. The soldiers are armed with bows, javelins, or sabres, but the apes have generally no weapons except their formidable claws : a few of them have clubs, sabres, or branches of trees.

Peristyle No. 1.—Here is represented the march of warriors mounted on birds, horses, tigers, and fabulous animals; the horses of the chiefs are led by the bridle. On the right the soldiers are advancing towards the scene of combat in the centre; but here there are no fantastic animals.

Peristyle No. 2.—The bas-reliefs of this peristyle represent the combat between the king of the apes and the king of the angels, and the death of the former. Close by is a boat filled with rowers, all with long beards, and some of them attired in the Chinese fashion : the group is admirable for the natural positions and for the expression given to the faces. A cock-fight, and women at play with their children, are also represented. It is in these bas-reliefs that the highest degree of skill is shown.

---

* These sculptures probably represent the story of the Hindu Ramdyana, of great reputation among Buddhist nations. The *angel* is Ramana, Tyrant of Ceylon; and the King of the Monkeys, Hanuman Rama's General.

Other subjects follow, the meaning of which I could not discover.

On the south side, to the left hand, is a military procession—bodies of soldiers headed by chiefs, some mounted on elephants, others on horseback, and each corps carrying different arms, lances, halberds, javelins, sabres, and bows. On the right are two series, one representing the Hindu Paradise Swarga, the other the Hindu infernal regions Naralma. A crowd of persons are entering Paradise, and are received in palanquins: they have with them banners, fans, parasols, and boxes for holding betel, without which even Paradise would not be perfect happiness to a Cambodian.

A triumphal march. Paradise.—The elect seated on a magnificent dais, surrounded by a great number of women, with caskets and fans in their hands, while the men are holding flowers and have children on their knees. These appear to be all the joys of Paradise.

The punishments of the infernal regions, on the contrary, are varied and numerous; and while the elect, who are enjoying themselves in Paradise, are all fat and plump, the poor condemned beings are so lean that their bones show through their skin, and the expression of their faces is pitiful and full of a most comic seriousness. Some are being pounded in mortars, while others hold them by the feet and hands; some are being sawn asunder; others are led along, like buffaloes, with ropes through their noses. In other places the *comphubal* (executioners) are cutting men to pieces with sabres; while a crowd of poor wretches are being transfixed by the tusks of elephants, or on the horns of rhinoceros. Fabulous animals are busy devouring some; others are in irons, and have had their eyes put out.

In the centre sits the judge with his ministers, all sabre in hand, and the guilty are dragged before them by the hair or feet. In the distance is visible a furnace and another crowd of people under punishment, being tortured in divers ways—impaled, roasted on spits, tied to trees and pierced with arrows, suspended with heavy weights attached to their hands and feet, devoured by dogs or vultures, or crucified with nails through their bodies.

These bas-reliefs are perfect; the rest are inferior in workmanship and expression.

On the east side, a number of men, divided into two equal groups, are represented as attempting to drag in contrary directions the great serpent or dragon with seven heads, while, in the centre, an angel stands looking on. Many angels are seen floating in the sky above, while fishes, aquatic animals, and marine monsters swim about in a sea visible beneath. The angel is seated on the celebrated mountain of Thibet, Pra Soumer, and in different places angels with several heads give assistance to those pulling the serpent. The king of the apes, Sdach Soa, appears also here.

To the right is a military procession and a combat, the chiefs being mounted on elephants, unicorns, griffins, eagles with peacocks' tails, and other fantastic animals, while winged dragons draw the cars.

On the northern side is portrayed a combat, and procession, with drums, flutes, trumpets, tam-tams, and organs
said to be Chinese; a king, mounted on the shoulders of
a hideous giant, who holds in each hand by the foot a
fighting giant. All the chiefs take part in the combat,
standing, some on tigers, others in cars.

Near the central peristyle is a figure of the king, with
a long beard; on each side are courtiers with clasped
hands.

To the right appears a military procession, a combat,
griffins, eagles with peacocks' tails, a dragon with seven
heads and a tower on his back—the king letting fly an
arrow, standing on the back of a giant with tail, claws,
and beak.

Second Story.—The first gallery on the west side is
connected with the second by two other smaller galleries,
40 metres long, and which are themselves connected by
two colonnades in the form of a cross, and supporting two
vaulted roofs.

Four rows of square columns, each hewn out of a single
block of stone, those in the inside row being 4 metres
14 centimetres high and 45 centimetres thick; those on
the outside being 3 metres 10 centimetres high, and
rather smaller at the top than at the base. The little
gallery on the right is filled with statues representing
persons in the act of worshipping idols, some of these
being of wood, others of stone. Many of the statues are
4 metres in height, and the greater number of them must
be of great age, to judge from their state of dilapidation,

in spite of the hardness of the stone. In the centre is
a statue of the famous leprous king, and by his side, in a
posture of adoration, are two statues of priests, with faces

Drawn by M. Thérond, from a Sketch by M. Mouhot.

PAVILION IN THE INTERIOR OF THE TEMPLE OF ONGCOR-WAT.

full of expression. These are real chefs-d'œuvre. At no
great distance is a small statue of his queen.

Here are found two pavilions of extremely elegant architecture, with porticoes and staircases at each end.

There is a second gallery, with four towers at each end and three porticoes and staircases on each side. This gallery is raised on a base 5 metres 10 centimetres high, the ledge of which forms a terrace 74 centimetres broad.

There are neither columns nor bas-reliefs here, but the walls have imitation windows with twisted bars; the gallery is half dark, receiving very little light except through the doors. There are idols, both of stone and bronze, on pedestals, with their hands held out to receive gifts from their worshippers.

Central part.—A raised terrace leads to the foot of the great staircase, and forms a cross, the arms of which lead to two small pavilions with four porticoes and staircases. The base of this part is admirably executed, both as to general effect and in detail. There are twelve staircases, the four in the middle being 6 metres wide, and having 39 steps.

The building forms a square, each side of which is 56 metres 60 centimetres, and at each angle is a tower. A central tower, larger and higher, is connected with the lateral galleries by colonnades covered, like the galleries, with a double roof; and both galleries and colonnades are supported on a base one metre from the floor of the interior courts.

Opposite each of the twelve staircases is a small portico with four colums, 4 metres 50 centimetres high,

Vol. I. p. 298.

CENTRAL PORTICO OF THE GREAT TEMPLE OF ONGCOR-WAT.

Drawn by M. Thérond, from a Sketch by M. Mouhot.

and 47 centimetres in diameter. Windows, similar in form and dimension to those of the other galleries, are on each side, and have twisted bars carved in stone.

In front of each colonnade, with an entrance in the tower, is a dark and narrow chapel, to which there is an ascent of eight steps. These four chapels do not communicate with each other. Each contains an idol 4 metres in height, sculptured in the solid wall, at whose feet is another nearly 2 metres long, representing Samanakodom sleeping. The central tower is 33 metres high from the pavement of the gallery, and 50 from the basement of the building.

What strikes the observer with not less admiration than the grandeur, regularity, and beauty of these majestic buildings, is the immense size and prodigious number of the blocks of stone of which they are constructed. In this temple alone are as many as 1532 columns. What means of transport, what a multitude of workmen, must this have required, seeing that the mountain out of which the stone was hewn is thirty miles distant! In each block are to be seen holes $2\frac{1}{2}$ centimetres in diameter and 3 in depth, the number varying with the size of the blocks; but the columns and the sculptured portions of the building bear no traces of them. According to a Cambodian legend, these are the prints of the fingers of a giant, who, after kneading an enormous quantity of clay, had cut it into blocks and carved it, turning it into a hard and, at the same time, light stone by pouring over it some marvellous liquid.

All the mouldings, sculptures, and bas-reliefs appear to have been executed after the erection of the building. The stones are everywhere fitted together in so perfect a manner that you can scarcely see where are the joinings; there is neither sign of mortar nor mark of the chisel, the surface being as polished as marble. Was this incomparable edifice the work of a single genius, who conceived the idea, and watched over the execution of it? One is tempted to think so; for no part of it is deficient, faulty, or inconsistent. To what epoch does it owe its origin? As before remarked, neither tradition nor written inscriptions furnish any certain information upon this point; or rather, I should say, these latter are as a sealed book for want of an interpreter; and they may, perchance, throw light on the subject when some European savant shall succeed in deciphering them.

RUINS IN THE PROVINCE OF ONGCOR. MOUNT BAKHÊNG.

A temple, about 100 metres in height, built of limestone has been erected on the top of Mount Bakhêng, which is situated two miles and a half north of Ongcor-Wat, on the road leading to the town. At the foot of the mountain are to be seen, among the trees, two magnificent lions, 20 centimetres in height, and each formed, with the pedestals, out of a single block. Steps, partly destroyed, lead to the top of the mountain, whence is to be enjoyed a view so beautiful and extensive, that it is not surprising that these people, who have shown so

much taste in their buildings, should have chosen it for
a site.

On the one side you gaze upon the wooded plain and
the pyramidal temple of Ongcor, with its rich colonnades,
the mountain of Crome, which is beyond the new city,
the view losing itself in the waters of the great lake on
the horizon. On the opposite side stretches the long chain
of mountains whose quarries, they say, furnished the
beautiful stone used for the temples; and amidst thick
forests, which extend along the base, is a pretty, small
lake, which looks like a blue ribbon on a carpet of verdure. All this region is now as lonely and deserted as
formerly it must have been full of life and cheerfulness;
and the howling of wild animals, and the cries of a few
birds, alone disturb the solitude.

Sad fragility of human things! How many centuries
and thousands of generations have passed away, of which
history, probably, will never tell us anything: what riches
and treasures of art will remain for ever buried beneath
these ruins; how many distinguished men—artists, sovereigns, and warriors—whose names were worthy of immortality, are now forgotten, laid to rest under the thick dust
which covers these tombs!

The whole summit of the mountain is covered with
a coating of lime, forming a vast smooth surface. At
regular intervals are four rows of deep holes, in some of
which still stand the columns that formerly supported
two roofs, and formed a gallery leading from the staircase
to the principal part of the building, and the transverse

branches of which were connected with four towers, built
partly of stone, partly of brick. Judging from the details
of the work, and the state of the stone, which in many
places crumbles at a touch, this building belongs to a
period much anterior to that of many of the other monuments. Art, like science, was then in its infancy;
difficulties were surmounted, but not without great efforts
of labour and intelligence; taste was of a grand description, but genius was not in proportion; in a word, the
temple of Mount Bakhêng appears to have been the
prelude to civilization, while that of Ongcor-Wat was
probably its climax.

In the two towers, which are least dilapidated, and
which the modern worshippers have covered with a
thatched roof, the old one having fallen in, are large idols
rudely fashioned, and bearing marks of great age. In
one of the other towers is a large stone, the inscription on
which is still visible; and on the exterior wall is carved
the figure of a king with a long beard, the only portion of
bas-relief remaining.

A wall surrounds the top of the mountain. Bakhêng
has also its Phrâbat, but it is a facsimile of recent origin.
The building is quadrangular, and composed of five stories,
each 3 metres high. That at the base is 68 metres
square. They form so many terraces, which serve as bases
to seventy-two small but elegant pavilions; and they are
enriched with mouldings, colonnades, and cornices, but no
sculpture. The work is perfect; and from its good state
of preservation would seem to be of a more recent date

than the towers. It is evident that each of these little
pavilions formerly contained an idol.

Each side of the square has a staircase 2 metres wide,
with nine steps to each story, and lions on each terrace.
The centre of the terrace formed by the last story is only
a confused mass of ruins from the fallen towers.   Near
the staircase are two gigantic blocks of very fine stone,
as polished as marble, and shaped like pedestals for
statues.

END OF VOL. I.

LONDON: PRINTED BY W. CLOWES AND SONS, STAMFORD STREET,
AND CHARING CROSS.

TRAVELS

IN THE

CENTRAL PARTS OF INDO-CHINA

(SIAM),

CAMBODIA, AND LAOS,

DURING THE YEARS 1858, 1859, AND 1860.

BY THE LATE

M. HENRI MOUHOT,

FRENCH NATURALIST.

IN TWO VOLUMES.—VOL. II.

WITH ILLUSTRATIONS.

LONDON:

JOHN MURRAY, ALBEMARLE STREET.

1864.

CONTENTS OF VOL. II.

CHAPTER XVIII.

APPENDIX.

ILLUSTRATIONS TO VOL. II.

———◆◆———

TRAVELS IN INDO-CHINA,

ETC.

CHAPTER XIII.

ONGCOR THÔM (ONGCOR THE GREAT)—SURROUNDING WALL—
TRIUMPHAL ARCH.

HALF-A-MILE beyond Bakhêng are the ruins of Ongcor-Thôm. A partly-destroyed road, hidden by thick layers of sand and dust, and crossing a large ditch, half filled with blocks of stone, portions of columns, and fragments of sculptured lions and elephants, leads to the gateway of the town, which is built in the style of a triumphal arch.

These remains are in a tolerable state of preservation, and are composed of a central tower, 18 metres high, surrounded by four turrets, and flanked by two other towers connected together by galleries. At the top are four immense heads in the Egyptian style; and every available space is filled with sculpture. At the foot of the great tower is a passage for carriages; and on each side of it are doors and staircases communicating with the walls, the whole building being constructed of sandstone.

The outer wall is composed of blocks of ferruginous stone, and extends right and left from the entrance. It is about 24 miles square, 3 met. 80 centimet. thick, and 7 met. high, and serves as a support to a glacis which rises almost from the top. At the four cardinal points are doors, there being two on the east side. Within this vast enclosure, now covered with an almost impenetrable forest, are a vast number of buildings, more or less in ruin, which testify to the ancient splendour of the town. In some places, where the heavy rains have washed away the soil, or where the natives have dug in search for treasure, may be seen immense quantities of porcelain and pottery.

PREA SAT LING POUN.

Within the enclosure of Ongcor Thôm, and two miles from the west gate, are to be seen through the trees the tops of the high towers of a building called by the Cambodians " Prea sat Ling poun," that is to say, " The Pagoda where they play hide and seek." It is a collection of 37 towers of unequal size, connected by galleries which cross each other perpetually, and form a labyrinth through which it is not easy to find one's way. A long shallow ditch, crossed by four roads leading to the principal entrances, surrounds it on all sides. Beyond the ditch rises the wall of a gallery, of which the exterior colonnades and the roof are only a mass of ruins, over which you must climb to reach the interior. This wall is still intact: it is about 120 metres long, and forms a square round the pagoda. About 1 metre from the ground are visible, in places where the blocks fallen from the roof have not hidden everything, various bas-reliefs carved in the thickness of the wall: they are not surmounted by cornices as at Ongcor-Wat, by which it would seem as if they had never been finished.

Besides the four principal entrances there were other doors at unequal distances in this gallery, but singularly enough many of them have been walled up. The gallery was connected with the main body of the building by four smaller ones opposite each of the great doors, and forming a covered way to the interior; but all these galleries are destroyed.

The second enclosure is 65 metres square, and each front is composed of five towers, connected by galleries. The central and corner towers are the largest: they are about 13 metres high. High galleries connect the centre tower with the intermediate ones, which again are connected with those at the corners by galleries of a less elevation.

On each side are seven staircases, of six steps each, and leading either to towers or galleries: these galleries are covered by a triple roof: a central one 7 metres high, resting on an outer wall, and on columns 2 metres in height; an exterior roof on a double row of columns; and a third resting on a very low wall, pierced with numerous large windows looking on to a narrow interior court.

On the exterior of the wall, which on one side sustains

the high roof, are a series of bas-reliefs, surrounding the whole gallery. They are sculptured in the thickness of the wall, and are curious from the scenes and costumes they represent. These scenes are drawn more from the sacred books of the people than from their history; for men with ten heads and twenty arms, fantastic animals, griffins and dragons, are favourite subjects. The men all wear the langouti, and often nothing beside, and have the ears pierced and hanging on their shoulders: many have long beards.

In the vestibules of the towers, and in the high galleries near them, are kings and queens seated on a rich dais, with a numerous court, and surrounded by persons carrying parasols, fans, standards, and caskets : there are likewise many musicians with drums, flutes, and harps.

In the galleries are represented several boats' crews fighting; while underneath are fishes disputing for the bodies of the slain. There are also in the same galleries persons in attitudes of adoration, with clasped hands, before a figure of Samonakodom.

In another part is a long procession : the king is in a large open carriage, divided into three compartments, he being in the centre one, and his wives in the two others. This carriage has six wheels and two shafts, which rest on the shoulders of eight men. The chiefs are mounted on elephants or horses, or seated in carriages drawn by four led horses, and by their side march a numerous company bearing standards, parasols, and caskets.

The bas-reliefs at the east and north sides represent

similar scenes, as well as many of the fabulous men and
animals which are to be seen in those at Ongcor-Wat.
In numerous places the water, trickling through holes in
the roof, has so obliterated the carving that the subjects
can no longer be recognised. This gallery, with its sixteen
towers, is connected with another only 3 metres distant;
and this last has five towers on each side, of which the
three in the middle face the exterior towers. The interior
of the gallery with its three roofs receives no light but
by the doors, and is so dark that torches are necessary
when it is visited. The gallery, sustained by two rows of
columns and by an exterior wall, has no bas-reliefs. The
towers, which are built at equal distances, are thus disposed: the largest at the angles, two smaller ones next to
them, and one of medium size in the centre.

The middle of the terrace is occupied by a large tower
connected with the gallery by two others, only about a
metre distant. The central tower is circular at the base,
is 20 metres in diameter, and nearly 40 metres high, and
has on each side a turret. A colonnade supporting a roof,
now in ruins, surrounds it: the columns, each of which is
hewn out of a single block of stone more than 40 metres
high, are still standing. Four doors lead to the interior.
Outside this tower, between each two doors, are three
chapels, constructed out of the thickness of the wall, and
having no communication with each other, nor with the
exterior. In nearly every one of them is a full-length
statue of Samanokodom seated on a pedestal.

On visiting this place you behold on every side the tops

of these numerous towers, and the roofs of the galleries,
intermingled with large trees, creepers, and thistles, which
invade the courts, the terraces, and other parts ; and you
have at first some difficulty in comprehending the arrange-
ments of the different buildings.   It is only after a long
examination that you perceive the symmetry of them as a
whole, and that these thirty-seven towers and numerous
galleries are all in regular order.   Some parts are in good
preservation ; others have been dealt hardly with by time,
in spite of the immense size of the blocks of stone, and
the skill with which they are united ; and the condition
of this stone, ready to crumble to powder, seems to prove
that this structure was anterior to Ongcor-Wat.

Like it, it is built of sandstone, and the roofs are very
similar, only that, in place of the pointed stones ranged
in courses at Ongcor, these are embellished, at about
two-thirds of their height, with four gigantic sculptured
heads.

The roof is terminated by a very elegant embrasure,
a feature not belonging to the other temple.   Every door
in the building is sunk, and many of them are admirably
carved, displaying scenes full of expression, skilfully
arranged, and exquisitely delicate in detail.   They represent various subjects : worshippers prostrated before their
idols, musicians and comedians performing pantomimes,
chariots filled with warriors standing up, and drawn by
horses galloping : in some instances they appear to be
running races.

Not far from this labyrinth are three platforms close

together, each occupied by a colossal idol of stone, and
gilt. These idols appear to be of modern date; but at
their feet are assembled a number of others, some uninjured, some broken, collected from among the ruins. On
one of the platforms are several stones fixed in the ground;
on one of which is a long undecipherable inscription.

PHIMÉNAN ACA. THE PALACE OF THE ANCIENT KINGS.

Three walls at some distance from each other, and each
bounded by a moat, surround what remains of the palace
of the ancient kings. Within the first enclosure are two
towers connected by galleries, which form four sides, like
a triumphal arch. The walls are of ferruginous stone,
and the length of each block forms the thickness of the
wall. The towers and galleries are of sandstone.

A hundred metres from the angle of the square formed
on the north side by the wall, is a singular building, consisting of two high terraces, and communicating with the
outer wall by another terrace half in ruins.

In a cavity recently made by excavations, are visible
large sculptured blocks, which seem to have fallen from
the top. The walls, still intact, are covered with bas-
reliefs, disposed in four rows, one above another, each
representing a king seated in the Oriental fashion, with
his hands resting on a broken poignard, and by his side
a number of women. All these figures are covered with
ornaments, such as very long earrings, necklaces, and
bracelets. Their costume is the langouti, and all wear

high head-dresses terminating in a point, and apparently composed of precious stones, pearls, and gold and silver ornaments.

On another side the bas-reliefs represent combats ; and here are children with long hair tied up like the savages of the East. Everything here, however, yields in beauty to the statue of the leprous king, which is at the end of the terrace. The head, admirable in its nobility, regularity of feature, and gentle yet proud expression, must have been the work of the most skilful sculptor of the country, in an age when many, doubtless, evinced great talent. A small moustache covers his upper lip, and his hair falls in long curls over his shoulders ; but the whole body is naked, and without ornament. One foot and one hand are broken.

Prea sat sour pŕôt.

About 1200 metres in front of the building just described is one called " Prea sat sour prôt," and said to have been the royal treasury. It is square, and consists of sixteen towers connected by galleries, but nearly all in ruins : the doorways and walls are ornamented with sculpture, as in the other remains. It served, they say, as a depository for the crown jewels. The Cambodians also believe that ropes were stretched from one tower to another, on which dancers exercised their skill in the presence of the king, who, seated on one of the neighbouring terraces, enjoyed their performances. All traditions being lost, the natives invent new ones, according to the measure of their capacity.

The centre of the interior of the third enclosure is occupied by an immense esplanade, supported by walls formed of magnificent blocks of stone, sculptured and surrounded by staircases. The ground is level; but in the excavations that had been made I remarked large masses of carved stone.

Not far from this esplanade is a square building in tolerable preservation, the basement composed of great blocks of ferruginous stone, as are the staircases, of which there are four, one on each side; but they are so steep, narrow, and worn away that it is difficult to climb them. The base supports small galleries, very narrow, and having windows with carved bars. The stones and every doorway are covered with inscriptions.

In the centre of the gallery rises a ruined tower, approached by four staircases, as awkward to ascend as the others just mentioned. Near the doors are some figures of women, standing with flowers in their hands. This building appears very old: the stone is crumbling away like rotten wood.

Prea sat Fiao Saïe.

On the banks of the river which skirts the eastern side of Ongcor Thôm are several remains. The first you come to is Fiao Saïe, two or three hundred metres from the water's edge. Large and deep ditches surround it on all

sides ; and when these have been crossed you arrive in
front of a terrace 45 metres long, and 2 metres 50 centimetres in width.   Four rows of columns 1 metre high are
all that is left standing.   Those in the middle rows are
square, the others are fluted, with capitals.   This terrace
leads to a square formed by four galleries, each 20 metres
long: the one facing the terrace has three porticoes with
doors and staircases, while in the centre, and at each
corner of the gallery, are towers.

Another gallery, 40 metres long, leads from the central
tower to another larger one, where, on a high pedestal,
is placed the principal idol.   On each side of this tower
are three staircases, with porticoes projecting four or five
metres, and supported by six high columns.   All the
windows have been ornamented with twisted bars, many
of which still remain.   By the side of each door are carved
columns, every block being cut and polished with infinite
patience and art.   There are some bas-reliefs portraying a
lion devouring a stag, dances, pantomimes, worshippers
before idols, &c.   As at Ongcor-Wat, the building is
entirely composed of great blocks of sandstone.

Prea sat Iheur Manone Tireada, or the Temple of the Angels.

This little pagoda is only about 150 metres from the
preceding, and, according to tradition, was formerly a
celebrated school for Buddhist theology.   At the east is
the principal entrance, which consists of a gallery 18

metres long, with a portico in the centre, and staircases.
A second gallery, 30 metres long, terminated by a tower,
extends from the centre of the other, and at about two-
thirds of its length open out on either side porticoes and
staircases.   There are two other small buildings north and
south, and a third behind the tower.   That on the south
is in good preservation, but receives no light except
through a single door.   This pagoda has been built with
smaller stones than the other temples: in its architecture
and details it much resembles Fiao Saïe.

THE BRIDGE.

Near Iheur Manone Tireada is a bridge of very ancient
date, in a fair state of preservation, excepting the parapet
and a portion of the roadway, which are a mass of ruins;
but the piers and arches still remain.   The piers are
formed of sandstone, some of the blocks being long, others
square, and placed irregularly ; a few only are carved.

This bridge, with its fourteen narrow arches, may be
about 42 or 43 metres in length, and 45 metres wide.

The river, instead of flowing under its arches, runs now
along the side, its bed having been altered by the shifting
of the sand, which has so accumulated around the piers
and fallen stones, that a great portion of the former is
concealed.

This bridge must have served as a communication
between Ongcor the Great and the high road, which,

traversing the province from east to west, took afterwards a southerly direction.

Prea sat Kéo.

Two hundred metres from the bridge rise, amidst the
forest, the imposing ruins of Prea sat Kéo, to reach which
you have to cross a deep moat. This done, you arrive at
the exterior wall, which has four entrances formed by
elegant pavilions, with staircases of eight steps leading to
a terrace raised nearly 2 metres from the ground; from
this you pass into a low narrow gallery with numerous
interior windows ornamented with twisted bars. This
gallery surrounds the building, and you ascend to it by a
staircase leading to a second terrace. Three other terraces,
each more than 3 metres 50 centimetres wide, rise one
above another, supported on blocks of well-cut sandstone.

Each terrace forms a perfect square, the sides of the
first measuring each 30 metres in length. A staircase, 15
metres high and $3\frac{1}{2}$ metres wide, leads to the top; and
a wide parapet to the staircase serves as a pedestal for
four statues of lions, more or less injured. In the centre
of the upper terrace is a lofty tower, and there are four
smaller ones at the corners. Each tower has four porticoes
with staircases, which rest on a base 7 metres high, and
these towers are reached by staircases of twenty-two steps.
From them a magnificent view is obtained over the surrounding forest. They, as well as their bases and stair-

cases, are built of great blocks of granite arranged in
regular tiers, and joined together in the most perfect
manner.   There is little sculpture, and the doorways have
been left unfinished.   The towers are without roofs, and
perhaps never had any.   The whole building appears very
ancient, judging by the condition of the stone, which in
many places is falling to pieces.

PONTÉEY TA PROUM.—TOWN OF TA PROUM.

On the road before mentioned are two towns containing
some remarkable buildings.   These towns, each of which
is enclosed by walls forming a square, almost touch each
other, being only about 20 metres apart.   The walls are
of ferruginous stone, surmounted by a coping of carved
sandstone resembling a cornice, above which are serrated
stones, giving a very finished appearance to the wall.

The smallest of these towns is called Pontéey Kedey
(Town of Kedey); the other, Pontéey ta Proum.

The town of Ta Proum has seven gateways in the style
of triumphal arches, formed by a central tower at the
entrance and by lateral galleries.   As at Ongcor the
Great, a deep track is worn in the roadway beneath by
the passage of vehicles.   The interior of the town is completely deserted; no one enters it except the Cambodians
from a hamlet outside the enclosure, who cultivate a few
rice-plantations.   In the centre are the ruins of a large
and splendid monument, which has suffered greatly by
the hand of time, and perhaps also from barbarous inva-

sions. The ruins are surrounded by a double wall of
ferruginous stone and by deep moats; and at every entrance are galleries with porticoes. A long gallery, 120
metres on each side, and with porticoes at the middle and
at each end, goes quite round the building. Exteriorly,
on each side, are two detached towers about 10 or 15
metres from the ruins. This gallery is formed by an
interior wall and colonnades supporting a vaulted roof,
which in many places has fallen in, and most of the
columns are overthrown.

On the opposite wall are large bas-reliefs, forming series
of subjects, set in a magnificent framework, which is in so
good a state of preservation that the delicacy of the execution can be appreciated. As for the bas-reliefs themselves,
they are much injured, not so much by time as by some
barbarous hand, for everywhere are marks of the hammer
or pickaxe. Leaving this gallery on the western side,
you enter a long court, in which are three detached towers,
and on the opposite side are similar towers.

Several of these, which are from 8 to 10 metres high,
and well preserved, are real works of art. The mandarins
of the provinces of Ongcor and Battambong are at present
occupied in taking two of them to pieces, in order to
transport them to Bangkok, the king having issued orders
to that effect, and appointed one of the mandarins to carry
them out.*

---

* In a letter from M. Silvestre, missionary at Battambong, to
M. Mouhot, but which he never received, the murder of this mandarin is mentioned.

Beyond, extends a second rectangular gallery, connected with the first by three parallel galleries and two transverse ones. At the points where they intersect are ten towers, placed, like the galleries, in an odd and unsymmetrical fashion. The perfect preservation of several parts of these last, and the ruinous state of others, seem to mark different ages.

One of the towers and several of the galleries are constructed of ferruginous stone, the others of sandstone. The architecture of the galleries is the same as that of Ongcor-Wat, a double roof with colonnades. All the building is on one floor. This temple, which, after Ongcor-Wat, is the largest of all, is situated in a desert place, and lost amidst a forest; an exuberant vegetation has overgrown everything, galleries and towers, so that it is difficult to force a passage.

Ruins in the Province of Battambong.

The principal ruins of this province are those of Bassette, Banone, and Watêk. I visited Bassette twice, before going to Ongcor and after; but all I could bring away was the design of a bas-relief in perfect preservation, carved on a block of sandstone 1 metre 50 centimetres long, forming the top of a doorway in a brick tower. The whole place is so ruinous, that one might suppose some enemy had done his utmost to demolish it, or that one gazed at the results of an earthquake. A thick vegetation, the haunt of fierce animals, has sprung up, and we found it quite impossible to discover the plan of the buildings. Galleries have disappeared under the ground, and the bases of doorways are to be seen 2 metres above.

The only portion which remains at all perfect is an erection 25 metres long and 6 metres wide, divided in two parts by an interior wall, the ends of which are in the form of a tower. It is built entirely of stone, and the exterior bears traces of fine carving on the tops of the doors and on the cornices; inside, the walls are bare, and almost all the stones chipped and injured. The windows have been ornamented with twisted bars, of which only a few traces remain.

On the ground inside lies a large broken stone, 5 decimetres wide and 2 thick, having on each side inscriptions apparently similar; this, and two small fractured idols are the sole remains of Buddhism at Bassette. The subjects, most frequently occurring over the doors, represent men with long beards, seated, and wearing high conical head-dresses, the hands either resting on the hilt of a poignard or crossed one over another, elephants with four heads, and other fanciful creatures.

A little beyond this enclosure is another, bounded by a wall of sandstone, a single block forming the thickness; it appears to have been only 75 centimetres high, and to have served as a kind of terrace. Within this enclosure are some magnificent columns, some still standing, others overthrown; doorways, the upper portions of which alone are visible above the ground; here and there fragments of sculptured stone, towers and walls nearly destroyed, and a beautiful dry basin, 18 metres square and above 2 metres deep, to which you descend by flights of steps extending the entire length of each side.

Bassette is believed to have been the occasional resi-dence of the ancient sovereigns. Battambong is com-paratively modern. It is scarcely a century since Bassette was the centre of a numerous Cambodian population, which has entirely disappeared in consequence of the frequent hostilities between Cambodia and Siam, the inhabitants being led away captive by the conquerors, who often employed this method of peopling the desert parts of their country. It is thus that, in Siam and Laos, entire provinces are to be found, of which the great mass of the population are of Cambodian origin.

The river which formerly flowed near Bassette has been banked up, and a new settlement, peopled from Penom-Peuh, Udong, and other places, formed in the place now called Battambong. Bassette is nine miles from this place, and about as far from the mountains.

Banone.—Ascending the river again for about forty miles from Battambong in a southerly direction, you arrive at a mountain standing somewhat isolated, but forming part of the ramifications of the great chain of Pursat. At the foot is a miserable pagoda of recent origin, and in the environs a few hamlets, while on the summit are the ruins of Banone.

Eight towers are connected with galleries, and communicate on two sides by a wall with a central tower nearly 8 metres in diameter. The buildings are all on one floor, and built of sandstone, and appear of the same date as Bassette. Although there is nothing about them especially remarkable, what remains of the galleries displays fine workmanship, and great taste and skill in construction.

Banone must have been a temple, for there are still in the central tower, and in two smaller ones connected by a gallery, a great number of enormous Buddhist idols, probably as ancient as the building itself, and surrounded by many divinities of less size. At the foot of the neighbouring mountains is a deep cavern in the limestone rock, from the roof of which hang some beautiful stalactites. The water dropping from these is considered sacred by the Cambodians, who attribute to it, amongst other virtues, that of imparting a knowledge of the past, present, and future. Devotees consequently resort hither in pilgrimage, from time to time, to gain information as to their own fate or that of their country, and address their prayers to the numerous idols scattered about on the ground or placed in the cavities of the rocks.

Wat-Ek.—This temple is about six miles on the other side of Battambong, and is in tolerably good preservation. The architecture of the galleries is full of beauty, and that of the tower very imposing; but neither here nor at Banone are you met by the singular grandeur and mag-

nificence which make so great an impression on you in
visiting Ongcor and most of the other ruins.

Wat-Ek is situated in an immense plain, bounded north
and east by the beautiful mountains of Pursat and
ramifications of those of Chantaboun.

CHAPTER XIV.

A KNOWLEDGE of Sanscrit, of "Pali," and of some modern languages of Hindostan and Indo-China, would be the only means of arriving at the origin of the ancient people of Cambodia who have left all these traces of their civilization, and that of their successors, who appear only to have known how to destroy, never to reconstruct. Until some learned archæologist shall devote himself to this subject, it is not probable that aught but contradictory speculations will be promulgated. Some day, however, the truth will surely appear and put them all to flight. I myself, having nothing but conjecture to rest upon, advance my own theory with diffidence.

Nokhor has been the centre and capital of a wealthy, powerful, and civilized state, and in this assertion I do not fear contradiction from those who have any knowledge of its gigantic ruins. Now, for a country to be rich and powerful, a produce relatively great and an extended commerce must be presumed. Doubtless, Cambodia was formerly thus favoured, and would be so at the present day under a wise government, if labour and agriculture were encouraged instead of despised, if the ruling powers exercised a less absolute despotism, and, above all, if slavery were abolished—that miserable institution which is a bar to all progress, reduces man to the level of the brute, and prevents him from cultivating more than sufficient for his own actual wants.*

The greater part of the land is surprisingly fertile, and the rice of Battambong is superior to that of Cochin China. The forests yield precious gums, gum-lac, gamboge, cardamoms, and many others, as well as some useful resins. They likewise produce most valuable timber, both for home use and for exportation, and dye-woods in great variety. The mines afford gold, iron, and copper.

Fruits and vegetables of all kinds abound, and game is in great profusion. Above all, the great lake is a source of wealth to the whole nation; the fish in it are so incredibly abundant that when the water is high they are actually crushed under the boats, and the play of the oars is frequently impeded by them. The quantities taken there every year by a number of enterprising Cochin Chinese are literally miraculous. The river of Battambong is not less plentifully stocked, and I have seen a couple of thousand taken in one net.

Neither must I omit to mention the various productions which form so important a part of the riches of a nation, and which might be here cultivated in the greatest per-

---

* This is equally true of Cambodia and of Siam, the former country being tributary to the latter.

fection. I would especially instance cotton, coffee, indigo, tobacco, and the mulberry, and such spices as nutmegs, cloves, and ginger. Even now all these are grown to a certain limited extent, and are allowed to be of superior quality. Sufficient cotton is raised to supply all Cochin China, and to allow of some being exported to China itself. From the little island of Ko-Sutin alone, leased to the planters by the King of Cambodia, the transport of the cotton produce employs a hundred vessels. What might not be accomplished if these were colonies belonging to a country such, for example, as England, and were governed as are the dependencies of that great and generous nation ?

Battambong and Korat are renowned for their silken "langoutis" of brilliant and varied colours, both the material and the dyes being the produce of the country.

A glance at the map of Cambodia suffices to show that it communicates with the sea by the numerous mouths of the Mekong and the numberless canals of Lower Cochin China, which was formerly subject to it; with Laos and with China, by the great river.

These facts being established, whence came the original inhabitants of this country? Was it from India, the cradle of civilization, or was it from China? The language of the present natives is that of the old Cambodians or Khendome, as they call the people who live retired at the foot of the mountains and on the table-lands, and it is too distinct from Chinese to render the latter supposition possible. But whether this people originally came from the north or from the west, by sea, and gradually making their way up the rivers, or from the land, and descending them, it seems certain that there must have been here other ancient settlers, who intro-duced Buddhism and civilization.   It would appear as though these had been succeeded by some barbarous race, who drove the original inhabitants far into the interior, and destroyed many of their buildings.   At all events, it is my belief that, without exaggeration, the date of some of the oldest parts of Ongcor the Great may be fixed at more than 2000 years ago, and the more recent portions not much later.   The state of decay of many of these structures would indicate even a greater age; but they probably date from the dispersion of the Indian Buddhists, which took place several centuries before the Christian era, and which led to the expatriation of thousands of individuals.

All that can be said respecting the present Cambodians is, that they are an agricultural people, among whom a certain taste for art still shows itself in the carved work of the boats belonging to the better classes, and their chief characteristic is unbounded conceit.

It is not so among the savages of the east, called by the Cambodians their elder brothers.   I passed four months among them, and, arriving direct from Cambodia, it seemed like entering a country comparatively civilized. Great gentleness, politeness, and even sociability—which, to my fancy, bore evidence of a past refinement—struck me in these poor children of nature, buried for centuries in their deep forests, which they believe to be the largest portion of the world, and to which they are so strongly attached that no inducement would tempt them to move. At the risk, then, of this portion of my notes being passed over by many readers, I shall enlarge a little upon these people, my own observations being aided by the information afforded me by the missionaries who have for years resided among their different tribes.

When looking at the figures in the bas-reliefs at Ongcor, I could not avoid remarking the strong resemblance of the faces to those of these savages. And besides the similar regularity of feature, there are the same long beards, straight langoutis, and even the same weapons and musical instruments.

Almost all the fruit-trees of the neighbouring countries are found, though in small numbers, among them; and they have some good species of bananas, which are unknown beyond the limits of their forests.

Having a great taste for music, and being gifted with ears excessively fine, with them originated the tam-tam, so prized among the neighbouring nations; and by uniting its sounds to those of a large drum, they obtain music tolerably harmonious. The art of writing is unknown to them; and as they necessarily lead a wandering life, they seem to have lost nearly all traditions of the past. The only information I could extract from their oldest chiefs was, that far beyond the chain of mountains which crosses the country from north to south are other " people of the high country "—such is the name they

give themselves; that of *savage* wounds them greatly—
that they have many relations there, and they even cite
names of villages or hamlets as far as the provinces
occupied by the Annamite invaders. Their practice is to
bury their dead.

I extract the following account of the Bannavs—which
applies to most of the tribes inhabiting the mountains
and table-lands between Tonquin and Laos, Cochin China
and Cambodia—from a letter of M. Comte, missionary in
Cochin China, who recently died amongst them after a
residence of several years :—

" To what race do the Bannavs belong? That is the
first question I asked myself on arriving here, and I must
confess that I cannot yet answer it; all I can say is, that
in all points they differ from the Annamites and Chinese;
neither do they resemble the Laotians or Cambodians, but
appear to have a common origin with the Cédans, Halangs,
Reungao, and Giaraïe, their neighbours. Their counte-
nances, costumes, and belief are nearly the same; and
the language, although it differs in each tribe, has yet
many words common to all; the construction, moreover,
is perfectly identical. I have not visited the various
tribes of the south, but from all I have heard I conclude
that these observations apply to them also, and that all
the savages inhabiting the vast country lying between
Cochin China, Laos, and Cambodia belong to the same
great branch of the human family.

" The language spoken by the Bannavs has nothing

in common with that of the Annamites. Very simple in
its construction, it is soft, flowing, and easy.

" These people manufacture the saucepans in which
they cook their rice and wild herbs, the hatchets, pickaxes, and pruning-bills, which comprise all their agricultural instruments, the sabres which serve them as
weapons, and the long-handled knives used for various
kinds of work in which they excel. Their clay calumets,
tastefully ornamented with leaves or other devices, are
the production of the most skilful among the tribe. The
women weave pieces of white or black cloth, which they
use for coverings, and which, coarse as they are, form the
principal article of commerce between the Bannavs and
the Cédans.

" The villagers who live on the banks of the river
Bla make light canoes, which are both solid and graceful,
out of the trunks of trees. Such are the principal articles
produced by the Bannavs, who are more backward than
any of the other tribes, having little inventive genius.

" The Giaraïe, their neighbours on the south, show
much taste and aptness in all they do; their clothes are
of a finer texture than those spun by the Bannavs, and
are sometimes embellished with designs which would be
admired even in Europe. The iron which they forge is
also wrought into more elegant forms, and is more finely
tempered; and they manufacture some articles in copper.
Very superior to the Reungao, they do not perhaps surpass
the Halangs.

" The Cédans are a tribe of iron-workers, their country abounding in mines of this metal. The inhabitants of more than seventy villages, when their agricultural labours are over, busy themselves in extracting and working the ore, which they afterwards dispose of in the shape of hatchets, pickaxes, lances, and sabres.

" Amongst all the dwellers in a Bannav village, even more than among the other natives, there exists a very decided spirit of community. Thus, no family will drink wine without inviting others to join them, as long as the quantity will hold out; and on killing a pig, goat, or buffalo, the possessor divides it into as many portions as there are families, reserving for himself a share very little larger than the others. No one is forgotten in this distribution, from the youngest child to the oldest man. The deer and wild boar taken in the chase are divided in the same way, the hunters retaining only a rather larger portion in consideration of their labour and fatigue. I have actually seen a fowl divided into forty or fifty parts. Even if the children catch a serpent, a lizard, or a mouse in their little expeditions, you will see the oldest of them, on returning, portion it with strict impartiality amongst the party. These customs might have been borrowed from the early Christians had these savages ever heard of them. The other tribes also observe them, but less scrupulously.

" Not only does general censure follow any criminal act, but severe penalties, such as slavery or exile, are imposed for lying. Even suicide—instances of which you occasionally find among them—has a stigma affixed to it in their penal code; any one who perishes by his own hand is buried in a corner of the forest far from the graves of his brethren, and all who have assisted in the sepulture are required afterwards to purify themselves in a special manner.

"This legislation is far from being deficient in morality and wisdom, but unfortunately on certain points it is tainted with superstition, and has opened a large door to numberless injustices, and sometimes provoked cruel strife. On the subject of witchcraft they are particularly credulous: nearly every misfortune is attributed by them to the malice of certain persons whom they believe gifted with the power of influencing their fate; superstition serves as a guide to seek out the guilty individual, and when he is supposed to be discovered, he is usually sold for a slave, or a heavy ransom is exacted.

"The Bannavs believe in the existence of a multitude of spirits, some mischievous to man, others beneficent. According to their creed, every large tree, every mountain, every river, every rock, almost everything, has its particular genius; but they seem to have no idea of a superior being, sovereign and Creator of all things.

"If you ask them respecting the origin of mankind, all they tell you is, that the father of the human race was saved from an immense inundation by means of a large chest in which he shut himself up; but of the origin or creator of this father they know nothing. Their traditions do not reach beyond the Deluge; but they will tell you

that in the beginning one grain of rice sufficed to fill a
saucepan and furnish a repast for a whole family.   This
is a souvenir of the first age of the world, that fugitive
period of innocence and happiness which poets have called
the golden age.

"They have no very fixed ideas on the subject of
rewards and punishments in a future life.   They believe
in the immortality of the soul, which, after leaving the
body, they imagine wanders about the tombs and adjacent
mountains, often terrifying the living by nocturnal appear-
ances, and finally loses itself for ever in the shadowy
depths of the regions of the south.

" All their religion consists of sacrifices and vows, vain
and endless observances performed in the hope of warding
off misfortune, alleviating suffering, and retarding the
hour of death; for, as with all Pagans, the foundation
of their religion is terror and egotism."

On my return from my excursion amongst the Stiêns,
M. Fontaine, whom I met at Pinhalú, was so kind as
to present me with his journal, kept during a residence of
twenty years among various savage races, and which I
hope some day will see the light; and he likewise
favoured me with the following remarks on the dialects
of several of these tribes :—

" The language of the Giaraïe and that of the Redais
bear a strong resemblance to each other: the two tribes
are only separated from each other by the river Bong,
which flows between them in a westerly direction, after
running for some distance from south to north and

watering the lands of the Candians or Bihcandians, whose
language also resembles in some degree that of the tribes
just mentioned. The dialect of the Bonnavs or Menons
does not appear to me to have any similitude to the
others, nor even to those of the tribes farther north.

"After a sojourn of several years among these tribes, I
was forced, on account of my health, to go to Singapore.
I was astonished, after a little study of Malayan, to find
in that language a number of Giaraïe words, and many
more bearing a strong resemblance to words in that dialect; and I doubt not this similarity would be found still
more remarkable by any one who thoroughly studied both
languages. The resemblance also of the language of the
Thiâmes, the ancient inhabitants of Isiampa, now in the
province of Annam, to that of these tribes, leads me to
believe that they must all have sprung from the same
root."

The information I obtained from the Stiêns accords
perfectly with these remarks of M. Fontaine: — "The
Thiâmes," they said, "understand our language very well,
but the Kouïs, who live beyond the great river, speak
exactly the same language as ourselves." M. Arnoux,
another missionary in Cochin China, who has long resided
amongst these savage tribes, speaks in the same way respecting the language. To M. Arnoux also I owe the
exact latitude of many places on the map, and a great
deal of topographical information about the whole country;
and it affords me great pleasure here to express my gratitude and my esteem for his character.

" The languages of the Sedans," says he, " of the Reun-
gaos, and of the Italhans are almost identical, although
often varying slightly even in the same tribe: the dialect
of the northern Sedans is somewhat different from that
of the southerns, and the Stiengs of Brelum speak differently from those farther to the east.

" The Bannav and the Bannam are nearly the same;
the Bannav and Sedan much alike; generally only the
terminations differ, but there are words in each not to be
found in the other.   M. Fontaine found that the Ieboune
and Braon strongly resemble the Bannav.   I cannot
speak personally about the Giaraïe, Nedais, Bonous, and
Bih; but doubtless others can."

I myself remarked many Stiên words like the Cambodian, especially in the western districts, where there exists
some commerce between the two countries.   To all this
must be added that the Siamese, Laotian,* and Cambodian seem to be sister languages: more than a fourth
part of the words, especially those expressing intellectual
things, are exactly the same in each.

In the course of this work I have cited several passages
from the Life of the Abbé Gagelin, who died a martyr
in Cochin China, and which was published by Abbé
Jacquenet: in it mention is made of savage races on the
coast of Siam and in the environs of Kompat (Cambodia).
I have sought in vain for them, and no one has ever
heard them spoken of.   Probably the missionary was

* Lao means ancient.

deceived by his servants, who were Annamites, and they always call the Cambodians and Siamese savages (Noye Uhen, inhabitants of the woods), while they give themselves the appellation of citizens.

Notwithstanding all my efforts to discover the traces of the probable migrations of the Jewish people through Siam and Cambodia, I have met with nothing satisfactory excepting a record of the judgment of Solomon, which, as I before stated, was found by M. Miche, Bishop of Laos and Cambodia, to be preserved *verbatim* in one of the Cambodian sacred books. To all my questions on this subject I received the same answer, "There are no Jews in the country." Nevertheless, among the Stiêns, I could not but be struck by the Hebrew character of many of the faces.

In 1670 Cambodia extended as far as Isiampa; but the provinces of Lower Cochin China, as Bien-hoa, Digne-Theun, Vigue Laon, Ann Djiann, and Ita-Tienne—all at one time conquered and annexed—have, for more than a century, shaken off their dependence on Cambodia; and the language and ancient Cambodian race have entirely disappeared in those districts. The different states have now their limits and sovereigns entirely independent of each other. Cambodia is, however, to a certain extent tributary to Siam, but in no degree to Annam; and I cannot understand how, at the present day, the French newspapers, even the 'Moniteur de la Flotte,' still less how our admiral in those seas, should habitually confound these two countries.

The suppositions of the Abbé Jacquenet, which I have already quoted and to which I was disposed to give credence, seem to fall before the more accurate information which I have obtained concerning the religion of the Thiâmes or Isiampois. It must be allowed that the only vestiges of Judaism found among them are equally met with amongst Mahometans. They have priests, temples, practise circumcision, abstain from pork, and frequently pronounce, with the greatest veneration, the words Allah and Mahomet. They themselves declare that their present religion was brought to them from Malaisia —that priests still come to them from thence and visit them from time to time. I had this information from some Cambodians of Battambong, who, having been taken prisoners in the wars with the Cochin Chinese, passed eight years in Isiampa. One of them, a blind man, who appeared to me to be remarkable for good sense and judgment—an exceptional case in this country—seemed especially to merit confidence. These facts, and others which I collected regarding the religion of the Thiâmes, who until 1859, the time of their flight, inhabited Cambodia, lead me to infer that the Abbé Gagelin was in error. I was certainly told of two sects into which the tribe was divided ; but the only distinguishing point between them was that one ate pork and the other did not.

The Thiâmes must formerly have occupied several important districts in Cambodia, principally on the banks of the tributary of the Me-kong. Thus, on the shores of Touli Sap, or the great lake, not far from Battambong, is

a place called Campong Thiâme (shore of the Thiâmes).
More to the south, near Campong Tchnam, the village
where the custom house of Cambodia is erected, is an
island called Isle of Thiâmes. According to tradition, the
whole banks of the river, as far as Penom-Peuh, were formerly inhabited by these people; and to this cause is to
be attributed the complete absence of remains in these
localities.

The mountains of Dom-rêe, situated a little way to
the north of Ongcor, are inhabited by the Khmer-dôme, a
gentle and inoffensive race, although looked upon as
savages by their brethren of the plain. These latter are
the Somrais: they speak the Cambodian language, but
with a different pronunciation. Beyond are the provinces,
formerly belonging to Cambodia, but now Siamese, of
Souréne, Song Kac, Con Khan, Nan Kong, and Ongcor-
Eith or Korat.

According to popular belief, the king, if he should
cross the great lake, is sure to die in the course of the
year.

Whilst the present sovereign was prince he paid a visit
to Ongcor, and seeing some of the Somrais, said, "These
are my true subjects, and the stock from which my
family sprang." It seems that, in fact, the present dynasty
did so.

The Cambodians give the following account of the introduction of Buddhism among them. Samanokodom left
Ceylon and went to Thibet, where he was very well
received; from thence he went among the savages, but,

not meeting with encouragement from them, he took refuge
in Cambodia, where he was welcomed by the people.

A circumstance worthy of remark is that the name of
Rome is familiar to nearly all the Cambodians: they pronounce it Rouma, and place it at the western end of the
world.

There are among the Giaraïe two great nominal chiefs,
called by the Annamites Hoa-Sa and Thorei-Sa, the king
of fire and the king of water.   The kings of Cambodia
and Cochin China send to the former chief, every four
or five years, a small tribute as a token of respectful
homage, in consideration of the ancient power of which
their ancestors have despoiled him.   The king of fire, who
appears to be the more important of the two, is called
Eni (grandfather) by the savages, and the village where
he resides bears the same name.   When this "grandfather" dies, another is chosen, sometimes one of his sons,
sometimes a stranger, the dignity not being hereditary.
His extraordinary power is attributed, according to M.
Fontaine, to Beurdao, an old sabre wrapped in rags, and
having no other sheath.   This sabre, say the Giaraïe, is
centuries old, and contains a famous spirit (Giang), who
must certainly have a good digestion to consume all the
pigs, fowls, and other offerings brought to him.   It is
kept in a certain house, and whoever ventures to look at
it dies suddenly, the sole exception being Eni himself, who
has the privilege of seeing and handling it unharmed.
Every inhabitant of the village has to act as sentinel in
turn at this house.

D 2

Eni wages war on no one, and is assailed by none; consequently his attendants carry no arms when they go
round to collect offerings.   Most of the people give something, cloth, wax, pickaxes; anything is accepted.

I have written these few notes on Cambodia, after returning from a long hunting expedition, by the light of a torch,
seated on my tiger-skin.   On one side of me is the skin
of an ape just stripped off; on the other, a box of insects
waiting to be arranged and packed; and my employment
has not been rendered easier by the sanguinary attacks of
mosquitoes and leeches.   My desire is, not to impose my
opinions on any one, especially with regard to the wonderful architectural remains which I have visited, but simply
to disclose the existence of these monuments, which are
certainly the most gigantic, and also to my mind display
a more perfect taste than any left to us by the ancients;
and, moreover, to collect all the facts and traditions
possible about these countries, hoping they may be useful
to explorers of greater talent and fortune.   For, I doubt
not, others will follow in my steps, and, aided by their own
government and by that of Siam, advantages denied to
myself, will gather an abundant harvest where I have
but cleared the ground.

But, after all, my principal object is natural history,
and with that study I chiefly occupy myself.   I have
written, as I said before, in leisure hours, when resting
from my fatigues, with a desire to implant in the breasts
of others a love for the great works of Nature, and to
benefit those who, in the quiet of their homes, delight to

follow the poor traveller; who, often with the sole object
of being useful to his fellow-men, or of discovering some
insect, plant, or unknown animal, or verifying some point
of latitude, crosses the ocean, and sacrifices family, comfort, health, and, too often, life itself.

But it is pleasant to the man devoted to our good
and beautiful mother, Nature, to think that his work, his
fatigues, his troubles and dangers, are useful to others, if
not to himself. Nature has her lovers, and those alone
who have tasted them know the joys she gives. I can-
didly confess that I have never been more happy than
when amidst this grand and beautiful tropical scenery,
in the profound solitude of these dense forests, the stillness
only broken by the song of birds and the cries of wild
animals ; and even if destined here to meet my death, I
would not change my lot for all the joys and pleasures of
the civilised world.

CHAPTER XV.

After a sojourn of three weeks within the walls of Ong-cor-Wat in order to make drawings and plans, I returned to Battambong. There I inquired for some means of transport to Bangkok, but, on different pretexts, I was detained more than two months before I could get away, in spite of the assistance of the viceroy. At last, on the 5th March, I set off with two waggons and two pair of powerful buffaloes, which had been taken wild, and trained up to the yoke, and were strong enough to sustain the fatigues of a journey at this season.

This time I carried along with me a complete menagerie; but of all my prisoners a pretty young chimpanzee, which, after slightly wounding it, we had succeeded in taking alive, was the most amusing. As long as I kept him in my room, and he could amuse himself with the numerous children and other visitors whom curiosity brought to look at him, he was very gentle; but as I was obliged on the journey to fasten him at the back of one of the waggons, he became frightened, and used ever effort to break his chain, continually screaming, and trying to hide himself. After a time, however, he got accustomed to his position, and was quiet and docile as before.

Our guns on our shoulders, I and my young Chinese Phrai followed or walked before the waggons, occasionally finding some sport as we skirted the forest. As for my other servant, when we reached Pinhalú he begged to be allowed to return to Bangkok by our former route; so, not wishing to retain him against his will, I paid his expenses home, and wished him happiness.

Scarcely had we proceeded a mile when our drivers asked my permission to stop for supper, saying that afterwards we could set out again, and travel part of the night. I at once consented, knowing it to be a custom with the Cambodians, before departing on a long journey, to make their first halt not far from their village, that they may return home to shed a last tear, and partake of a farewell glass.

Before the oxen were even unyoked, the families of our drivers were all collected round me, the whole party talking at once, and begging me to take care of their relations, to save them from robbers, and give them medicine if they had a headache. They all then took their evening meal together, washing it down with some glasses of arrack which I gave them; after which we resumed our journey by a magnificent moonlight, but treading in a bed of dust which reached to our ankles, and raised a thick cloud round our waggons.

We encamped part of the night near a small piece of water, where some custom-house officers are stationed—

three poor wretches—whose duty it is to arrest the depre-
dators who lie in wait for the buffaloes and elephants
coming down here from the lake and neighbouring districts. Those among us who had mats, spread them on
the ground, and lay down; those who had none, piled up
grass and leaves for beds.

For three days we travelled northward until we reached
Ongcor-Borige, chief town of a province of the same
name; but, surprised by darkness and a heavy storm, we
were compelled to halt at the outskirts. The next morning, as we were leaving the place, we fell in with a caravan of thirty waggons conveying rice to Muang-Kabine,
whither we were ourselves going; so my Cambodians
fraternised with the party, all breakfasting together, and
two hours afterwards we set off again at the head of this
line of waggons.

There is here an immense plain, almost a desert, which
in the best season takes six days to cross with elephants,
and twelve with waggons. As for us, we set out on the
5th March, and only reached Muang-Kabine on the 28th;
and oh! what we suffered from ennui, from heat, from
attacks of mosquitoes, and want of water. In addition to
these miseries my feet became like a jelly; and, when we
arrived at our destination, I could scarcely drag myself
along, or keep up with the slow but regular step of the
buffaloes.

Some days before reaching Muang-Kabine we had to
ford a small river, the Bang-Chang, and here we obtained
some good water; but all the rest of the journey we had

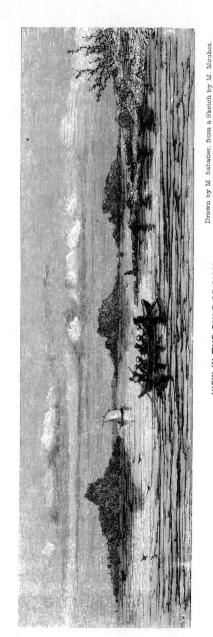

VIEW IN THE GULF OF SIAM.

Drawn by M. Sabatier, from a Sketch by M. Mouhot.

nothing but the water from the muddy pools, serving for
baths and drinking-places to all the buffaloes of the caravan. When I drank it, or used it for cooking or tea, I
purified it with a little alum, a better method than filtering.
Every day some accident happened to our waggons, which
was one cause of our being so long on the road.

On our arrival at Muang-Kabine we found great excite-
ment prevailing on account of a recent discovery of gold-
mines, which had attracted to the place a number of
Laotians, Chinese, and Siamese. The mines of Battambong, being less rich, are not so much frequented. From
Muang-Kabine I continued my route to Paknam, where
I hired a boat to take me to Bangkok.

The first day's navigation was very tedious, the water
being shallow, and the sand-banks in many places bare,
but the day following we were able to lay aside our poles,
and take to the oars. The stream takes a bend towards
the south, and empties itself into the gulf a little above
Petrin, a district which produces all the sugar of Siam,
which is sold at Bangkok.

This canal connects the Menam and the Bang-Chang,
which afterwards takes the name of Bang-Pakong; it is
nearly sixty miles in length, and was the work of a clever
Siamese general, the same who, twenty years ago, retook
Battambong from the Cochin-Chinese. He is also noted
for having constructed a fine road from Paknam to
Ongcor-Borige, the place where the great inundations
have their limit. This road I could not make use of, for

at this season I should have found neither water nor grass for my oxen.

On the banks of the Bang-Pakong are several Cambodian villages, peopled by prisoners from Battambong; and along the canal, on either side, is a mixed, and for this country numerous population, of Malays, Laotians from the peninsula, and Laotians from Vien-Chan, a district on the banks of the Mekong, north-east of Korat, and now depopulated by frequent revolts.

Although overburdened with taxes, yet, to judge from their clean and comfortable dwellings, and a certain air of well-doing which reigns in these villages, the inhabitants must enjoy some degree of prosperity, especially since the impulse given to commerce by the Europeans settled in the capital.

The water was so thickly covered with weeds that our progress was much impeded, and we were three days in the canal; while, after May, it only takes the same time to go from Paknam to Bangkok.

On the 4th April I returned to the capital, after fifteen months' absence. During the greater part of this time I had never known the comfort of sleeping in a bed; and throughout my wanderings my only food had been rice or dried fish, and I had not once tasted good water. I was astonished at having preserved my health so well, particularly in the forests, where, often wet to the skin, and without a change of clothes, I have had to pass whole nights by a fire at the foot of a tree; yet I have not had a single

Drawn by M. Bocourt, from a Sketch taken by M. Mouhot in the residence of the Prime Minister.

CEREMONY, ON A YOUNG SIAMESE COMING OF AGE, OF THE REMOVAL OF THE TUFT.

attack of fever, and been always happy and in good spirits, especially when lucky enough to light upon some novelty. A new shell or insect filled me with a joy which ardent naturalists alone can understand; but they know well how little fatigues and privations of all kinds are cared for when set against the delight experienced in making one discovery after another, and in feeling that one is of some slight assistance to the votaries of science. It pleases me to think that my investigations into the archæology, entomology, and conchology of these lands may be of use to certain members of the great and generous English nation, who kindly encouraged the poor naturalist; whilst France, his own country, remained deaf to his voice.

It was another great pleasure to me, after these fifteen months of travelling, during which very few letters from home had reached me, to find, on arriving at Bangkok, an enormous packet, telling me all the news of my distant family and country. It is indeed happiness, after so long a period of solitude, to read the lines traced by the beloved hands of an aged father, of a wife, of a brother. These joys are to be reckoned among the sweetest and purest of life.

We stopped in the centre of the town, at the entrance of a canal, whence there is a view over the busiest part of the Menam. It was almost night, and silence reigned around us; but when at daybreak I rose and saw the ships lying at anchor in the middle of the stream, while the roofs of the palaces and pagodas reflected the first rays of the sun, I thought that Bangkok had never looked so beautiful. However, life here would never suit me, and the mode of locomotion is wearisome after an active existence among the woods and in the chase.

The river is constantly covered with thousands of boats of different sizes and forms, and the port of Bangkok is certainly one of the finest in the world, without excepting even the justly-renowned harbour of New York. Thousands of vessels can find safe anchorage here.

The town of Bangkok increases in population and extent every day, and there is no doubt but that it will become a very important capital: if France succeeds in taking possession of Annam, the commerce between the two countries will increase. It is scarcely a century old, and yet contains nearly half a million of inhabitants, amongst whom are many Christians. The flag of France floating in Cochin China would improve the position of the missions in all the surrounding countries; and I have reason to hope that Christianity will increase more rapidly than it has hitherto done.

I had intended to visit the north-east of the country of Laos, crossing Dong Phya Phai (the forest of the King of Fire), and going on to Hieng Naie, on the frontiers of Cochin China; thence to the confines of Tonquin. I had planned to return afterwards by the Nékong to Cambodia, and then to pass through Cochin China, should the arms of France have been victorious there. However, the rainy season having commenced, the whole country was inundated, and the forests impassable; so it was neces-

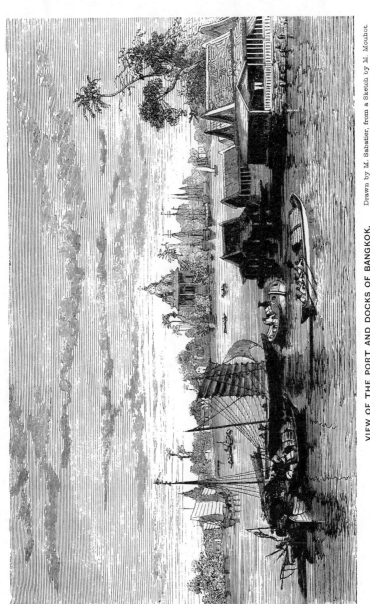

VIEW OF THE PORT AND DOCKS OF BANGKOK.   Drawn by M. Sabatier, from a Sketch by M. Mouhot.

with the great river to the north-east of the town, and
leads to some Laotian and Xieng villages bearing the
name of _Xxx_. These are no other than the tribes called
Penoms by the Cambodians, _Kha_ by the Siamese, and
Moï by the Annamites,—all words simply signifying
"savages."

The whole chain of mountains which extends from
the north of Tonquin to the south of Cochin China,
about 100 miles north of Saigon, is inhabited by this
primitive people, divided into tribes speaking different
dialects, but whose manners and customs are the same.
All the villages in the immediate neighbourhood are
tributary; those nearest to the town supply workmen for
buildings erected for the king and princes, and these are
heavily taxed. Others pay their tribute in rice.

Their habitations are in the thickest parts of the
forests, where they only can find a path. Their cultivated
grounds are to be seen on the tops and sides of the
mountains; in fact, they employ the same means as wild
animals to escape from their enemies, and to preserve
that liberty and independence which are to them, as to
all God's creatures, their supreme good.

Yesterday, and the day previous, I was presented to
the princes who govern this little state, and who bear
the title of kings. I know not why, but they displayed
for my benefit all they could devise of pomp and
splendour.

The Laotians of Leuyé appear to me more industrious
than the Siamese, and, above all, possess a much more

sary to wait four months before I could put my project in
execution.   I therefore packed up and sent off all my
collections, and after remaining a few weeks in Bangkok
I departed for Pechaburi, situated about 13° north lat.,
and to the north of the Malayan peninsula.

On the 8th May, at five o'clock in the evening, I sailed
from Bangkok in a magnificent vessel ornamented with
rich gilding and carved-work, belonging to Khrom Luang,

Drawn by M. Bocourt, from a Photograph.

**PORTRAIT OF KHROM LUANG, ONE OF THE BROTHERS OF THE
KING OF SIAM.**

one of the king's brothers, who had kindly lent it to a
valued friend of mine.   There is no reason for concealing
the name of this gentleman, who has proved himself a
real friend in the truest meaning of the word; but I rather

embrace the opportunity of testifying my affection and gratitude to M. Malherbes, who is a French merchant settled at Bangkok. He insisted on accompanying me for some distance, and the few days he passed with me were most agreeable ones.

The current was favourable, and, with our fifteen rowers, we proceeded rapidly up the stream. Our boat, adorned with all sorts of flags, red streamers, and peacocks' tails, attracted the attention of all the European residents, whose houses are built along the banks of the stream, and who, from their verandahs, saluted us by cheering and waving their hands. Three days after leaving Bangkok we arrived at Pechaburi.

The king was expected there the same day, to visit a palace which he has had built on the summit of a hill near the town. Khrom Luang, Kalahom (prime minister), and a large number of mandarins had already assembled. Seeing us arrive, the prince called to us from his pretty little house; and as soon as we had put on more suitable dresses we waited on him, and he entered into conversation with us till breakfast-time. He is an excellent man, and, of all the dignitaries of the country, the one who manifests least reserve and hauteur towards Europeans. In education, both this prince and the king are much advanced, considering the state of the country; but in their manners they have little more refinement than the people generally.

Our first walk was to the hill on which the palace stands. Seen from a little distance, this building, of

European construction, presents a very striking appearance; and the winding path which leads up to it has been
admirably contrived amidst the volcanic rocks, basalt, and
scoria which cover the surface of this ancient crater.

About twenty-five miles off, stretches from north to
south a chain of mountains called Deng, and inhabited
by the independent tribes of the primitive Kariens.
Beyond these rise a number of still higher peaks.   On
the low ground are forests, palm-trees, and rice-fields, the
whole rich and varied in colour.   Lastly, to the south and
east, and beyond another plain, lies the gulf, on whose
waters, fading away into the horizon, a few scattered sails
are just distinguishable.

It was one of those sights not to be soon forgotten, and
the king has evinced his taste in the selection of such a
spot for his palace.   No beings can be less poetical or
imaginative than the Indo-Chinese; their hearts never
appear to expand to the genial rays of the sun; yet they
must have some appreciation of this beautiful scenery, as
they always fix upon the finest sites for their pagodas and
palaces.

Quitting this hill, we proceeded to another, like it an
extinct volcano or upheaved crater.   Here are four or
five grottoes, two of which are of surprising extent, and
extremely picturesque.   A painting which represented
them faithfully would be supposed the offspring of a fertile
imagination; no one would believe it to be natural.   The
rocks, long in a state of fusion, have taken, in cooling,
those singular forms peculiar to scoria and basalt.   Then,

after the sea had retreated—for all these rocks have risen from the bottom of the water—owing to the moisture continually dripping through the damp soil, they have taken the richest and most harmonious colours. These grottoes, moreover, are adorned by such splendid stalactites, which, like columns, seem to sustain the walls and roofs, that one might fancy oneself present at one of the beautiful fairy scenes represented at Christmas in the London theatres.

If the taste of the architect of the king's palace has failed in the design of its interior, here, at least, he has made the best of all the advantages offered to him by nature. A hammer touching the walls would have disfigured them; he had only to level the ground, and to make staircases to aid the descent into the grottoes, and enable the visitor to see them in all their beauty.

The largest and most picturesque of the caverns has been made into a temple. All along the sides are rows of idols, one of superior size, representing Buddha asleep, being gilt.

We came down from the mountain just at the moment of the king's arrival. Although his stay was not intended to exceed two days, he was preceded by a hundred slaves carrying an immense number of coffers, boxes, baskets, &c. A disorderly troop of soldiers marched both in front and behind, dressed in the most singular and ridiculous costumes imaginable. The emperor Soulouque himself would have laughed, for certainly his old guard must have made a better appearance than that of his East Indian

Drawn by M. Bocourt, from a Photograph.

GROTTO AT PECHABURI.

brother. Nothing could give a better idea of this set
of tatterdemalions than the dressed-up monkeys which
dance upon the organs of the little Savoyards. Their
apparel of coarse red cloth upper garments, which left
a part of the body exposed, in every case either too
large or too small, too long or too short, with white shakos,
and pantaloons of various colours; as for shoes, they were
a luxury enjoyed by few.

A few chiefs, whose appearance was quite in keeping
with that of their men, were on horseback, leading this
band of warriors, whilst the king, attended by slaves, slowly
advanced in a little open carriage drawn by a pony.

I visited several hills detached from the great chain
Khao Deng, which is only a few miles off. During my
stay here it has rained continually, and I have had to
wage war with savage foes, from whom I never before
suffered so much. Nothing avails against them; they let
themselves be massacred, with a courage worthy of nobler
beings. I speak of mosquitoes. Thousands of these cruel
insects suck our blood night and day. My body, face,
and hands are covered with wounds and blisters. I would
rather have to deal with the wild beasts of the forest.
At times I howl with pain and exasperation. No one
can imagine the frightful plague of these little demons, to
whom Dante has omitted to assign a place in his infernal
regions. I scarcely dare to bathe, for my body is covered
before I can get into the water. The natural philoso-
pher who held up these little animals as examples of

parental love was certainly not tormented as I have been.

About ten miles from Pechaburi I found several villages inhabited by Laotians, who have been settled there for two or three generations. Their costume consists of a long shirt and black pantaloons, like those of the Cochin Chinese, and they have the Siamese tuft of hair. The women wear the same head-dress as the Cambodians. Their songs, and their way of drinking through bamboo pipes, from large jars, a fermented liquor made from rice and herbs, recalled to my mind what I had seen among the savage Stiêns. I also found among them the same baskets and instruments used by those tribes.

The young girls are fair compared with the Siamese, and their features are pretty; but they soon grow coarse, and lose all their charms. Isolated in their villages, these Laotians have preserved their language and customs, and they never mingle with the Siamese.

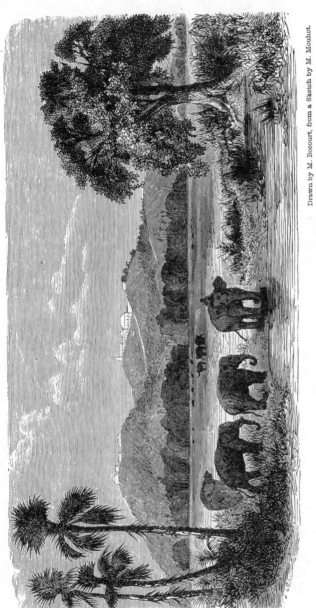

VIEW OF THE MOUNTAINS OF PECHABURI.

Drawn by M. Bocourt, from a Sketch by M. Mouhot.

PAVILION CONTAINING THE ASHES OF THE LATE KING OF SIAM IN THE GARDENS ATTACHED

Drawn by M. Therond, from a Sketch by M. Mouhot.

CHAPTER XVI.

AFTER a sojourn of four months among the mountains
of Pechaburi, known by the names of Makaon Khao,
Panam Knot, Khao Tamoune, and Khao Samroun, the last
two of which are 1700 and 1900 feet above the level
of the sea, I returned to Bangkok to make the necessary preparations for my new expedition to the north-
east of Laos, my intended route being to the basin of
the Mekong, towards the frontier of China. I had an
additional motive for coming here again, namely, to get
cured of that annoying complaint the itch, which I caught
at Pechaburi; how, I really cannot guess, for, in spite of
the mosquitoes, I bathed regularly two or three times a
day; but I hope that a short course of rubbing with
sulphur ointment, and proper baths, will effect a cure.
This, one of the ills of a traveller's life, is, however,
trifling in comparison with the misfortune of which I have
just heard. The steamer 'Sir James Brooke,' in which
Messrs. Gray, Hamilton, and Co., of Singapore, had sent
off all my last boxes of collections, has foundered at the
entrance of that port. And so all my poor insects, which

have cost me so much care and pains for many months, are lost for ever — some of them rare and valuable specimens, which, alas ! I shall probably never be able to replace.

Two years ago, about this same season, I was nearly in the same place where I now am, on the Menam, some leagues north of Bangkok. The last floating shops, with their almost exclusively Chinese population, are beginning to disappear, and the banks of the river are assuming a monotonous aspect, although from time to time, through the brushwood and foliage of the bananas, the roof of some hut is visible, or the white walls of a pagoda, prettily situated, and surrounded by the modest dwellings of the priests.

It is the season of fêtes; the stream is covered with large and handsome boats, decorated with gilding and carved work, with true oriental gorgeousness; and among them the heavy barges of the rice-merchants, or the small craft of poor women going to the market with bananas and betel-nuts. It is only on festivals, and a few other occasions, that the king, princes, and mandarins display their riches and importance. The king was on his way to a pagoda to offer presents, followed by his whole court. Each of the mandarins was in a splendid barge, the rowers being dressed in the most brilliant colours. A number of pirogues were filled with soldiers in red coats. The royal barge was easily to be distinguished from the rest, by the throne surmounted by a canopy terminating in a pinnacle, and by the immense quantity of carving and

THE BAR OF THE RIVER MENAM.

Drawn by M. Sabatier, from a Sketch by M. Mouhot.

Drawn by M. Catenacci, from a Sketch by M. Mouhot.
CLOCK TOWER AT BANGKOK.

gilding about it. At the king's feet were some of his
children, and he waved his hand to every European whom
he saw.

All the ships at anchor were adorned with flags, and
every floating house had an altar covered with various

objects, and with odoriferous woods burning on them. Amidst all these fine barges, one was remarkable for its simplicity, and the good taste with which the rowers were dressed,—a uniform of white cloth, with red cuffs and collar. It belonged to Khrom Luang, the king's brother, a good, courteous, and intelligent prince, ever ready to protect Europeans to the utmost of his power; in a word, a gentleman.

Most of the dignitaries, generally fat men, were lying lazily on triangular embroidered cushions, in their splendid boats, upon a kind of dais, surrounded by officials, women, and children, kneeling, or lying flat, in readiness to hold out the golden urns which serve them for spittoons, or their betel-boxes or teapots, all made of the same precious metals by the goldsmiths of Laos and Ligor. The boats have generally from eighty to a hundred rowers, with the head and greater part of the body bare, but wearing a large white scarf round the loins, and a brilliant red *langouti;* they all raise their paddles simultaneously, and strike the water in regular time, while at the prow and stern are stationed two other slaves, one dexterously managing a long oar which serves as a rudder, the other on the watch to prevent a collision with any other boat. The rowers continually raise a wild, exulting cry, "Ouah! ouah!" while the steersman utters a louder and more prolonged one, which rises above the voices of the rest. Many boats also are to be seen crowded with women, musicians, or parties carrying presents. The *coup d'œil* is certainly charming.

Drawn by M. Sabatier, from a Sketch by M. Mouhot.

SCENE ON THE RIVER MENAM, NEAR BANGKOK.

F 2

From time to time appears, amidst the picturesque assemblage, the boat of some European, always to be recognised by his "chimney-pot" or silk hat.

Drawn by M. Sabatier, from a Sketch by M. Mouhot.

A PRIEST IN HIS BOAT.

All these scenes passed rapidly away, and, before long, I could only hear the distant sounds of the music, and see a few scattered boats adorned with streamers, passing

up or down the river, being often skilfully managed by
girls and very young children, who amused themselves
by racing. It is evident, from the careless gaiety of these
people, that they do not suffer the frightful poverty
but too often met with in our large cities. When his
appetite is satisfied—and, for that, all that is necessary
is a bowl of rice, and some fish seasoned with capsicum
—the Siamese is lively and happy, and sleeps without
care for the morrow; he is, in fact, a kind of Laz-
zaroni.

My friend M. Malherbes accompanied me for a few
hours' sail from Bangkok, and then we parted with a
warm clasp of the hand, and, I confess, not without tears
in both our eyes, trusting that destiny might reunite us
here or elsewhere. My friend's light boat glided rapidly
down the stream; in a few minutes he was out of sight,
and I was again left alone—for how long a period being
quite uncertain. I rarely allow myself to dwell on the
subject; but separations are painful to the traveller who
has left behind him all he holds most dear in the world,
—family, country, home, and friends,—to visit countries
inhospitable, and in many ways dangerous, without
comfort or companionship. It is equally painful to think
that, during long months, his impatient family are living
in anxiety, and forming a thousand conjectures as to his
fate. I know what awaits me, having been warned both
by the missionaries and the natives. During the last
twenty-five years, only one man, as far as I know, a
French priest, has penetrated to the heart of Laos, and

Drawn by M. Théroud, from a Photograph.

THE NEW PALACE OF THE KING OF SIAM, BANGKOK.

he only returned to die in the arms of the good and
venerable prelate, Mgr. Pallegoix. I know the discomfort,
fatigue, and tribulations of all sorts to which I am again
about to expose myself; the want of roads, the difficulty
of finding means of conveyance, and the risk of paying
for the slightest imprudence by a dangerous or even
fatal illness. And how can one be prudent when compelled to submit to the hardest life of the forest, to
suffer many privations, and to brave all inclemencies of
the weather? Nevertheless, my destiny urges me on, and
I trust in the kind Providence which has watched over me
until now.

Only a few hours before my departure from Bangkok,
the mail arrived, and I received news of my dearly loved
family, which consoled me for the misfortune I sustained
in the loss of my collections. Thanks, thanks, my good
friends, for the pleasure you gave me before starting, by
the expression of your warm and constant affection; I
shall not forget you in my solitude.

I shall continue during my journey to take notes of all
my little adventures, very rare, alas! for I am not one
of those travellers who kill a tiger and an elephant at
one shot; the smallest unknown shell or insect is more
interesting to me; however, on occasion, I do not object
to a meeting with the terrible inhabitants of the forest,
and more than one have known the range of my rifle and
the calibre of my balls.

Every evening, enclosed in my mosquito curtains,
either in some cabin or at the foot of a tree, in the jungle

Drawn by M. Rousseau, from a Photograph.

KUN MOTTE, A SIAMESE NOBLE AND SAVANT.

or by the river bank, I shall talk to you, my friends; you shall be the companions of my journey, and it will be my greatest pleasure to confide to you my impressions and thoughts.

Scarcely had my friend M. Malherbes left me, when I discovered, in the bottom of my boat, a box, which he had contrived to place, unknown to me, among my packages; a fresh proof of his kindness, for he had already sent me three cases when I was at Pechaburi. I found it to contain some dozens of Bordeaux, as much cognac, boxes of sardines, biscuits, and a number of other things, which would recall to me, were I ever likely to forget it,

Drawn by M. Catenacci, from a Photograph.

BUILDING FOR THE INCREMATION OF THE QUEEN OF SIAM.

the true and considerate friendship of my countrymen, so valuable to one far from home.

I also carry with me most agreeable *souvenirs* of another excellent friend, Dr. Campbell, of the Royal Navy, attached to the British Consulate; and am very grateful to Sir R. Schomberg, the English Consul, who has shown me much attention and sympathy. Here let me, likewise, express my obligations to Mgr. Pallegoix, to the American Protestant missionaries, and, indeed, to most of the Consuls and resident strangers, who have all shown me kindness; and I would particularly mention the name of M. D'Istria, the new French Consul.

Let me say, in passing, that I am cured of the itch, which I suspect my servants had caught in wandering about the villages, and had communicated to me, in spite of my scrupulous cleanliness.

The banks of the Menam are covered with splendid crops, the periodical inundations rendering them as fertile as those of the Nile. I have four Laotian rowers; one of them was in my service for a month two years ago, and he now begged to be allowed to attend me throughout my journey, telling me I should find him very useful. After a little hesitation I have engaged him, so now I shall have three servants. My good and faithful Phrai has never left me, luckily for me, for I should find it difficult to replace him; and, besides, I am attached to the lad, who is active, intelligent, industrious, and devoted to me. Deng — which means "The Red" — his companion, is another Chinese whom I brought from Pecha-

Drawn by M. Bocourt, from a Photograph.

SAYA VISAT, HEAD OF THE CHRISTIANS AT BANGKOK.

buri. He knows English pretty well; not that incomprehensible jargon of Canton, "You savee one piccey boy, lartel pigeon," &c. (You know a clever boy, &c.) He is very useful to me as interpreter, especially when I wish to comprehend persons who speak with a great piece of betel between their teeth. He is likewise my cook, and shows his skill when we want to add an additional dish to our ordinary fare, which occasionally happens when some unfortunate stag comes within range of my gun, or I bring down a pigeon, or even a monkey, a kind of game not much to my taste, though highly esteemed by my Chinese, as well as wild dog and rat. Every one to his taste.

This attendant of mine has one little defect, but who has not in this world? He now and then takes a drop too much, and I have often found him sucking, through a bamboo cane, the spirit of wine from one of the bottles in which I preserve my reptiles, or laying under contribution the cognac presented to me by my friend Malherbes. A few days ago he was seized with this devouring thirst, and, profiting by my absence for only a few minutes, he opened my chest, and hastily laid hands on the first bottle which presented itself, great part of the contents of which he swallowed at one gulp. I came back just as he was wiping his mouth with his shirt-sleeve, and it would be impossible to describe his contortions and grimaces as he screamed out that he was poisoned.

He had had the bad luck to get hold of my bottle of ink; his face was smeared with it, and his shirt pretty well sprinkled. It was a famous lesson for him, and I think it will be some time before he tries my stores again.

The wages I give at present are ten ticals each per month, which, allowing for exchange, amounts to nearly forty francs per month. This in any other country would be good pay; but here I should find great difficulty in finding any other men to accompany me, were I to offer them a tical a day.

I soon reached the mountains of Nephaburi and Phrabat, with their pure clear atmosphere, the weather being pleasant and a fresh wind blowing. All nature

looks smiling, and I feel exhilarated and happy. At
Bangkok I felt stifled and oppressed. That town does
not awaken my sympathies. Here my heart dilates, and
I could fancy I had grown ever so much taller since I
arrived. Here I can breathe, I live, amid these beautiful hills and woods; in cities I seem to suffocate,
and the sight of so great a number of human beings
annoys me.

I stopped yesterday at Ayuthia to see Father Larmandy, and, after a night passed beneath his hospitable
roof, proceeded on my way towards Pakpriau. The whole
day after our departure we passed by fields and rice-
plantations on both sides of the river. All the country,
till within two miles of Ayuthia, is inundated; there,
only, the ground begins to rise a foot above the waters.
Already, in several places they are beginning to cut the
rice, and in a fortnight the whole population, male and
female, will be busy with the harvest.

At present most of them are availing themselves of
the short time left them to enjoy the " far niente," or
visit the pagodas with offerings to the priests, which
consist principally of fruit and yellow cloth; the latter
intended to afford a supply of raiment for them while
they are travelling; as, during several months of the dry
season, they are allowed to quit their monasteries and
go where they like.

October 20.—Having reached Thama Triestard at
night, we slept at the entrance of the village, and early
this morning I stopped my boat before the house of Khun

PORTICO OF THE AUDIENCE HALL AT BANGKOK.

Drawn by M. Clerget, from a Photograph.

Pakdy, the kind chief who, two years ago, accompanied me to Phrabat. The worthy man was not a little surprised to see me, and could scarcely believe his eyes, for he had heard that I had died at Muang-Kabuic. We soon renewed our acquaintance, and I was pleased to find that his regard for me, especially when stimulated by a glass of cognac, had survived the lapse of time. Poor Khun Pakdy! if I were King of Siam—which Heaven forbid!—I would name you Prince of Phrabat, or rather resign my throne to you.

He gave immediate orders to prepare breakfast for me; then, on finding that I was going to Korat, he remembered that he had promised again to be my companion if I brought him a gun from Bangkok. "If it were only worth three ticals it would do," said he; but seeing only the same percussion guns, "You have not brought me one," he observed; "but never mind, I will go with you all the same." It was only when I told him that I should make but a very short stay at Korat, and intended to proceed farther on into places where he would doubtless have to "tighten his belt," and that I did not wish him to lose his comfortable mandarin's *embonpoint*, that I succeeded in checking his enthusiastic devotion. But when he heard that we should be obliged to sleep among the woods by the light of the stars, he turned the conversation.

As soon as we had breakfasted I returned to my boat to escape his rather too demonstrative conversation, and the noisy eulogiums he continued to pour upon me.

From hence are visible the beautiful chain of hills which extend from Nephaburi, and which, I conjecture, join those of Birmanie and the Deng mountains, which do not appear more than fifteen miles off, and awaken a host of agreeable recollections. I feel sure the fine season has arrived; the air is pure, the sky serene, and the sun shines almost constantly.

Saohaïe, October 22.—I have not yet reached Pakpriau, and already I have met with, and begun to suffer from, the annoyances inevitable in a country like this, inundated during a great part of the year, and in which the means of travelling are so difficult to obtain, particularly when one is burdened with an extra, though indispensable, quantity of luggage.

During the two days I have been here I have lodged in the boat of a Chinese who was at first afraid to receive me; and I may consider myself fortunate in meeting with any resting-place. Yesterday I paid a visit to the governor, who resides in an old hut, repulsively dirty, about two miles from the spot where I landed. Although this is the most important place in Saraburi, this wretched dwelling, and a few scattered huts belonging to agriculturists, are all the houses I have seen; there is no bazaar, and no floating shops. From time to time petty merchants come to sell or exchange salt and other articles of absolute necessity; or a few Chinese with small stocks of *langoutis*, arrack, cloth, Siamese dresses, and bowls, which they barter for skins, horns, or rice. These dealers sometimes go as far as Boatioume.

The current was so strong, that in a quarter of an hour
we reached the residence of the mandarin whose acquaintance I had made on my former journey, and who, in
return for a present I had given him, had promised me,
in the event of my going to Korat, to furnish me with
even a hundred attendants, if I needed as many.   I
announced to him my intention of visiting Khao-Khoc,
fixed upon two years ago by the King of Siam as a
desirable place for a fortress to 'which he might retire,
in case the too active Europeans should seize upon his
capital—which, let me whisper, would be very easy to do,
and would only require a handful of our brave Zouaves
accustomed to an African sun.

I was all the better received by the mandarin, that I
asked for nothing ; for I had already engaged a boat, the
owner of which wished to return to Khao-Khoc in two
days.   I had projected a trip to Patawi, but at this season
the roads are impassable, so that I was forced to abandon
the idea.

A great number of the inhabitants of this province
are natives of Laos, and are principally captives brought
from Vien Chang after the insurrection there.   The provinces of Boatioume and Petchaboune are peopled by
Siamese, for Laos proper only commences at M'Lôm.
Boatioume, Petchaboune, Sôm, and some other provinces
in the north and east, are governed by Siamese mandarins of rank more or less elevated ; that is to say,
several of them have the power of life and death, and are

then considered as viceroys. The most distant provinces belong to the empire of Siam, and form a part of it.

Petchaboune is particularly noted for its tobacco, which is reckoned the best in Siam; and a commerce in this article is carried on with Bangkok in spite of the extreme difficulty of communication; for in the time of the inundations, when boats of some size are able to come up here, the contending against a very strong current is the labour of a month; while in the dry season only very small boats can be used, as, frequently, they have to be dragged over the sand, or carried past the rocks, which in many places cause rapids and obstruct the navigation. This commerce is chiefly in the hands of the Siamese of Petchaboune, who arrive at Pakpriau towards the end of the rainy season, to exchange their tobacco for betel and other articles.

The province of Saraburi is very populous, and in the southern districts a great quantity of rice is produced, but the quality of it is inferior to that of Pechaburi, which is considered very good, and is regularly bought by the Siamese dealers, who afterwards carry it to Bangkok. As is the case all over the country, there is great difficulty in arriving at a correct estimate of the population, which is scattered along the banks of the stream.

Saohaïe is the starting-point for all the caravans going to Korat. Another road, from Muang-Kabuic, also leads to this ancient Cambodian town; but it is little frequented, except by the Laotians of the locality.

Whilst writing I was interrupted by the unexpected visit of the governor, who was on his way to a pagoda to make an offering of dried fruits, and passed an hour in my cabin. He was in a large and elegant pirogue more than 30 metres long, for which I would have given his house and all its appurtenances. He sent for the owner of the boat which was to take me to Khao-Khoc, and gave him some instructions for the chief of that place, adding, " I have sent no letter, because I know that M. Mouhot made himself respected when here two years ago, and will doubtless do the same there." I could not but offer him some small presents in acknowledgment of this slight service, which might or might not be of use to me. I therefore gave him a pair of spectacles mounted in tortoiseshell, a bottle of scent, and one of brandy; and I prepared for him a sedative mixture, as he begged for some medicine for his rheumatism. Happy Raspail! who, with his " system," can assuage suffering even in these distant lands.

In return, he promised to give me a pony when I wanted to go to Korat, besides other useless things; but he will probably forget these promises, for here it is the custom of the rich to accept everything even from the poorest, but very rarely to give away. However, were it not for peculation and presents, how could these mandarins live? Their salary — when they have one — would condemn them to a state of leanness which would not only drive them to despair, but cause them to be looked upon as unsuitable for their places.

VOYAGE TO KHAO-KHOC.—DONG PHYA PHAI (FOREST
OF THE KING OF FIRE).

I am now en route for Khao-Khoc, in the boat of a
Chinese merchant, a worthy person, who, luckily for me,
does not intoxicate himself with opium or arrack.   He
intends going as far as Boatioume, but the current is so
strong that I doubt if he will be able to proceed higher
up the river than Khao-Khoc; for, in spite of his four
rowers, and the aid of my two men—(I sent away my Laotian, who found it too great fatigue to row, and preferred
sleeping and smoking)—we have been nearly carried away
at every bend of the river and at the frequent rapids.

The weather, which I trusted was settled, has changed
during the last three days, and every afternoon, about
four or five o'clock, we have a violent shower.   Last
evening I was seized with a more severe headache than
any I have had since I entered the country, and my first
impression was that I had been attacked by fever, which,
in the rainy season, there is so much cause to dread in
the neighbourhood of Dong Phya Phai.   It proceeded,
however, only from the heat of the sun, to which I had
been all day exposed, and was dissipated by the freshness
of the night air at the prow of the boat.   In the morning
I felt as well as usual.

They tell me that to-morrow I shall see Khao-Khoc, and
I shall not be at all sorry.   The little boat is so encumbered with our united baggage, that the fraction of space
left for me forces me to all sorts of constrained and un-

comfortable positions; and these twelve days of tedious navigation have fatigued me much. And what a place this is! The air is damp, unwholesome, and dreadfully heavy; one's head burns, while one's body is at one time covered with perspiration, and at another a cold shivering comes on.

After four days of excessive toil we entered a gorge through which the river passes, which, even at this season, is here not more than 90 metres wide. Torrents of rain, bursting suddenly upon us, forced us to stop rowing, and take refuge under our roof of leaves. The rain lasted all night, and a wretched night it was for the poor men, who, having yielded to me the front of the boat, were all crammed together in the cabin, and, after all their fatigues under a burning sun, were unable to obtain a moment's sleep, but lay groaning under the suffocating atmosphere and the attacks of legions of mosquitoes.

At daybreak about a hundred strokes of the oar brought us past a new bend in the river, and we found ourselves before Khao-Khoc. This place has, in my humble opinion, been badly chosen by the kings of Siam for their stronghold and retreat in case of an European invasion of the south. In the event of this occurring, they would abandon Bangkok; and, certainly, as whoever possesses that town is master of the whole country, no one would be likely to come and molest the kings in their solitude.

Two or three miles below Khao-Khoc I observed a kind of landing-place, and a house of mediocre appearance, bearing the pretentious appellation of palace, although

built only of leaves and bamboo. This is Rabat Moi.
At Khao-Khoc, although the second king often visits it,
there is no landing-place, nor even steps cut in the
steep banks to aid the ascent.

Immediately after landing I set off to look for a lodging,
having been informed that I should find numerous vacant
houses belonging to mandarins, amongst which I might
make my choice. My men and I hunted amid the
brushwood, often sinking up to our knees in mud, but
could discover only seven or eight Laotian huts, the
inhabitants of which form the nucleus of the population
of this future stronghold, now peaceful and hospitable
agriculturists, who would be deeply afflicted, and still
more terrified, if ever their echoes should repeat the roar
of cannon and varied sounds of war. As for the royal
habitations, I could not reach them, for the whole ground,
excepting a strip about fifty feet broad next the river, is
a swamp; and the narrow paths are obstructed by bushes
and tall grass, which had had time to grow during the six
or eight months that have elapsed since the King has
visited the place.

Not being able to find a lodging, some men from the
village joined us, and we all set to work to cut down bamboos, with which to construct one, which was soon accomplished; and in this hut, open to every wind, we took up
our abode.

I was told that a white elephant had just been taken
in Laos, and had been sent off to Bangkok under the
care of a mandarin.

All the inhabitants of the village, amounting perhaps to about fifty, have brought their children to me, begging for remedies; some for fevers, others for dysentery or rheumatism. I have not heard of any cases of leprosy here, as at Khao-Tchioulaü, but the children are repulsively dirty; they are covered with a coating of filth, which makes them resemble little negroes, and the greater number of them are shaking with fever.

The site of my hut is in a valley, formed by a belt of mountain-chains, running from Nephaburi and Phrabat, and connected with those of the peninsula and of Birmah. Mount Khoc is distant a kilometre from the left bank of the river, and stretches out in the form of a semicircle, afterwards joining the mountains which run eastward towards Korat, and M'Lôm, and Thibet. Facing Mount Khoc, other mountains rise abruptly from the right bank, and then extend in an easterly direction.

As soon as my dwelling was finished, which was neither a long nor a costly job, we slung up three hammocks, and then betook ourselves to prepare a place for insect-catching, the end of the rainy season being the best time for this work. We accordingly cut down a great number of trees, a hard and painful task in this climate, where the sun, drawing up the humidity from all the surrounding marshes, makes one feel as if in a stove or hothouse; but our labours have been abundantly repaid by a rich harvest of specimens. Beetles of the longicorn tribe abound here; and to-day I have filled a box with more than a thousand new or rare insects. I have even been

Drawn by M. Sabatier, from a Sketch by M. Mouhot.

LAOTIAN HOUSE.

fortunate enoguh to replace some of the more valuable
kinds which were destroyed or injured by sea-water on
board the 'Sir James Brooke.' The villagers come every
day to bring me "beasts," as they call them, grasshoppers, scorpions, serpents, tortoises, &c., all presented
to me at the end of a stick.

The sanitary condition of the place is dreadful. The rains are now less abundant, and the river has fallen more than twenty feet. They tell me that at Boatioume it is so narrow that the branches of the trees on the two banks touch and form an arch overhead. The mountains are of calcareous rock, and are covered with a fertile vegetation, but everywhere bear the traces of the water which anciently covered them. From the top you can imagine the former limits of the ocean, and see that the plain to the south was then submerged, and that all these heights formed capes or islands. I found close to their base, under a stratum of soil, banks of fossil coral and sea-shells in a good state of preservation.

The north wind now makes itself frequently felt, although the south-east and south-west winds resume their sway at times, and bring back the rain; but the heat of the nights gradually diminishes, and now, after three o'clock in the morning, I can bear a covering, and am glad to wrap myself in my burnous. My two men suffer occasionally from attacks of intermittent fever, and often complain of cold in the stomach; indeed, death lays so many snares for us here, that he who escapes may think himself lucky.

At last we breathe a pure and delicious air. It is now mid winter; since the day before yesterday a fresh north wind has blown, and at night the thermometer has gone back to 18° centigrade. All the evening I have been walking by the river, wrapped in a warm burnous, with the hood up; and this is a pleasure I have not enjoyed since I was at Phrabat, two years ago.

One must have passed sleepless nights, suffocating with the extreme heat, in order to appreciate the comfort of sleeping under a woollen covering, and, above all, without the necessity of waging incessant war on the dreadful mosquitoes. Phrai and Deng wear their whole wardrobe both night and day, and I have seen them dressed in red flannel and with felt hats, when you might take them for Garibaldians, as far, that is to say, as their costume is concerned, for their appearance otherwise is far from war-like; however, they are not wanting in a kind of courage which has its own merit. They dance and sing round a good fire, and open their eyes with astonishment when I tell them that I have seen rivers larger than the Menam frozen over so hard that the heaviest vehicles could go upon them with safety,* and others on which whole oxen have been roasted;† and that men and animals often die of cold.

My little "Tine-Tine" says nothing, but creeps under my counterpane and sleeps at his ease; only if Phrai torments him by lifting the cover, he shows his teeth. Ungrateful being that I am, I have not yet spoken of this little companion who is so faithful and attached to me—of this pretty "King Charles," whom I brought from home. All the Siamese, and especially those who have no

---

* In Russia, on the Neva.   † On the Thames at London.

children, are very fond of the little creature, notwithstanding their general aversion for dogs. Theirs, however, are usually half savage. I much fear that my poor
dog will come to an untimely end, and be trampled under
foot by some elephant, or devoured at a mouthful by a
tiger.

For the last few days we have feasted; our provisions
were beginning to fail, but the fish are now coming up
the river, and we take them by hundreds. Certainly
they are not much larger than sardines, but in an hour
we took six or eight basketfuls, and my two boys have
enough to do to cut off their heads and salt them.

All the children of the neighbourhood, most of whom
are still kept at the breast, come frequently to bring me
insects, in exchange for a button or cigarette, for it is a
common thing for them to leave their mother's breast to
smoke. Were they not so dirty, they would be nice-
looking; but I am afraid of touching them, lest I should
again catch the itch.

The Laotian is as superstitious as the Cambodian, and
perhaps more so than the Siamese. If a person falls ill
of a fever, or, indeed, is ever so slightly indisposed, they
believe it to be owing to a demon who has entered his
body. If any matter in which they are engaged goes
wrong, or an accident happens when hunting, fishing, or
cutting wood, it is the fault of the demon. In their houses
they carefully preserve some object, generally a simple
piece of wood, or some parasitic plant, whose form they
fancy bears a resemblance to some part of the human

body; and this is constituted their household god, and prevents evil spirits from entering, or, at least, causes them speedily to depart.

Every day we go out on our collecting expeditions; but while we are seeking insects or birds, the sound of our voices, or the report of our guns, repeated by the mountain echoes, brings forth the wild beasts from their dens. Yesterday, after a long and fatiguing excursion, during which we had killed some birds and one or two monkeys, we were returning home quite worn out, when we reached a small clearing in the forest, and here I told my two boys * to take a little repose at the foot of a tree, while I went to hunt for insects.

Suddenly I heard a sound as of some animal gliding through the thick underwood. I looked round, at the same time loading my gun, and then crept quietly back to the tree where my servants lay asleep, when I perceived a large and beautiful leopard taking his spring to clear the brushwood, and pounce upon one of them as he lay all unconscious. I fired, the shot striking the animal in the right shoulder. He gave a tremendous leap, and rolled over among the bushes, which much embarrassed his movements. However, he was but wounded, and still dangerous, if my second ball did not kill, or at least cripple him. I fired again, and hit him between the shoulders; the ball lodged in the heart, and he fell dead almost instantaneously. The terror of my two poor fol-

---

* The word "boy" is generally used by me to denote a male servant.

Drawn by M. Bocourt, from a Sketch by M. Mouhot.

lowers, suddenly awakened by the report of my gun
so close to their ears, was only equalled by their pleasure when they saw the creature extended lifeless before
them.

Another year has flown, a year chequered for me, as
for others, with joy, anxiety, and trouble; and to-day my
thoughts turn especially to the few who are dear to me.
From more than one loving heart arise, I feel sure, on
this day, good wishes for the poor traveller, and from no
one more warmly than from you, my dear father. You
long for my return; so writes my brother in his last
letter, forwarded to me from Bangkok. But I am only
commencing my new campaign; would it be like a good
soldier to leave on the eve of the engagement? I am at
the gates of the infernal regions, for so the Laotians and
Siamese designate this forest, and I have no spell to
terrify the demons which inhabit it, neither tiger's teeth
nor stunted stag-horn; nothing but my faith in and love
for God. If I must die here, where so many other wan-
derers have left their bones, I shall be ready when my
hour comes.

The profound stillness of this forest, and its luxuriant
tropical vegetation, are indescribable, and at this midnight
hour impress me deeply. The sky is serene, the air
fresh, and the moon's rays only penetrate here and there,
through the foliage, in patches, which appear on the
ground like pieces of white paper dispersed by the wind.
Nothing breaks the silence but a few dead leaves rustling to the earth, the murmur of a brook which flows

over its pebbly bed at my feet, and the frogs answering
each other on either side, and whose croaking resembles
the hoarse barking of a dog. Now and then I can distinguish the flapping of the bats, attracted by the flame of
the torch which is fastened to a branch of the tree under
which my tiger-skin is spread ; or, at longer intervals, the
cry of some panther calling to its mate, and responded
to from the tree-tops by the growling of the chimpanzees, whose rest the sound has disturbed.

With a sabre in one hand and a torch in the other,
Phrai pursues the fishes in the stream, and he and his
shadow reflected on the rocks and water, as he stands
there making sudden darts, and crying out "hit" or
"missed," might easily be mistaken by the natives for
demons.

I cannot shake off a feeling of sadness which a few
hours of sleep and a long chase to-morrow will probably
dissipate ; yet, at the moment, I cannot forbear asking
myself, how will this year end for me? Shall I accomplish
all I have in view? shall I preserve that health without
which I can do nothing? and can I surmount all the
difficulties which oppose themselves to me, and of which
not the least is the difficulty of finding any means of
conveyance?

And you, my dear father, be not too anxious as to my
fate, but preserve that tranquillity, hope, and love of God,
which alone can make men strong and great: with this
help and support, our reunion will not be long delayed.
Courage then, and hope ! our perseverance and efforts will

be recompensed. And thou, invisible link, which, in spite of distance, unites hearts, bear to all those dear to me a thousand embraces, and fill them with all those thoughts which at all times give me strength, and supply joy and consolation in my saddest and most dreary hours. To all, then, a happy new year! and may I bring back safe and sound my poor young followers, who have been such faithful and devoted companions; and who, although already rather weakened by fever and incipient dysentery, are still full of gaiety and energy, and as much attached to me as ever.

Five or six leagues north of Khao-Khoc is Mount Sake, and two miles farther all habitations cease, and there is complete solitude as far as Boatioume. The banks become more and more picturesque; here are calcareous rocks, covered in places with a ferruginous crust, and whence flow streams endowed with petrifying properties, while hills, rising abruptly to a great height, contain grottoes ornamented by stalactites; there, are beds of sand, islands on which sport in the sun a crowd of iguanas; everywhere, a rich vegetation, mingled with tufts of bamboo, in which fight and squabble the chimpanzees, on whom Phrai exercises his skill, and which afford him a delicious repast.

We embarked in a very light pirogue, and, during the first day, passed the boats from Petchaboune, which had left Khao-Khoc the night before; for the current is still rapid, even though the water is so low that in many

places you have to drag the boat over the sand, and poles
have to be used instead of oars.

Tigers, which are rare at Khao-Khoc, are more common
in the environs of Boatioume, where they destroy many
of the cattle.

CEMETERY AT BANGKOK.

Drawn by M. Catenacci, from a Photograph.

CHAPTER XVII.

On the 28th February, 1861, I arrived at the town of Chaiapume, and presented myself before the governor to request his permission to hire some elephants or oxen to enable me to continue my journey. I showed him my French passport, and also gave him the letter from Khrom Luang, and another from the Governor of Korat; but all in vain. He replied that, if I wanted oxen or elephants, there were plenty in the forest. I might easily have done without the assistance of this functionary, and procured animals from people in the village; but they would have made me pay two or three times the ordinary price, and my purse was too slenderly filled to allow of my submitting to this extortion, which would probably be repeated at every station.

The only thing left me to do, therefore, was to retrace my steps, and, leaving one of my servants at Korat with

my baggage, to return to Bangkok and claim aid from the
consul, the ministers, or the king himself; for there is
a treaty between the Governments of Siam and France,
concluded by M. de Montigny, which obliges the king to
afford assistance and protection to the French, and especially to missionaries and naturalists. It was a sad loss
of time for me, and might occasion me serious inconvenience; for, if I were delayed, the rainy season might
surprise me in the midst of the forests before I could
reach a healthier region, and the consequences might be
fatal. However, I was forced to submit, and I returned
to Bangkok.

It cost me some time and trouble, and I found it
needful to make some valuable presents before I succeeded in my object; but at last I obtained more
stringent letters to the governors of the provinces of Laos,
and left Bangkok once more, after having experienced
for a fortnight the kind hospitality of my friend Dr.
Campbell, one of the best men I ever met with: his
goodness, friendliness, and British frankness, won my
heart and my esteem.

After all this loss of time and great expense I went
again to Korat, where I was well received by the governor;
and he gave me, in addition to my other letters, one for
the mandarins of all provinces under his jurisdiction,
commanding them to furnish me with as many oxen and
elephants as I might require. The greater part of the
inhabitants, with Phrai at their head, came out to meet

Drawn by M. Catenacci, from a Photograph.

BUILDING ERECTED AT THE FUNERAL OF THE QUEEN OF SIAM.

me, and several gave me presents—sacks of rice, fish, fruits, or tobacco, all in abundance.

Speaking to me of his journey to Korat, Dr. House, the most enterprising of the American missionaries at Bangkok, and the only white man who has penetrated so far for many years, told me that he found everything disappointing. I could have said the same, if, like him, I had started with any illusions; but I had a good idea of the forest, which I had already passed at several points, as at Phrabat, Khao Khoc, and Kenne Khoé, and amidst whose deleterious shades I had already spent one night. Nor did I expect to find towns amidst its thick and almost impenetrable masses of foliage, through which one can distinguish nothing beyond a distance of a few feet.

I have lately again passed ten successive nights in this forest. During our journey through it, all the Chinese in the caravan, happy to find themselves still among the living, at every halting-place hastened to draw from their baskets an abundance of provisions wherewith to make a comfortable repast: then choosing, for want of an altar, some large tree, they laid out their dishes, lighted their matches, burned a quantity of gilt paper, and, kneeling down, murmured their prayers. Both on entering and leaving the forest they erected a shed of leaves and sticks interwoven, and raised upon four bamboo stakes, intended as a sort of chapel, in which they placed a number of offerings, in order, as they said, to drive away demons and save them from death.

As for the Laotians, I have found them, although superstitious, very courageous, especially those who traverse this forest eight or ten times a year. Some of them even venture to awake the "King of Fire" by bringing down game or shooting at robbers: yet death, even in the best season, carries off one or two out of every ten who travel here. I think the number of those who fall victims to this terrible journey must be considerable in the rainy season, when every torrent overflows its bounds; the whole soil is soaked, the pathways nothing but bogs, and the rice-grounds covered with several feet of water. After five or six days' walking through all this, with feet in the mud, the body in a profuse perspiration, and breathing a fetid atmosphere, hot as a stove and reeking with putrid miasma, what wonder that many sink and die?

Two Chinese in our caravan arrived at Korat in a frightful state of fever. One I was able to save by administering quinine in good time, but the other, who appeared the strongest, was dead almost as soon as I heard of his being ill.

We halted at five o'clock in the evening and encamped on a little hill, where, in the absence of grass, our poor oxen could only appease their hunger with leaves from the shrubs. The river, which flows down from these hills, is the same which runs near Korat, and on the opposite bank was encamped another caravan with more than 200 oxen,

In a gorge of the mountain, and on the almost inaccessible heights, I found a small tribe of Karians who formerly inhabited the environs of Patawi, and who, for the sake of preserving their independence, live here in seclusion; for the dread of fever prevents the Siamese from penetrating to their haunts. They have neither temples nor priests; they raise magnificent crops of rice, and cultivate several kinds of bananas, which are only found among tribes of the same origin. Many of the inhabitants of the neighbouring districts appear to be ignorant of their very existence. It is true they are of migratory habits; others say that they pay a tribute in gum-lac, but the Governor of Korat and several chiefs of the province of Saraburi, seemed to me profoundly ignorant on the subject.

The following morning, an hour before sunrise, after having counted the oxen dead from fatigue and exhaustion, which would serve for food to the wild beasts, and repacked our goods, we resumed our march. Towards eleven o'clock, having quitted Dong Phya Phai, we entered a long tract of ground filled with brushwood and tall grass and swarming with deer, and here, before long, we halted near a stream.

The next day, after making a détour of some miles to the north to find a pass, we ascended a new chain of hills running parallel to the last, and covered with blocks of sandstone; and here the vegetation was extremely luxuriant. The air was fresh and pure, and, thanks to repeated ablutions in the running streams, those of the

party whose feet had suffered most at the beginning of
the journey found them greatly improved.

The monkeys and hornbills began to be heard again,
and I killed several pheasants and peacocks, and an eagle,
on which our guides feasted. Beyond these mountains
the soil becomes sandy again and vegetation scanty. We
encamped once more on the banks of the river of Korat,
300 metres from a village dignified by the name of chief
town of the district.

The last range of hills which we crossed still displays
itself like a sombre rampart, above which tower the
dome-like and pyramidal summits of others farther in the
distance.

Our guides are all Laotians from the neighbourhood
of Korat, and their leader is unremitting in his care and
attention towards me. Every evening he prepares my
place for the night, levelling the ground and cutting down
branches which he covers with leaves, and I am thus
raised from the earth and protected from the dew. These
guides lead a hard life, tramping in all seasons along
these wretched roads, having scarcely time, morning and
evening, to swallow a little rice, and having but little
sleep at nights, tormented by ants, and exposed to the
attacks of robbers, against whom they have constantly to
be on their guard.

Every day we met one or two caravans of from eighty
to a hundred oxen, laden with stag and panther skins,
raw silk from Laos, *langoutis* of cotton and silk, peacocks'

Drawn by E. Thérond, from a Sketch by M. Mouhot.

BIVOUAC OF M. MOUHOT IN THE FORESTS OF LAOS.

tails, ivory, elephants' bones, and sugar; but this latter article is scarce.

The country presented much the same kind of aspect for four days after leaving the forest. We passed through several considerable villages, in one of which, Sikiéou, are kept six hundred oxen belonging to the king. The journey from Keng-Koë to Korat occupied ten days. The Chinese quarter of this latter town contains sixty or seventy houses, built with bricks dried in the sun, and surrounded by palisades nine feet high, and as strong as those of a rampart.

These precautions are very necessary, for Korat is a nest of robbers and assassins, the resort of all the scum of the Laotian and Siamese races. Bandits and vagrants, escaped from slavery or from prison, gather here like the vultures and wolves which follow armies and caravans It is not that they enjoy complete immunity, for the governor, son of Bodine, the general who conquered Battambong and the revolted provinces, is viceroy of the state, has absolute power of life and death, and is, they say, very severe, cutting off a head or a hand with little compunction. But still it is Siamese justice, "non inviola:" there are neither gendarmes nor police; the person robbed must himself arrest the offender and bring him before the judge. Even his neighbour will give no assistance in the capture.

It was necessary to look out for a dwelling, and I applied to the Chinese, hoping to find a house rather larger than the one where Phrai had settled himself

with my luggage, and I had not much difficulty in
doing so.

At the end of the Chinese quarter, which is the bazaar,
commences the town properly so called, which is enclosed
by a wall of ferruginous stone and sandstone, brought
from the distant mountain—a work which I at once recognised as that of the Khmerdôm.   Within is the residence
of the governor and those of the other authorities, several
pagodas, a caravanserai, and a number of other houses.
A stream of water, eight metres wide, crosses the town
and is bordered by little plantations of betel and cocoa-nut
trees.

The real town of Korat does not contain more than
five or six thousand inhabitants, including six hundred
Chinese.   The Siamese I found impertinent and disagreeable, the Chinese friendly and kind.   It was the contrast
between civilization and barbarism—between the mass of
vices engendered by idleness, and the good qualities cultivated by habits of industry.   Unfortunately, however,
the money acquired by these indefatigable merchants
furnishes the means of gratifying their baneful propen-
sities, gambling and opium-smoking.

Stretched on a carpet in some shed they lie, thin and
emaciated-looking, playing at cards, or else, plunged in
a kind of lethargy, they surrender themselves to the
influence of the seductive drug in their dark and filthy
hovels, lighted only by a single lamp.   Yet, in spite of
their gambling, most of them grow rich, though they
generally begin poor, and with goods lent to them by

some countryman from his shop, and a few voyages frequently suffice to make their fortunes.

The merchants who bring silk, which, though of
inferior quality, is an important article of commerce,
come from Laos, Oubone, Bassac, and Jasoutone.

The entire province of Korat comprises a number of
villages, and more than eleven towns, some containing
as many as fifty or sixty thousand inhabitants. This little
state is simply tributary, but on condition of furnishing
the first and most considerable levy of men in case
of war.

The tribute consists of gold or silver, and in several
districts, amongst others those of Chaiapume and Poukiéan, amounts to eight ticals a head. Some pay in
silk, which is weighed by the mandarins, who, as with
the cardamom at Pursat, and the *langoutis* at Battambong,
buy a further quantity on their own account, and at their
own price.

Elephants are numerous, and a great many are brought
from the north of Laos as far as Muang-Lang. I should
think there must be more than a thousand of these
animals in each province. Oxen and buffaloes were
formerly exceedingly cheap, but the distemper, which
has for some years committed great ravages among the
herds, has doubled or tripled the price. They are brought
southward from the extreme north of East Laos, and even
from the frontiers of Tonquin.

I went to see a temple nine miles east of Korat, called
Penom-Wat. It is very remarkable, although much in-

ferior in grandeur and beauty to those of Ongcor. The
second governor lent me a pony and guide, and, after
crossing extensive rice plantations, under a vertical and
fiery sun, we reached the spot to which my curiosity
had attracted me, and which, like an oasis, could be recognised a long way off by the freshness of its cocoa-trees
and its rich verdure. I did not arrive there, however,
without having taken an involuntary bath. In crossing
the Tekon, which is nearly four feet deep, I, in order to
escape a wetting, tried to imitate Franconi, by standing
on my saddle; but, unluckily, according to the custom
of the country, this was fastened on by two pieces of
string, and in the middle of the stream it turned and
sent me head foremost into the water. But there was
no worse result from the accident than my having to
remain for half an hour afterwards dressed in Siamese
fashion.

Penom-Wat is an interesting temple 36 metres long by
40 wide, and the plan resembles a cross with tolerable
exactness. It is composed of two pavilions, with vaulted
stone roofs and elegant porticoes. The roofs are from
seven to eight metres in height, the gallery three metres
wide in the interior, and the walls a metre thick. At each
façade of the gallery are two windows with twisted bars.

This temple is built of red and grey sandstone, coarse
in the grain, and in some places beginning to decay. On
one of the doors is a long inscription, and above are
sculptures representing nearly the same subjects as those
at Ongcor and Bassette.

RUINS AT PAN BRANG, CHAIAPUME.

Drawn by M. Catenacci, from a Sketch by M. Mouhot.

In one of the pavilions are several Buddhist idols in stone, the largest of which is 2 metres 50 centimetres high, and actually covered with rags.

You might here easily imagine yourself among the ruins of Ongcor. There is the same style of architecture, the same taste displayed, the same immense blocks polished like marble, and so beautifully fitted together, that I can only compare it to the joining and planing of so many planks.

The whole building is, without doubt, the work of the Khmerdôm, and not an imitation, and must be as old as the illustrious reigns which have left the traces of their grandeur in different parts of the empire. The exterior is not equal to the interior. Penom was the temple of the Queen, so say the Siamese; that of the King, her husband, is at Pimaïe, a district about 30 miles east of Korat.

To consult any existing maps of Indo-China for my guidance in the interior of Laos would have been a folly, no traveller, at least to my knowledge, having penetrated into east Laos, or published any authentic information respecting it. To question the natives about places more than a degree distant would have been useless. My desire was to reach Louang-Prabang by land, to visit the northern tribes dependent on that state, and then again to descend the Mekong to Cambodia. Setting out from Korat, I had but to proceed northwards as long as I found practicable roads and inhabited places; and if I could not go by a direct route to Louang-Prabang, I should only have to diverge to the east when I judged it necessary.

I was again delayed a few days at Korat before I could obtain elephants, in consequence of the absence of the viceroy; but on his return he received me in a friendly manner, and gave me a letter of introduction to the governors of the provinces under his jurisdiction. He likewise furnished me with two elephants for myself and servants, and two others for my baggage; so at last I was able to set out for Chaiapume. Before I started, the Chinese with whom I lodged gave me the following advice: — "Buy a tam-tam, and, wherever you halt, sound it. They will say, 'Here is an officer of the king;' robbers will keep aloof, and the authorities will respect you. If this does not answer, the only plan to get rid of all the difficulties which the Laotian officials will be sure to throw in your way is to have a good stick, the longer the better. Try it on the back of any mandarin who makes the least resistance and will not do what you wish. Put all delicacy aside. Laos is not like a country of the whites. Follow my advice, and you will find it good."

I was, however, much better received on my second visit to Chaiapume, and required neither tam-tam nor cane. The sight of the elephants and the order from the viceroy of Korat made the mandarin as supple as a glove, and he provided me with other elephants for a visit to some ruins existing about 3 leagues north of the town, at the foot of a mountain. The superstitious Laotians say that these ruins contain gold, but that every one who has sought for it has been struck with madness.

Two roads lead from Chaiapume to Poukiéan; the first, across the mountains, is so excessively difficult, that I decided on taking the other, which, however, is much longer. The first day we started at 1 o'clock, and reached a village named Non Jasiea, where we were overtaken by a fearful storm. We sheltered ourselves as well as we could, and arrived before night at the entrance of a forest where we slept.

For five days we were compelled to remain in the forest on account of the weather; it rained great part of the day, and throughout the night; the torrents over-flowed, and the earth was nothing but a sea of mud. I never in my life passed such wretched nights, as all the time we had to remain with our wet clothes on our backs, and I cannot describe what we suffered. The snow hurricanes, so frequent in Russia, and which nearly killed me when in that country, seemed trifling miseries in comparison. My poor Phrai was seized with a dreadful fever two days before reaching Poukiéan, and I myself felt very ill.

The passage of the mountains was easy, and the ascent very gradual; blocks of stone obstruct the road in various parts, but our oxen and elephants made their way without much difficulty. I had bought a horse for myself at Korat.

The vegetation, though not thick, is beautiful: the trees, many of which are resinous, are slender, the stems

being seldom more than a foot or two in diameter, and
often 25, 30, and even 40 metres in height. Under their
shade are to be seen great numbers of deer, and tigers
are not uncommonly met with. In the mountains are
many elephants and rhinoceros. We found immense beds
of stone, and in some places saw small brick buildings
containing idols. During the journey one of my chests
was thrown to the ground by the movements of the
elephant, and broken to pieces, as, unfortunately, were
all the contents, consisting of instruments, and bottles of
spirit of wine containing serpents and fishes.

Poukiéan is a smaller village than Chaiapume. I met
with a friendly reception from the governor, who had
just returned from Korat, and had heard of my intended
journey. Poverty and misery reign here; we cannot find
even a fish to purchase; nothing but rice; and as soon
as my faithful Phrai is on his legs again we shall leave
the place.

Tine-Tine attracts the most attention. The people
do not, as we pass, cry out first, "Look at the white
stranger," but "A little dog!" and every one runs to see
this curiosity. My turn comes afterwards.

In these mountains the Laotians make offerings to
the local genii of sticks and stones.

The same chain of hills which, from the banks of
the Menam, in the province of Saraburi, extends on one
side to the southern extremity of the peninsula, on the
other encircles Cambodia like a belt, runs along the
shores of the gulf, and forms a hundred islands; stretches

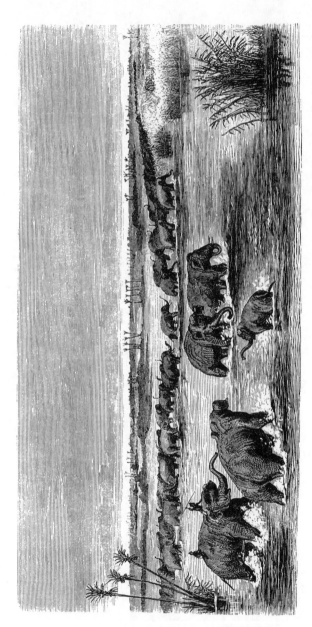

ELEPHANTS BATHING.

Drawn by M. Bocourt, from a Sketch by M. Mouhot

directly northwards, continually increasing in size, and spreading its ramifications towards the east, where they form a hundred narrow valleys, the streams flowing through which empty themselves into the Mekong.

The rains had commenced on my second entrance into Dong Phya Phai, and I was greeted by a perfect deluge, which continued with intervals of two or three days; but this did not stop me, although I had to pass through a country still more to be dreaded than this forest, and where no one goes willingly.

In all this mountainous region elephants are the only means of transport. Every village possesses some, several as many as fifty or a hundred. Without this intelligent animal no communication would be possible during seven months of the year, while, with his assistance, there is scarcely a place to which you cannot penetrate.

The elephant ought to be seen on these roads, which I can only call devil's pathways, and are nothing but ravines, ruts two or three feet deep, full of mud; sometimes sliding with his feet close together on the wet clay of the steep slopes, sometimes half buried in mire, an instant afterwards mounted on sharp rocks, where one would think a Blondin alone could stand; striding across enormous trunks of fallen trees, crushing down the smaller trees and bamboos which oppose his progress, or lying down flat on his stomach that the cornacs (drivers) may the easier place the saddle on his back; a hundred times a day making his way, without injuring them, be-

tween trees where there is barely room to pass; sounding
with his trunk the depth of the water in the streams or
marshes; constantly kneeling down and rising again, and
never making a false step. It is necessary, I repeat, to
see him at work like this in his own country, to form
any idea of his intelligence, docility, and strength, or how
all those wonderful joints of his are adapted to their
work—fully to understand that this colossus is no rough
specimen of nature's handiwork, but a creature of especial
amiability and sagacity, designed for the service of
man.

We must not, however, exaggerate his merits. Probably the saddles used by the Laotians are capable of
great improvement; but I must admit that the load of
three small oxen, that is to say, about 250 or 300 pounds,
is all that I ever saw the largest elephants carry easily,
and 18 miles is the longest distance they can accomplish with an ordinary load. Ten or twelve miles are the
usual day's work. With four, five, or sometimes seven
elephants, I travelled over all the mountain country from
the borders of Laos to Louang-Prabang, a distance of
nearly 500 miles.

All this eastern portion, with the exception of a few
villages filled with "black-bellied savages" — so called
from the manner in which they tattoo themselves—is
inhabited by the same race, the "white-bellied Laotians,"
who call themselves Laos, and are known by this
name to all the Siamese, Chinese, and surrounding
nations.

CARAVAN OF ELEPHANTS CROSSING THE MOUNTAINS OF LAOS.

Drawn by M. Bocourt, from a Sketch by M. Mouhot.

The black-bellied or western Laotians are called by
their eastern brethren by the same name which, in Siam
and Cambodia, is bestowed on the Annamites, Zuène,
Lao-Zuène. The only thing that distinguishes them is,
that they tattoo the under part of the body, principally
the thighs, and frequently wear the hair long and knotted
on the top of their heads. Their language is nearly
the same, and differs little from the Siamese and Eastern
Laos, except in the pronunciation, and in certain expres-
sions no longer in use among the former.

I soon found that, but for the letter from the governor
of Korat, I should have met everywhere with the same
reception as at Chaiapume; however, this missive was
very positively worded. Wherever I went, the authorities
were ordered to furnish me with elephants, and supply
me with all necessary provisions, as if I were a king's
envoy. I was much amused to see these petty provincial
chiefs executing the orders of my servants, and evidently
in dread lest, following the Siamese custom, I should use
the stick.

One of my men, to give himself importance, had tied
one of these bugbears to the arms which he carried, and
the sight of it alone sufficed, with the sound of the tam-
tam, to inspire fear, whilst small presents judiciously
distributed, and a little money to the cornacs, procured
me the sympathy of the people.

Most of the villages are situated about a day's journey
from one another, but frequently you have to travel for
three or four days without seeing a single habitation,

and then you have no alternative but to sleep in the jungle. This might be pleasant in the dry season, but, during the rains, nothing can give an idea of the sufferings of travellers at night, under a miserable shelter of leaves hastily spread over a rough framework of branches, assaulted by myriads of mosquitoes attracted by the light of the fires and torches, by legions of ox-flies, which, after sunset, attack human beings as well as elephants, and by fleas so minute as to be almost invisible, which assemble about you in swarms, and whose bites are excessively painful, and raise enormous blisters.

To these enemies add the leeches, which, after the least rain, come out of the ground, scent a man twenty feet off, and hasten to suck his blood with wonderful avidity. To coat your legs with a layer of lime when travelling is the only way to prevent them covering your whole body.

I had left Bangkok on the 12th of April, and on the 16th of May I reached Leuye, the chief town of a district belonging to two provinces, Petchaboune and Lôme. It is situated in a narrow valley, like all the towns and villages through which I have passed since I left Chaiapume.

This is the district of Siam richest in minerals; one of its mountains contains immense beds of magnetic iron of a remarkably good quality. Others yield antimony, argentiferous copper, and tin. The iron only is worked, and this population, half agriculturists, half artisans, furnish spades and cutlasses to all the surrounding pro-

CORDIER

Drawn by M. Thérond, from a Photograph.

"PARK" OF ELEPHANTS, EXTERNAL VIEW.

vinces, even beyond Korat. Yet they have neither foundries nor steam-engines, and it is curious to see how little it costs an iron-worker to establish himself in a hole about a yard and a half square hollowed out close to the mountain.

They pile up and smelt the mineral with charcoal: the liquified iron deposits itself in the bottom of the cavity, and there hollows out a bed, whence they withdraw it when the operation is completed, and carry it home. There, in another cavity they make a fire, which a child keeps alive by means of a couple of bellows, which are simply two trunks of hollow trees buried in the ground, and upon which play alternately two stopples surrounded by cotton. These are fixed to a small board, and have long sticks for handles, to which are attached two bamboo hollow canes which conduct the air into the cavity.

In several localities I discovered auriferous sand, but only in small quantity. In some of the villages the inhabitants employ their leisure time in searching for gold, but they told me that they hardly gained by this work sufficient to pay for the rice they ate.

In this journey I have passed through sixty villages, numbering from twenty to fifty houses each; and six small towns, with a population of from four to six hundred inhabitants. I have made a map of all this part of the country.

Since leaving Korat I have crossed five large rivers which fall into the Mekon, the bed of which is more or less full according to the season. The first of these, 35 metres wide, is called the Menam Chie, lat. 15° 45′; second, the Menam Leuye, 90 metres wide, lat. 18° 3′; third, the Menam Ouan, at Kenne-Tao, 100 metres in width, lat. 18° 35′; fourth, the Nam Pouye, 60 metres, lat. 19°; fifth, the Nam-Houn, 80 or 100 metres wide, lat. 20°.

The Chie is navigable, as far up as the latitude of Korat, from May to December; the Leuye, the Ouan, and the Houn are only navigable for a very short distance on account of their numerous rapids; neither is there any water-communication between the Menam and the Mekon in Laos or Cambodia, the mountains which separate them forming insurmountable obstacles to cutting canals.

The Laotians much resemble the Siamese: a different pronunciation and slow manner of speech being all that distinguishes their language. The women wear petticoats, and keep their hair long, which, when combed, gives the younger ones a more interesting appearance than those have who live on the banks of the Menam; but, at an advanced age, with their unkempt locks thrown negligently over one temple, and their immense goîtres, which they admire, they are repulsively ugly.

Little commerce is carried on in this part of Laos. The Chinese inhabiting Siam do not come as far, owing to the enormous expense of transporting all their merchandise on elephants. Nearly every year a caravan arrives from Yunnan and Quangsee, composed of about

LAOTIAN GIRLS. Drawn by M. Bocourt, from a Photograph.

a hundred persons and several hundred mules.   Some go to Kenne Thao, others to M. Nâne and Chieng Maï.   They arrive in February, and leave in March or April.

The mulberry does not thrive in these mountains; but in some localities this tree is cultivated for the sake of furnishing food to a particular insect which lives upon its leaves, and from which is obtained the lague or Chinese varnish.

All the gum-benzoin which is sold at Bangkok comes from the northern extremity of the state of Louang Prabang, and from a district tributary both to Cochin China and Siam, and peopled rather by Tonquinites than Laotians.

On the 24th of June I arrived at Paklaïe, lat. 19° 16′ 58″, the first small town on my northward route.   It is situated on the Mekon, and is a charming place; the inhabitants seem well off; the houses elegant and spacious,—larger, indeed, than I have seen before in this country; and everything betokens a degree of prosperity which I have also remarked wherever I have stopped since.   The Mekon at this place is much larger than the Menam at Bangkok, and forces its way between the lofty mountains with a noise resembling the roaring of the sea and the impetuosity of a torrent, seeming scarcely able to keep within its bed.   There are many rapids between Paklaïe and Louang Prabang, which is ten or fifteen days' painful travelling.

I was tired of my long journey on elephants, and was

anxious to hire a boat here, but the chief and some of
the inhabitants, fearing that I might meet with some
accident, advised me to continue my route by land. I
therefore proceeded as far as Thadua, ninety miles farther north, and during eight days passed through much
the same style of country as before, changing one valley
for another, and crossing mountains which became more
and more elevated, and being more than ever annoyed
by the leeches. We were, however, no longer compelled
to sleep in the jungle, for every evening we reached some
hamlet or village, where we found shelter either in a
pagoda or caravanserai.

As among the Grisons or the mountains of the Valais,
the whole population, from Dong Phya Phai to this
district, who drink the water of the mountain rivulets,
are disfigured by immense goîtres; but the men are not
so subject to them as the women, who rarely escape.

I have only passed through one village where any
serious ravages are committed by the tigers. There is
one danger, which may be serious, incident to travelling
with elephants in a region like this. Usually, among
the caravan there are one or two females, followed by
their young, who run about from one side to another,
playing or browsing. Now and then one of them stumbles
and falls into a ravine, and immediately the whole troop
jump down after him to draw him out.

In a letter which I wrote from Cambodia I described
the Mekon river as imposing, but monotonous and unpic-
turesque; but in this part of the country it presents a

very different appearance. Where it is narrowest the
width is above 1000 metres, and it everywhere runs
between lofty mountains, down whose sides flow torrents,
all bringing their tribute. There is almost an excess of
grandeur. The eye rests constantly on these mountain
slopes, clothed in the richest and thickest verdure.

On the 25th of July I reached Louang Prabang, a
delightful little town, covering a square mile of ground,
and containing a population, not, as Mgr. Pallegoix says
in his work on Siam, of 80,000, but of 7000 or 8000 only.
The situation is very pleasant. The mountains which,
above and below this town, enclose the Mekon, form here
a kind of circular valley or amphitheatre, nine miles in
diameter, and which, there can be no doubt, was anciently
a lake. It was a charming picture, reminding one of the
beautiful lakes of Como and Geneva. Were it not for
the constant blaze of a tropical sun, or if the mid-day heat
were tempered by a gentle breeze, the place would be a
little paradise.

The town is built on both banks of the stream, though
the greater number of the houses are built on the left
bank. The most considerable part of the town surrounds
an isolated mount, more than a hundred metres in height,
at the top of which is a pagoda.

Were they not restrained by fear of the Siamese, and
their horror of the jungles so prolific of death, this princi-
pality would soon fall into the hands of the Annamites,
who now dare not advance nearer than seven days'
journey off. A beautiful stream, 100 metres wide, unites

with the great river to the north-east of the town, and
leads to some Laotian and savage villages bearing the
name of *Fie*. These are no other than the tribes called
Penoms by the Cambodians, *Khu* by the Siamese, and
Moï by the Annamites, — all words simply signifying
" savages."

The whole chain of mountains which extends from
the north of Tonquin to the south of Cochin China,
about 100 miles north of Saigon, is inhabited by this
primitive people, divided into tribes speaking different
dialects, but whose manners and customs are the same.
All the villages in the immediate neighbourhood are
tributary; those nearest to the town supply workmen for
buildings erected for the king and princes, and these are
heavily taxed. Others pay their tribute in rice.

Their habitations are in the thickest parts of the
forests, where they only can find a path. Their cultivated
grounds are to be seen on the tops and sides of the
mountains; in fact, they employ the same means as wild
animals to escape from their enemies, and to preserve
that liberty and independence which are to them, as to
all God's creatures, their supreme good.

Yesterday, and the day previous, I was presented to
the princes who govern this little state, and who bear
the title of kings. I know not why, but they displayed
for my benefit all they could devise of pomp and
splendour.

The Laotians of Leuye appear to me more industrious
than the Siamese, and, above all, possess a much more

adventurous and mercantile spirit; and although, both physically and morally, there are great points of resemblance, yet there exist shades of difference which distinguish them at once, and are apparent in their dialect, or rather patois, and in their manners, which are more simple and affable. They are all much alike in features ; the women have round faces, small noses, large almond-shaped eyes, thick hair, the mouth large and strongly-marked; but the men do not exhibit so great a diversity of race as they do in Siam.

Alas! what a journey my fragile collection of specimens, so difficult to gather together, has still to take, and what various accidents may befall them ! Those who in museums contemplate the works of Nature do not think of all the perseverance, trouble, and anxiety required before they are safely brought home.

The Laotians have not the curiosity of the Siamese, and ask me fewer questions. I find them more intelligent than either the latter race or the Cambodians, and among the villagers especially there is a curious mixture of cunning and simplicity. They do not as yet seem to me to merit their reputation for hospitality,—a virtue which appeared to be much more practised in Siam. I should never have obtained any means of conveyance without the letter from the Viceroy of Korat, and my experience has been that they are less respectful, but at the same time less importunate, than the Siamese.

The ground between Leuye and Kenne Thao is hilly, but traversed without difficulty. The formations are cal-

careous rocks, sandstone, slaty sandstone, and lime mixed
with clay; the sandstone in long beds, not in blocks.
In the streams I found stones, not boulders, but with sharp
angles.

The Chinese and Indians alone traffic here; it requires
a day's journey to conclude the smallest bargain, and a
whole village is assembled to make sure that the money
is not spurious. On my route here I have not met a
single Siamese, but in every village have seen Birmans,
Kariens, and people from Western Laos. I have found
men in Lao-Pouene moulded like athletes and of hercu-
lean strength, and thought that the King of Siam might
raise in this province a fine regiment of grenadiers. In
all the villages I have visited, the inhabitants, including
even the priests, set to work to collect insects for me, glad
to receive in return a few copper buttons, glass beads, or a
little red cloth.

At Paklaïe, which I have already mentioned as a
pretty town, I had the pleasure of again seeing the beautiful stream, which now seems to me like an old friend:
I have so long drunk of its waters, it has so long either
cradled me on its bosom or tried my patience, at one
time flowing majestically among the mountains, at another
muddy and yellow as the Arno at Florence.

The road between Kenne Thao and Paklaïe is dreadful.
You have to force your way along a narrow path, through
a thick jungle, and sometimes there is no path at all, or
else it is obstructed by bamboos and branches which
interlace and often catch hold of your saddle. Every

moment you are in danger of being hurt by them; our hands and faces were covered with scratches, and my clothes torn to pieces.

Muang-Moune-Wa.—This place is surrounded by mountains. I am very feverish and tremble with cold, although the thermometer shows 80 degrees of heat. I am getting tired of these people, a race of children, heartless and unenergetic. I sigh and look everywhere for a man, and cannot find one; here all tremble at the stick, and the enervating climate makes them incredibly apathetic.

15th August, 1861.—Nam Kane. A splendid night; the moon shines with extraordinary brilliancy, silvering the surface of this lovely river, bordered by high mountains, looking like a grand and gloomy rampart. The chirp of the crickets alone breaks the stillness. In my little cottage all is calm and tranquil; the view from my window is charming, but I cannot appreciate or enjoy it. I am sad and anxious; I long for my native land, for a little life; to be always alone weighs on my spirits.

Louang Prabang, 29th August, 1861.—My third servant, Song, whom I had engaged at Pakpriau, begged me to allow him to return to Bangkok in the suite of the Prince of Louang Prabang, who was going there to pay tribute. I did all I could to induce him to remain with me, but he seemed to have made up his mind to go; so I paid him his wages, and gave him a letter authorising him to

receive a further sum at Bangkok for the time occupied
by his return journey.

Same date. Song is gone. How changeable we are!
He was always complaining of cold or had some other
grievance, and I cared less for him than for my other
servants—but then I had not had him long. Yesterday,
however, when he asked permission to go, I was vexed.
Either he has really suffered much here from illness, or
has not been happy with me; perhaps both. I hired a
boat to take him to the town, and my good Phrai accompanied him there this morning, and recommended him
from me to a mandarin whom I knew. I gave him all
that was necessary for his journey, even if it lasts three
months, and on his arrival at Bangkok he will receive
his money. On taking leave he prostrated himself before
me; I took hold of his hands and raised him up, and then
he burst into tears. And I, in my turn, when I had bid
him farewell, felt my eyes fill, nor do I know when I
shall be quite calm, for I have before me, day and night,
the poor lad, ill in the woods, among indifferent or cruel
people. He has a great dread of fever, and, if he had
been taken ill here and died, I should have reproached
myself for keeping him ; and yet, if it were to come over
again, I almost fancy I would not yield to his desire to
leave me. He was confided to me by the good Father
Larmandy. May God protect the poor boy, and preserve him from all sickness and accidents during his
journey !

I reached Louang Prabang on the 25th of July. On the 3rd of August I was presented to the King and to his cousin. On the 9th of August I left Louang Prabang and travelled eastwards.

26th.—The thermometer rose to 92° Fahr. This is the maximum I have noted this month, 71° being the minimum.

CHAPTER XVIII.

THE dress of the Laotians differs little from that of the Siamese. The people wear the *langouti* and a little red cotton waistcoat, or often nothing at all. Both men and women go barefoot: their head-dresses are like the Siamese. The women are generally better-looking than those of the latter nation: they wear a single short petticoat of cotton, and sometimes a piece of silk over the breast. Their hair, which is black, they twist into a knot at the back of the head. The houses are built of bamboos and leaves interwoven and raised upon stakes, and underneath is a shelter for domestic animals, such as oxen, pigs, fowls, &c.

The dwellings are, in the strictest sense, unfurnished, having neither tables nor beds, nor, with few exceptions, even vessels of earth or porcelain. They eat their rice made into balls out of their hands, or from little baskets plaited with cane, some of which are far from unartistic.

The crossbow and *sarbacane* are the arms used in hunting, as well as a kind of lance made of bamboo, and

Drawn by M. Janet Lange. from a Sketch by M. Mouhot

LAOTIAN WOMAN.

sometimes, but more rarely, the gun, with which they are very skilful.

In the hamlet of Na-Lê, where I had the pleasure of killing a female tiger, which with its partner was committing great ravages in the neighbourhood, the chief hunter of the village got up a rhinoceros-hunt in my honour. I had not met with this animal in all my wanderings through the forests. The manner in which he is hunted by the Laotians is curious on account of its simplicity and the skill they display. Our party consisted of eight, including myself. I and my servants were armed with guns, and at the end of mine was a sharp bayonet. The Laotians had bamboos with iron blades something between a bayonet and a poignard. The weapon of the chief was the horn of a sword-fish, long, sharp, strong, and supple, and not likely to break.

Thus armed, we set off into the thickest part of the forest, with all the windings of which our leader was well acquainted, and could tell with tolerable certainty where we should find our expected prey. After penetrating nearly two miles into the forest, we suddenly heard the crackling of branches and rustling of the dry leaves. The chief went on in advance, signing to us to keep a little way behind, but to have our arms in readiness. Soon our leader uttered a shrill cry as a token that the animal was near; he then commenced striking against each other two bamboo canes, and the men set up wild yells to provoke the animal to quit his retreat.

A few minutes only elapsed before he rushed towards

us, furious at having been disturbed.   He was a rhinoceros
of the largest size, and opened a most enormous mouth.
Without any signs of fear, but, on the contrary, of great
exultation, as though sure of his prey, the intrepid hunter
advanced, lance in hand, and then stood still, waiting
for the creature's assault.   I must say I trembled for him,
and I loaded my gun with two balls ; but when the
rhinoceros came within reach and opened his immense
jaws to seize his enemy, the hunter thrust the lance into
him to a depth of some feet, and calmly retired to where
we were posted.

The animal uttered fearful cries and rolled over on his
back in dreadful convulsions, while all the men shouted
with delight.   In a few minutes more we drew nearer to
him ; he was vomiting pools of blood.   I shook the chief's
hand in testimony of my satisfaction at his courage and
skill.   He told me that to myself was reserved the honour
of finishing the animal, which I did by piercing his throat
with my bayonet, and he almost immediately yielded up
his last sigh.   The hunter then drew out his lance and
presented it to me as a souvenir; and in return I gave
him a magnificent European poignard.

Oubon and Bassac lie W.N.W. from M. Pimaï.   It
takes eight days in the rainy season to travel from this
last town to Oubon, two more to reach Bassac.   To
return occupies at least double that period, the current
being excessively strong.

The Ménam-Moune at Pimaï is 75 metres wide in the
dry season; in the rainy season it is from 6 to 7 metres

A CHIEF ATTACKING A RHINOCEROS IN THE FOREST OF LAOS.

Drawn by M. Janet Lange, from a Sketch by M. Mouhot.

in depth. There are in this district iron, lignites, and trunks of petrified trees lying on the ground, which even from a very short distance look like fallen trees in a natural state.

Mgi-Poukham, inhabited by the Soués, is six days' journey from Korat in a south-easterly direction.

In the dry season the navigation of the river is impeded by sandbanks: at some points the stream is tolerably wide, but in others choked with sand.

From Korat to Pimaï, on an elephant, occupies two days: from Korat to Thaison, two; to Sisapoune, two; to Josoutone, two days; to Oubon, four days; to Bassac, four.

Direction E.N.E. from Korat; Poukiéau, N. of Chaia-pume; Pouvienne, ten degrees E. of Chaiapume; Dong-kaïe, N.E. by E. of Chaiapume; M. Louang Prabang, N. of Chaiapume.

From Chaiapume to Vien-Tiane is fifteen days' journey on foot towards the N. and nine degrees E. M. Lôm, N.W. of Chaiapume; Petchaboune, W.N.W. of Chaia-pume; Bassac, E.S.E.

Bane Prom, a mountain situated in a valley nine miles across, is nearly 300 metres high. Bane Prom, a town. Menam Prom, a river nearly 2 metres deep and 40 wide, rises in M'Lôm, and empties itself in the Menam Chie, in the province of Koukhine. Bane-Rike, between Poukiéau and Kone-Sane, four geographical leagues from each place. Menam-Rike is a torrent which empties itself into the Prom.

The vegetation is monotonous — everywhere resinous trees, chiefly of small size. There is a complete absence of birds; insects are in great number and variety, musquitoes and ox-flies in myriads. I suffer dreadfully from them, and am covered with swellings and blisters from their bites; and they torment our beasts so much that we sometimes fear it will drive them mad. The sensibility of the skin of the elephant is extraordinary, but these creatures are very skilful in brushing off their tormentors by means of a branch held in their trunks. I do not know what would become of me without these good and docile animals, and I cannot tell which to admire most, their patience or intelligence.

From Kone-Sane to Vien-Tiane is eight good days' journey in a north-easterly direction.

To M'Lôm, four days W.N.W.

To Petchaboune, four days W.S.W.

To Kôrat, four days E.S.E.

To Chaiapume, four days E.S.E.

To Poukiéau, four days E.S.E.

To Leuye, three days' rapid travelling N.N.E. over mountains.

From Kone-Sane to Koukhène, two days' rapid journey E.S.E.

From Koukhène to Chenobote, one day's journey S.E.

On the road from Kone-Sane to Leuye, near the former place, is a stream called Oué-Mouan, and a torrent, Oué-Kha.

Bane-Nayaan, a village, five geographical leagues off,

two days' journey, with high mountains to cross, difficult
of ascent for the elephants.   On the first day your course
is over peaked mountains, volcanic, and like those of the
Khao Khoc.   The next day you meet with calcareous and
volcanic hills; in the valleys sandstone, jungle, and fertile
ground.

Mgi-Lôm, four days' journey west of Bane-Nayaan.
From this last place to Bane-Napitone runs the stream
Oué-Yan.

Menam-Fon-Khau, passed over twice, a geographical
league.

In the provinces of Kone-Sane and of Leuye a great
number of the inhabitants are affected with goître.   Is
this caused by the water from the mountains and the
mineral substances with which it is impregnated?   I
suppose so.

From Bane-Napitone to B. Proune you have to cross
high mountains.   Half way up one of these is a fine view
extending over a wooded plain to the north-west in the
direction of Nong Khaï, and bounded at a distance of
twenty-five or thirty miles by a chain of mountains; whilst
in every other direction you are surrounded by hills varying in height from 300 to 900 feet.   The sandstone and
chalky rocks of these heights have taken most picturesque
forms.

From B. Proune to B. Thiassène runs a stream five
leagues long, in a north-westerly direction, and which is
navigable for boats.   It flows on towards Leuye, and
empties itself in the Mekon at M. Sione-Kane, which is

ten degrees N.N.E. of N. Thiassène. From B. Thienne to Leuye are hills easy to climb, with vegetation similar to those of Chantaboune and Brelum, forests of bamboo: the rocks are calcareous, with a small mixture of sandstone.

The Menam-Rope and Menam-Ouaie are two large rivers, deep in the rainy season, which empty themselves into the Menam-Leuye: also several torrents. Villages: Bane-Kataname, Bane-Poune, Bane-Nahane, Bane-Pathiou.

From Bane-Thienne to Nong Khane you go in an easterly direction. Bane-Poua is the first village in a four days' journey: here are forests, jungles, and a small hill. The plain is barren and desolate in appearance.

Towns and provinces of Louang Prabang in coming down: Thienne-Khane, Nong-Kaïe, Saïabouri, Outène, Lakhone-Penome, Mouke-Dahane, Emarate, and Bassac.

I am literally pillaged by these petty mandarins and chiefs of villages, and have to give away guns, sabres, lead, powder, colours, pencils, and even my paper; and then, after having received their presents, they will not put themselves out of their way to do me the smallest service. I would not wish my most deadly foe, if I had one, to undergo all the trouble and persecution of this kind which I have encountered.

The Laotian priests are continually praying in their pagodas; they make a frightful noise, chanting from morning to night. Assuredly they ought to go direct to Paradise.

Between Oué-Saïe and Thienne-Khane the villages

are : Bane-Tate, B. Oué-Sake, B. Na-Saor, B. Poun, B. Na-Poué, Nam-Khane, near B. Nmïen; near Kenne Thao, between Bane Nam-Khane and Bane-Noke, is a torrent called Nam-Kheme.

Observations taken at Kéte-Tao: Vienne-Thiane, eastward; Mg. Nane, N.N.W.; Tchieng-Maïe, N.W.; Louang Prabang, N. of Kenne Thao.

Mg. Dane-Saie, four days' journey W.S.W. of Bane-Mien; Lôme, four days' journey W.S.W. of Bane-Mien.

Villages: Bane Thène, Nha-Khâ—two roads; Nâ-Thon —two roads; Nâ-Di, Nâ-Moumone, Nâ-Ho, Bane Maïe, B. Khok.

The river Menam-Ouan runs in a north-westerly direction to within a day's journey of the Menam-Sake. A high mountain lies between them.

In Lôme the villages are: Bane Tali, B. Yao, B. Khame, B. Pouksiéau, B. Name-Bongdiéau, B. Nong-Boa, B. Na-Sane-Jenne, B. Nam-Soke, B. Ine-Uun, Dong-Saïe, Bane Vang-Bane, B. Nang-Krang, Mg. Lôme-Kao, Bane Koué-Nioune.   Between M. Lôme-Maïe and Thiene-Khame are Bane Oué-Saïe, B. Rate, B. Na-Shî, B. Oué-Pote, B. Na-Sao, B. Loke, B. Na-Niaô, Thiene-Khame.

Between Kenne Thao and Bane Mien are B. Kone Khêne, B. Pake-Oué, B. Khène-Toune.

The Mekon is ten leagues east of Kenne Thao.

M. Phitchaïe eight days' journey west from Bane-Nmien.

At Bane-Nmien I found the Laotians even more ungrateful and egotistical than elsewhere; they not only will give you nothing—one has no right to expect it—but after taking presents from you, they will make you no return whatever.

The Menam-Ouan rises at Dane-Saïe, S.S.W. from Kenne Thao, and joins the Mekon E.N.E. from that town.

From Kenne Thao to Louang Prabang is a distance of seven geographical or ten ordinary leagues, and a journey of ten or eleven days, quick travelling.

Mg. Pakhaie is north of Kenne Thao. From this place to Bane-Na-Ine is one day's journey; to Bane-Moun-Tioum two days.

Near this latter place, where I have found a greater number of insects than anywhere else in my travels here, is the river Nam-Shan. It is a continual ascent to this part.

Near Bane-Na-Ine auriferous quartz occurs. The jungle here is thick.

Villages in the neighbourhood of Moun-Tioume, consisting of from fifteen to thirty huts: Bane-Hape, a league to the north; Rape-Jâ, the same distance southwards; Tate-Dine, one league to the north-east; Nam-Poune, half a league south-east.

In Bane Moun-Tioume are twenty-six houses.

Route from B. Moun-Tioume to B. Kouke-Niéou:—This last village is composed of eighty houses. There is in it an abandoned pagoda, and it is environed by woods and hills. A stream, called the Nam-Peniou, flows past it and joins the Nam-Shan. There is plenty of rice on the hills, but not in the plains.

From Bane-Kouke-Niéou* there are continual hills.
We are tormented by immense numbers of leeches and
ox-flies.   The jungle is as thick as in Dong Phya Phai.
We passed the night on the banks of a stream, the Nam-
Koïe, which we had several times crossed, but could get
no sleep on account of the leeches; and the following
night, by the same river, we were equally pestered.

Bane-Oué-Eu is a small hamlet in the immediate
vicinity of Kouke-Niéou-Paklaïe, a very pleasant town,
apparently prosperous.   The houses are clean and elegant.

Paklaïe is two geographical leagues distant from Muang-
Moune-Wâ.   The district is very mountainous, with rice-
grounds on some of the slopes.   We several times had to
cross the Laïe, which is 35 metres wide, and rushes along
like a torrent, with a great noise.   There are, about here,
many precipices.   It was wonderful to see the elephants
climb, descend, and hang on by their trunks to the rocks
without ever making a false step.

I have quite an admiration and regard for these noble
animals.   How remarkable are their strength and intelligence!   What should we have done without them amidst
these vast forests and rugged mountains?

Mgi-Roun, district of M. Louang, a day's journey
W.N.W. of Mgi-Moune-Wâ; there are seventy houses
in it.

The villages near to Moune-Wâ are Bane-Bia, 2 miles

---

* At Kouke-Niéou I sold my horse for 13 ticals, as he could no
longer climb the hills, which became more and more difficult.

westward; Bane-Name-Pi, two days' journey; Thiême-Khâne, one day; B. Nam-Kang, one day. These villages are all on the road from Mgi-Moune-Wâ to Phixaïe. This place lies W.S.W. from Muang-Moune-Wâ, and five days' journey off, and three days' journey from Nam-Pate. The country between Mgi-Moune-Wâ and Nam-Pate is mountainous; from the latter place to Phixaïe is also hilly ground, and is part of the direct line from Bangkok to Mgi-Louang.*

From Mgi-Moune-Wâ to Bane-Nakhau is a good day's journey over a mountain country, through woods of resinous trees and high grass; but the jungle predominates. Auriferous sand occurs in the Nam-Poune; also, though less rich, in the Nam-Ouhan and other streams.

Bane-Phêke and B. Nalane lie between B. Nakhan and Mgi-Nam-Poune.

Mgi-Nane is six days' journey W.N.W. of Moune-Wâ. The first day, to Mgi-Roun; second day, through woods and crossing streams, to Nan-Pi (here are black-bellied Laotians); third day, Bane-Khune; fourth day, Bane-Dhare; fifth day, B. Done; sixth day, Tuke.

3rd September.—We left Bane-Nakhau, and arrived about midday at a rice-field, where we passed the night. All the women here have goîtres, often enormous and most repulsive. Even young girls of nine or ten are to be seen with them, but rarely the men.

---

* These particulars were received by me at Moune-Wâ from inhabitants of Nam-Pate.

About Tourair there are woods and thick jungles, and
the river Nam-Poune, 60 metres broad, runs near.   The
hills here are of moderate height.   I saw some pretty
young girls with intelligent faces; but before the females
attain the age of eighteen or twenty their features become
coarse, and they grow fat.   At five-and-thirty they look
like old witches.

Two rivers unite here, the Nam-Poune from the west,
and the Nam-Jame from the north.

On my route from B. Nakhau to B. Na-Lê, I spent
the night of the 4th of September in a hut at B. Nakone.
On the 5th I reached B. Na-Lê, passing through several
hamlets, Na-Moune, Na-Koua, and Na-Dua.   Bane-Na-
Lê contains only seven houses.

The streams are, first, the Nam-Jame, crossed and re-
crossed several times; the Nam-Quême, Nam-Itou, Nam-
Pâne; the Nam-Khou, near Bane-Nakone.

The road lies across high mountains, with jungles full
of monkeys uttering their plaintive cries.   I was told of a
royal tiger at Na-Lê, which, in the space of four months,
had killed two men and ten buffaloes.   I had the satisfaction of killing the tigress.

5th September, 1861.—From this date M. Mouhot's
observations cease; but until the 25th of October he
continued to keep his meteorological register.

The last dates inscribed in his journal are the following :—

20th September.—Left B . . . . . . p.

28th.—An order was sent to B . . . ., from the council

of Louang Prabang, commanding the authorities to prevent my proceeding farther.

15th October. 58 degrees Fahr.—Set off for Louang
Prabang.

16th.—. . . . . . .

17th.—. . . . . . .

18th.—Halted at H . . . .

19th.—Attacked by fever. *

29th.—Have pity on me, oh my God . . . .!

These words, written with a trembling and uncertain
hand, were the last found in M. Mouhot's journal. His
faithful Phrai asked him several times if he did not wish
to write anything to his family, but his invariable answer
was, "Wait, wait; are you afraid?" The intrepid traveller never for one moment thought that death was near;
he had been spared so far, and he doubtless thought he
should recover, or he might have made an effort to write
again. He died November 10th, 1861, at 7 o'clock in the
evening, having been previously insensible for three days,
before which time, however, he had complained of great
pains in his head. All the words which he uttered during
the delirium of the last three days were in English, and
were incomprehensible to his servants.

He was buried in the European fashion, in the presence
of his two servants, who never left him. It is the custom
of the country to hang up the dead bodies to the trees,
and there leave them.

---

* The handwriting of this entry is evidently much affected by his
state of weakness.

This account of the last illness of my dear brother I received from his friends at Bangkok, particularly Dr. Campbell, to whom his two faithful servants hastened at once to give all details. His collections and other property they took to M. d'Istria, the French consul. Dr. Campbell kindly took charge of the manuscripts, and transmitted them to his widow in London.

The family of M. Mouhot have already expressed their gratitude to those who were useful and kind to the traveller. The two good servants who remained with him to the last also merit their thanks; and, if these lines should fall into the hands of Phrai, I wish him to know how much gratitude and esteem we feel for him, and for his companion Deng. We wish them every happiness in return for their devotion to my dear brother.

C. MOUHOT.

SIAMESE MONEY.

APPENDIX.

APPENDIX.

LIST OF THE NEW SPECIES OF MAMMALS DISCOVERED
BY THE LATE M. MOUHOT IN CAMBODIA AND SIAM.

By Dr. Albert Günther.

a. Monkeys.

1. *Hylobates pileatus.*

Male.—Black: back of the head, back of the body, and front
hind legs greyish; forehead and circumference of the black
spot on the crown paler grey: hands and tuft of long hair round
the organ of generation white.

The three specimens in this state are all nearly of the same
size, and appear to be adult. They only vary slightly in the
size of the coronal spot, and in the extent of the white colour on
the hands.

Female.—White: back brownish white, slightly waved; a
large ovate spot on the crown, and a very large ovate blotch on
the chest, black.

These specimens are all of one size, and appear to be adult;
three have the teats well developed. They vary in the size of
the black chest-spot, and in the colour of the whiskers,
thus :—

a, b. White : spot on the chest moderate, reaching only half-
way down the abdomen : whiskers on side of face white.

c. Brownish: spot on chest larger, reaching further down the abdomen: sides of the face black: a few black hairs on the throat.

d. Brownish: side of the face, under the chin, and the whole of the throat, chest, and belly black: teats well developed.

Young.—Uniform dirty white, without any black spot on chest or head.

All those varieties were found by M. Mouhot on a small island near Cambodia. (Described by Dr. J. E. Gray, Proc. Zool. Soc., 1861, p. 135.)

b. CARNIVORES.

2. *Herpestes rutilus.*

Grizzled chestnut-brown, variegated with black and white rings on the hairs: the head and limbs darker chestnut, with scarcely any hair, and very narrow white rings: lips and throat, and under part of the body, uniform duller brown; the nape with longer hairs, forming a broad short crest.

Cambodia. (Gray, Proc. Zool. Soc., 1861, p. 136.)

c. SQUIRRELS.

3. *Sciurus Mouhotii.*

Grizzled grey brown, with pale rings: lips, chin, throat, and under side of body and inside of limbs white: the upper part of the sides with a longitudinal black streak, edged above and below with a narrow white line: tail blackish, whitish washed, hairs elongate, brown, with two broad black rings and a white tip: ears simple, rounded.

The species differs from most of the squirrels of the size, in the three streaks being on the upper part of the back, and in the dark colour between the two colours of the upper and under surface.

Cambodia. (Named by Dr. J. E. Gray, after M. Mouhot, and described in Proc. Zool. Soc., 1861, p. 137.)

4. *Sciurus splendens.*

All the specimens are bright red bay.

Var. 1.—All over dark, and very intense red bay, with a white spot on each side of the base of the tail.

Var. 2.—Top of the head and tail, like var. 1, dark and very intense red bay : side of the back, under sides of the body, and tip of the tail paler red bay, without any white spot at the base of the tail.

Var. 3.—Uniform pale bay, like the side of var. 2 : tail and middle of the back rather darker and brighter : tail without pale tip or white basal spot.

Var. 4.—Crown, middle of the back, and tail dark intense red bay : throat, chest, and under side paler red bay, like var. 2, 3 : cheeks, shoulders, and thighs, and outsides of the fore and hind legs brown, grizzled, with yellow rings on the hairs : side of the body rather greyish red.

Cambodia. (Gray, Proc. Zool. Soc., 1861, p. 137.)

5. *Sciurus siamensis.*

Bright red-brown, grizzled, with elongate black tips to the longer hairs, each of which is marked with a broad subterminal yellow band. These black hairs are more abundant and have broad pale rings on the rump, outside of the thighs, and especially on the lower part of the tail, where they nearly hide the general red colour. The terminal half of the tail bright chestnut-brown, without any black hairs or pale rings. The throat, breast, belly, lower part of sides, inner side and edge of the legs, uniform bright red-brown : ears rounded : whiskers black : feet covered with short close-pressed hairs.

(Gray, Proc. Zool. Soc., 1859, p. 478.)

d. Ruminants.

6. *Tragulus affinis.*

Similar to T. javanicus in colour, but rather smaller and much paler, and the side of the neck similar in colour to the side of the body : the belly is white, with a brown streak on each side of the central line : the head is smaller. It is larger than *T. kanchil;* very much paler; and the neck is not blacker and grizzled. A specimen of the species has been in the British Museum, as above named, for many years : it is said to have come from Singapore; but that probably was only the port of transit. It may be only a small pale local variety of *T. kanchil.*

Six specimens, adult, all exactly similar, and one young, have been collected by M. Mouhot. (Gray, Proc. Zool. Soc., 1861, p. 138.)

7. *Cervulus cambojensis.*

There are the forehead covered with hair and the horns of a Muntjack in the collection sent by M. Mouhot from Cambodia : it is very much larger than any specimen of that genus in the British Museum collection, and is probably a distinct species.

The horns are thick, nearly straight, with a short, thick recurved branch on the outer part of the front side, near the base, and one of them has a somewhat similar callosity on the hinder side on the same level. Hair of forehead very rigid, close pressed, dark brown, with narrow yellow rings. (Gray, Proc. Zool. Soc., 1861, p. 138.)

LIST OF THE NEW SPECIES OF REPTILES DISCOVERED
BY THE LATE M. MOUHOT IN SIAM AND CAMBODIA.

By Dr. Albert Gunther.

a. Tortoises.

1. *Geoclemys macrocephala.*

The shell oblong, rather depressed, entirely three-keeled, olive-
brown : the keels subcontinued, nearly parallel; the middle
one higher and more distinct behind; the lateral ones, near
the upper edge of the shields, continued, ending abruptly on the
hinder edge of the third lateral discal shield : the hinder lateral
and central shield only marked with a slight convexity : the
margin entire, yellow edged : the under side yellow, with black
triangular spots : the sternum flat, very indistinctly keeled on
the side.

Animal black olive, head large; crown flat, covered with a
single smooth plate, purplish-brown, with two streaks from
middle of the nose; the upper edging the crown, the other the
upper part of the beak, and with two streaks from the hinder
edge of the orbit ; the lower short and interrupted, extended
on the temple ; the upper broader and continued over the ear,
along the side of the neck; two close streaks under the nostrils
to the middle of the upper jaw, and two broad streaks dilated
behind, down the front of the lower jaw, and continued on the
edge of the lower jaw behind : the nape and hinder part of the
side of the lower jaw covered with large flat scales : the rest
of the neck and legs covered with minute granular scales : the
front of the forelegs covered with broad band-like scales : the
toes of the fore and hind feet rather short and thick, covered
above with broad band-like scales. (Gray, Proc. Zool. Soc.,
1859, p. 479, pl. 21.)

2. *Cyclemys Mouhotii.*

Shell oblong, pale yellow; back flattened above, with a dark-edged keel on each side: the vertebral plates continuously keeled, and rather tubercular in front: the margin strongly dentated: nuchal shield distinct. (Gray, Ann. and Mag. Nat· Hist., 1862, x. p. 157; Günth., Rept. Brit. Ind., pl. 4, fig. D.)

3. *Trionyx ornatus.*

Back of the young animal, in spirits, brown, with large, unequal-sized, irregularly disposed black circular spots: head olive, with symmetrical small black spots on the chin, forehead, and nose: throat and sides of neck with large, unequal-sized, irregular-shaped, and nearly symmetrically disposed yellow spots: legs olive, yellow spotted in front: sternum and under side of margin yellow: sternal callosities not developed.

A single specimen has been found by M. Mouhot in Cambodia, which is now in the British Museum. (Described by Dr. J. E. Gray, Proc. Zool. Soc., 1861, p. 41, pl. 5.)

b. LIZARDS.

1. *Draco tæniopterus.*

Tympanum not scaly: nostrils above the face-ridge directed upwards: a low longitudinal fold on the neck: scales on the back of equal size, obscurely keeled: gular sac covered with large smooth scales, uniformly coloured: wings dark-greenish olive, with five arched black bands, not extending to the margin of the wing, some being forked at the base. (Günth., Proc. Zool. Soc., 1861, April 23, and Ind. Rept., p. 126, pl. 13, fig. E.)

2. *Acanthosaura coronata.*

The upper orbital edge serrated, without elongate spine posteriorly; a short spine on each side of the neck; a yellowish-
olive band edged with black across the crown, from one orbital
edge to the other; an oblique, short, yellowish band, broadly
edged with brown, from below the orbit to the angle of the
mouth.

This and the following species belong to the genus *Acantho-
saura*, as defined by Gray (Catal. Liz. p. 240). The tympanum
is distinct; a short spine between it and the dorsal crest, which
is rather low; no femoral or præanal pores: a short spine
behind the orbital edge, and separated from it by a deep notch:
back and sides covered with small smooth scales, slightly turned
towards the dorsal line, and intermixed with scattered larger
ones which are keeled: belly and legs with larger keeled scales:
tail slightly compressed at the base, the rest being round, and
without crest; all its scales are keeled; those on the lower side
being oblong, and provided with more prominent keels: throat
without cross-fold, and without distinct longitudinal pouch: a
slight oblique fold before the shoulder. (Günth., Proc. Zool.
Soc., 1861, April 23, and Ind. Rept., p. 149, pl. 14, fig. E.)

3. *Acanthosaura capra.*

The upper orbital edge not serrated, terminating posteriorly
in a long moveable horn: no spine above the tympanum or on
the side of the neck: nuchal crest high, not continuous with the
dorsal crest, which is rather elevated anteriorly: crown and
cheek without markings.

The tympanum is distinct: no femoral or præanal pores: back
and sides covered with small smooth scales, which become gradually larger and more distinctly keeled towards the belly: no
large scales intermixed with the small ones; only a few appear

to be a little larger than the rest : tail slightly compressed at the base, surrounded by rings of oblong, keeled scales : throat expansible ; a very slight fold before the shoulder. (Günth., Ind. Rept., p. 148, pl. 14, fig. F.)

4. *Physignathus mentager.*

Dorsal crest not interrupted above the shoulder; interrupted above the hip : caudal crest as high as that on the back : no large scales on the side of the neck : sides of the throat with large convex or tubercular scales.

A high crest, composed of sabre-shaped shields, extends from the nape of the neck to the second fifth of the length of the tail, being interrupted above the hip : scales on the back and the sides of equal size, very small, with an obscure keel obliquely directed upwards ; those on the belly smooth, on the lower side of the tail rather elongate ; strongly keeled : tympanum distinct : throat with a cross-fold : orbital edges and sides of the neck without spines : tail transversely banded with black.

One stuffed specimen is 30 inches long, the tail taking 21. (Günth., Proc. Zool. Soc., 1861, April 23, and Ind. Rept., p. 153, pl. 15.)

5. *Tropidophorus microlepis.*

Snout rather narrow and produced : scales on the back strongly keeled, the keels not terminating in elevated spines : back of the tail with two series of moderately elevated spines, the series not being continuous with those on the back of the trunk : scales of the throat smooth, or very indistinctly keeled : tail with a series of plates below, which are much larger and broader than the scales of the belly : three large præanal scales : a single anterior frontal shield (internasal). (Günth., Proc. Zool. Soc., 1861, April 23, and Ind. Rept., p. 76, pl. 10, fig. A.)

c. Snakes.

Simotes tæniatus.

Scales in nineteen rows. Brownish-olive, with a brown longitudinal dorsal band enclosing an olive-coloured line running along the vertebral series of scales; another brownish band along the side of the body; belly whitish, chequered with black.

One loreal shield, one anterior and two posterior oculars; eight upper labials, the third, fourth, and fifth of which enter the orbit; 155 ventral plates; anal entire; 44 pairs of subcaudals. Head with the markings characteristic of the genus: each half of the dorsal band occupies one series of scales and two halves; the lateral band runs along the fourth outer series, touching the third and fifth. (Günth., Proc. Zool. Soc., 1861, April 23, and Ind. Rept., p. 216, pl. 20, fig. A.)

d. Newts.

Plethodon persimilis.

Black, white-speckled, the specks closer and more abundant on the sides; the hind-toes elongate, unequal. Tail compressed.

This is the first species of Newts which has been discovered in Continental India; it is exceedingly like the *Pl. glutinosus* from North America, but the hind toes are rather longer and more slender. (Gray, Proc. Zool. Soc., 1859, p. 230, c. tab.)

LIST OF THE NEW SPECIES OF FRESH-WATER FISHES DISCOVERED BY THE LATE M. MOUHOT IN SIAM AND CAMBODIA.

By Dr. Albert Günther.

1. *Toxotes microlepis.*

D. $\frac{5}{13}$. A. $\frac{3}{17}$. L. lat. 42. L. transv. $\frac{6}{14}$.

In the general habit and in all the generic characters the present species completely agrees with *T. jaculator ;* the snout, however, is much shorter, its length being scarcely more than the diameter of the eye, and considerably less than the width between the orbits. The diameter of the eye is one-fourth of the length of the head. The length of the base of the anal equals exactly that of the dorsal. One of the largest scales covers two-thirds of the eye.

The colour may prove to be subject to as much variation as in the other species. The specimens described are yellowish, with greenish back and yellowish caudal. There is a series of four black blotches on each side : the anterior is the smallest, and situated on the upper extremity of the præoperculum ; the third is the largest, and placed opposite the dorsal spines ; a narrow blackish band round the base of the caudal ; a round black spot on the posterior angle of the dorsal ; the anal and the ventrals are black.

(Günth., Fishes, ii. p. 68.)

2. *Eleotris siamensis.*

D. 6 | 10. A. 9. L. lat. 90.

Twenty-two longitudinal series of scales between the origin of the posterior dorsal and the anal, forty transverse ones be-

tween the anterior dorsal and the snout. The height of the
body is contained six times and two-thirds in the total length,
the length of the head four times. Head broad, depressed,
with the snout obtuse; the lower jaw is prominent, and the
maxillary extends to behind the vertical from the centre of the
eye. Teeth in villiform bands. The diameter of the eye is
one-seventh of the length of the head, one-half of that of the
snout, and of the width of the interorbital space. A small
barbel on each side of the upper jaw; the head is covered with
small scales; there are about ten between the posterior angle of
the orbits; the snout is naked. Dorsal and anal fins much lower
than the body: one-half of the caudal is covered with thin
scales; its length is contained five times and a half in the
total. Brown: the lower parts whitish, minutely punctulated
with brown: two oblique dark stripes on the cheek, radiating
from the eye. Dorsal fins variegated with blackish, the other
fins uniform blackish; a black ocellus, edged with whitish, on
the upper part of the root of the caudal fin.

						Lines.
Total length	..	..	..	..	..	60
Height of the body	..	..	..	..	..	9
Length of the head	..	..	..	..	..	15
Diameter of the eye	..	..	..	..	..	2
Length of the caudal fin	..	..	..	..	11

(Günth., Fish., iii. p. 129.)

3. *Osphromenus siamensis.*

D. $\frac{7}{8}$. A. $\frac{11\text{-}12}{33\text{-}35}$. L. lat. 42. L. transv. $\frac{12}{16}$.

When we take the origin of the dorsal fin as the highest point
of the upper profile, and the base of the last anal spine as the
lowest of the abdomen, the depth between these two points is
one-half of the total length (the caudal not included). The

length of the head is three times and two-thirds in the same
length. The snout is broader than long, equal to the diameter
of the eye, which is one-fourth of the length of the head. The
interorbital space is convex, wider than the orbit. Mouth very
small, rather protractile; præorbital, with its extremity truncated and serrated: angle of the præoperculum serrated; there
are two or three series of scales between the eye and the angle
of the præoperculum. The dorsal fin commences nearer to the
root of the caudal than to the end of the snout; it has six
strong spines, which increase in length posteriorly, the last
being longer than one-half the length of the head. Caudal
emarginate; the anal is nearly entirely scaly, and terminates
immediately before the caudal. The longest ventral ray extends beyond the extremity of the caudal, and has three or
four rudimentary rays in its axil.

The colour is greenish on the back, silvery on the sides and
on the belly. A black spot on the middle of the body in the
vertical from the origin of the dorsal, below the lateral line; a
second on the middle of the root of the caudal. The soft dorsal
and caudal with brown dots; anal yellowish, with lighter spots,
and sometimes with brownish dots.

This description is taken from specimens which are from three
to four inches long.

(Günth., Fishes, iii. p. 385.)

4. *Osphromenus microlepis.*

D. $\frac{3}{10}$. A. $\frac{10}{39}$. L. lat. 60. L. transv. $\frac{12}{22}$.

The height of the body is one-half of the total length (without caudal), the length of the head two-sevenths; the profile
of the nape is convex, that of the head rather concave. The
snout is somewhat depressed, broader than long, with the lower
jaw prominent; the interorbital space is convex, nearly twice

as wide as the orbit, the diameter of which is one-fifth of the
length of the head, and less than that of the snout. Præorbital triangular, with the lower margin serrated; there are five
series of scales between the orbit and the angle of the præoperculum. The entire lower margin of the præoperculum and a
part of the sub- and inter-operculum are serrated. The dorsal
fin commences on the middle of the distance between the snout
and the root of the caudal; its spines are moderately strong,
the length of the third being more than one-half of that of the
head. Caudal emarginate; more than one-half of the anal fin
is scaly; it terminates immediately before the caudal. The
longest ventral ray extends beyond the extremity of the caudal,
and has three rudimentary rays in its axil. Immaculate: back
greenish, sides and belly silvery; the soft dorsal and caudal
with brownish dots.

Total length six inches.

(Günth., Fishes, iii., p. 385.)

5. *Catopra siamensis.*

D. $\frac{13}{15}$.   A. $\frac{3}{9}$.   L. lat. 27.   L. transv. $\frac{5\frac{1}{2}}{13}$.

The height of the body is contained twice and a third in the
total length, the length of the head thrice and a third; head as
high as long. Snout rather shorter than the eye, the diameter
of which is one-fourth of the length of the head, and equal to
the width of the interorbital space. The lower jaw is scarcely
longer than the upper, and the maxillary extends slightly beyond the anterior margin of the orbit. Two nostrils remote
from each other, both very small. Præorbital and angle of the
præoperculum slightly serrated; opercles, throat, and isthmus,
entirely scaly. The dorsal fin commences above the end of the
operculum, and terminates close by the caudal; its spines are
very strong, and can be received in a groove; the fifth, sixth,
and seventh are the longest, not quite half as long as the head;
the last spine is shorter than the penultimate; the soft dorsal

is elevated and scaly at the base. The second anal spine is exceedingly strong, rather stronger and longer than the third, and not quite half as long as the head; the soft anal is similar to the soft dorsal. Caudal fin rounded, slightly produced, one-fourth of the total length; its basal half is scaly. Pectoral rather narrow, as long as the head without snout. The ventral is inserted immediately behind the base of the pectoral; it has a strong spine, and extends to the vent.

Scales minutely ciliated : the upper part of the lateral line terminates below the last dorsal rays, the lower commences above the third anal spine.

Gill-membranes united below the throat, not attached to the isthmus, scaly. Four gills, a slit behind the fourth; pseudo-branchiæ none.

The jaws, vomer, palatines, and upper and lower pharyngeals are armed with bands of small villiform teeth. Very remark-able are two large, ovate, dentigerous plates, one at the roof, the other at the bottom of the mouth, in front of the pharyngeals; these plates are slightly concave in the middle, pavimentated with molar-like teeth, and have evidently the same func-tion as the pharyngeal dentigerous plates of the true Pharyn-gognathi.

Total length 52 lines.

(Günth., Proc. Zool. Soc., 1862, June 24.)

6. *Ophiocephalus siamensis.*

D. 42.   A. 27.   L. lat. 65.   L. transv. $\frac{5}{11}$.

Large teeth in the lower jaw, on the vomer and the palatine bones. The height of the body is contained six times and four-fifths in the total length; the length of the head three times and two-fifths; the length of the caudal six times. The width of the interorbital space is more than the extent of the snout, and two-ninths of the length of the head. Cleft of the mouth wide the maxillary not extending to the vertical from the posterior margin of the eye (in old specimens it probably reaches to below that margin). There are eleven series of scales between the eye and the angle of the præoperculum; scales on the upper surface of the head of moderate size. The pectoral extends to the origin of the anal fin, and its length is less than one-half of that of the head: the ventral is not much shorter than the pectoral; greenish-olive, with darker streaks along the series of scales; a light longitudinal band from the eye to the middle of the caudal fin; two series of alternate darker blotches, one above the light band, the other below; side of the head with three oblique brown bands; dorsal and anal fins with oblique blackish stripes; caudal with blackish spots: the lower side of the head blackish, with white spots. (Günth., Fishes, iii., p. 476.)

7. *Mastacembelus argus.*

D. $\frac{32}{60}$.   A. $\frac{3}{56}$.

Præoperculum with two or three spines. The maxillary does not extend to the vertical from the anterior margin of the eye. Vertical fins continuous: brownish black, with white bands and round white spots: a band from the occiput, along the middle of the back, passing into the white margin of the vertical fins: a second band above the eye, interrupted and lost on the side of the back: a third from the angle of the mouth, passing into a series of spots, which is continued to the caudal: another series of spots along the side of the belly; the soft dorsal with a series of six spots: pectoral black at the base and near the margin. (Günth., Fishes, iii. p. 542.)

8. *Cynoglossus xiphoideus.*

D. 120.   A. 98.   V. 4.   L. lat. 135.

Three lateral lines on the left side, the upper and lower separated from the middle by twenty or twenty-one longitudinal series of scales: a single line on the right side. Two nostrils: one between the posterior parts of the eyes, the other in front

of the lower eye. Eyes separated by a concave space, the width
of which is more than that of the orbit; the upper eye considerably in advance of the lower : lips not fringed. The length
of the snout is contained twice and a third in that of the head,
the angle of the mouth being behind the vertical from the posterior margin of the eye, and nearer to the gill-opening than to
the end of the snout. The rostral hook terminates below the
front margin of the eye. The height of the body is contained
four times and two-thirds in the total length, the length of the
head five times and a half. The height of the dorsal and anal
fins is two-sevenths of that of the body. Uniform brownish-
grey. (Günth., Fish., iv. p. 495.)

ON AN APPARENTLY UNDESCRIBED SPIDER FROM COCHIN CHINA.

By Dr. Albert Günther.

——◆◆——

Cyphagogus Mouhotii.

Cephalothorax subovate, covered with fine, short, dense hairs,
with a transverse groove between cephalic and thoracic portion,
and with a deep impression in the middle of the upper surface
of the latter.

Eyes eight, unequal in size, disposed thus ·. : : :; the four
middle occupy a slight protuberance in front of the cephalothorax, whilst the lateral are the smallest, and situated on the side
of its anterior part.

Falces articulated vertically, rather compressed, with a non-
denticulated claw of moderate size at their extremity; the claw
is received in a sheath at the lower end of the falces, the edges
of the sheath being provided with some horny spines of unequal
size. Maxillæ flat; the outer margins of both together form a
card-like figure; their lower extremity is hairy; sternal lip be-

tween the maxillæ, elongate elliptical. Sternum ovate, covered with rather coarse hairs. Palpi of moderate length : the terminal joint is rather longer than the two preceding together, and armed with a minute non pectinated claw.

Legs rather robust, tapering, very unequal in length, the two anterior being nearly equally long, but much longer than the two posterior : the fourth is longer than the third : each is armed with a pair of minute claws.

Abdomen club-shaped, anteriorly produced into a very long, thin, cylindrical process, which is twice bent, so that its basal half is leaning backwards on the back of the abdomen, whilst its terminal half is directed upwards and forwards, terminating in a slight cuneiform swelling : this singular appendage is covered with a leathery, fine hairy skin, like the lower parts of the abdomen. The cephalothorax being united with the abdomen at no great distance from the spinners, the anterior portion of the abdomen, with its appendage, is situated vertically above the thorax. The abdomen is nearly smooth above, and covered with very fine hairs below ; it terminates in an obtuse point directed upwards.

Six spinners in a quadrangular group immediately before the vent : the anterior and posterior pair are of moderate size : the third pair is very short, and situated between the posterior spinners.

Two branchial opercula : tracheal opercula absent.

Dimensions.

		Lines.
Length of cephalothorax		4
,,	abdomen to the first bend of the appendage	12
,,	appendage from its first bend	10
,,	falces	$1\frac{1}{3}$
,,	palpus	$4\frac{1}{3}$
,,	terminal joint of palpus	$1\frac{2}{3}$
,,	first leg	16
,,	second leg	16_3
,,	third leg	9
,,	fourth leg	$10\frac{1}{2}$

Colour brownish yellow: extremities of the legs and of abdominal appendage and sternum blackish brown: upper parts of the abdomen yellow: two black bands round the femur of the first leg.

A single female specimen of this spider was obtained by the late M. Mouhot in the Lao Mountains of Cochin China. Its form is so extraordinary that we have not hesitated to refer it to a new genus, *Cyphagogus*.

DESCRIPTION BY M. LE COMTE DE CASTELNAU OF A NEW AND GIGANTIC CARABIDEOUS INSECT DISCOVERED BY M. MOUHOT IN LAOS.

(Communicated by the Count to the 'Revue et Magasin de Zoologie.' 1862. No. 8. Paris.)

Among the magnificent insects that M. Mouhot collected during the few months of his stay in Laos, the first place is claimed by the beautiful Carabus which forms the subject of this paper, and which I have named *Mouhotia gloriosa* after my unfortunate countryman.

This splendid insect is black, with a large border of flame-colour at the sides of the thorax and of the elytra; this is covered with longitudinal striæ, formed by a double row of punctures. The thorax is hollowed behind, smooth on the top, with the lateral border a brilliant coppery-red; it presents a small longitudinal stria in the middle of its disk, and the anterior angles are very prominent.

It much resembles Pasimachus and Emydopterus, but is distinguished from them; firstly, by the maxillary palpi, of which the last joint is broad, flat, angular on the inner side, and rounded at the end, this joint being a little longer than the one before it; secondly, by the labrum, which is wide, short, and indented on the exterior side; and thirdly, by the labial

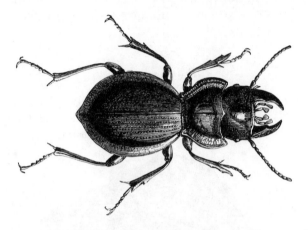

palpi, which have their last joint in the same form as the maxillary, but longer and hatchet-shaped. The mandibles are very strong, moderately arched, striated transversely, and with a strong tooth on the inner side; the jaws are also striated and obtuse at the ends. The head is similar to that of Pasimachus, the thorax is heart-shaped, the elytra oval, with angles towards the joints not strongly marked, convex, and a little serrated behind; the claws are powerful, with a strong tooth on the outer side of the middle of the tibiæ of the centre pair.

This insect is one of the most magnificent Carabidæ known, and is nearly two inches in length. The collection in the British Museum contains a fine specimen of it.

DESCRIPTIONS OF TWO NEW SPECIES OF LAND-SHELLS
DISCOVERED BY M. MOUHOT IN THE INTERIOR OF
CAMBODIA.

Helix cambojiensis.

Shell sinistral, deeply umbilicated, conoidly globose, rather
inflated; upper portion of the whorls of a rich-toned transparent chestnut colour, edged at the sutural margin with purple

black; lower portion of the whorls white, turning to a delicate
straw-colour by the overlying of a shining, transparent, horny
epidermis, encircled below the periphery and around the umbilicus with two very decided, broad, rich purple black bands;
whorls six, corrugately puckered throughout at the sutural margin, the first four whorls very densely granosely wrinkle-striated
in the direction of the lines of growth, the striæ gradually dis-
appearing on the fifth whorl; aperture lunar-orbicular; lips
simple, reflected partly round the umbilicus.

Out of two thousand species of *Helix* at present known, the
only one of the same type as *H. Mouhoti* is the large *H. Brookei*,
collected by Mr. Arthur Adams, in company with Sir Edward
Belcher, on the mountains of Borneo, during the voyage of the

' Samarang,' and described by Mr. Arthur Adams in the ' Zoology '
of that expedition. *H. Mouhoti*, of which Mr. Stevens has received a few specimens in various stages of growth, is even
larger and more inflated than *H. Brookei*. In adult specimens
the last whorl measures 6½ inches in circumference, 3 inches in
diameter, and the shell is about 2 inches high. It differs from
H. Brookei in being conspicuously, but not broadly, umbilicated,
and in the mature lip not being in the least degree reflected at
the margin. The lip itself (not the margin) is reflected at its
junction with the body-whorl, partly round the umbilicus, as in
the *Nanina* form of the genus. But the most striking feature
of the species is the colouring. In *H. Brookei* the lower half
of the whorls is of a uniform dark chestnut-colour; in *H.
Mouhoti* it is pure white, turned to a bright straw colour by the
overlying of a shining horny epidermis, encircled immediately
below the periphery by a broad, rich, purple-black band, somewhat like the bands of the large Philippine *Bulimus Reevei*,
but even broader and more defined on the white ground. The
region of the umbilicus is also deeply and as definitely stained
with the same purple-black colour. As in *H. Brookei*, all the
specimens of *H. Mouhoti* are sinistral, or what is more commonly called reversed.

Bulimus cambojiensis.

This shell is either sinistral or dextral, cylindrically ovate,
thick, stout and pupoid in the spire, bluish-white, tinged with a
watery fawn-colour, and clouded throughout with oblique zigzag
flames of the same colour, darker, but very undefined and washy;
whorls seven, smooth, rather bulbous, faintly impressed con-
cavely below the suture; aperture ovate, of rather moderate
dimensions, overlaid in a very conspicuous manner across the
body-whorl, and over a very thickly reflected lip, with a callous,
opaque, milk-white deposit, which in the interior is stained with
a beautifully iridescent violet-rose. This fine species, of which

Mr. Stevens has received several specimens, measuring nearly 3 inches in length by 1½ inch in width, is a most characteristic example of a type of the Malayan province of the genus, represented by the old *Bulimus citrinus* of Brugnière; and it has been named after its well-authenticated place of habitation, because the species is, in all probability, confined to that locality. The islands adjacent to Cambodia have been pretty well ransacked; and we have nothing like it in species either from them or from the contiguous mainland of Siam on the west, or Cochin China on the east. This particular type of the genus appears, however, abundantly at the Moluccas, in *B. citrinus*; and at Mindanao, the southernmost of the Philippine Islands, in *B. maculiferus*. Like these two species, *B. cambojiensis* occurs with the shell convoluted either to the right or to the left. The shell is both larger and stouter than that of *B. citrinus*, differently painted, and especially characterized by its mouth of iridescent violet-rose, or what is now fashionably termed " Solferino " colour.

These descriptions are from the pen of Lovell Reeve, Esq., F.L.S., &c., and were communicated by him to ' The Annals and Magazine of Natural History.' See vol. vi. p. 203.

The annexed plate contains representations of several other new and interesting species of land shells discovered by M. Mouhot, and named by Dr. Pfeiffer, but which have yet to be described.

New Land Shells discovered by M. Mouhot.

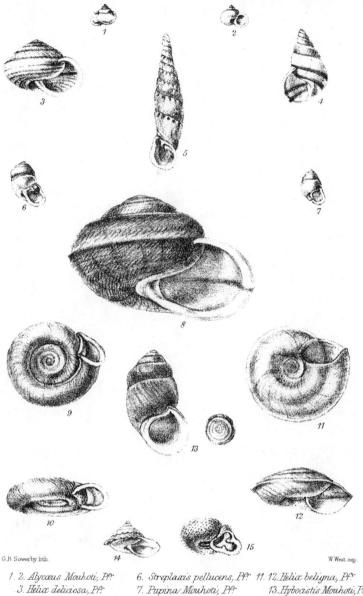

G.B. Sowerby lith.

W. West imp.

1. 2. *Alycæus Mouhoti*, Pfr.   6. *Streplaxis pellucens*, Pfr.   11. 12. *Helix beligna*, Pfr.
   3. *Helix deliciosa*, Pfr.   7. *Pupina Mouhoti*, Pfr.   13. *Hybocistis Mouhoti*, Pfr.
   4. *Bulimus Römeri*, Pfr.   8. *Helix illustris*, Pfr.   14. *Trochatella Mouhoti*, Pfr.
   5. *Clausilia Mouhoti*, Pfr.   9. 10. *Helix Laomontana*, Pfr.   15. *Helix horrida*, Pfr.

ATMOSPHERICAL OBSERVATIONS.

January. — THE month of January at Bangkok is generally
the coolest in the whole year. The thermometer generally
ranges from 58° to 60° Fahr. in the morning. The wind is
sometimes N. or N.E., and at others S.S.W. or S. The rainy
season ends in the latter part of October; the water has fallen
in the rivers, which have not overflowed since the middle of
December; therefore at this time of the year one can walk along
the banks, which are pleasant. The paths are visible and in
a good state for travellers, and there is less danger, even in
the interior of the country, of being attacked by jungle fever.
There is often fog in the morning, but yet it is not unhealthy.
The weather has been fine all the month, excepting one or two
rainy days towards the middle.

February.—During this month the wind frequently blows from
the N.E. or E., though sometimes from S.S.W. The weather
is fresh, agreeable, and healthy. It is the month which the
Buddhist pilgrims choose to visit Phrabat, where they imagine
they can trace the prints of Buddha's feet. It is the best time
for crossing the jungles and the plains, for the banks are all
raised high above the water and the earth is perfectly dry. If
the wind blows from the S. for a few days, as it sometimes
does, the heat becomes overwhelming for the time. There are
also occasionally, as in January, two or three rainy days towards
the middle of the month.

March.—This month is hotter and drier than the two preceding ones; there is less freshness. The wind blows generally
from the E.N.E., S., or S.S.W., and often with great violence
during the day: the Siamese call it Som Won (wind of the
shuttlecock), of which game they are very fond, and one hears
everywhere their noise mingled with cries of admiration from

the people. Violent storms, accompanied by rain and thunder, generally mark the equinox; after that the weather becomes hot and dry. The thermometer sometimes rises as high as 93 in the middle of the day, but the nights are still pleasant.

April.—April is the hottest month of the year. The first part is generally dry, with E. or S. winds, but changes about the middle to N.E. and S.W. In the latter part of the month the excessive heat is tempered by some refreshing rains. Although the sun is very powerful during the day, the nights at Bangkok are cool. This month is not so healthy for Europeans as the three which precede it, and dysentery makes great ravages.

May.—This month is considered one of the most rainy of the year, though sometimes July and September are more so. The rain rarely lasts all day, and there are sometimes intervals of two or three fine days. In this month the people prepare their ground and sow their rice.

June.—During the whole of this month the wind blows constantly either from the S., W., or S.W. The jungles at this season are fatal to travellers, especially to Europeans, who would do wisely to avoid them and to pass this the rainy season at Bangkok, which is one of the healthiest of the tropical towns.

July.—In July sweet and refreshing breezes blow from the W. and S., but more rain falls than in June. There are sometimes very hot days, when the thermometer rises very high, but still in Siam this month is considered tolerably healthy.

August.—The same as July.

September.—This is a month of almost incessant rain, and it is very rare to have two or three consecutive fine days.

October.—Everything is inundated, some of the streets of Bangkok are transformed into canals, and the rivers everywhere overflow their banks. The first part of this month is as rainy as the preceding one.

November.—The Siamese now complain of the cold, but the Europeans rejoice in it, for the N.E. wind begins to blow. There are still some rainy days at the beginning of the month, and some hot ones. These transitions of temperature give rise to colds and catarrhs. At the end of the month the wind changes to the S.W.

December.—This is the best month to commence travelling on the rivers. Occasionally there is thunder and rain, but altogether it is considered a healthy month.

METEOROLOGICAL REGISTER kept during the month of October 1861, and up to the sixth day after M. MOUHOT was attacked by fever.

Louang Prabang (Laos).

Dates.	Fahr. 8 A.M.	Reaumur.	Fahr. 3 P.M.	Reaumur.	Fahr. 8 P.M.	Reaumur.
1	73	18	84	..	80	..
2	72	..	85	..	78	..
3	73	18	81	22⅓	76	20
4	75	..	80	22	75¼	20
5	73	18	81	24¾	75¼	20¼
6	75½	20	79	20	75	20
7	73	19	77	20½	74	..
8	72	18½	83	23¼	72¼	18½
9	73	19	79	20	74	19
10	74	19½	83	23	74	19
11	72	18	83½	23¼	74	19
12	72	18¼	79½	21½	72	18
13	70	15½	78	21	70	17½
14	63	14½	79	21½	65	15
15	60	13	72	18	60	15
16	60	13	83½	23½	70	17
17	64	14½	83½	22	70	15
18	64	14½	86	23½	70	18
19	69	17	85	24	71½	17½
20	70	15½	89	25	74	19½
21	73	19	90	26	74	19
22	71	18	86	23½	71	18
23	73	19	87	25	70	18
24	68	16½	88	25	..	..

TALE.

Translated from the Chinese by M. Henri Mouhot.

———•◇•———

In a Chinese village lived two cousins, both orphans: the eldest, who was called Moû, was cunning and egotistical; the other, on the contrary, was goodness and simplicity itself; he was called A-lo-Sine. The time for ploughing the fields arrived: A-lo-Sine possessed a buffalo, while Moû had only a dog. An idea struck him, and he went to his cousin and said, " I bring you my dog; give me your buffalo: my dog will plough your field, which is not very large, and you will see that you will have very fine rice."

A-lo-Sine consented, and worked so well with the dog that his rice was first-rate, while the field ploughed by the buffalo produced hardly anything.

Moû, then, full of spite, went by night into his cousin's field, and set fire to it: A-lo-Sine saw the flames, and, unable to repress his despair, uttered piercing cries, and rolled in the field.

Some apes, who were marauding in a neighbouring field, witnessed this spectacle, and said to each other, " That must be a god, since the fire does not hurt him." They accordingly drew near him, took him by the feet and arms, and carried him to the top of a mountain, where they laid him down, plunged in a deep sleep. The monkeys then piled up rice and delicious fruits, and bowls of gold and silver of extraordinary beauty and value, and then left him to return to the fields.

At last he awoke, and thought no more of his misfortune, seeing around him so many treasures: he gathered them all up, and returned to his hut, full of joy.

Moû, seeing him so happy, followed him, and, at the sight of the gold, "Heavens!" cried he; "my cousin as rich as a prince: give me something."

"No," replied A-lo-Sine, "I will not; for you are wicked, and you set fire to my field."

Moû then went to his own field, and set fire to that also, and imitated all that his cousin had done: he wept, cried, and, like him, threw himself into the flames. Five monkeys, one of them a young one, who were feasting close by, drew near him, curious to see what he was about. "He is a god," said they, also; "the flames have spared him. Let us carry him away." No sooner said than done. Each monkey seized one an arm, the other a leg, and they set off.

They reached a neighbouring wood; but there the little monkey began to cry out, "I want to help to carry him also." "But there is nothing of him to hold by," said the mother. The little monkey, however, continued to cry, and at last seized Moû's long tress of hair, and put himself at the head of the procession.

But this hurt Moû, and he tried to disengage his hair. The young monkey began to cry again. "Ah, you are angry; stay there, then," said all the others, and they threw him into a prickly bush.

Moû had great trouble in extricating himself from his disagreeable position; and it was nearly evening when he reached home, all covered with blood.

"Well, cousin, have you also some gold and silver?" said A-lo-Sine, on seeing him. "Ah! I am thoroughly punished for the harm I did you," replied Moû. "I bring back nothing but needles: call the women to take them out of me."

TALE.

TRANSLATED FROM THE CHINESE BY M. HENRI MOUHOT.

———◆◇◆———

THERE lived formerly in a Chinese village an old couple who had no children; and one day the husband put himself in a violent passion with his wife for never having had any, and even beat her. The poor old woman rushed out of the house, crying, and ran a long way. A priest of Buddha met her accidentally, and asked her what had happened to her. " My husband was angry to-day, and beat me, because we had no children," replied she. " Listen," said the priest; " I will make you happy! Dig in this earth and knead it" (it was clay). The woman obeyed, and the priest then sat down, and with his fingers moulded nine little figures. " The first," said he, " will have long ears and very quick hearing; the second, a piercing sight; the third, a skin so hard that he will not feel any blow; the fourth will stand fire without hurt; the fifth will have an enormous head, as hard as iron; the sixth, legs long enough to cross the deepest stream; the seventh, feet as large as those of an elephant, for walking in mire; the eighth, an immense stomach; and the ninth, a nose as long as a pipe, from which jets of water will issue at command. Now," continued the priest, " go home, and every year eat one of these children." The old woman bowed several times, professing her gratitude and happiness; then she returned home; but in her joy, instead of contenting herself with one child, she eat up all nine at once. Her stomach, which had begun to swell at once, grew every month bigger and bigger, and became frightful. The husband was beside himself with joy, and was very kind to his wife.

At last the day of delivery arrived: the father received the first child, and ran to wash him in the stream; but there came a second. "Another!" cried the father, and ran again to the river. Returning, he found a third, then a fourth. He opened his eyes and cried, "Really this is quite enough : what can we give them to eat ?" But the whole nine made their appearance on the same day.

All were prodigies : they grew rapidly; never cried; eat enormously, and began to run about in two months. But the old man did not know what to call them all; and one day he complained to his wife that he could not distinguish them one from another, got in another passion, and struck her again. The old woman ran away, crying, again, and went to find the priest who had helped her before. "Why do you cry now ?" said he. "My husband has so many children now that he does not know what names to give them." "You are very foolish," replied he, "not to be able to distinguish them by the gifts they possess. Call one 'Quick-ear,' another 'Hard-head,' and so on for the others."

The old man had calmed down when his wife returned; but debts accumulated as the children grew up. At last they became strong and fearless.

One day a creditor came and asked for money. "I have none," replied the old man. He persisted in this reply, and at last turned the creditor out of the house. A few days after, this man collected several of his friends, and went again to the old man, declaring he would seize one of the children, and whip him. "Quick-ear" had heard all, and "Piercing-eye" had mounted to the top of a tree and seen all that was going on. They decided that "Hard-skin" would be the best to go, and the creditor succeeded in binding him and taking him away. But every cane broke on his back, without hurting him : at last they took an immense cudgel, but this broke in the same way; and seeing that it was lost time to beat him, they let him go home.

But a few days after, the creditor came back, determined to

kill one of the children with boiling water. "Quick-ear" heard the project, and "Invulnerable" was left at home, and consequently carried off. They threw him into a boiler full of water; and in about an hour, when they opened it, the child raised his head. "What, not yet dead!" cried the creditor, in a fury, and he made up a larger fire, but "Invulnerable" was still alive. They made it still hotter, but the next day their wood was exhausted, and they let him go free, saying that Buddha protected him. "This is very sad," said the creditor; "I cannot get my money; I cannot get my money: I will write a letter to Heaven, to beg that fire may be sent down to burn the house of my debtor." He did so accordingly; but "Quick-ear," who heard the plot, warned "Fountain-nose," who thereupon took care to water the roof. The thunderbolt fell, but glided from the roof to the ground. All the children joined their strength, and lifted it, chained it up, and placed it in the house.

"Is it possible," cried the creditor, "that they are not all dead? I must throw one of them into the sea." This time it was "Stilt-bird's" turn. The boat in which they placed him had not gone far from the shore when a storm arose and upset it, and all the men were drowned, with the exception of "Stilt-bird," who escaped, thanks to his long legs. However, his brothers feared for him, and sent "Big-head" to the shore, where he found him fishing, and having already caught so many fish that he did not know where to put them. Luckily "Big-head" had his hat, which they filled, and returned home with an immense load. "Large-feet" went to cut wood to fry it with; but "Great-stomach" eat it all up before his brothers had hardly had time to begin. "Weeping-eyes" began to cry, and an inundation ensued, in which many of the neighbours perished.

Meanwhile, all the children were out searching for food, and the mother was left at home alone. She, seeing the thunderbolt chained in a corner, unfastened it. Immediately it rose in the air, then, falling again, struck the poor woman, and killed her.

FABLE.

Translated from the Chinese by M. Henri Mouhot.

Firmness and presence of mind often make heroes of cowards, and rescue them from great dangers, while rashness is generally fatal.

In the midst of a thick and virgin forest, where everything seemed to slumber, an elephant began to utter doleful howlings, and a tiger replied by others still more dreadful, which froze all the other animals with terror. Monkeys, stags, and all the inhabitants of the neighbourhood, ran groaning to seek refuge at the tops of the trees, or in the depth of the woods, or in their dens. The elephant himself ran with all his speed, when on his way he met a hare, who stopped him, and said, " Why do you run thus, without aim and without reason ? " "What! did you not hear the frightful roaring of the tiger ? Would you advise me to stay here and be devoured ? " " Stay here, and have no fear ; I will answer for it that no harm happens to you," said the hare ; " only sit down, that I may jump on your back." The elephant goodnaturedly approached and extended his four legs ; then the hare jumped up, having first put into his mouth a piece of betel.

" Now, get up again," said he, " and you will see that all will go well." He then proceeded to give the elephant further counsel, and afterwards let out along his back a long stream of saliva, reddened by betel. Soon the tiger came up. " What are you coming to seek here ? " said the hare, as the tiger stopped to look at them. " Do you not see that this elephant is not too much for me alone; and do you think I will share with you?" The tiger drew aside, behind a tree, to watch what passed. The hare then seized hold of the elephant's ear, made him roar, and seemed perfectly master of his prey, and busy at his work. "Heavens! how strong he is!" said the tiger; but still he drew near. "Wait a minute, and I will come to you," cried the hare, looking as though preparing to spring, and the tiger, struck with terror, turned and ran away. A chimpanzee, seeing him running away in such terror, burst out laughing. "What! you laugh at my misfortune?" cried the tiger. "I have just escaped from death, and you do not pity me." "How so? I should like to see the beast who frightened you; take me to him."

"What! to be devoured? no."

"Do not be afraid; I will get on your back, and will not leave you: we will fasten our tails together, if you like; and thus united we shall run no risk!" The tiger was persuaded by these words, and they both returned to the elephant. The hare seemed still busy at his work: he had chewed a new piece of betel, and had made another stream, red as blood, on the elephant's back. "You dare to come back!" cried he, in an angry tone, to the tiger. "You knew I had only just enough here for myself, and yet you want to carry away my prey from me; you deserve to be punished."

At these words the elephant uttered a piercing cry; the hare made an enormous bound on his back; and the tiger, struck with terror, rushed precipitately away at full speed, saying to the chimpanzee, "Now, you see; you laughed at my fears, and we both narrowly escaped death." But the chimpanzee did not hear; for in the tiger's precipitate retreat he had fallen off his back, struck himself against a bamboo, and died, cursing his rashness with his last sigh.

THE HARE AND THE SNAIL.

FABLE.

TRANSLATED FROM THE CHINESE BY M. HENRI MOUHOT.

————◇•————

FORMERLY, according to the Siamese, hares had thick ears; but a certain day one of these animals, having more legs than memory, met a snail dragging himself painfully along the ground, and in a moment of pride sought to humiliate him. "Why, little one, where are you going at this pace?" said he. "To the beautiful rice-fields of the next village." "But, my poor fellow, you will be a long time reaching them. Why did not Nature furnish you with legs like mine? Confess you envy me. How long, now, do you think it would take me to get there?"

"Perhaps longer than it would take me, though you pity me so much," replied the snail, coldly.

"You jest, do you not?"

"No."

"Well, will you bet about it?"

"Willingly."

"What will you bet?"

"Whatever you like."

"Well, then, if you win you shall nibble my ears; for you cannot eat me; and if you lose I will eat you: will that suit you?"

"Perfectly."

"Then set off; for I will give you a start."

While the hare began to browse the snail set off at his slow pace, and went to his brother, who was a little way off, and to him he communicated a pass-word, which he in turn told to another, and so on along the whole line which the betters had to travel, so that it quickly reached the end.

Soon the hare, having satisfied his hunger, and feeling strong, set off, and flew over the ground, calling to the snail, whom he believed to be close by. "Ohé!" answered he, from a long way off. "Oh, he is already far on the way," cried the hare, who set off again like an arrow. In a few minutes he stopped and called again: "Ohé," answered a voice still farther on. "Really, he goes very quickly," thought the hare, and he set off again. A quarter of an hour after, he stopped, quite out of breath. "Now," said he, "I may rest; I must be far in advance; but I will call and see. "Ohé! snail." "Ohé!" replied a voice a long way on. "Oh! I must be quick; I shall lose my bet," murmured the hare. He ran, and ran, and at last stopped, quite exhausted, only a few yards from the fields. "Snail," cried he, faintly: "what! you are returning from the place? Unfortunate that I am, I have lost my bet;" and he made vain efforts to get up and escape, but, alas! his strength failed him, and the snail pitilessly gnawed his ears.

Since that day the hare always avoids damp places, for fear of meeting one of the creatures who punished him for his pride.

TALE.

TRANSLATED FROM THE CHINESE BY M. HENRI MOUHOT.

THERE lived formerly in a small town in China a singular couple, of a description still met with, for the Chinese progress very slowly. The husband was noted for his folly, and the wife for her cunning. "Always remember," she used constantly to say to her husband when he went out, "that all people with long noses, in the form of an eagle's beak, and bending downwards, are good-for-nothings, beggars, cheats, and, worse still, bad paymasters, coiners of false money, false-swearers, and will go to hell; while people with small turned-up noses are good, and will go straight to heaven. Therefore, that you may not lose, sell only to these last; for, I repeat to you, the others are bad."

Every day the husband went out, and passed from street to street, examining the passers-by, but never addressing any but those who had their heads raised to look at something, so that he very seldom sold anything.

One day, when he was observing noses as usual, he saw a man reading a placard which was placed very high. "That man will go straight to heaven," thought he; "his nose is so much turned up. Will you buy some clothes, good man?" said he. "Clothes! you see I have some." "But you appear to me the most honest man I ever saw" ("I never saw such a nose," he added to himself); "and I should like to sell you a whole suit; my wife makes them herself." "Well, what is the price?" "Of my wife?" "No; of the clothes." "Two kóóu" (about ten francs). "But why do you come into this retired place to sell your clothes, when there are so many people elsewhere?" "Oh! I went to those places; but all the people had long, bent, and eagle-shaped noses, you see! and I only sell to snub-nosed people." "I do not understand you; why will you not sell to people with long noses?" "My wife who is a very clever woman, told me that all people with long, eagle-shaped noses are knaves." "Really, yóur wife is very sharp, and I understand you now. Well, my friend, I will buy your clothes; but as I have no money with me, I will pay you to-morrow. You have only to come to my house; I live near here. You will see a hurdle covered with eggs, a flag at the end of a mast, and a little plantation of betel." "Very well; that will do."

The merchant went home to his wife, and told her he had sold to a man with a snub nose. "Where is the money?" said she. "I have not got it yet, but I shall be sure to have it to-morrow. I am to go where I see a hurdle covered with eggs, a flag on a mast, and a little betel plantation." The next day the wife said, " Go for your money." He went, but could not find the house; and after long searching he came home again. " Have you the money ? " said the wife. " No, I could not find the house." " Well, I will go myself to look for it. If I am not back in an hour, you will know that I am drowned." After an hour, as his wife did not return, the man took the sieve with which he usually sifted his rice, and set off to the river, which he began to try to empty with it. A passer-by asked him what he was doing. " I am emptying the river," replied he; " for my wife is drowned, and she had on her best yellow bonnet." " Nonsense ! " said the other; " I just met her walking with a man who had a snub nose."

THE DAMIER, OR CAPE PIGEON.

Procellaria Capensis.

DURING a long voyage, when for months you have seen nothing but water and sky, the smallest novelty which appears and promises variety for the eye and the mind, though only for a few minutes, is joyfully welcome. Sometimes it may be a stormy petrel, flying like a swallow, skimming through the air in a hundred different directions, and seeming to play in that element; sometimes a ring-tail, which, with its piercing cry like that of a hawk, appears a messenger from the sun to bid the bold navigator welcome to the tropics, hovers for a few minutes over the ship, and then flies off with a jerk and disappears.

Sometimes are to be seen numerous blowers, who pass and repass the ship with bounds; or perhaps a whale, which almost stupefies you with the noise he makes as he displaces the water in rising to the surface to breathe : at another time it is some hungry shark, who, following in the wake of the ship, lets himself be caught by the bait thrown out to him, and which, when hoisted with great difficulty on deck, lashes it with his tail and looks formidable even after death; and this is a good take for the sailors, who divide the spoil and feast on it.

But of all the creatures dear and familiar to sailors, none rejoices him more than the faithful companion who, more than 3000 miles before he doubles the Cape of Good Hope or Cape Horn, appears to his sight, swims in the water, grazes a thousand times the hull or the rigging, pleases his eye by its particoloured plumage, and announces to him calm and tempest.

This bird, called by the French " *Damier*," by the English the *Cape Pigeon*, and "*Peintada*" by the Portuguese, is the Cape Petrel, or *Procellaria capensis* of naturalists.

Gifted with great powers of flight, though less than other petrels, from morn till night, and often even a part of the latter when the moon is full, it is seen in the wake or alongside of the ship, describing in its flight, in which scarcely any movement is apparent, a thousand evolutions, sometimes touching the great waves which seem ready to overwhelm it, the moment after reappearing far above them, always wheeling about and careless of the storm.

The sight of this flight and of all these evolutions is most pleasing, and one involuntarily thinks of a graceful skater flying over the ice at his utmost speed, and seeking to attract admiration.

The whole life of this bird is perpetual movement, a constant chase after a scarce and insignificant prey. Unlike the swallow, who has his hours of pleasure and of amorous warbling, and nights of sleep in his warm nest, the Cape pigeon, pressed by hunger and by his ravenous appetite, only rests for a few minutes at a time at rare intervals during the day, in order to recruit his strength, and at night, rocked by the stormy wave, must find but little sleep.

Neither does the Cape pigeon know the delight of a peaceful retreat in a favourite spot sheltered by thick foliage or long reeds; and while most birds confine themselves to a limited district, where they are almost certain to be found at the same season, and to which they invariably return at the disappearance of the frosts which have chased them away for a time, this one, a sailor by nature, has for its domain an immense empire, namely the greatest part of the Atlantic, Pacific, and Indian oceans, and has to brave night and day, at one time an icy wind, and at another the rays of a burning sun.

But in a state of liberty nothing living is often unhappy, and the foreseeing Providence, who knows how to satisfy the wants of his creatures, also knows how to create joys for them, where we see nothing but trouble and misery. In like manner the industrious workman and the hardy traveller experience, perhaps, of all men the most lively joys; to them repose would be the greatest suffering.

Although inseparable companions of the sailor, it is not certainly for the pleasure of his society, nor for that afforded by the sight of the ship, that the petrels follow it, but for the certainty of finding in the scraps thrown overboard, as well as in the number of shells in the wake of the ship, food more abundant than he would discover elsewhere in the water. Nothing can equal their voracity but the quickness and vivacity with which they catch sight of the smallest prey and seize it even amidst a stormy sea. From a great distance, and long before the albatross, and the other descriptions of petrels which are often to be seen with the Cape pigeons, have remarked it, they see and pounce on it, and have generally swallowed it before the jealous rivals who follow them have been able to overtake them. The sense of smell does not here come in aid of that of sight, for they often pounce on a piece of wood or something of that description which falls from a vessel, and only abandon it when convinced by the touch that it is not fit for food. Their greediness is such that they will often let themselves be taken in dozens with hooks; no sooner are they on deck than they disgorge a thick liquid the colour of linseed oil.

When these birds rest on the sea and let themselves be tossed about by the waves, their appearance, dimensions, form, and colour of plumage strongly resemble our domestic pigeons, and hence the English seamen, struck with the similarity, have given them the name of Cape pigeons. Their size varies; the largest measuring more than 18 inches English from the beak to the tip of the tail, and rather more than a foot in circumference.

They are generally seen in great numbers only in stormy weather and in rather high latitudes. In the winter season—that is, during our June, July, and August—they follow the ships constantly between 23° S. lat. and 31° and 103° E. long.

Is it not a wonderful thing and worthy of admiration that the instinct with which this bold little navigator is endowed guides him safely through this vast space, where there is nothing to serve him as a landmark, enables him to rejoin his comrades if accidentally separated from them, and teaches him every year when the warm season returns to recognise and find the island or the solitary rock where he was born, and where in his turn he will bring up his young ones; while man, with his maps, his books, his nautical instruments, and in spite of all his long experience, has such difficulty in finding his way across the ocean? And yet we think that our intelligence raises us above the animals. This is what confounds and overwhelms the scholar when he seeks to fathom the great mysteries of creation.

THE ALBATROSS.

—•◦•—

A WISE and bountiful Providence has taken care to people
the most distant and desert parts of the globe, whether covered
with eternal snow or impenetrable forests.   In the waters of
the ocean are, as well as in our fields and woods, creatures
which rejoice the eyes of man and provide for his wants.   Of all
these creatures none are more charming and pleasing than the
birds ; endowed either with melodious voices or brilliant plumage, or with some other charm or quality, such as vivacity,
quickness and grace of movement, and power of flight ; all have
attractions for us ; and even in our museums, in spite of their
faded plumage and often altered forms, they are still objects
of admiration, not only to the learned naturalist, but to men
who care little for other beautiful sights.

But if leaving the cabinet we visit Nature herself, penetrate
into the heart of the forests, climb the rocks, or visit the shores
and the ocean, then our admiration grows stronger and more
deep.

Of all birds there is none which exercises a greater influence
over the mind of man, or causes greater astonishment, than the
albatross, so celebrated by voyagers from the earliest times.
The albatross ! The word recalls to the navigator a thousand
souvenirs ; as the name of some bloody battle in which he has
taken part, or of some general who has led him to victory,
awakens those of the soldier.   It recalls to the memory of the
sailor the principal incidents of an existence passed between
calm and tempest ; he feels himself transported in thought to
the time when the first albatross was signalled, and passengers
and sailors turned their gaze eagerly towards the spot where,
like a proud man of war, cradled by the rolling waves, advanced

the powerful sailer against whom the storm rages in vain, and who, far from avoiding, seems to court it.

To this first souvenir succeed many others; there is the dead calm, which in the tropics has often detained his vessel inactive for weeks, as though chained under the burning sky, where the eye seeks in vain for a cloud, and the only sound that meets the ear is the heavy flapping of the sails against the masts as the ship rocks; a calm often more to be feared and more dangerous than the most terrible tempest, for it renders the crew inactive, impatient, and bad-tempered. But the first sight of the albatross indicates a coming change and wind to be expected. There is also the memory of painful and too sudden transitions from equatorial heat to the cold of high latitudes; that also of hours of dreadful anxiety when the storm broke out in all its violence, of the contest between winds and waves, and of the albatross hovering over the latter, as though chosen an umpire between these two formidable antagonists. The albatross inhabits the southern hemisphere of the Atlantic Ocean from the 25° or 26° of latitude, also both Pacifics, but is rarely seen farther north, and has never been known beyond the tropics; it is in the seas which bathe the three southern capes that they are seen in the greatest numbers.

It often happens, however, when the winter is mild and the weather fine, that very few are seen until you reach the 40°. They lay their eggs on some deserted southern shore; the female lays only one, and feeds her little one for nine months without leaving it, so much need has it of its mother's help.

There is much difficulty in the classification of the palmipeds, which exhibit a great number of varieties.

The beak of the albatross is long and very strong; the upper jaw furrowed at the side and much curved; the lower one sharp, smooth, and truncated at the end; the nostrils, formed by two tubes opening outwards, are lateral and placed in a groove.

The tarsi are short, but very thick, and ending in three front toes much palmated; the wings are long and narrow.

There are probably four distinct species of albatrosses.

1st. The wandering albatross, *Diomedea exulans*, which measures ten feet with the wings spread; it has a white head, the wings and belly being spotted with white, grey, and chestnut brown; the beak is the colour of horn. This species varies much in size, and still more in colour and plumage, which is more or less mixed with grey or brown, and sometimes even entirely white; this depends doubtless on the season, the sex, and the age.

2nd. The epauletted albatross, *Diomedea epomophera*, which is smaller than the common albatross. His head, neck, body, back, and rump are snowy white, while the feathers of his wings are perfectly black, with the exception of a large white lozenge-shaped spot on each; the beak is yellowish. Some naturalists believe these to be only the young of the ordinary kind.

3rd. The yellow-beaked albatross, *Diomedea chlororhyncos*. This species I have myself taken with a hook; his head, belly, and neck are brilliantly white, his back and the plumage of the wings a deep brown grey, the beak yellow, and the feet bluish grey; the rump is white, and as well as the underpart of the tail is bordered by a wide black line.

4th. The sooty albatross, *Diomedea spadicea* of Forster, which is the size of the common albatross, and of a uniform deep chestnut-colour.

CAMBODIAN VOCABULARY.

A.

Abandon (to)	Lĕng, chol.
Abhor (to)	Sââp.
Approach (to)	Dâl.
Abstinence .. .. Abstain (to)	} Tam.
Accept (to)	Iotuol.
Accompany (to)	Iam.
Accomplish (to)	Ihúruéch hoì.
Accustom oneself (to)	Ihlap.
Accuse (to)	Shŏdéng.
Acid	Ehu.
Admire (to)	Ehhugăl.
Adore (to)	Ihoui băngeom.
Adultery	Bap phit propon Ki.
Afflict (to)	Lruey chot chaw chot.
Age	Acŏschhnam.
Announce (to)	Srăp, pram.
Appease (to)	On.
Appetite	Comléan Klileán.
After	Ĕcroí.
Arid	Sngnot, comynot.
Arm	Crùóng predăp.
Army	Iăp.
Arrive (to)	Dâl.
Assembly	Chumnam.

Assemble (to)	Chumnam Kenéa.
Audacity	}Ihean.
Audacious	
August	Mahu.
Also	Dél.
Altar	Balang, as-prĕn.
Agile	Chuery.
Air	Acos.
Add (to)	Thêm.
Aloes	Jadam.
Alum	Saĕpchu.
Amuse oneself (to)	Ling.
Ancient	Chus.
Ass	Satliá.
Angel	Firĕuda.
Angle	Chrung.
Animal	Săt.
Avarice	Comnaut.
Advocate	Sma Kedey.
Abortive (to be)	Relutcõn.
Arm	Phlu.
Aim	Vong.
Ashes	Phe.
Ask (to)	Som.
Above	Lù ê lù.
And	Non.
Awake (to)	Dăs.
Arrow	Prúeup.
Agreeable	Totuol.
Appearance	Cŏmnăp.
According to	Tam.
Always	Ruéy (iún ruey reáp darăpton muc).
Anger	Conhong.
Amongst	Erang.

Across .. .. Totùng.
Already .. .. Hoi.

B.

Bitter .. .. Loving.
Before .. .. Mum.
Bathe (to) .. .. Ngut tin.
Breath .. .. Dâng hina.
Bold .. .. Tahéan.
Broom .. .. Bombãs.
Bamboo .. .. Resey.
Banana .. .. Chá.
Banquet .. .. Car si.
Beard .. .. Puk mŏt.
Boat .. .. Iui.
Build (to) .. .. Sâhy, thú phtĕn.
Beat (to) .. .. Véag.
Beautiful .. .. Sââ.
Benediction .. .. Prăe pór.
Beast .. .. Sat.
Blue .. .. Khín.
Beef .. .. Cũ.
Bushel .. .. Ihang-Iao.
Box .. .. Hêp.
Bottle .. .. Săr phdŏe.
Button .. .. Leu.
Branch .. .. Mie.
Brick .. .. Ot.
Break (to) .. .. Rei.
Burn (to) .. .. Dot.
Buffalo .. .. Crebey.
Black .. .. Khnaun.

Bone .. .. Cheóng.

Bread .. .. Nam.

Basket .. .. Conchir.

Blade .. .. Lompeng.

Book .. .. Sombot.

Bed .. .. Domnéc.

But .. .. Pê.

Bad .. .. Bap, chomngú.

Breast .. .. Dă.

Beg (to) .. .. Som teau.

Better .. .. Cheang, lus.

Bite (to) .. .. Kham.

Be born (to) .. .. Cót.

Bee .. .. Khmum.

Bark (to) .. .. Sru.

Buy (to) .. .. Iink.

Business .. .. Domnor.

Bow .. .. Ehme.

Batatas .. .. Eomlong.

Bridge .. .. Spreau.

Behind .. .. Croi, ê croi.

Back .. .. Hhnang.

Be (to) .. .. Non-mêan, Chèn.

Big .. .. Phom.

Broil (to) .. .. Hang.

Bird .. .. Sat liar.

Blood .. .. Chheàm.

Blow (to) .. .. Phlŏm.

Betray (to) .. .. Kebăt.

Bark .. .. Sombok.

Brother (elder) .. .. Bâng.

Brother (younger) .. .. .. Phŏôn.

C.

Come (to)	Moc Dăl.
Cottage	Catôm.
Corpse	Khmoch.
Cage..	Irung.
Case	Hêp.
Calk (to)	Bàt.
Calm oneself (to)	On.
Cambodia	Sroch Khmêr.
Cambodian	Khmêr.
Country	Neal.
Canal	Preê.
Comb	Suét.
Cask	Thâng.
Cardamom	Crevanh.
Cause	Het dòm.
Cold (a)	Cââc.
Cup	Chan.
Conduce (to)	Tôm.
Cloth	Souipăt.
Cough	Cââc.
Commotion	Revàl.
Cut (to)	Cat.
Conquer (to)	Chhnĕa.
Conquered	Chănh.
Clothing	Ao.
Carriage	Retĕ.
Centipede	Kaêp.
Circle	Vong.
Coffin	Mochhus.
Chain	Chervăi.
Choir	Sach.
Change (to)	Prê.

P 2

Coal	Khîung.
Chastity	Sel.
Cat	Chhma.
Chief	Mechàs, héay.
Chinese	Swe chèn.
Cholera	Rŏmbâl.
Clear	Thla.
Clock	Condong.
Cocoa-nut	Dong.
Combat (to)	Chebang.
Commencement	Dòm.
Count (to)	Rắp.
Consent (to)	Prom.
Console (to)	Tŭo Săo.
Clay	Deyót.
Crowd	Fông, cânbân.
Crow	Khoêi.
Cord	Khse.
Coast	Khaeng.
Cotton	Crebas.
Colour	Sombar.
Cut	Cap, cat.
Crown	Mocŏt.
Call (to)	Han.
Clean	Saat.
Cry (to)	Tŏui.
Carry (to)	Chun, Rĕc sêng.
Clean (to)	Nos leáng.
Cloud	Sapŏc.
Chew (to)	Bièm.
Cold	Rengia.
Cricket	Chungret.
Clock	Novea.
Custom	Chebăp, Tomlăp.

Create (to) .. .. Bângeat.
Cry .. .. Sâmléng.
Cry (to) .. .. Srêc.
Cook (to) .. .. Dam.
Copper .. .. Spŏn.
Cymbal .. .. Lông, Khmŏ.
Crab .. .. Pomgeong.
Church (temple) .. .. Preă-Vihear.
Carry away (to) .. .. Roc ton.
Coat (to) .. .. Leap.
Child .. .. Coming.

D.

Descend (to) .. .. Chô.
Desire (to) .. .. Sângvat, Châng.
Destroy (to) .. .. Pombat.
Debt .. .. Bomnàl.
Diviner .. .. Achar.
Daybreak .. .. Prealum, Preahean.
Delicate .. .. Ton.
Different .. .. Titey.
Difficult .. .. Cra.
Disciple .. .. Cŏn Sŏs.
Dearth .. .. Âmnât.
Dispute (to) .. .. Chhlŏ prokêe.
Doubt .. .. Moutûl.
Dysentery .. .. Chomngú mual.
Do (to) .. .. Thu.
Dung .. .. Ach.
Dress (to) .. .. Prăeae.
Damp .. .. Som.
Drunk .. .. Sreving.
Day .. .. Thugay.

Deliver (to) .. .. Preeol.

Doctor .. .. Cruthnam, pet.

Despise (to) .. .. Măcngeáy.

Deride (to) .. .. Sôch, châm-ôn.

Die (to) .. .. Slăp.

Dwarf .. .. Tua.

During .. .. Compung.

Dust .. .. Ehuli.

Dare (to) .. .. Héan.

Dote (to) .. .. Trŭl.

Dove .. .. Rŭs.

Dig (to) .. .. Hal.

Drum .. .. Seôr.

Delay (to) .. .. Ângvéng.

Dye (to) .. .. Cherlŏc.

Darkness .. .. Tângcap.

Draw (to) .. .. Téanh.

Deceive (to) .. .. Bŏn chhăt.

Dear .. .. Thlay.

Dew .. .. Ânsóm.

Deaf .. .. Câ.

Dream .. .. Sâp.

Dog .. .. Chkê.

Door .. .. Shóĕ.

Drink (to) .. .. Elinear.

Duck .. .. Iea.

Dream (to) .. .. Zăl Sap.

E.

Exchange (to) .. .. Dôr.

Efface (to) .. .. Lap.

Equal .. .. Smó.

Elephant .. .. Tamrey.

Endure (to) .. .. Ăt, ȯn.

Engage (to) .. .. Pobuol.

Enemy .. .. Satron-Khmang.

Enter (to) .. .. Chôl.

Envy (to) .. .. }Chernêu.
Envy .. ..

Example .. .. Kébuon.

Exhort (to) .. .. Boutun méan.

End .. .. Chông.

Evening .. .. Lŏngéach.

Easy .. .. Ngeáy.

End .. .. Long-âs.

Eye .. .. Phnée.

Egg .. .. Pong-sut.

Ear .. .. Erechiéc.

Equal .. .. Mytrey.

Eat (to) .. .. Si, pisa, chhăn, soi.

Even .. .. Smó, dock.

Everywhere .. .. Săp ăulú.

Eagle .. .. Antri.

Earth .. .. Dey, Preă thorni.

F.

Face .. .. Mŭc.

Feeble .. .. Comsoi.

Family .. .. Crua.

Famine .. .. Âmnăt.

Fatigue .. .. Nuèy.

Fault .. .. Tus.

Female .. .. Nhi.

Ferocious .. .. Sahan.

Fire .. .. Phlâng.

Fever	Cran.
Figure	Muc.
Flower	Phŏm.
Faith	Chommia.
Forest	Prey.
Fresh	Rehoi.
Front	Thngos.
Fruit	Phle.
Float (to)	Ândet.
Freeze (to)	Câc.
Fat	Thop.
Frog	Ong Kêp.
Food	Ahur Sâbiĕng.
Friend	Keló.
Formerly	Pidom.
Firewood	Os.
Finger	Day.
Fast	Buos.
Fast (to)	Si buos.
Free	Neaĕ Cheá.
Far	Chhngai.
Falsehood	Câhâc.
Frightful	Noiai.
Forget (to)	Chŭs bât côrna.
Fly	Rug.
Fishing	Bap.
Fish (to)	Stuch trey, Dóc non.
Father	A puc.
Few	Eech.
Fear	Khlach.
Full	Peuh.
Feather	Slap, mems.
Foot	Chung.
Fish	Eyey.

Fowl .. .. Món.
Fill (to) .. .. Bampenh.
Fool .. .. Lengong.
Follow (to) .. .. Tam, dòr tam.
Firebrand .. .. Rengûc.
Fall (to) .. .. Duol-thleăc.
Find (to) .. .. Roi ban.
Face .. .. Mac.
Flesh .. .. Sach.
Field .. .. Prê.
Figuratively .. .. Chŏt.
Fear (to) .. .. Khlàch.
Fly (to) .. .. Luèch.
Fly (to) (like a bird) .. .. .. Hòr.

G.

Gold .. .. Meas.
Gunpowder .. .. Démsón.
Go (to) .. .. Tou.
Greedy .. .. Luphu.
Good .. .. Lââ, chiá, písa.
Grind (to) .. .. Boh.
Girdle .. .. Crevat.
Garlic .. .. Ketym Sá.
Grasshopper .. .. Chungret.
Go out (to) .. .. Chenh.
Green .. .. Khién, baí tong.
Glass (a) .. .. Péng Kên, Kên.
Go to bed (to) .. .. Dec.
Grow (to) .. .. Sbec.
God .. .. Prĕa.
Give (to) .. .. Oi, chun.
Grief .. .. Chhu.

Girl .. .. Consrey.

Gun .. .. Comphlûng.

Gain (to) .. .. Ban chonménch.

Guard (to) .. .. Reăesa.

Glove .. .. Teăc.

Generous .. .. Chôt tuléay.

Ginger .. .. Khnhey.

Glutton .. .. Luphu.

Gum .. .. Chor.

Govern (to) .. .. Tac tîng.

Governor .. .. Chanfai sroč.

Grave .. .. Ânisăng.

Grain .. .. Crŏp.

Great .. .. Thôm Kepŏs.

Graft .. .. Crechâc.

Guide (to) .. .. Nóm.

Grass .. .. Smau.

Garden .. .. Chomca, chebar.

Gladness .. .. Ngeay.

H.

Hunger .. .. Comléan.

Hungry (to be) .. .. Khléan.

Helm .. .. Changcôt.

Hail .. .. Prŭl.

Habit .. .. Tomlăp.

Hatchet .. .. Puthae.

Hate (to) .. .. Săâp.

Haricot .. .. Sondêe.

Harmonious .. .. Pirŏ.

High .. .. Kepŏs.

Hour .. .. Mong, Teunc.

Hideous	Acrăc, asron.
Honour (to)	Rŏp an.
Horror (to have an) of	Kepum.
Half	Chomhieng conmat, pheac condat.
Hard	Rùng.
Hell	Morok.
Hear (to)	Lú.
House	Phtêa.
Husband	Phodey.
Honey	Tác khmum.
Host	Phnhién.
Humble	Suphéap réap téap.
Here	Nĕ ênĕ.
Heavy	Thngŏn.
Hundredweight	Hap.
Holy	Arahán.
His	Rônthuc.
Hold (to)	Can.
Hole	Prŏhong.
Heat	Cadau.
Horse	Sê.
Hair	Sôc.
Heart	Bêdông.
How much	Ponman.
How	Doehmedéch?
Horn	Sneng.
Hang (to)	Phiuor.
Hair (of animals)	Merues.
Heap (to)	Bomol.
Have (to)	Mean.
Happiness	Boran-Lays.
Hide (to)	Puvu.
He	Veá Cǎt.

Heaven .. .. Mie.
Him .. .. Châng.

I.

Ignorant   .. .. Khlan.
Island .. .. Că.
Image .. .. Comnur.
Imbecile .. .. Chicuat.
India .. .. Pon, suey.
Impost .. .. Srŏc Keling créas.
Indicate (to) .. .. Bânghanh.
Inundate (to) .. .. Lich.
Inscribe (to) .. .. Cat.
Insipid .. .. Sap.
Instant .. .. Mŏ pŏnlú.
Instruct (to) .. .. Predan, Pourieu.
Insult (to) .. .. Promat pikhèat.
Intelligence .. .. Praehuha.
Intention .. .. Chŏt.
Interdict (to) .. .. Khŏt.
Interest (of money) .. .. Lar prăe.
Interpret (to) .. .. Prêpasa.
Interrogate (to) .. .. Suor, donding.
Introduce (to) .. .. Boŭchôlnòm.
Invite (to) .. .. Anchùnh.
Ill .. .. Chhu.
Illness .. .. Chumgŭ.
If .. .. Bó.
In order that .. .. Oi.
Idle .. .. Khchìl.
Idleness .. .. Comchil.

In .. .. Kenong.
Incense .. .. Comnhau.
Is .. .. Còt.
Inhabit (to) .. .. Non, công.

J.

Join (to) .. .. Phehăp.
Joy .. .. Âmnâr.
Joyous .. .. Ar, sabai, sremŏc sŏc sabai.
Judge .. .. Chmrom.
Judge (to) .. .. Cat săch Kedey.
Just .. .. Tiéng Trâng.
Jump (to) .. .. Sut.

K.

Kiss (to) .. .. Thŏp, ap.
King .. .. Luong, sdăch.
Know (to) .. .. Déng, chê.
Kill (to) .. .. Sâmlûp.
Knife .. .. Combit.
Kneel (to) .. .. Lut cháng cong.
Knee .. .. Cháng cong.

L.

Labour .. .. Phehuor.
Lake .. .. Touli Sap.
Leave (to) .. .. Lêng, chol.
Layman .. .. Crehŏs.
Lamp .. .. Chiêng Kién.

Language	Pasa.
Language	Ândut.
Language (of a country)	Pasa.
Large	Tuléay.
Lick (to)	Lit.
Light	Sral.
Leper	Chomugu, Khlong.
Leprous	Comlong, Khlong.
Letter	Âcâr, sombăt.
Leaven	Tambê.
Lip	Pepir.
Liberty	Lâmpey.
Line	Poutŏt.
Line (fishing)	Sontŭch.
Limpid	Thla.
Lion	Sóng.
Law	Crŏt, viney.
Long	Véng.
Let (to)	Chuol.
Lean	Siom.
Lead (to)	Dóc, nóm.
Lie (to)	Căhăc cŏmphŭs.
Leaf	Slŏr.
Left	Chhnéng.
Lose (to)	Bâng, bât.
Little	Eoch.
Ladder	Chóndór.
Light (to)	Och.
Lead	Somnar.
Low	Iéap.
Like	Suró.
Lend (to)	Khchey.
Lawsuit	Kedey.
Lower (to)	Lontéep.

Learn (to) .. .. Lù, rién.
Look at (to) .. .. Múl.
Laugh (to) .. .. Soch.
Learned .. .. Méac, prach.
Lord .. .. Âmmechûs, mechäs.
Like .. .. Smó, doch.
Love (to) .. .. Srelant.
Life .. .. Aios.
Live (to) .. .. Rŏs.

M.

Malay .. .. Churéa.
Male .. .. Chnmul.
Malediction .. .. Bŏndasa.
Misfortune .. .. Ândarai, piér, lombac.
Mandarin .. .. Maman.
Mango .. .. Soai.
Manner .. .. Iĕang.
Marsh .. .. Bóng, trepang.
Marry (to) .. .. Souipĕa apea pipéa.
Mark .. .. Sâmcól.
Morning .. .. Prŭc.
Medicine .. .. Thnamsangcon.
Meditate (to) .. .. Niŭ, rompúng chon chieng.
Mingle (to) .. .. Leay.
Member .. .. Thnac thang.
Mercury .. .. Bârât.
Mother .. .. Medai, mê.
Merit .. .. Bŏn.
Marvellous .. .. Chôm lû.
Measure (to) .. .. Vàl.
Midnight .. .. Atréat.

Mirror	Conchâe.
Model	Kebuon.
Month	Khe.
Monastery	Vât.
Mountain	Phnom.
Mount (to)	Lòng.
Musquito	Mus.
Mutton	Chiêm.
Murmur	Khsâp, Khsién.
Music	Phlêng.
Mat	Còntil.
Mad	Chimat.
Man	Menus.
Milk	Tiù dă.
Moon	Khê (prĕa-Chăn).
Miser	Comnaut.
Much	Chrón.
Mouth	Môt.
Mud	Phoc.
Mills	Bôs, tomboa.
Money	Srae.
More	Lus, Cheang.
Meat	Săch.

N.

Net	Uon.
Narrow	Chang-ièt.
Nail	Dêc ail.
Neck	Kho.
Now	Êlounĕ.
Noon	Hmgay trâng.
Not	Com.

Nine .. .. Thmey.
Nose .. .. Chermo.
Nest .. .. Somboi.
Name .. .. Ehhnaô, neàm.
No .. .. Ei.
Nourish .. .. Anchein.
New .. .. Crăp.
Naked .. .. Srat.
Night .. .. Yap.
Nail .. .. Creehâi.
Near .. .. Chut.
Needle .. .. Mòchul.
Native Priest .. .. Meăc, nìng prĕa sâng.

O.

Obey (to) .. .. Sdăp, doi Toudap.
Observe (to) .. .. Mal.
Obtain (to) .. .. Ban.
Offend (to) .. .. Ehú tuč.
Offer (to) .. .. Chun.
Onion .. .. Ketym.
Ounce .. .. Eomlong.
Opposite .. .. Eo-tung.
Orange .. .. Croch.
Order (to) .. .. Bângcáp.
Open (to) .. .. Bòc.
One .. .. Muey.
Old man .. .. } Chăs.
Old .. .. }
Other .. .. Sitey-tiĕt, e tiét.
Oil .. .. Preńg.
Oar .. .. Cheo.

Often	Chrondâng, chron créa.
Owl	Eitui.
Of	Si âmpi.
Overflow	Compŏi.
Oath	Sâmbât.

P.

Pride	Comnoi.
Pagoda	G. vihéar.
Pair	Cû.
Palace	Vang, Preă-montir.
Palm-tree	Dóm tenot.
Peacock	Canghoc.
Paper	Credas.
Paradise	Sthan suor, phimean.
Pardon (to)	Ât tus.
Priest	Sâng Kreach.
Porringer	Chan.
Perceive (to)	Khŭuh.
Pray (to)	Phéavĕanea, sot thor.
Prayer	Ehór pheavinia.
Prison	Erung.
Price	Tomlay.
Profit	Chomniuh.
Profound	Chron.
Promise (to)	Sămŏt.
Prompt	Ranăs.
Prostrate oneself (to)	Crap.
Punish (to)	Toctus.
Partake (to)	Chec.
Pass (to)	Huvs.
Poor	Pibac.

Pay (to) .. .. Sâng.

Paint (to) .. .. Cuor.

Pelican .. .. Eung.

Pierce (to) .. .. Ehlu, thleay.

People .. .. Reas.

Perhaps .. .. Proman.

Pound (to) .. .. Bŏc.

Pipe .. .. Khsier.

Prickly .. .. Hór, mat.

Place .. .. Dăc, tuò.

Pity (to) .. .. Anót, anot

Please (to) .. .. Săp.

Pleasure .. .. Âmnâr sôc sabai.

Plank .. .. Cadar.

Plant (to) .. .. Dam.

Poison .. .. Ehnam pal.

Pepper .. .. Mŏreih.

Polished .. .. Reling.

Pork .. .. Chrue.

Pursue (to) .. .. Ehuli.

Pomegranate .. .. Tetum.

Pupil .. .. Crôm Sôs.

Pincers .. .. Eăngeap.

Power .. .. Amnach.

Preach (to) .. .. Eisna.

Prepare (to) .. .. Riép.

Plane (to) .. .. Chhus.

Perspiration .. .. Rhûs.

Perspire (to) .. .. Bêe nhús.

Perforated .. .. Thlu, dăch.

Preserve (to) .. .. Eue reaisa.

Pine-apple .. .. Monós.

Perceive (to) .. .. Klrúuh.

Print (to) .. .. Bă pum.

Play (to) ... ... Líng.
Place ... ... Tach.
Pound (weight) ... ... Neal.
Put (to) ... ... Dăc, tuo.
Piece ... ... Comnap.

Q.

Queen ... ... Khsatrey.
Question (to) ... ... Dondeng.
Quit (to) ... ... Léng, léa.
Quick ... ... Chhăp.

R.

Reason ... ... Sack Kedey.
Row (to) ... ... Cheo.
Rank ... ... Chuor.
Raze (to) ... ... Côr.
Rat ... ... Condor.
Ray ... ... Reăcsemey.
Recently ... ... Âmbauh.
Receive (to) ... ... Totuol.
Recompense ... ... Rongvoú.
Rent ... ... Viéch.
Rule (to) ... ... Soi réach.
Regret (to) ... ... Sdai.
Religion ... ... Sassena.
Repent (to) ... ... Chhu chăt.
Reply (to) ... ... Chhlói.
Respect (to) ... ... Cat Khlach.

Remain (to) .. .. Non.
Restore (to) .. .. Sañg viuh.
Rouse (to) .. .. Dàs.
Revolt (to) .. .. Kebăt.
Rich .. .. Câăc.
Riches .. .. Sombat tròp.
River .. .. Prêe, stùng.
Rice .. .. Iron. Ângeâ. Ḃai.
Roast .. .. Thang.
Red .. .. Crehâm.
Route .. .. Thlon.
Roof .. .. Tambâl.
Rain .. .. Phliéng.
Run .. .. Răt.
Rain (to) .. .. Phliéng.
Rotten .. .. Laoy.
River .. .. Touli.
Ripe .. .. Eam.
Read .. .. Sot.
Rainbow .. .. Anthua.
Ring .. .. Anchién.
Relation .. .. Bang phoon, sach uheat.

S.

Spit (to) .. .. Sdâ Pruvs.
Strengthen (to) .. .. Chuol.
Spider .. .. Ling peáng.
Sit down (to) .. .. Ângmi.
Sharp .. .. Sruéch.
Sharpen (to) .. .. Sâmbiéng.
Smell .. .. Eum Keloń.

Shadow	Molâp.
Storm	Phiu.
Straw	Chamboṅg.
Speak (to)	Sredey—Nieáy.
Sweep (to)	Bas.
Stick	Iâmbâng.
Shine (to)	Phlú.
Seal	Ira.
Slander (to)	Chombon.
Soul	Prea lúng.
Smelling	Amnach, p. bâzmey.
Set out (to)	Eau.
Stone	Ehmâ.
Sweet	Saân.
Straight	Eraṅg.
Squirrel	Compr̆oc.
Still	Etiér.
Swell (to)	H̆om.
Send (to)	Pró, phnô.
Shoulder	Sma.
Sword	Sâmsér.
Stuff	Sompat.
Star	Pheai.
Study (to)	Rień.
Split (to)	Su.
Son	Cou Pros.
Strong	Khlang.
Strike (to)	Meay.
Son-in-law	Côu prusa.
Swallow	Trechiéc cam.
Shame	Khmas.
Swear (to)	Sebât.
Shine (to)	Phlu.
Slander (to)	Sredey dám.

Sea	Sremăt.
Sparrow	Chap.
Show (to)	Bânghanh.
Soft	Som.
Swim (to)	Hêl.
Snow	Ap.
Sing (to)	Chrieng.
Seek (to)	Roc.
Scissors	Contray.
Sew (to)	Dér.
Short	Keley.
See (to)	Sâmléng.
Shore	Mót compong.
Stream	Stûng.
Sand	Khsach.
Sabre	Dan.
Sacrifice	Buchéa.
Seize (to)	Toc, chap.
Season	Câughê.
Salary	Chhnuol.
Sob (to)	Tuéuh.
Satiety	Châet.
Sauce	Sômlâ.
Savoury	Pisa.
Seal	Era.
Seal (to)	Prelâc âmbêl.
Saw	Anar.
Saw (to)	Ar.
Scribe	Smién.
Sculptor	Chhleăc.
Shake (to)	Ângruom.
Succour (to)	Chuey.
Secretary	Smień.
Sow (to)	Prô, sap.

Serpent	Pôs.
Sieve	Chuey.
Sex	Ângiochéat.
Silent	Sngiém.
Silk	Pré.
Soldier	Pôl, tahéan.
Sun	Ehngay.
Sound (to)	Phsâm.
Sulphur	Eeá.
Suffer (to)	Spoń thor.
Soil (to)	Chhú, ât.
Suspicion	Montúl.
Statue	Rup.
Stimulate	Âutóng.
Succession	Mârdăc.
Sugar	Seâr.
Suffice (to)	Lemon.
Supplicate (to)	Ângvâr.
Support (to)	Ât.
Suspend (to)	Phiuor.
Stoop (to)	Pontēep Khluon Êng.
Soon	Chhăp.
Silent (to be)	Non sugiém.
Steep (to)	Trom.
Sell (to)	Lŏc.
Stomach	Khiâl.
Smooth (to)	Smó, reling.
Say	Sredey.
Small pox	Ot.
Shed (to)	Chăk.
Saucepan	Chhang, keteă.

T.

Take (to)	Yoi.
Tail	Cŏntui.
Think (to)	Niŭ, rompûng chŏuchúng.
Thus	Hêt nê.
Then	Eŭp.
To-day	Ehngay nĕ.
Thin	Siom.
Trade	Ehneúh prô.
Thunder	Routèa.
Taste (to)	Shlŏc.
Tear (to)	Reliĕr.
To-morrow	Sŏă.
Tooth	Ehmeúh.
Teach (to)	Predan.
Together	Kenéa.
Thick	Crăs.
Thorn	Soŭla.
Tin	Somnăr Pahang.
Trust (to)	Dêc.
Take care (to)	Réacsa.
Tipsy	Chăêt, srevońg.
Tobacco	Ehnăm chŏc.
Table	Tang.
Try	Prońg.
Tax	Pŏn, suey.
Testimony	Bŏntál.
Tempest	Phin.
Temple	Preă viheár.
Time	Cal, pileá, vileá.
Thibet	Preă, sumér.

Tiger	Khla.
Thee	Êng, preă, sedêng.
Thunder	Phiôr, roŭteă.
Torch	Chôulô.
Torrent	Stung.
Tortoise	Ândoc.
Touch (to)	Pŏl.
Tower	Preă-sat.
Turn (to)	Vil.
Translate (to)	Prê.
Traffic	Chomnuénh.
Transcribe (to)	Châmlâng.
Tremble (to)	Nhór.
Trumpet	Erê.
Throne	Cŏl.
Too much	Pic.
Troop	Fóng, cân-bân.
Tile	Kebúong.
Turbulent	Repus.
Town	Pŏnteéy.
True	Prăcăt; Arăng.
Thing	Rebâs.
Travel (to)	Dór.
Toad	King cok.
Twin	Cŏn Phlô.
There	Ênŏ, nŏ.
Tear	Eŭć Phneé.

U.

Undergo (to)	Mărdăc.
Uproar	Vôr.
Ulcer	Bŏs.

Universe	Lu key.
Unite (to)	Phsăm.
Urine	Tuc uŏum.
Usage	Tomlóp.
Use (to)	Pro.
Useful	}Preioch.
Utility	
Understand (to)	Yŏl.
Useless	Ât preíoch.
Upright	Chhor.
Untie (to)	Srai.
Under	Crom, ê crom.
Ungrateful	Smŏr.
Ugly	Airâc.

V.

Very	Năs.
Vague	Relŏc.
Vessel	Sâmpon, capol.
Vaunt (to)	Uot.
Vase	Chan.
Vein	Sesay.
Venom	Pŭs.
Virtue	Cousâl, bŏn.
Victory	Chhneă.
Virgin	Prommăchărey.
Village	Phum.
Violent	Khlang.
Violet	Sâmbôr soag.
Violin	Chăpey.
Visit (to)	Suor.
Vow	Bâmmăn.

Vow (to)	Bân bâmmăn.
Veil	Sounoiéa.
Veil (to)	Bang.
Voice	Sâmleng.
Vomit (to)	Cunot.
Voracious	Lupha.
Vice	Bap, tus.
Vegetable	Poule pongea.

W.

When	Calna.
Who	Nana.
What	Oy ? Sat ay ?
Wake (to)	Phuheăc.
Wisdom	Samphi.
Winding	Chhăp.
Work	Car.
Work (to)	Thú car.
Watch (to)	Retrit tetrut.
Wind	Khiâl.
Worm	Chŏulin dûngeon.
Well (a)	Andong.
Word	Peac.
Why	Debâtay.
We	Túng.
Work	Chĕang.
Water (to)	Sroch.
Wait (to)	Ohâm.
Wash (to)	Pongeon.
Water-closet	Leáng.
When	Căl, calêna, compung.
Wicked	Bap, Chomugú.

Walk (to) .. .. Dór.
World .. .. Long.
Word .. .. Peác.
Wall .. .. Comphiñg.
Water .. .. Tŭć.
Write (to) .. .. Săcer.
Wife .. .. Propôn.
Wake (to) .. .. Dăs.
Wave .. .. Touli.
Wager .. .. Phnŏl.
War .. .. Sŏc.
Wine .. .. Sra.
Wish (to) .. .. Châng.
Warm .. .. Cadan.
Warm (to) .. .. Prap.
White .. .. Sâ.
Wound .. .. Rebuos.
Wood .. .. Srey.
Where .. .. Êna.
Woman .. .. Srey.
Widower .. .. Pomaí.

Y.

Yes .. .. Chŭs, bât, côrna.
Year .. .. Chhnam.
Yellow .. .. Lúóng.
Young .. .. Coming.
Yesterday .. .. Mŏsăl.

Z.

Zeal .. .. Chhú chaăl.
Zinc .. .. Sămnăr pang Krey.

NAMES OF THE NUMBERS.

1 .. .. Muey.	30 ... Sumsăp.
2 .. .. Pir.	40 .... Sêsŏp.
3 .. .. Bey.	50 .... Hosăp.
4 .. .. Buon.	60 .... Hocsăp.
5 .. .. Prăm.	70 .... Chêtsăp.
6 ... Prămmuey.	80 .... Pêtsŏp.
7 .. .. Prämpil.	90 .... Cansăp.
8 .. .. Prămbey.	100 .... Mŏ roi.
9 .. .. Prambuon.	200 .... Pir roi.
10 .. .. Dăp.	300 .... Bey roi.
11 .. .. Mŏtŏn Dăp.	400 .... Buon roi.
12 .. .. Pirtŏn dăp.	500 .... Prăm roi.
13 .. .. Beytŏn dăp.	600 .... Prămmuey
14 .. .. Buontŏn dăp.	roi.
15 .. .. Prămtŏn dăp.	&c.
16 .. .. Prămmueytŏn dăp.	1,000 .. .. Mŏ pŏn.
17 .. .. Prămpiltŏn dăp.	2,000 .. .. Pir pŏn.
18 .. .. Prămbeytŏn dăp.	&c.
19 .. .. Prămbuontŏn dăp.	10,000 .... Mŏ mŭn.
20 .. .. Mŏphey, or Bien Phey.	100,000 .... Mŏ sên.
21 .. .. Mŏphey muey, or Phey muey.	1,000,000 .... Mŏ côt.
22 .. .. Mŏphey pir, or Phey pir.	10,000,000 .... Mŏ béan.
23 .. .. Mŏphey bey, or Phey bey. &c.	100,000,000 .... Mŏ a Kho.
	1,000,000,000 .... Mŏ puni.

CARDINAL POINTS.

North	Ê chûng, Tùs udăr.
South	Ê thbong, Tus ê bor.
East	Ê cát, Tus ê cát.
West	Ê lich, Tus ê chém.

SEASONS.

Rainy Season ..	Cânghê or redon phliéng.
Hot or Dry Season	Cânghê or redon cadan.
Winter	Cânghê or redon rengèa.

THE DAYS OF THE WEEK.

Sunday .. .. .. Atŭt.	Thursday .. .. Prěa-hŏs.
Monday .. .. .. Chan.	Friday .. .. .. Sŏc.
Tuesday .. .. .. Âng Kéar.	Saturday .. .. .. San.
Wednesday .. .. Pût.	

THE NAMES OF THE MONTHS.

1. March .. .. .. Chêt.	7. September .. Asôch.
2. April .. .. Pisac.	8. October .. .. Cârdŏc.
3. May .. .. Chis.	9. November .. Méac Khsér.
4. June .. .. Asat.	10. December .. Bŏs.
5. July .. .. Srap.	11. January .. Méac thŏm.
6. August .. .. .. Phetrebot.	12. February .. Phăl cun.

CYCLE OF TWELVE YEARS.

1. Pig .. .. .. Côr.	7. Serpent .. .. Méa Sanh.
2. Rat .. .. .. Chût.	8. Horse .. .. Méa mê.
3. Ox .. .. .. Chhlom.	9. Goat .. .. Méa mê.
4. Tiger .. .. .. Khal.	10. Monkey .. .. Voê.
5. Hare .. .. .. Thâ.	11. Cock .. .. Roca.
6. Dragon .. .. Rung.	12. Dog .. .. .. Chô.

PRONUNCIATION OF THE CAMBODIAN VOWELS.

a, ă, ã; é, ê; i; o, ó; u, ú.

a. This is pronounced like the English word, "Palm."

ă. This is pronounced short; as, "Mat."

ã. This is something between the *a* and the *o*; it is pronounced like a very open *o*.

é. This is pronounced like our close *e*; as, "Men."

ê. This is pronounced like our open *e*; as, "He."

i. This is pronounced also like our *e*.

o. This is pronounced like our *o*; as, "Go."

ó. This is pronounced like *eu* in "Liqueur."

u. Like *ou*, in "You."

ú. This is pronounced like *u*.

DIPHTHONGS.

Ai, ei, oi, ôi, ói. This is pronounced with a single emission of sound.

Ay, ey, oy, óy, ui, úi. This is pronounced with two emissions of sound, as, a-ï, e-ï, o-ï, u-ï, u-ï.

Cha, ché, chi, cho, chu. This is pronounced as Tia, tié, tii, tio, tiu; with a single emission of sound.

Chha, chhé, chhi, chho, chhu. This is pronounced as Thcha, thché (etc.), with a strong aspiration.

Kha, khe, khi, kho, khu. This is pronounced as Ka, ke, ki (etc.), with a strong aspiration.

Nha, nhe, nhi, nho, nhu. This is pronounced as Nia, Nie (etc.), with a single emission of sound.

Pha, phe, phi, pho, phu. This is pronounced as pa, pe, pi (etc.)., with an aspiration.

Nga, nge, ngi, ngo, ngu. This is pronounced hard.

Tha, thé, thi, tho, thu. Hard, and with an aspiration.

THE LORD'S PRAYER IN CAMBODIAN.

O' Preă dâ công lu mic, apuc Túng Khnhŏm oi: Túng Khnhŏm ângvâr Preă-âng, som oi ûs neăc phâng têng núng cot sesór preă néam Preă-ang: som oi preă-nocor Preă-âng ban Tûng Khnhŏm. Som ai rebal méan non dey thú tam preă hartey Preă-âng dock lú mic. Ahar Túng Khnhŏm săp thngay som ai Túng Khnhŏm ban thngai nê: hoï som pros bap Túng Khnhŏm dock iung Khnhŏm ăt tus neăc êna mian tus núng Túng Khnhŏm: hoï som pum ai Túng Khnhŏm doi comnach: tê aî Túng Khnhŏm ban ruéch âmpi ândărai teăng puâng. Amén!

LETTERS FROM M. MOUHOT.

To Samuel Stevens, Esq.

[To be communicated to the Royal Geographical Society.]

Brelum, among the Savage Stiêns, lat. N. 11° 46' 30",
long. W. 103° 3', merid. of Paris, 15th October, 1859.

Dear Mr. Stevens,

I profit by a favourable opportunity which has just presented itself to write you a few hasty lines to let you know that I am alive. For the last two months I have been living with the savage Stiêns amidst their immense forests, the latitude being precisely as I have stated above, and here I have passed the season most favourable for collecting insects and land shells. In spite of the letter given to me by the King of Cambodia, ordering all the chiefs of the Srok Khmer, or Cambodian villages, to furnish me with the means of transport on my journey, I experienced much difficulty, as frequently neither buffaloes nor carts were to be found in the hamlets through which I passed. My journey took me a month to accomplish, which is about three times as long as it would have taken me on foot.

On the 21st July, after having descended the great arm of the Mekon from Pinhalú, a village about nine miles from the capital, and in lat. 11° 46' 30" N. and long. 103° 3 W. merid. of Paris, as far as Penom Peuh, a commercial town filled with Chinese, and situated at the conflux of two streams, I ascended

the great Cambodian River, the water of which is still low, as
all through the country the rainy season is two months later
than usual. The Mekon is studded with islands, of which many
are eight or nine miles long and more than a mile broad;
such is the large and beautiful island of Ko-Sutin, where I
arrived after five days' journey. I estimate the width of the river
to be about three miles. Pelicans are found on its waters, often
in flocks of more than fifty, and storks, sea swallows, and other
aquatic birds, abound in the shallow parts of the river. The
general aspect of this mighty river is, however, rather sombre
than gay, although doubtless there is something imposing in
the rapidity of its waters, which run like a torrent. Few boats
are to be seen on it, and its banks are almost barren (the forests
being more than a mile distant), and, being constantly undermined by the water, fall down at the least shock, and this is generally all that you can see or hear. The Menam is much more
gay and animated.

The rapids and cataracts commence about thirty or forty
leagues north of Ko-Sutin, on the confines of Laos, and it is
there necessary to leave the large boats and take to canoes,
which as well as the luggage are often obliged to be carried on
men's backs.

The current of the Mekon is so strong that at certain times
of the year you can go little more than a league a day, and the
rowers often seek for fire in the evening at the very place
where they cooked their rice in the morning. I ascended it
in a small boat with three rowers, but at every bend of the river
we had the greatest trouble to make any progress, and were
frequently obliged to hold on by the rushes to prevent our
being carried away by the current. Eight days after leaving
Pinhalú I reached Pemptiélan, a large Cambodian village, where
I found it necessary to take to land travelling.

There still remained 150 miles to travel in carts, all in
an easterly direction. I was well received by the mandarin

at the head of affairs in this part of the country, and was able
to set out again in two days.

The first day our conveyances upset, and I feared that we
should be unable to proceed; there were continually dreadful
bogs, quagmires, and marshes, in which the carts sank up to the
axletrees and the buffaloes to their bellies. Fortunately on the
following day the road improved, but for three weeks all that
was visible was a few scattered rice-fields round the villages, and
we had to make our way through a marshy plain, covered with
thick and dark woods, which reminded one of the enchanted
forest of Tasso, and it is easy to understand that the imagination of a pagan race peoples these gloomy solitudes with evil
spirits. Twenty times in an hour the men who accompanied
us were obliged to raise the large branches and cut down the
trunks which obstructed our passage, and sometimes we had to
make a new path for ourselves.

The Cambodians were all much surprised at seeing us journeying towards the Stiêns at the worst time of the year, for in
that country the rainy season had commenced, and even those
who live nearest dare not venture there; and had I not brought
with me from Siam my two young servants, I could not for
any money have found a single individual to accompany me.
Even they felt great repugnance to proceed—for in Siam, Cambodia bears a terrible reputation for unhealthiness, and unhap-
pily both for them and for myself they were attacked with fever
in the forests, since which, instead of receiving any help from
them, I have had two patients to nurse.

Passing through a village peopled by a barbarous race of
Annamites, I ran great risk of being taken prisoner by them,
and being sent to finish my researches in a dungeon. Last year
the carriages belonging to a French missionary were completely
rifled, and the men sent with ropes round their necks to Cochin
China. I loaded all my guns, and gave one to each of my men:

our firm appearance, no doubt, frightened them, for we were not attacked.

In spite of the heat, the fatigue, and privations inseparable from such a journey, I arrived among the Stiêns in perfectly good health as far as I was concerned, and here I found a settlement of Catholic missionaries from Cochin China. It would have been impossible to go further, for I could neither find means of transport nor provisions, for at this time of the year the poor savages have consumed all their rice, and have nothing to live upon but herbs, a little maize, and what they can catch in the chase. I therefore accepted the hospitality offered to me with much kindness by a good priest. In a few weeks the rainy season will be over, the nights will become cold, and for several months insects will be found, and after that will come the turn of the birds, with which I shall exclusively occupy myself.

My departure from here will depend upon circumstances; perhaps I shall myself be the bearer of this letter to Pinhalú, perhaps I may be detained here some months by the bad state of the roads and the impossibility of procuring vehicles during the rice-harvest.

If you ask who are this strange people, living retired on the table-lands and mountains of Cambodia, which they appear never to have quitted, and differing entirely in manners, language, and features from the Annamites, Cambodians, and Laotians, my answer is that I believe them to be the aborigines of the country, and that they have been driven into these districts by the repeated inroads of the Thibetians, from whom they evidently descend, as is proved by the resemblance of features, religion, and character.

The whole country from the eastern side of the mountains of Cochin China as far as 103° long., and from 11° lat. to Laos, is inhabited by savage tribes, all known under one name, which signifies "inhabitants of the heights." They have no attachment to the soil, and frequently change their abode; most of the villages are in a state of continual hostility with each other, but they do not attack in troops, but seek to surprise each other, and the prisoners are sold as slaves to the Laotians.

Their only weapon is the cross-bow, which they use with extraordinary skill, but rarely at a distance of more than twenty paces. Poisoned arrows are used only for hunting the larger animals, such as elephants, rhinoceros, buffaloes, and wild oxen, and with these the smallest scratch causes death, if the poison is fresh : the strongest animal does not go more than fifty paces before it falls; they then cut out the wounded part, half roast it without skinning or cutting it up, after which they summon the whole village by sound of trumpet to partake of it. The most perfect equality and fraternity reign in these little communities, and the Communists would here find their theories reduced to practice and producing nothing but misery.

The strongest European would find it difficult to bend the bow which the Stiên, weak and frail as he appears, bends without effort, doubtless by long practice.

They are not unacquainted with agriculture, but grow rice and plant gourds, melons, bananas, and other fruit-trees; their rice-fields are kept with the greatest care, but nearly all the hard work is done by the women. They seldom go out in the rainy season on account of the leeches, which abound in the woods to such a degree as to render them almost unapproachable; they remain in their fields, where they construct small huts of bamboo, but as soon as the harvest is over and the dry season returns they are continually out fishing or hunting. They never go out without their baskets on their backs, and carrying their bows and a large knife-blade in a bamboo handle. They forge nearly all their instruments from ore which they procure from Annam and Cambodia. Although they know how to make earthen vessels, they generally cook their rice and herbs in bamboo. Their only clothing is a strip of cloth passed between the thighs and rolled round the waist. The women weave these scarfs, which are long and rather pretty, and which when well made often sell for as much as an ox. They are fond of ornaments, and always have their feet, arms, and fingers covered with rings made of thick brass wire; they wear necklaces of glass beads, and their ears are pierced with an enormous hole, through which they hang the bone of an animal, or a piece of ivory sometimes more than three inches in circumference. They wear their hair long in the Annamite fashion, and knot it up with a comb made of bamboo; some pass through it a kind of arrow made of brass wire, and ornamented by a pheasant's crest.

Their features are handsome and sometimes regular, and many wear thick mustachios and imperials.

Quite alone and independent amidst their forests, they scarcely recognise any authority but that of the chief of the village, whose dignity is generally hereditary. For the last year or two the King of Cambodia has occasionally sent the mandarin who lives nearest the Stiêns to their first villages, in order to distribute marks of honour to their chiefs, hoping little by little to subdue them, and to get from them slaves and ivory, and already he receives a small tribute every year. His emissaries, however, scarcely dare pass the limits of the kingdom, so fearful are they of the arrows of the savages and of the fevers which reign in their forests.

The Stiên is gentle and hospitable, and possesses neither the stupid pride of the Cambodian, nor the refined cruelty and corruption of the Annamite. He is the "good fellow" of the forest, simple and even generous; his faults are those common to all Asiatics, namely, cunning, an extraordinary power of dissimulation, and idleness; his great passion is hunting, and he leaves work to the women, but, unlike the Cambodians, robbery is very rare among them.

They believe in a supreme being, but only invoke the evil spirit to induce him to leave them in peace. They bury the dead near their dwellings. They do not believe in metempsychosis, but think that animals have also souls which live after their death, and continue to haunt the places they frequented in their lives. Their superstitions are numerous; the cry of an owl, or the sight of a crow, just as they are about to set off on a journey, they consider a bad augury, which is sufficient to turn them from their plans.

When any one is ill they say it is the demon tormenting him, and keep up night and day a frightful uproar round him, which only ceases when one of the bystanders falls as in a fit, crying out, " He has passed into me, he is stifling me." They then question the new patient as to the remedies which must be employed to cure the sick man, and as to what the demon demands to abandon his prey. Sometimes it is an ox, a pig, too often a human victim; in the latter case they pitilessly seize on some poor slave, and immolate him without remorse.

They imagine that all white people inhabit secluded corners of the earth in the midst of the sea, and often ask if there are any women in our country. When and how I can return to Cambodia and Siam I am ignorant, and I dare not think of the difficulty I shall experience among the rude and stupid Cambodians in transporting my treasures. What heartbreaking jolts my boxes of insects will receive! What palpitations I shall feel each time some rough fellow takes them to place on the oxen, elephants, or his own back! Poor soldiers of science! these are our trophies, and in the eyes of some people find as much merit as a piece of silk fastened to a pole; and what pains, patience, and solicitude is necessary to procure them! therefore I believe my anxiety as to my collections will be understood by the lovers of nature.

Pinhalú, 20th December, 1859.

P.S.—I arrived last evening at Pinhalú, in perfect health, and am now about to go northward to visit the famous ruins of Ongcor and then return to Bangkok, so I have little time to give you any details as to what I despatch from Komput and Singapore. I am not quite satisfied; for birds are scarce here, and I have but a small number; besides, my boxes as I feared have been much knocked about; I sent them off to Komput on men's backs. On my return to Bangkok I will send you some good maps of this almost unknown country.

To Samuel Stevens, Esq.

[To be communicated to the Geographical Society of London.]

Khao Samoune, Province of Pechaburi (Siam).
Lat. N. 13° 4', long. 100°.   15th June, 1860.

In my last letter, of March, 1859, I told you about two active volcanoes that I discovered in the Gulf of Siam, one in the little isle of Koman, lat. 12° 30' 29'' N., and long. 101° 50' 2'' W., mer. of Greenwich, and of the probable existence of others whose workings were latent and slow. Since then I have travelled through Cambodia, from north to south and from east to west, gone up the Mekon as far as the frontier of Laos, visited one of the savage tribes which live between these two countries and Cochin China, then crossed the great lake Touli Sap, explored the provinces of Ongcor and Battambong, which are full of splendid ruins, one of which in particular, the temple of Ongcor, is almost perfect, and, perhaps, unequalled in the world. I then passed from the Mekon to the Menam, and returned to Bangkok.

A low table-land, of which the gradual slope takes a week to ascend, separates the two rivers.

A chain of mountains, of which the highest peak is 6274 English feet above the level of the sea, extends to the S.W., joins the ranges of Chantaboun, Pursak, and Thung Yai, which are from 4000 to 5000 feet high, and reaches nearly to Komput and Hatienne; while to the north another small chain, joining the greater one of Korat, runs eastward, throws some ramifications into the provinces of Battambong and Ongcor Borege, which is 40 miles farther north, and bears the name of the mountains of Somrai.

Not being in direct communication with the Archæological Society, I wish to call your attention to the marvellous remains at Ongcor of the civilization of a great people.

The country is rich in woods and mines, and although thinly populated, produces enough cotton for the use of Cochin China, while the great lake, which abounds in fish, furnishes an immense quantity of this article also to China. Iron of a superior quality is also abundant, and the Kouis, an ancient tribe of a primitive race, living east of the Mekon, who speak the same language as the Stiêns, work it very industriously. There are also many other mines, rich in gold, lead, and copper, in the chains to the east and west; that of Pursak produces the beautiful cardamom, which, when transplanted, gives fine stems but no fruit.

Unluckily most of these mountains are frightfully unhealthy, and no one but those who have lived there from infancy can remain long among them with impunity.

In the island of Phu-Quor or Koh Trou, which belongs to Cochin China, and which is very near to Komput, there are rich mines of cannel coal. I was not able to get there, the war having rendered the people hostile and cruel to all white men; but my attention having been drawn to it by some ornaments worked in this mineral by the islanders, I procured two specimens, which I send you.

There are several extinct volcanoes in Pechaburi, four of

which I have ascertained to form part of the numerous detached and conical hills which are probably all ancient craters belonging to the great chain Khao Deng, which occupies all the northern part of the centre of the Malayan peninsula, and is inhabited by the Kariens, a primitive and independent people, who, like the Stiêns and other tribes, have doubtless been driven back to the mountains by the encroachments of the Siamese, and where the inclemency of the climate protects them against all attacks from their neighbours. The mountains are known in the country as the Na-Khou, Khao, Panom Knot, Khao Tamonne, and Khao Samroum. The last two are 1700 and 1900 feet above the level of the sea, and only a few leagues distant from each other. All these craters appear to have been originally upheaved ("craters of elevation" M. de Buch styles them) from the bottom of the water, at a period when all this part of the country, as far as the great chain, which I have not yet been able to visit, was under the sea.

Besides an immense volcanic cone, in part fallen in, and where the ground resounds under one's feet, each of the mounts has several lateral mouths and a number of fissures and chimneys, or passages, which bear evident traces of subterranean fires. They are entirely composed of trachytic rocks, scoria, lava, felspar, &c.

The Siamese have made temples of the largest of these caverns, which are of great depth and breadth, and extremely picturesque. One of the caverns of Samroum is quite inaccessible. Having descended to the depth of 20 feet by a chimney 2 feet wide at its mouth, and shut in between rocks, I found myself at the entrance of a deep cavern, but there all my efforts to proceed farther were defeated; a few steps from the entrance my torch suddenly went out, my breathing was checked, and I in vain fired my gun several times in order to disperse the foul air.

To M. Charles Mouhot (his Brother).

Bangkok, 13th October, 1860.

To you, my dear brother, I address my last letter before quitting Bangkok for my long journey to Laos. I have waited till the last moment for the steamer which ought to bring me letters from Europe, but unfortunately I am obliged to set out without receiving any answers to those which I sent in May, on my return from Cambodia. I fear that, once in the interior of the country, I shall have no means of sending letters; arm yourself, therefore, with patience, dear brother, and do not think me neglectful if you do not receive any; but be sure that I, alone in those profound solitudes, shall suffer more than you, from my ignorance of everything concerning those dear to me; and during the eighteen or twenty months which the journey will probably occupy I shall not see a European face nor hear a word which can recall to me my beloved country.

I have done everything in my power to obtain letters and passports from the French and Siamese authorities here, but all have been nearly useless. I have obtained nothing but a letter from the King's brother, who has the superintendence of the provinces north of Laos, and with that I trust to be able to get on. The good Dr. Campbell has supplied me with medicines of all kinds, and as I am nearly acclimatized, and have with me devoted followers—one particularly, Phrai, who would die for me—you may be easy on my account. Besides, and I really know not why, I have hitherto been much liked by the missionaries and natives, and I am sure it will be the same there. Fever does not kill all travellers. I have traversed many dangerous districts in my journey to Cambodia, and I am safe. Let us trust in God, my brother, that I shall be as fortunate in this expedition, and that we shall meet again. Nothing is requisite but courage, hope, and patience. I am sober, and drink nothing but tea. My food is the same as that of the

natives, dried fish and rice, and sometimes a little game which
I shoot, and roast on a spit after the fashion of the natives,
that is, by two bamboos stuck into the ground and another laid
horizontally on them, which is turned from time to time. My
amusements are hunting, arranging my collections, my drawings,
to which I devote a great deal of time, and of which some are
not bad, as you may judge by those sent to the Geographical
Society of London, and my journal; with those I pass many
pleasant hours. Besides, you know how I love nature, and am
only really happy in the woods with my gun, and that when
there, if I know you all to be happy, I have nothing to wish for.
I often think of our good old father, but as long as you are with
him I feel easy about him; you will make him bear my absence
patiently, repeat often to him how I love him, and how happy I
shall be when I can tell him about my long journeys. And
you, my brother, love and cherish your two dear children, my
little nephews; inculcate in them the love of nature, and teach
them to think that virtue is recompensed even here, and a good
conscience ennobles more than patents of nobility, or orders in
the button-hole; bring up your little ones in the love of God,
and of all that is good and great. Think and talk sometimes
with Jenny of the poor traveller. Adieu, my brother!

To Madame Charles Mouhot (his Sister-in-law).

Khao Khoc, 21st December, 1861.

An unexpected opportunity presents itself, my dear
Jenny, to send you a few words before proceeding farther. A
new year is about to commence : may you, my dear little sister,
experience in its course only joy and satisfaction; may your
interesting little family cause you unmixed happiness; in a

word, I desire every possible good for you. As for myself, I ask
nothing but the happiness of seeing you all again. Think occasionally of the poor traveller whom every day removes farther
and farther from civilization, and who for eighteen months or
perhaps two years is about to live alone in a strange place, where
I shall not have even the consolation of meeting those good
missionaries as at Brelum and in Cambodia.

You know my manner of life, so I shall not repeat it. The
heat and the musquitoes make a real hell of this place. Those
who praise it must have hard heads and skins, or else must
be comfortably lodged, and surrounded by an army of slaves.
They know nothing but its enjoyments. If there is one pleasant
hour in the morning and another in the evening, one must think
oneself lucky, for often there is no peace night or day. My pleasures are, first, liberty, that precious thing without which man
cannot be happy, and for which so many have fought and will
fight still; then, seeing so much that is beautiful, grand, and
new, and which no one has seen before me. From these I draw
my contentment. Thank God! my health is as good as when
I left you, although three years have passed over me.

Soon I shall be in Laos, and then, what strange things I shall
see daily! what curious beings I shall meet, to whom I shall be
equally an object of curiosity! I shall have delightful days,
then, perhaps, sad ones, if my servants have the fever, which
happens at intervals. If only to enliven these solitudes, I could
have you here, my dear Jenny, or if I could sing like you,
or even like a nightingale! Sometimes I do make use of my
falsetto voice, and hum the beautiful airs of Béranger, and
feel strengthened by the sublime odes of that great man of
genius.

Two or three thin volumes—I say thin, for the white ants
have eaten the greater part of them—and a few old newspapers
(new to me) compose my library; but I have blank paper,
which I fill as I best can; it is an amusement, at least; and if it

turn out of no other use than to serve to amuse you all, I shall
be satisfied, for I am not ambitious.   I dream as I smoke my
pipe, for I must confess that I smoke more than ever.

Well! the musquitoes and thorns will still be my companions
for a long time.   It is my own choice, and I shall never complain as long as God grants to all of you the joy and happiness
I wish for you.

How I shall accomplish the long journey before me I know
not; probably with oxen and elephants; but if even I have to
go on foot I care not, so that I reach there, for I have determined to drive away even the devil, should I meet him
here.

To M. Charles Mouhot.

Khao Khoc, near Pakpriau (Siam), 23rd Dec. 1860.

My dear Brother,

This is the sixth letter I have written, and written on
my knees; and in this heat, and tormented by musquitoes, it is
an affair of as many days.   Do not complain, therefore, if this
is short.   Khao-Khoc is a mountain nine or ten leagues north
of Pakpriau, which I visited two years ago, and where I have
been waiting two months for the roads to become passable, in
order to reach Korat, and then Laos.   I have made a fine collection of coleoptera, particularly some remarkable longicorns.
I have but few shells or birds; nevertheless, the collection is
precious, and, although less numerous than the one at Pechaburi, it is quite equal to it.   I have been lucky enough to replace a great part of the insects that were lost in the *Sir J.
Brooke*.

I remain perfectly well, but my two poor lads suffer from
time to time with intermittent fever; quinine, however, generally stops it, and I hope the change of air will do them good.

The brave fellows do their work none the less cheerfully, and they love me, and are quite devoted to me.

I am only waiting for the arrival of my letters, through the medium of my good friend Dr. Campbell, to set out, because when I have once started I fear none of your letters will reach me.

I think I shall explore the Mekon, and go up as far as China, if circumstances are favourable, and trust to bring back from this journey many rare and precious things. I bought at Bangkok many articles to give to those who shall aid me, such as red and white cloth, brass wire, glass beads, needles, spectacles, &c.

28th Dec.—The night before my departure for Korat. All the good news I have received from Europe and from Bangkok has made me joyful. I have just received with your letters a mass of papers. Every one is kind to me, and that is very pleasant. My friend Malherbe has sent me some *caporal*, which I had not enjoyed for a long time; he had just received some from France, along with some pipes, and a precious extract of sarsaparilla, invaluable for cooling the blood heated by the climate, the food, and the troublesome musquitoes of which I have spoken so often. I shall require another elephant to carry all the red cloth sent to me by Mr. Adamson, and which will be invaluable in Laos, as the people delight in it. I was moved even to tears at so many marks of kindness from people who hardly know me.

To M. Charles Mouhot.

Korat, 26th January, 1861.

I have been three days at Korat, which is about 140 miles east-north-east of Pakpriau,—that is, nearly in the same longitude as Battambong.

The journey, which I performed on foot, in company with a caravan of 400 oxen carrying merchandise, lasted ten days, from four in the morning to sunset, deducting only a few hours in the middle of the day. My feet are in a bad state from crossing the mountains, but, nevertheless, I enjoyed my journey.

On these uplands, which are more than 4000 feet high, the air is pure and pleasant, the nights are fresh, and the early morning almost cold.

During these ten days I have collected but little, and my expenses have been greater than I calculated on. Within the last two years everything has doubled in price; but the governor appears honest; he paid me a visit, which cost me a pair of spectacles, some engravings, and other little things, but he has promised me conveyances, and a letter to the chief of another province, who will provide me with elephants.

My health is excellent, and I hope it will remain so; my servants are better. I am surrounded by a crowd of curious gazers, who fill up my hut.

TO M. CHARLES MOUHOT.

Saraburi (Siam), 24th February, 1861.

You will be astonished, my dear friend, to see my letter dated from Saraburi, instead of from Laos. When I reached Chaiapume, I went to the governor with my letters, and asked him to lend me elephants to enable me to continue my journey, that being the only method of travelling among these mountains; but he refused me decidedly, and consequently I have been forced to retrace my steps. Here one can do nothing without the help of the people in power.

I therefore returned to Korat, and established Phrai in a

hut which I hired of a Chinese; and went myself to Bangkok, to
procure from the authorities orders to the different governors
of provinces to aid me instead of throwing obstacles in my
way.

From Korat I had the pleasure of travelling with an amiable
mandarin of Bangkok, who had been to fetch a white elephant
from Laos, and who had conceived a great friendship for me.
He travelled in great style; the caravan was magnificent; we
had more than sixty elephants, two of which were placed at my
disposal, one for my own use, and one for my servants.

Finding myself in the good graces of this mandarin, I told
him why I was going to Bangkok, and he promised to obtain for
me all I wanted.

When I reached Saraburi I found all the governors of Laos
and the first mandarins of Bangkok assembled there to take care
of the white elephant. The Siamese, being very superstitious, and
believing in metempsychosis, think that the soul of some prince
or king has passed into the white elephant; they have the
same belief as to white apes and albinoes, consequently they
hold them all in great respect. They do not worship them,
for the Siamese recognise no God, not even Buddha, but they
believe that a white elephant brings luck to the country.

During the whole journey the men were busy cutting down
branches to make his passage easy; two mandarins fed him with
different kinds of cakes in golden dishes, and the King came
out to meet him.

I owe, therefore, to the white elephant the most satisfactory
letters which I have obtained, and which have cost me my best
gun and nearly 300 francs in presents; but I might have had
to give much more, and, as I am going to Bangkok, I can replenish my stock. As for the poor elephant, he was so much
cared for and so well fed, that he died of indigestion.

It is a terrible affliction, and all the mandarins and other dignitaries collected here are in great grief about it.

To Madame Mouhot (his Wife).

Saraburi, 24th February, 1861.

My dear Annette,

You will be much surprised on receiving this letter to see it dated from Saraburi, for if you have received the one I wrote in January, you must believe me to be already in Laos. But man proposes, and God disposes. However, to reassure you, I must begin by saying that I am in perfect health, and full of strength and hope. All goes well with me.

I had in fact reached Laos. I arrived at Korat after a tedious and troublesome journey, for I had only a few oxen for my baggage, and was forced to walk myself. From there I went to Chaiapume, and here an animal of the mandarin species made himself great, and under the pretext of having no elephants refused me the means of going further, and was so rude and impolite to me that I determined at once to return and protest against the very insufficient protection which had been granted to me. Indeed, I could do nothing else, not being able to go on. The elephant which had brought me to Chaiapume took me back to Korat, and there I found a mandarin from Bangkok, who had been sent to fetch a white elephant which had been taken in Laos. I begged him to let me join his party, and he lent me two elephants, one for my servant and luggage, and one for myself. I left Phrai at Korat, with the greater part of my possessions, having hired a room for him in the house of a Chinese, and a week afterwards found myself back at Saraburi, in company with this strange divinity (who, by the way, had more black than white about him), and of the grand personage who had been sent to escort him, and who had showered on him every kind of attention during the journey. He had an escort of fifty foot soldiers and several on horseback. As for me, I wanted for nothing ; at every halt the mandarin sent me ducks, fish, fruit, sweetmeats, &c., and he was also kind enough to allow me eight men as night-guards to watch round my fire. In return, I discovered for him in the mountains large quantities of copper, and even gold, which delighted him.

The whole province of Saraburi was in motion to do honour to the white elephant; the King and all his court are coming here; the ministers are here already to watch over him. I decided, therefore, to apply to the Siamese, hoping to obtain more from them than from the Europeans; and yesterday, hearing of the arrival of Khrom Luang, the King's brother, I hastened to address myself to him. He, however, had only passed through, and was gone to Prabat, to join the King. However, I found here the man I wanted, the mandarin who has most interest in Laos, and without a letter from whom it would have been difficult to proceed. I did not know him, but I went to him to ask about the Prince, and told him what I wanted. "I am your man," said he; "the Prince can only give an order for me to write a letter, such as I will give you, if you like." I accepted gladly, and promised him in return my double-barrelled gun, which I could easily replace, "if he would only furnish me with the means of travelling through Laos without expense, and would bring the Chaiapume mandarin to reason." The poor governor of Saraburi was with us, and had to remain more than an hour amidst a number of others kneeling on the bare ground, while I was seated on the mat of the mandarin, by his side, eating sweetmeats and drinking tea, while he dictated a letter in which he called the governor of Chaiapume a fool, and threatened to deprive him of his office, and of this letter I was to be the bearer; and he promised me another general one on the morrow, in which he stated that if I did not receive efficient aid it might bring on a war; and this he also repeated to all the chiefs present. My cause was gained, and I could plainly see that our affairs must be going on well in Cochin China; the echo of the cannon had its effect in Siam. However, I had pro-

mised him my gun, and evidently he wished to have it before he
gave me the letters. This morning, therefore, I took it to him
all cleaned and furbished up. He was delighted with it, and gave
me at once the letter for Korat and Chaiapume, and to-morrow I
am to have one which will carry me all through Laos without any
expense but a few ticals to the cornacs. Without this, judging by
what I had to pay for an elephant from Korat to Chaiapume, my
purse would have been exhausted by the time I reached the
north of Laos, and I should not have had the means of returning
without sending to Bangkok to ask for help, which would have
been a work of difficulty, and, what is worse, I should have been
exposed all along the route to the insolence of these arrogant
mandarins. Now, they will all humble themselves before me,
taking me for some important personage sent by the Emperor
Napoleon or Queen Victoria to collect butterflies, insects, and
birds for them. I shall no longer travel on foot, but on
elephants, and shall want for nothing. Agree, then, with me,
that out of evil comes good, or rather, that God does all for the
best. When at Chaiapume I found myself obliged to retrace my
steps, after so many fatigues, and so great a waste of money, I
was only downcast for a few minutes; God almost immediately
inspired me with the idea that all would turn to my advantage,
and this persuasion never left me again. Unaccountably to myself, I was gayer on my return than I had been in coming,
although then I was everywhere well received and kindly
treated by the people. Even after my discourteous reception
at Chaiapume, all the inhabitants came to see me, to bring me
little presents, and to express their regret that they could not
aid me from fear of their chief. The head of the monastery
took me to see some ruins similar to those in Cambodia, and
gave me a tiger-skin; and all along the road I experienced the
same kindness, and numbers came to me to ask for advice and
various remedies.

The Chinese are all my friends. When I returned to this

town, you should have seen them all run out to see me, and those at whose houses I had stopped were full of inquiries as to my affairs, and crying out "Ah! here is the gentleman back again." The next day would be their New Year's Day, which they keep as a feast as we do Christmas. "I have come back to feast with you to-morrow," replied I; and the next day I was so loaded with cakes and other good things that I have not finished them yet.

You must arm yourself with patience, dear Annette, for I have not yet finished. I learned this morning that a French ship of war is at Paknam, I presume for the purpose of taking back the Siamese Ambassador who has been so long expected in France. The king must be delighted, for he has a great dread of any quarrel with France or England now that he has seen their power. They may very probably come here, and at the risk of losing three days I shall wait and see, for, doubtless, the officer would receive me well, and do more for me than the Consul did. After that, I shall go to Bangkok, where I shall remain only a day, in order to buy a few necessaries in which I was beginning to run short, such as camphor, shoes, cloth, and a gun, and to get a little money, 50 or 100 ticals, from M. Adamson, who will willingly advance it to me, as he promised; and above all, to receive all the dear letters from home, of which a number must be lying at Dr. Campbell's.

My useless voyage to Chaiapume diminished my resources, and it would be great pity that the want of a few hundred francs should force me to return before I have completed my journey, and before I have finished collecting what will amply repay all my expenses.

In a few days I will add a line to this letter to tell you the result of my interview with the officer, and of my journey to Bangkok. I shall hear news also from your letters; let them only be good, and I shall be happy. I must now close my letter for to-day, my dear Annette; some day you will see my journal, and read all my adventures in detail. I can write no more to-day, but only repeat my assurance that I am perfectly well, in spite of all trials, thanks to my prudence and sobriety. Show this letter or anything that is interesting in it to all friends. I speak only of my own affairs, but you know I am not changed. And yet a few words of love would doubtless be more prized by you, but were I to write a thousand I could not express half the love with which my heart is filled for you all; indeed I fear to begin, for that would have no end. I write all this on my knees; my back aches, and now I must go and seek some repose. Au revoir! I trust soon to send you still better news than this. I embrace you a thousand times from the bottom of my heart, as well as all those dear to us, and am ever

Your devoted husband,

H. MOUHOT.

To Madame Mouhot.

Saraburi, 25th February, 1861.

My very dear Annette,

I reached Korat two days ago, and in four more I hope to be able to proceed northward. I have been obliged to travel on foot, not having been able to procure elephants at Saraburi; my baggage was carried by oxen. I feel perfectly well, and experience so little fatigue that on the day of my arrival here I walked about till evening.

I write you these few lines only to set your mind at ease, for — surrounded from morning till night by curious gazers who have never before seen a European—it would be difficult to enter into details, but, in truth, my journey furnished but few. I travelled with Laotians, and found them very kind; in a few days I shall be in the heart of their country, and think I shall find them superior to the Siamese. I regret that this letter will be short, but I have little to tell since I wrote last; when I am quietly settled in some little hut in the midst of a village, I can write at my ease if an opportunity presents itself.

Be easy on my account, dear Annie, and feel sure that God will not abandon me; all my confidence is in Him, and this will never deceive me. He will sustain and protect you also, and this assurance gives me strength.

Adieu, my good Annette; take great care of yourself. I embrace you tenderly, and am ever your devoted and affectionate husband,

H. MOUHOT.

P.S.—I shall set off to-morrow. Yesterday I visited an old pagoda; there is another, but to which I shall not be able to go, as it would cost me 9 ticals, and take several days, and I shall be obliged to be excessively economical. Yesterday I had a visit from a mandarin, the viceroy of the province. He was very amiable, and promised me a letter, but the people are so kind that I have really no need of it, and even the disagreeable ones I manage to gain over.

Adieu, my love. Do not forget me, but do not be uneasy. May God grant to you the same tranquillity and confidence that I feel and make you as happy as I am. Do not complain of the shortness of this letter; you cannot imagine how I am pestered by gazers and idlers.

Embrace your dear mamma for me, to whom I wish good health; say everything kind to Kate, &c. Once more, adieu, and au revoir! Your devoted HENRI. I shall write whenever I find an opportunity.

To Madame Charles Mouhot.

Louang Prabang (Laos), 23rd July, 1861.

Now, my dear Jenny, let us converse together. Do you know of what I often think when every one around me is asleep, and I, lying wrapped in my mosquito-curtains, let my thoughts wander back to all the members of my family? Then I seem to hear again the charming voice of my little Jenny, and to be listening once more to 'La Traviata,' 'The Death of Nelson,' or some other of the airs that I loved so much to hear you sing. I then feel regret, mingled with joy, at the souvenirs of the happy—oh, how happy!—past. Then I open the gauze curtains, light my pipe, and gaze out upon the stars, humming softly the 'Pâtre' of Béranger, or the 'Old Sergeant,' and thinking that one day I may return Corporal or Sergeant of the battalion of Naturalists.

Perhaps all this does not interest you, but you may feel sure that I do not forget you nor your children; so let me, my dear child, talk to you as we used to talk in the old times as we sat by the fire. When shall we do so again?

In another year, or perhaps two, dear Jenny, I shall think of returning to you all for some time. Shall you be very angry, my dear little sister, when I say that it will be with regret? —for I should wish to visit the whole of the mountains that I can see from my window. I say "window," but here such a luxury is unknown : I live in a shed without either doors or windows—a room open to every wind.

I would wish, I repeat, to cross the whole network of mountains which extend northward, see what lies beyond them, visit China or Thibet, and see the Calmucks or the Irkoutsk. But, alas! I cannot trust my dear insects. I say "my dear insects" as you would say "my dear children" to the king of Louang Prabang.

How does all go on at Jersey?—for I hope that you are still

there. Your children form your happiness, and you can dis-
pense easily with travelling, or with those people commonly
called "friends"—nothing is so general as the name, or so
rare as the reality—and you are right; yet I consider a true
friend as a real treasure. I may be wrong, for man is so constituted as always to long for what he has not, but I wish I
had friends around me here; these places, now often gloomy,
would please me more.

I hoped that at the king's return I should have the happiness
of hearing from you; but I am told that his journey will occupy
a year, and before that time I shall be away from here.

I hope, my little friend, that all is well with you. Embrace
your dear children for me, and talk to them sometimes about
their uncle "Barberousse," who often thinks of them in this
distant land, and is collecting stories for their amusement on
his return. Ask C—— what I shall bring him—a monkey, a
sabre to cut off M——'s dolls' heads—no, that would give him
warlike ideas, and I do not like our modern soldiers—or a
tiger-skin for a carpet. I have several. And your pretty little
M——, will she have an ape, a fan, some Chinese slippers
(for she must have feet which would be small even in China),
some marabout feathers, or a cane to keep her brothers in
order?

Adieu, adieu! Au revoir! Do not forget me.

To Madame Mouhot.

Laos, Louang Prabang, 27th July, 1861.

During my journey through the forests I enjoyed in
anticipation the pleasure I should enjoy on reaching Louang
Prabang, the capital of the province of Laos, in writing you
good long letters containing all details of my journey; but

I reckoned without my host, and it will be several weeks before I can enjoy any repose, or carry my wishes into execution.

In the villages through which I passed no great degree of curiosity was manifested; but here, where the population is greater, I am surrounded by a compact and curious crowd, which extends even to the walls of a pagoda adjoining the caravanserai where I am lodged by the favour of his Majesty the King. Besides, I, in my turn, see people of various nations and tribes who excite my curiosity. Judge, therefore, if it be easy to collect my ideas. However, I profit by the occasion of the king's departure for Bangkok in a few days to pay his tribute, and who has offered to take charge of any letters for me, to give some signs of life to you.

You will be happy to hear that I have accomplished this troublesome journey satisfactorily, without the loss of a single man, and without any personal illness. Indeed, my health has been very good, which is more than I can say for my servants, who are so kind and devoted to me. I am even astonished at myself, having gone through the mountainous district which separates the basin of the Menam from that of the Mekon, a place much dreaded by the Siamese, and covered with virgin-forests like those of Dong Phya Phia, without having had a single touch of fever, or, indeed, any indisposition, with the exception of *migraine*, caused by the heat of the sun, and having my feet in a very bad state.

I bless God for the favour granted to me of having accomplished these perilous journeys, and trust wholly to His goodness for the future.

I am now more than 250 leagues north of the place where two years ago I first drank the waters of the Mekon. This immense stream, which is larger here than the Menam at Bangkok or the Thames below London Bridge, flows between high mountains with the rapidity of a torrent, tearing up in the

rainy season the trees along the banks, and breaking with a
noise like that of a stormy sea against the rocks, which form
a number of frightful rapids.

I arrived here only the day before yesterday, after a journey
of four months and ten days; but I stopped in several places,
for I often found fields ready to cut in the rice-grounds that
the mountaineers cultivate on the slopes of the mountains, and
when the crops are cut down insects abound.

My collections made during the journey are very valuable
and beautiful, and I have a great number of new species, both
entomological and conchological, with which, if they only reach
London in safety, our friends will be delighted. All the beautiful kinds that I was asked for, but which elsewhere are so
rare that with great trouble I was only able to procure one or
two specimens, I have now in great abundance, and also many
new sorts. Here I hope to do still better.

They are all savages in this province, and I have just
received a visit from two young princes remarkable for their
stupidity.

I have suffered little from the heat, in spite of the season,
which is easy to understand, as I have been always amidst thick
forests or on mountains. In the valleys the air is heavy, and
the heat overwhelming; but everywhere the nights were so
fresh that my wraps were useful and almost indispensable. In
a few months we shall probably want fire. I prefer this
climate to that of the South; there are few mosquitoes (that
plague of the tropics and especially of Siam) in comparison
with other places—indeed, in some of these parts I have not
found any.

Thanks to the Governor of Korat, who gave me an excellent letter to the mandarins, I have travelled at little expense;
without it, I should have paid much more, and have suffered
every kind of inconvenience. Everywhere I have been furnished

with elephants (as many as seven in some provinces), an escort, guard, and plenty of provisions.

I had this morning an audience of the great body of State Mandarins, like the House of Peers with us. Twenty of them were assembled in a vast caravanserai, and presided over by the eldest prince. You may form some idea of the dignity of these gentlemen by the drawing which I will send to you.

My plan is to pass six or eight months of the good season in the neighbouring villages, in order to complete my collection, and next January or March I will try to go north or east, where I shall pass a few more months amidst the Laotian tribes. Probably I shall go no farther, for China would be a barrier to me on the north, and Cochin China on the east. I shall then return here, and go down the Mekon in July or August, 1862, the time when the waters are high, and shall thus reach Korat in a few weeks. I am yet uncertain whether I shall stop there, whether I shall explore the eastern part of the river, or whether I shall go to Cambodia. All my movements depend upon circumstances that may arise. I shall try to profit by all that are favourable, and that will contribute to give interest to my journey.

Do not be anxious when you think of your poor friend the traveller, for you know that up to the present time everything has prospered with him: and truly I experience a degree of contentment, strength of soul, and internal peace, which I have never known before.

[*Same Letter.*]

Louang Prabang, 8th August, 1861.

No event could have caused more sensation here than the arrival of "the long-bearded stranger." From the humblest to the greatest—for even here are distinctions of rank—every one

looks on a " white " as a natural curiosity, and they are not yet
satisfied with looking—nothing is talked of but the stranger.
When I pass through the town in my white dress, to go to the
market or to visit the pagodas or other interesting places,
the people crowd round me, and look after me as long as they
can catch a glimpse of me. Everywhere I go complete silence
reigns, and I am treated as though I were a sovereign or prince,
and the council, by order of the king, have given to me as to
them power of life or death over his subjects. Poor people!
why can I not raise you from the abasement into which you
have fallen? I am overwhelmed with presents of all kinds in
return for the slightest favour shown to these unfortunate
people. They seem to me some of the most to be pitied that I
have seen; even the women and children are opium-eaters:
they might really be called a nation of crétins.

The heat is greater here than any I have felt; when the.sun
shines, and there has been no rain for several days, I find it
worse than at Bangkok; still the nights are generally pleasant,
and from the month of December to the end of March I am
told that it is really cold.

To M. Charles Mouhot.

Louang Prabang, West Laos, 27th July, 1861.

As you will have the opportunity, my dear brother, of
reading my other letters, I shall not write to you at length;
but, nevertheless, I must give you some details as to my journey
to Laos, although I cannot tell whether the crowd of curious
gazers around me will permit me to write as I would wish; if
not, you must blame them and not me.

On the 10th April I wrote you from Korat, and I think you
must also have received a message which I sent to you by a
good and honest Chinese, who has been very useful to me, and

from whom I have received more help and kindness than from any other of the mandarins.

I was not then in good spirits, for I doubted whether I should be able to accomplish the journey for which I had already suffered so many annoyances, one of which was having to return to Korat to procure more useful letters than those which I had taken with me on starting. At last I obtained one from the Viceroy of Korat, which was the only one of service to me, and which sufficed to secure me aid and protection during my whole journey to Laos.

From Korat to Bangkok you know that I travelled in company with an animal who has a title equal to that of the greatest Siamese mandarin, and who was served by two inferior mandarins, who gave him his meals composed of cakes, biscuits, and sweetmeats out of golden dishes; and who had slaves sent before him to clear the way and cut down the brushwood and branches, for this elephant, according to the Siamese superstition and ignorance, possesses the soul of some deceased prince or king. They called him a white elephant, but in reality he had only a few spots of that colour on his body. Alas! The king and all his mandarins are now in mourning, for the object of their worship died of indigestion. Poor beast and poor king!

I have travelled a long way since I last wrote, and God has protected me. I crossed the mountains and went through the most dreaded jungles in the rainy season without losing a man, and without having suffered myself. My travelling expenses were comparatively small to what they might have been; everywhere I was furnished gratis with elephants, escorts, guards, and provisions (rice and fowls), as though I were an envoy from the king, and all this owing solely to a letter from the Viceroy of Korat.

I have made a good collection of coleoptera, and have procured a number of excessively rare and beautiful species.

I have also obtained some very rare and interesting conchological specimens. As for animals, I have but few; some monkeys and a good many serpents.

In a week I shall be settled in a new place, where I intend to spend four or five months, and by the end of the year I trust to have 4000 insects.

The Mekon is a large and beautiful stream, full of rocks, which form frightful rapids in the rainy season. I shall descend it at the season when the waters are high, and when the navigation though dangerous is easy and rapid. I can then reach Cambodia in a month if I like, but I am undecided whether or not I shall go eastward towards the 15th degree of latitude.

It seems to me, my dear brother, that my happiness would be complete if I could have good news of you all; but, alas! more than a year must elapse before I shall hear. The last letters I received were in January; yet I am resigned, since I willingly embraced this career, which has been the dream of my whole life, for you remember how in our young days, when we still had the happiness of a tender mother to guide us, and impress on us, by her example, virtuous principles, religion, and the love of mankind, we delighted to roam the woods of our dear native place, to draw from nature, and how I stuffed the birds that we took in snares or nets.

That time is long passed, my friend, but I trust in God, who will I hope watch over you. I think of you every day in my solitude, and in the long nights when we bivouac beside the fires lighted to keep off the wild beasts, a scene of which I will send you a drawing before long.

What are your dear children doing? I picture to myself all the happiness they give you and your dear Jenny; she is well I hope. Ah! my friend, protect them all with a tender affection, and endeavour by your love, your care, and your example, to render them all happy and good.

There is one subject on which I can hardly write, that of our dear old father; it would make me too sad to think he was not happy; console him for my absence, write to him often, repeat to him how much I love him, that he is always associated in my thoughts with the memory of our good and worthy mother. But I have no need to recommend all this to you: have you not ever been good to him, a worthy son? therefore I am without anxiety on this point.

I do not speak to you of any of my physical sufferings, for I hold mental ones to be the only ones worth thinking of; but you may imagine that one cannot make a four months' journey on elephants, who toss and shake one like a stormy sea, without fatigue, and that the heat, the long bad nights generally passed at the foot of some tree, and the wretched food, are all painful. But what matters all this? I am used to it, and my patience is inexhaustible. In truth, this life is happiness to me; how joyful I am when I find a new insect, or see a monkey fall from a tree! I do not therefore complain. The nights here are pleasant, and the mosquitoes not numerous.

The men of this nation are dull and apathetic and full of small vices. The women are generally better, and some of them are even pretty in spite of their yellow skins, but they have little idea of modesty. The men and women all bathe together without any clothing. But for the people, Louang Prabang would be one of the most charming places in the world: the lake of Geneva does not present scenes more beautiful than many here by the river.

After waiting for ten days I have at length been presented to the king with great pomp. The reception room was a shed such as they build in our villages on fête-days, but larger and hung with every possible colour. His Majesty was enthroned at one end of the hall, lazily reclining on a divan, having on his right hand four guards squatting down, and each holding a sabre: behind were the princes all prostrated, and farther off the

senators, with their backs to the public and their faces in the
dust; then in front of his Majesty was your poor brother,
dressed all in white, and seated on a carpet, with teacups,
basins, and spittoons in silver placed by his side, contemplating
this grotesque scene, and having some trouble to preserve his
gravity as he smoked his pipe. This visit cost me a gun for
the king and various small presents for the princes, for one
cannot travel here without being well furnished with presents
for the kings, princes, and mandarins. Luckily it is not here
as in Siam; the natives are willing to help me, and for a few
inches of brass wire I get a beautiful longicorn or some other
insect, and these are brought to me on all sides: thus I have
succeeded in largely increasing my collection, but five pieces of
red cloth have disappeared already.

The day after my first audience I had another from the
second king, who wished also for a present. I sought among my
stock, which anywhere else would cause me to be taken for a
dealer in old stores, and found a magnifying glass and a pair of
old-fashioned spectacles with round glasses, which make him
look like a gorilla without hair, a little cake of soap (he had
great need of it), a bottle of eau-de-cologne, and a bottle of
brandy. This last was opened on the spot and duly appreciated. You see all this is expensive, but I am obliged to
pay these good people, and the king has been kind to me, and
is going to carry my letters for me. It is lucky that he does
not understand French; for if at Bangkok the same system of
postal curiosity was carried on as was established in Europe by
the great king who betrayed La Vallière, I should be hung from
the highest tree they could find, without even a warning. I
afterwards distributed among the princes some engravings
which I had bought at Bangkok—fine Cossack cavalry, lance in
rest; some Napoleons (the First), for which I gave a penny; and
some battles of Magenta, portraits of Victor Emmanuel and of
Garibaldi, very white, blue, and red, and some Zouaves; also

some brass-headed nails and some brandy; and it was quite
pleasing to see how delighted they were, regretting only that I
should go away before I had given them my whole stock.

To Samuel Stevens, Esq.

[To be communicated to the Royal Geographical Society.]

Louang Prabang, 1st August, 1861.
Lat. 20° 50', long. 102° 35' 3'', merid. Greenwich.

Dear Mr. Stevens,

Being entirely cut off from all communication with
Bangkok, from which I am nearly 700 miles distant, is the
only reason why you have not heard from me for so long a
time.

In January last I quitted the Siamese province of Saraburi, where during four months I had been making active
exertions in order to enable me to penetrate into Western Laos,
and to explore the basin of the Mekon. Unluckily in March
I was forced, after having at great expense proceeded 350
miles, to return to Bangkok, in order to claim more assistance
and protection than had hitherto been accorded to me, and a
passport to counteract the difficulties continually thrown in my
way by the mandarins, a class not less jealous and greedy here
than in China. A letter of recommendation which had been
voluntarily given to me (on my departure in October, 1860)
by the Khrôme Louang Wougsâ, who is considered to be the
prince best disposed towards Europeans in all Siam, and who
has the superintendence of all the country which I intended
to visit, turned out after all to be only a kind of letter of
Bellerophon's. In spite of all my entreaties and valuable
presents I obtained nothing better; still I set off again.

I have passed three times through the forest of the Dong Phya Phia, which separates Korat from the ancient Siamese provinces of the south and east. This thick jungle covers a space of thirty miles in breadth,—that is to say, the chain of mountains which separates the basin of the Mekon from that of the Menam.

After passing the mountains you reach a sandy and generally arid plain, where nothing is to be seen but resinous trees of stunted growth, bamboos, underwood, and sometimes only grass; but in some places a richer soil permits cultivation, and there fields of rice and bananas have been established. I found in this district both oligist and magnetic iron.

In the bed of a torrent I also discovered gold and copper in two different places. This district is rich and abundant in precious minerals, neglected or unknown until now, except by a small tribe of 400 or 500 Kariens, without doubt a remnant of the aborigines, who a short time ago, in order to preserve their independence, retired into almost inaccessible places, thirty or forty miles eastward of the tracts traversed by the caravans. Monkeys, panthers, elephants, and other wild beasts are the only inhabitants of this mountain, which the natives regard as the abode of death on account of its insalubrity.

Korat Ongcor Aithe of the Cambodians was formerly the bulwark of Cambodia on the north and west: a solid rampart supported by a large épaulement, the work of Khmer Dôme (the ancient Cambodians), still surrounds the town. It is at present governed by a Siamese mandarin of the first class, a kind of viceroy, but the ancient inhabitants have nearly disappeared, and it contains only about 300 Chinese or their descendants, small resident merchants, 300 other individuals who go about the country trading, and 1500 or 2000 Laotians, Cambodians, and Siamese, who, like wolves or jackals which follow an army or caravan, have come there from all parts of the kingdom, or have remained there after the wars of Laos and Cambodia, in order to lead a life in harmony with their inclinations, attacking travellers and Chinese merchants, in fact a band of miscreants, with few exceptions destitute of all good qualities.

In the environs are two temples, which would do honour to the founders of the Cambodian edifices : one of them is in good preservation, and of this I have made a drawing. The style, architecture, and workmanship are all alike; one would say that the same artists and workmen had drawn the plans and executed them. Again you see those immense blocks, beautifully cut, joined without cement, and covered with carving and bas-reliefs.

One of these temples is situated about thirty miles from the town, and is said to have been founded by a Queen; the other, nine miles to the east, is supposed to have been built by the King her husband. Much farther east it is said that there are others containing beautiful sculptures, but I have not been able to visit them, as they are out of my route.

Want of means for the easy and advantageous removal of merchandise, causes Korat to be the central market for all the eastern part of the country. There they bring all the silk of Laos, langoutis, skins, horns, ivory, peacocks' tails, &c., which the active Chinese merchants sell again at a good profit at Bangkok, notwithstanding all the taxes they have to pay, having brought from thence cotton and other useful articles of Chinese and European manufacture for the use of the natives. Thus there passes daily through the forest of Dong Phya Phia, on the average, a caravan of from 100 to 150 oxen. With protective instead of restrictive laws, and an enlightened and civilized government, this commerce would increase threefold in a very short time.

Notwithstanding the small population of Korat, it is the chief town of a province, or rather an extensive state, containing eleven towns or boroughs, chief towns of districts, and a great number of villages, more or less populated. Fifteen days' journey brings you from Korat to Bassac on the banks of the Mekon, and in the same latitude.

My intention was to proceed northwards, only stopping in the province of Louang Prabang, and then to descend the river as far as Cambodia. I hired elephants, and five days after, having passed through several villages inhabited by the descendants of ancient Siamese colonists who had taken refuge there in time of war, passing continually through forests of resin trees thinly scattered, I arrived at Ban Prang, a village where I discovered a ruined tower, and also the remains of an ancient temple. The next place I arrived at was Chaiapoune, the principal Laotian town in the north, and the chief town of the district. Here also I found ruins; but they were inconsiderable, and seemed more like a Laotian imitation than the work of Khmer Dôme. The inscriptions on the other temples in the province of Korat resemble those of Ongcor : here I found upon a block of broken slate-stone an inscription in Laotian characters, but which is unintelligible even to the inhabitants of the country. These, with some remains of idols and towers at the foot of a mountain in the district, were the only vestiges of that ancient civilization which I discovered in the north. Everything leads me to suppose that here also were the limits which separated the kingdom of Cambodia from that of Vieng Thiane, destroyed during the last war which the Siamese raised against the Western Laotians or *white-bellies*. It was in this district that I was stopped in my travels by the authorities of the country, who treated me with great rudeness, and who forbade the people to let me have any means of transport, even after seeing my passport. I was therefore obliged to retrace my steps, deploring the expense and loss of time in the best part of the year, and which will cause me serious inconvenience.

LETTERS ADDRESSED TO M. MOUHOT.*

From M. Guilloux.

Brelum, among the Stiêns, 12th August, 1859.

Dear M. Mouhot,

It must be allowed that you have plenty of courage; and before knowing you, I feel a strong interest in you; indeed, I feel as though I loved you already. You will be very welcome, and must share pot-luck with me, like a brother, will you not? I trust you will not be scandalized at any of our ways; for among the savages we live in rather an uncivilized fashion. But with good hearts all will go well.

Your servant Nhu arrived yesterday among the Stiêns at Brelum, quite tired with the journey, and with his feet in a sad state. A few days' rest, however, will restore him. He looks to me like a good fellow. You may be sure we shall take care of him, as well as of your little Chinese when he arrives.

You must never trust to the word of a Cambodian, dear M. Mouhot; they are terrible boasters.

You are two long days' journey from us, and will have to pass one night in the forest. We will try to send you one or two vehicles. These, with a good covering and a fire, will preserve you from injury from the night air. You say, too, that you are accustomed to sleep on the ground; it is well to be able to do everything.

Unluckily, my feet are very bad just now, or I should have been delighted to come and meet you. I will send the three

---

* Several of these letters were never received by M. Mouhot.

carriages — carriages! wretched carts rather! There will be
an Annamite seminarist to lead the caravan; he is a good fellow,
and clever at that kind of work. You can talk to him in
Latin. Two of the carts are drawn by oxen, and one by buffaloes; but if they are not enough to bring your luggage, ask the
Cambodians boldly for more, and show them your letter from
the king.

Our carts will arrive one day after the return of the Cambodians; when you arrive I will explain why. I trust that will be
soon. I wish you a good journey. Keep your gun loaded, for
animals of all kinds abound. But you will find here warm hearts,
patriotism, and, above all, no ceremony.

From M. Chas. Fontaine.

Pinhalú, Cambodia.

Dear M. Mouhot,

I think of you in your peregrinations, and I feel sure
that you must meet with many obstacles and difficulties; but
with patience, perseverance, and help from on high, a great deal
may be done.

As for myself, I have not got rid of my atony—for such is
my illness. At first I obtained some relief by means of opium
as an astringent and quinine as a tonic, and by great attention
to diet, living almost wholly on broth; a piece of meat, or
even an egg, throws me back for a week.

M. Guilloux set off in good health on the 9th January. He
tells me that you have promised to go and see his relations when
you return to France.

I shall never forget, dear M. Mouhot, the pleasure that I
experienced in the few days that I passed in your society; such
days are so rare in our missionary life.

All is quiet just now in Cambodia; the forts or redoubts

are guarded only by a few men.   Mgr. Miche is expected
to return from Komput about the end of March.   Shall I be so
happy as to receive news of you?   It would give me great
pleasure, and recall that which I have already experienced in our
meeting in this life.   Let us hope to be re-united, no more to
part, in a happier one.

Pray receive my kindest remembrances, and believe me,
dear M. Mouhot,

Your true friend in the Lord,

MARIE CHS. FONTAINE.

FROM M. CHAS. FONTAINE.

Singapore, 29th May, 1860.

MY VERY DEAR FRIEND, M. MOUHOT,

Your two kind and welcome letters, one from Battambong
on the 7th March, and the other from Bangkok on the 3rd
May, reached me when I was about three days' distance from
Singapore, where I had gone for my health, and which I reached
in April, after having passed the whole month of March in
Bangkok.

I must tell you that MM. Arnoux and Guilloux have been
able to buy five or six little savage children, and that they now
meet with a little more kindness from the natives than they did.
When France shall reign in Cochin China, and the natives can
shake off the yoke of the Cambodians, it is to be hoped that they
will be better disposed towards religion.   The king has already
discovered the mistake he made in attacking the Annamites,
who may fall upon him without dread of the French.   Mgr.
Miche thinks that the daily flight of the Cambodian soldiers
will avoid new provocation, and that the war may not take
place; but every one is on the *qui vive*.   The king has sent a

letter to ask for silence on the part of M. Miche. They are fawning curs now; but on the slightest return of good fortune, their arrogance will be redoubled.

You gave me much pleasure, dear M. Mouhot, by your promise to visit my family at Laval. If you go near there, I shall expect no less from your kindness.

I hope to see you again, either at Singapore or at Saigon, before your return to Europe. May the good God guide your steps and preserve your life in this country, where death finds so many victims! I beg it through the intercession of our common mother.

Believe in my cordial friendship.

Yours most truly, in Jesus and Mary,

M. CH. FONTAINE.

FROM M. GUILLOUX.

Among the Stiêns at Brelum, 1st October, 1860.

DEAR M. MOUHOT,

I received your welcome letter of the 4th May, and it is impossible to tell you the pleasure it gave me. I was much pleased to hear that you were still in good health. May the good God aid and bless your efforts, and send you home safe and well to your family and country!

I sympathize sincerely with you in your disappointment at not meeting at Bangkok with more kindness among those from whom you had a right to expect aid and protection, and who are paid well for that purpose. Alas! how weak we all are when we rely for aid only on men like ourselves. But you, dear M. Mouhot, do not do so; you know how to seek support from a higher source; and while you remain the submissive child of God, be sure He will not abandon you.

I went to Pinhalú last month, and brought back a young Annamite with me, but the poor fellow died.

You see I can travel; but I am not strong. I have been often ill since your departure; and M. Arnoux is going this time to undertake the journey to Cambodia. May God bring him back safe and well!

The affairs of Cochin China are very bad; debauchery and infamy are rife at Saigon. So many crimes cannot bring a blessing on the colony.

No news from China.

Adieu, dear M. Mouhot. Believe me ever one of your most faithful friends,

GUILLOUX.

FROM DR. CAMPBELL, R.N.

Bangkok, 15th Dec. 1860.

My DEAR M. MOUHOT,

Your letters of the 30th October and 20th November were duly delivered to me on the 12th instant. I was naturally rejoiced to find you continue in good health and spirits; and I sincerely trust you will be able, on each occasion you write, to give me a like favourable account.

Since you left there has been little or no change in Bangkok, the only domestic item I have to communicate being the recent marriage of Dr. Brady's eldest daughter to one of the missionaries named M‘Gilvary, who used to stay with Dr. House.

Only one European letter has arrived for you, but I enclose others from Mr. Wilson and Mr. Adamson, and, by the way, some newspapers from him and M. Malherbe. The latter will probably write to you; if so, I shall enclose his letter. The box from Europe also accompanies this letter. Luckily it has arrived in time; but I only received it yesterday. I forward you the evening mails just arrived by last vessel. I could send you all that have come to hand since you left; but as it is a voluminous paper, it would take up much space, and you might not care to wade through all of them, in spite of the stirring events in Europe. Garibaldi, you will perceive, has liberated Sicily, and all but done likewise for the Neapolitan kingdom. The King of Naples left his capital without firing a shot; but made a stand at Capua, where his Neapolitans and mercenaries made a determined though ineffectual resistance. The King of Sardinia in the mean time has invaded the Marches, and now it is believed the states of the Pope are wrested from him, Rome and the suburban villages alone being retained for him by the French army stationed at Rome. It is not believed that an attempt will be made to take Rome or Venice, as that would be encountering the two great military Continental Powers, Austria and France. And it is supposed that the aim of the King of Sardinia, in invading the states of the Church and Naples, is to prevent the too ardent Garibaldi from fulfilling his threat of no peace till the Quirinal and the palace of the Doges be emancipated. However, all this you will see by the papers herewith.

The China war is over. The combined forces advanced and took Pekin. The emperor fled; but a treaty has been signed, and a large sum as indemnity—though, I believe, not equal to the outlay—is to be given to the European belligerents.

A Dutch ship is now here with an ambassador to make a treaty.

At Bangkok we have had higher tides this season than there have been for several years. The place continues healthy.

I forward you some calomel as requested. Calomel is a good purgative, and it might be well occasionally to take one such in preference to others; but castor oil is the safest where there is any irritation of the bowels. In such cases it should alone be used; though, if you fancy there be derangement of the liver, it would be well to use the mineral.

M. Malherbe has made up his mind to stay in Bangkok. As soon as his successor comes out, he (M. M.) will live near Santa Cruz, at the house owned by Mr. Hunter.

There is a chance of the second king going to Saraburi shortly in a steamer; so, if I think newspapers would reach you before the Chinaman, I may send you some, if a mail arrives by that time. However, I shall not, you may depend upon it, forget to attend to your wishes; but I really fear, after leaving Korat, it will be difficult to send you letters. Even to Korat it will not be easy; but though you did not tell me to send thither, I will do so, if possible, within two or three months; after that date it would be precarious, and I shall not do so. However, you can often, by the governors, have an opportunity of writing to me; and if you have altered any of your plans, or think of doing so, let me know, so that I may forward news if an opportunity offers for doing so.

The articles sent are: one large box from Mr. Adamson, one small ditto from Malherbe, one ditto from England, one parcel of papers from Mr. Swainson, one ditto from myself; three letters (besides this one) are enclosed in the box from M. Malherbe, which I will seal after enclosing this. The calomel is also in the same box.

And now, wishing you a prosperous, pleasant journey, believe me,

Yours very sincerely,

Jas. Campbell.

P.S.—Remember, whenever you return, I shall expect you to come direct to my house, and make it your own.

From M. E. Silvestre.

Battambong, 26th Nov. 1860.

Dear M. Mouhot,

I had the honour of writing to you in September last; did you receive my letter? As I did not know the courier, and am ignorant whether his fidelity was to be depended upon, I do not wish to lose a sure occasion which presents itself of recalling myself to your remembrance.

It is now the end of the rainy season, and I think that you must have returned from your expedition. I trust it has been successful, and that you have not left your courage and good health behind you on the banks of the Mekon or in the forests of Laos.

I had promised to collect for you some " sinsei ;" but the ants, true Garibaldians, have annexed them during my journey to Pinhalú, and all that I have been able to collect since are as nothing compared to what the first rains brought with them. Such as they are, I send them to you; they are few in number, but for that you must blame the ants.

I have just had a visit from M. Miche and M. Arnoux. They only remained a few days; and in spite of his wish to see Ongcor, M. Arnoux was unable to go there.

They are raising troops here, preparing arms, and getting ready to assist the Cambodians against the Annamites. The death of the King of Cambodia will perhaps put an end to these fine projects.

The mandarin who was sent by the King of Siam to carry away the stones from Ongcor, and bring them to Bangkok, has been assassinated in the " Pra Sat Ea proum," and the mandarins of Ongcor are accused of the murder; but they say that those of Battambong had a hand in it. They have, therefore, all been sent for to Bangkok for judgment, and among them the son of

our late governor. You see we are not over tranquil here. The
war particularly terrifies my poor Battambongians.

Mgr. Miche is going to Bangkok in January or February;
perhaps you may be there.

Receive the assurance, &c.,

E. SILVESTRE.

<hr>

FROM M. LARNAUDIE.*

Pakprio, 25th January, 1861.

MY DEAR FRIEND, M. MOUHOT,

I have just received the two letters which you were kind
enough to write to me from Kong Khoc, containing enclosures
for MM. Arnoux and Silvestre. I much regretted not finding
you here, that I might have had the pleasure of seeing you once
more, and of conversing with you again before your departure
for Laos. I am glad to hear that you have been able to do
something at Khao-Khoc in spite of the advanced season.

I wish you much success in your new sphere of action. Do
you know that I sometimes envy you ? Do not forget to procure
some skins of the argus pheasant; I think it differs from those
of the Malayan peninsula. Take great care of your health; and
if you are in want of anything which can be sent to you by way
of Korat, write to me for it.

The young man who will give you this is a Christian and an
associate of Cheek-Ke; he is a worthy lad, and you may trust
him with your collections, if you have been able to make any
in going through Don Phya Phia. All the Laotians declare
that in that forest there is a kind of orang-outang which they

<hr>

* M. Larnaudie accompanied the Siamese Ambassador to Paris, as
interpreter, in 1860.

call Bua, and which they say is only to be distinguished from an old man by its having no joints in its knees. Among all their fables there is probably some truth; try to find out.

Excuse this scrawl; I write on my knees.

Your sincere friend,
LARNAUDIE.

FROM M. E. SILVESTRE.

Battambong, 4th January, 1862.*

DEAR M. MOUHOT,

Imagine my surprise and joy when, a week ago, a worthy Chinese from Korat entered my house, bringing me your letter of the 8th April. Blessed be God for granting you good health and courage. With these you can go far, even to the source of the Mekon; and if you return through Cambodia, with what pleasure I shall see you again! But your letter is dated more than eight months ago, and where are you now? I trust that the rainy season induced you to descend the Menam instead of the Mekon. Should you ever return to Battambong, you will find something new there. A pretty little church now replaces the old one; it is not yet quite finished, but I trust will be so very shortly.

Since I last wrote to you, grave events have taken place in Cambodia; the mandarins and people have risen against the young king in favour of his brother. It has been less a revolt than a universal pillage; nothing has been spared. Mgr. Miche had great trouble to guard his house, with the help of a young missionary and M. Aussoleil, for all the Christians fled. For a fortnight he was subject to constant attacks, and more than once saw sabres uplifted over his head; but his firmness

---

* This date is after M. Mouhot's death.

and bravery awed the mob, and he was lucky enough to preserve his house.

Some damage was done to the Annamite church at the end of the village.   M. Miche wrote letter after letter to the French commander in Cochin China, but his messengers were all murdered, or else robbed, and their boats taken away from them.

At last, out of six letters, one reached its destination, and two days after the French flag appeared in the rivers of Cambodia; and at Pinhalú, six or seven cannon-shots spread terror among the rebels for twenty-five leagues round.

The mandarins who had pillaged the village were fined, and since then the Christians in Cambodia have been respected; and a letter sealed by M. Miche is the best possible passport.   All this is well, you will say, and our countrymen did their duty.

You must excuse my lengthiness; at least, it will show that you are not forgotten at Battambong, but that we preserve here a happy remembrance of your too short stay.   May you return in a few months, and recruit after your fatigues.

I must conclude with offering you my good wishes on the new year, and praying God to have you always and everywhere in his holy keeping.

I am yours very sincerely,

E. SILVESTRE.

FROM M. MALHERBE.

Bangkok, 25th May, 1861.

MY DEAR FRIEND,

On my return from Singapore I was much astonished to hear that you had been forced to go back again, and was much pained to think of all the troubles and discomforts you must have had to endure.   How much I regret not having been with you!

perhaps I might have succeeded in persuading you against
making a new attempt, and have induced you rather to pass some
years here with me. Your task is a glorious one; but when life
is at stake, one must take care and not risk it rashly. In any
case do not attempt the impossible; and if your troubles recom-
mence, return here; you will always find a friend ready to receive
you.

Your letter from Korat reached me a few days ago. I thank
you for it; it gave me great pleasure. In a few days I shall set
out for Europe; but I have given my orders, and you will find
my house ready for you at any time of the day or night. If you
do not make use of it, I shall be really angry.

Every one here is interested for you, and asks for news of you.
Where are you now? Doubtless much fatigued and *ennuyé*
wherever you are; yet you must be travelling through a fine
country. If you want anything which it is possible to send you,
have no scruples; I have given my clerks all necessary instructions, if by chance or any unforeseen circumstance—such as may
easily occur on a journey—you find yourself in want of what
they call here "ticals." We are friends,—dispose freely of my
purse; we will divide like brothers. Do not be offended at this
offer, it comes from a heart devoted to you; therefore, have no
false pride. Ask, and I will help you.

The heat is dreadful just now, and every one is ill of
dysentery.

Au revoir, dear M. Mouhot. Take care of yourself, and do not
be discouraged by the dreadful climate. That we may have,
please God, many pleasant days together yet, is the earnest wish
of your real friend,

L. MALHERBE.

LETTERS ADDRESSED TO THE FAMILY
OF THE LATE M. MOUHOT.

From Dr. Campbell to Madame Mouhot.

Bangkok, April 7th, 1862.

My dear Madame Mouhot,

About three weeks ago I had the pleasure of forwarding a letter from your husband, and I mentioned the probability of a second one, written before the one sent, reaching me in time for this mail. This has been realized, and I enclose the letter referred to. News from Luang Prabang, up to the middle of November, have also reached Bangkok, and oh! my dear madam, what a sad duty devolves upon me in narrating certainties that have transpired since my last communication. Would that I had some relation in London to whom I could write and request him to call upon you, to divulge the painful truth that your husband—my valued friend—is, alas! now no more. It may perhaps in a measure tend to soothe your sorrow under this severe trial, to say that I never knew a person who was so universally esteemed as he was by the foreign community of this city; and that all who had the pleasure of his acquaintance deeply regret his sudden and premature loss. The last letter he wrote me was dated from Louang Prabang, on the 30th August; in it he was satisfied with his success, and altogether buoyant in spirits. He continued in the neighbourhood of the above-named city, which is the capital of north-east Laos, till the middle of October, when he returned to the city. On the 19th he has written in his journal, " Attacked with fever;" but his servant and the Laos official account of his illness make it the 18th. On the 29th he made an entry, but nothing subsequently, and departed this life on Sunday the 10th November, at 7 p.m., being twenty-eight days subsequent to the attack. His servants, after seeing him interred, commenced their journey hither, taking with them his baggage and everything he had collected. M. D'Istria, the present French Consul, has to officiate as administrator to the late M. Mouhot's estate, but has assigned to me the care of all your late husband's manuscripts and collections. These I thought of forwarding forthwith for Singapore, and thence, by the kindness of Mr. Pady, to Europe; but as I expect to leave for England on a short leave of absence by the middle of next month, I think it better to retain them till then, and convey them home myself.

On your late husband arriving here, he brought me a small parcel from Dr. Norton Shaw, Secretary to the Royal Geographical Society, Whitehall-place; and as it is only proper that the Society should be made aware of this martyr to science, I enclose two letters—the last he wrote me—for your perusal, and that they may be handed to the above-named gentleman for his information, forwarding, at the same time, the announcement of M. Mouhot's untimely death. On looking over the charts he has left behind him, I find Louang Prabang placed 3° to the north and about 1° to the east of that denoted in the map given by Bishop Pallegoix; but as it would be improper to write about his discoveries till you have received the documents, and given them to some person for publication, I shall not dilate further on that topic.

And now, my dear madam, I beg to tender you my sincere condolence under the heavy bereavement which it has pleased the Almighty to inflict upon you,

And remain yours very sincerely,

James Campbell.

From M. Ch. Fontaine, Missionary at Cochin China, to M. Charles Mouhot.

Foreign Missions, Paris, 128, Rue du Bac,
15th August, 1862.

Dear Friend,

Permit me to give you this title; all the sentiments expressed in your letter authorise it. What a worthy brother you weep for! and I, what an honoured friend!

I had the pleasure of knowing M. H. Mouhot. I saw him first at Bangkok, and six or eight months after at Pinhalú, in Cambodia, where he remained with us ten days, sharing with us our house and our table, which is always open to any worthy fellow-countryman whom chance may lead to those parts. In both places all our brotherhood were charmed to make the acquaintance of so devoted a scion of learning, so polished a Frenchman, and so exemplary a Christian. All these qualities rendered him dear to the whole of the missionaries who had the pleasure of his acquaintance; and it was a real happiness to us to render him any little service possible in the performance of the troublesome task which he had imposed upon himself, of exploring countries so wild and destitute of comfort.

On his return from among the Stiêns, where he met MM. Guilloux and Arnoux, this dear friend lavished on me the greatest care, and expended for me all his medical science; for I had then been several months suffering from the malady which afterwards obliged me to return to France to recruit.

He left us to go to Battambong to M. Silvestre, and at the parting we experienced the deepest regret at losing the society of a friend who had so much cheered our solitude. From Battambong he was to return to Siam, and thence to Birmah, Bengal, and Europe. I wrote to him several times, both from Bangkok, from Pinhalú, and from Singapore, where my illness had induced me to go to consult an English physician; but M. Mouhot had changed his plans; he wished to explore Laos, a country whose climate is always so fatal to foreigners. There God saw fit to summon him to a better world. This I read with great sorrow in a Parisian newspaper; it was an extract from a London journal.

When I was abroad I heard of the death of my father, then of that of my mother, and I declare that these two announcements did not make more impression upon me than did the news of the death of a man whose equal I had not met with for twenty years; and the thought of his death, without any help but that of his servants during his illness and in his last moments, was more than enough to bring tears to my eyes as I remembered this good and benevolent friend. Be assured, dear Sir, that my feelings are shared by all the brothers who knew him. The natives themselves must have felt regret at his death; for all who knew him had only praises to repeat of his conduct towards them; and all acknowledged his gentleness and generosity—both qualities invaluable in the eyes of those people.

Permit me, then, dear Sir, to unite my regrets to your grief, and to present my respects to Madame Mouhot, together with my warmest sympathy with her in her affliction; also with your father and your wife. Receive my thanks for your having honoured me with your friendship; and be assured of my desire to be useful to you if ever it should lie in my power.

MARIE CH. FONTAINE,
Missionary at Saigon, Cochin China.

P.S.—Twelve of us are about to set out for Indo-China, and I will not fail to express to Mgr. Miche and his companions the kind feelings which you express with regard to them. On the 20th we shall sail from Marseilles in the *Hydaspe*. Write to the Seminary of Foreign Missions, whence our correspondence will be forwarded to us. My family live at Laval, and you will be always welcome there.

From Mr. Samuel Stevens to M. Charles Mouhot.

Mr. Stevens has the honour to inform M. C. Mouhot that the collection made by his late brother in the mountains of Laos is very fine, particularly the insects and shells. Among the former are a great number of beautiful and new species, one of which, a splendid Carabus, has been described in the ' Zoological Review' at Paris, under the name of Mouhotia gloriosa, in compliment to the late lamented M. Mouhot. This name is very appropriate, as it is one of the most beautiful and remarkable beetles which has been seen for years. There is also a beautiful set of Longicorns, and other insects of the order of Coleoptera, of which a great number are new to science.

The land and fresh-water shells are also very beautiful. Among the former there are twenty-five different genera; eight or ten are quite new, and some of them very remarkable. They will shortly be described by Dr. Pfeiffer and others.

I can truly say that the insects and shells equal, if they do not surpass, the most beautiful collections I have ever received; and clearly demonstrate how rich a country for the naturalist lies between Siam and Cochin China.

There is also a small collection of birds and some monkeys, small animals, reptiles, and serpents in spirits, of which some are quite new.

The collection of insects and shells made in Cambodia was also very beautiful, and contained the large and fine *Helix Cambojiensis*, one of the best and most beautiful specimens known; also, the *Bulimus Cambojiensis*, and a splendid *Buprestida*, new and unique, besides a great number of others, new to science.*

---

* M. Mouhot, in his letters to his family, always spoke with the highest esteem of Mr. Stevens, to whom they now beg to offer their thanks for the honourable manner in which he has conducted everything connected with their unfortunate relative.

FROM M. MALHERBE TO M. CHARLES MOUHOT.

Bangkok, Nov. 1862.

DEAR SIR,

On my return from Java a few days ago, I found waiting for me your kind letter, for which I thank you, although I should have wished to make your acquaintance under happier circumstances. All consolation from me, I know, would be ineffectual. The friendship I felt for your brother was not that of a stranger, but rather as though he were a member of my family; and I felt most painfully the news which met me on my return, of his death so far away: for I had been pleasing myself with the idea of his return, and long before my arrival here had given orders for his reception, and that he should be welcomed as though I were present.

One great consolation to the survivors is the feeling of how much he is regretted; here he had not a single enemy, but every one spoke of him as the best of men. I vainly tried to dissuade him from undertaking this dangerous expedition, for I had already lost a dear friend in that country. He was treacherously assassinated there by his boatmen.

I am much pleased with the frank manner in which you offer me your friendship. I thank you, and accept it with all my heart.

PAPER READ AT

THE ROYAL GEOGRAPHICAL SOCIETY,

10TH MARCH, 1862.

LORD ASHBURTON, PRESIDENT.

M. MOUHOT traversed Cambodia from east to west, and
also ascended the Mekon river to the frontier of Laos. He
returned to the coast by crossing the water-parting between
it and the basin of the Menam river, and descending to
Bangkok.

The Mekon is a vast melancholy-looking river, three miles
broad, covered with islands, and flowing with the rapidity of a
torrent. Its shores are covered with aquatic birds, but its
waters are almost deserted by canoes.* A plain covered with
coarse herbage separates it from the forest by which Cambodia
is overspread, and which can rarely be traversed except by
cutting a way. That forest is exceedingly unhealthy.

M. Mouhot reached Brelum, a village in lat. 11° 58', long.
107° 12', inhabited by a secluded race of wild people, whose
customs are minutely described, differing in features from the
Cambodian and Laos tribes, and forming one of a series of
similar groups widely distributed in the less accessible parts
of Cochin China, Cambodia, and Burmah. They are believed
by M. Mouhot to be the aborigines of the land. Two Catholic
missionaries were resident at Brelum.

Subsequently the author visited the large Buddhist ruins of
Ongcor, of which he has brought back numerous sketches. He

---

* The war in Cochin China has prevented many of the Annamite
fishermen from coming down the Mekon to fish in the great lake, which is
one cause of its desertion.

speaks of the mineral wealth of Cambodia—its iron, gold, lead, and copper. In the islands of Phu-Quoc or Koh Tron, belonging to Cochin China and near to Komput, there are rich mines of coal, similar to our Cannel coal, from which ornaments are made. Several extinct volcanoes exist in Pechaburi, of heights not exceeding 2000 feet above the sea-level, and there are two active ones in an island called Ko-man, lat. 12° 30', long. 101° 50', in the Gulf of Siam.

Dr. Hodgkin stated that, besides the two letters, portions of which had been read, and the drawings and charts, M. Mouhot had likewise sent an elaborate description of the ruins which he found at Ongcor and in its vicinity. The plans on the table would give some idea of the magnitude of these ruins. A great part of the manuscript which accompanied them described their structure and workmanship. They were constructed chiefly of granite, and many of the stones were not only of very large size, but were elaborately carved. The workmanship of some of them was described as exquisite, and the designs not so deficient in artistic taste as one might suppose. Many of them represented imaginary animals, such as serpents with many heads; others, beasts of burden—horses, elephants, and bullocks. These temples were situated in a district which was now completely imbedded in a forest very difficult of access, and were so much in ruins that trees were growing on the roofs, and many of the galleries were in a state of great decay. The base and a large portion of the elevation were constructed of a ferruginous rock, but for the upper part blocks of granite were used—so exquisitely cut as to require no mortar to fill the interstices, and carved with relievos relating to mythological subjects indicative of Buddhism. M. Mouhot had copied some of the inscriptions, which from their antiquity the natives who accompanied him were unable to read. The characters so nearly resembled the Siamese that Dr. H. had no doubt that a skilful archæologist would have very little difficulty in deciphering them. He believed that the remains in question would be found equal in value to those which had recently been explored in Central America; and he felt convinced that when the descriptions were published, M. Mouhot would be thought deserving of great respect.

Mr. Crawfurd said it was about forty years since he visited the country, but his recollection of it continued vivid to this day. Most people knew very little about Cambodia; its very name was only familiar to us in that of its product, gamboge, which word was nothing else than a corruption of Cambodia. It was one of five or six states lying between India and China, whose inhabitants had lived under a second or third-rate civilisation at all times—never equal, whether physically, morally, or intellectually, to the Chinese, or even the Hindoos. At the present time Cambodia was a poor little state, having been encroached upon by the Siamese to the north, and by Cochin China to the south. M. Mouhot had given us an account of a country that no European had ever visited before. With respect to that gentleman's belief that certain wild tribes whom he described had descended from Thibet, he (Mr. Crawfurd) believed that his ethnology was at fault. For his part, he believed these wild people to be no other than natives of the country— mere mountaineers, who had escaped from the bondage, and hence from the civilisation, of the plain. Such people existed in Hindoostan, in Siam, in the Burmese empire, in Cochin China, and in China itself—in fact, they were of no distinct origin, but simply the natives in a rude, savage, uncivilised state.

With respect to the French, he did not know on what grounds they had gone to Cambodia. They had obtained possession of one spot which was eminently fitted for a settlement. The finest river in all India, as far as European shipping was concerned, was the river at Saigon, which he had himself ascended

about 14 miles, and found it navigable even for an old " seventy-
four." He believed it was the intention of the French to
attempt the conquest of the whole of Cochin China. If they
effected it, and occupied it, they would find it a monstrous difficulty. It would prove another Algeria, with the additional dis-
advantage of being 15,000 miles off instead of 500, and within
the torrid instead of the temperate zone. The climate was very
hot, the country was covered with forests, the malaria and the
heat rendered it unsuitable for the European constitution. If
they made an advance upon the Cochin Chinese capital, they
would find the enterprise one of great difficulty. From Saigon
to the northern confines of Cochin China the distance is 1500
miles, and the capital itself could not be less than 700 or 800
miles from Saigon, situated on a small river navigable only for
large boats, with a narrow mouth, and two considerable for-
tresses, one on each side, at its mouth. When they arrived,
they would find one of the largest and most regular fortifications
in the East. He believed it was the most regular, after Fort
William in Bengal, and a great deal larger than Fort William.
It was constructed by the French, and now they will have considerable difficulty in conquering their own work. The French
had a perfect right to be in Cochin China, and their being
there would do no harm, but rather good, however questionable
the benefit to themselves; for their presence amounted to the
substitution of a friendly and civilised power for a rude and
inhospitable one.

The drawings on the table were exceedingly curious and
interesting; they were admirably done, and exhibited representations of some remarkable monuments, evidently of Buddhist
origin. They reminded him very much, though inferior in
quality and beauty, of the monuments of the island of Java.
He never heard of volcanoes when he was in Cambodia, but he
had no doubt M. Mouhot's information was correct, though

it appeared he did not describe them from his own personal experience. He would add a word upon the alphabets which were on the table. The Cambodians had invented a written phonetic character, which they used at the present time; therefore there could be no difficulty in understanding a Cambodian manuscript. But there were several of those now exhibited which were of more or less antiquity. One of them seemed to be the alphabet which was used by the Cambodians in their religious rites. The figure of Buddha showed that the Cambodians were worshippers of Buddha.

To M. Charles Mouhot.

Montbéliard,* 13th June, 1862.

THE members of the "Société d'Émulation" at Montbéliard desire to express the deep regret which they have experienced at the premature death of their fellow-townsman M. Henri Mouhot. After a three years' journey in Cambodia and Siam, during which he devoted himself to researches which have been highly appreciated by the Geographical and Zoological Societies of London, he fell a victim at the early age of thirty-five to his love of science. His work remained unfinished, but it was gloriously commenced, and his name will not perish. The regret experienced by his friends is the greater from their conviction that had he lived he would have been still more an honour to his native town, and that the name of Mouhot would have ranked side by side with those illustrious ones which have already rendered Montbéliard famous in the department of Natural Science.

---

* Montbéliard is the birthplace of Cuvier and of Laurillard.

THE END.

LONDON: PRINTED BY WILLIAM CLOWES AND SONS, STAMFORD STREET, AND CHARING CROSS.

Oxford in Asia Hardback Reprints